Practical Ideas

for teaching writing as a process

Compiled and edited by

Carol Booth Olson
Codirector, University of California, Irvine/
California Writing Project

Prepared for publication by
The Staff of the Bureau of Publications
California State Department of Education

Publishing Information

Practical Ideas for Teaching Writing as a Process, which was compiled and edited by Carol Booth Olson, Codirector of the University of California, Irvine/ California Writing Project, was edited for publication by Theodore R. Smith, Editor in Chief, California State Department of Education. The book, which presents techniques and practical ideas for teaching students the stages in the writing process, was first published by the Department of Education in 1986 as a companion to its *Handbook for Planning an Effective Writing Program.* This new edition of the book has been revised and expanded to include new practical ideas for teaching writing, an index, and a list of references. Janet Lundin, an Assistant Editor in the Bureau of Publications, helped in the editing of this new edition, and she prepared the index and list of references.

Practical Ideas was prepared for photo-offset production by the staff of the Department's Bureau of Publications. Marguerite Wobschall designed the cover and prepared the artwork for the book, using a design created by Norman Wobschall. The typesetters were Anna Boyd, Leatrice Shimabukuro, and Ron Zacharias; and the editors who proofed the typeset copy were Ms. Lundin and Marie McLean. Russell Frank, Barbara Lyter, Marguerite Wobschall, Pat Chladek, and the Media Services Unit of the Department of Education provided most of the photographs used to illustrate the book. The other photographers whose work appears in the book are cited in the acknowledgments on page x.

Practical Ideas was published by the California State Department of Education, 721 Capitol Mall, Sacramento, California (mailing address: P.O. Box 944272, Sacramento, CA 94244-2720). The document was printed by the Office of State Printing and distributed under the provisions of the Library Distribution Act.

Copies of this publication are available for $6 each, plus sales tax for California residents, from Publications Sales, California State Department of Education, P.O. Box 271, Sacramento, CA 95802-0271. Any questions regarding the sale or distribution of the book should be directed to Marilyn J. Butts, Publications Sales Manager, at the address cited above or by phoning (916) 445-1260.

A list of other publications available from the Department of Education may be found on the last page of this book.

ISBN 0-8011-0671-0

EDPRESS

Contents

Foreword

Ernest Boyer captured, in the most precise words I have read on the subject, the idea that writing is at the core of all education: "Clear writing leads to clear thinking; clear thinking is the basis of clear writing." Recognizing, as Ernest Boyer does, that learning to write clearly has a direct relationship to thinking clearly, I made the improvement of student writing an integral part of the educational reform effort in California. And in identifying good, clear writing as a standard to be achieved in our schools, I asked that the standard be spelled out in both the Department's *Model Curriculum Standards: Grades Nine Through Twelve* and in the *English–Language Arts Model Curriculum Guide for Kindergarten Through Grade Eight.*

Those who prepared the standards for the high school level were very supportive of my request, and they developed this standard:

All students will learn that writing is a process that includes stages called prewriting, drafting, revising, and editing. These writing stages include higher level thinking processes, such as convergent and divergent thinking, analysis and synthesis, and inferential and evaluative skills.

The writers of the guide for the elementary school level were equally supportive of my request. They identified the importance of writing to a child's education in several ways, including this one:

Students become aware that writing is a means for clarifying thinking and that it is a process which embodies several stages, including prewriting, drafting, receiving responses, revising, editing, and postwriting activities, including evaluation.

By recognizing that students at all levels and abilities need to learn the process involved in developing a piece of writing, I also acknowledged the basic tenets of the California Writing Project that Jim Gray has outlined so well in the introductory section of this book. Jim is the director of the Bay Area Writing Project and the National Writing Project. The tenets also formed the foundation on which our *Handbook for Planning an Effective Writing Program* was developed.

Because of the significant contributions the *Handbook* has made to our reform efforts, I am pleased that we can offer teachers a companion book filled with practical ideas to use in helping their students understand better the process described in the *Handbook*—the process through which the act of writing is accomplished.

I congratulate Carol Booth Olson and all of those others who helped her place under one cover so many challenging thoughts regarding the teaching of writing and so many creative approaches—so many practical ideas—for helping students learn for themselves that clear writing does lead to clear thinking.

Bill Honig

Superintendent of Public Instruction

As a people who value the lessons of history, we must realize that our very survival depends primarily on our collective abilities to speak and write clearly and precisely and to be understood as we strive to understand others.

FROM BILL HONIG'S FOREWORD TO THE *HANDBOOK FOR PLANNING AN EFFECTIVE WRITING PROGRAM*

Preface

If you are looking for ideas for teaching writing as a process at all levels of the curriculum, this book was compiled for you. It is a collaborative effort on the part of teachers from and consultants to the University of California, Irvine/California Writing Project and special guest contributors. Their articles present some of the most innovative and influential strategies for teaching writing that have been presented at our annual Summer Institute on the Teaching of Composition.

The idea for the creation of this manuscript came to me one day when I was trying to figure out some way to organize and gain easy access to the wealth of information I had accumulated in the large three-ring notebooks (often affectionately referred to as *Big Blue*) that we spend five weeks filling to capacity during each summer institute. One shelf in my office is now lined with copies of *Big Blue,* which is loaded with techniques that teachers of writing, from kindergarten through the university, have used successfully in their classes. It occurred to me that it was about time to organize all this material and share it with teachers who had not had an opportunity to participate in a writing project or who, like me, need to construct a conceptual framework for the ideas they are already familiar with in order to make maximum use of them.

Because the concept of writing as a process has revolutionized the way that so many of us view the act of composing, structure our classes, and design our assignments, the stages of that process—prewriting, writing, sharing and responding, rewriting, editing, and evaluating—seemed like the most logical organization to use for this publication. In each section of the book, you will find well-known authors presenting specific techniques for teaching one of the stages of the writing process. I thought it would also be helpful for you to hear from classroom teachers who have implemented the ideas discussed. Therefore, following the description of each technique are commentaries in which you will find testimonials, applications of writing techniques at particular grade levels, descriptions of ways to modify assignments, new ideas which sprang from an original idea, and variations on a theme. These commentaries are intended for your use as points of departure as you experiment with the suggested approaches and develop your own lesson plans.

One of the most rewarding dimensions of the California Writing Project and the National Writing Project is the spirit of sharing inherent in the teacher-teaching-teacher model initiated by James R. Gray, Director of the Bay Area Writing Project, and discussed by him as part of the introduction to this book. You might say that this publication is a product of that process of sharing that takes place at every writing project site. But it is not meant as a replacement for that process. In fact, we hope it will encourage you to become involved in a summer institute or other available workshops and conferences in your area. Take what you can use. Use what you take to supplement what you already know and do well. Make the ideas that are presented your own by adapting them to your unique teaching style and classroom situation. And discuss them with your colleagues. If, as a result of your exposure to *Practical Ideas for Teaching Writing as a Process,* you come up with an overall approach or specific assignment that you would like to share, send it to me. There is always room for one more good idea in *Big Blue.*

CAROL BOOTH OLSON
Codirector, UCI Writing Project

Acknowledgments

Practical Ideas for Teaching Writing as a Process represents the work of many dedicated people over a period of several years. And first we thank all of the contributing authors whose work appears on the following pages. It was your practical and innovative ideas for teaching writing and your spirit of sharing that made this book a reality. On behalf of all those teachers who will benefit from your generous contributions, we thank you:

Lois Anderson, Carl Babb, Virginia Baldwin, Sandra Barnes, Trudy J. Beck, Ruby Bernstein, Sheridan Blau, Rich Blough, Linda Bowe, Joan Bower, Barbara Farrell Brand, William Burns, Pam Burris, Rebekah Caplan, Michael Carr, Evelyn Ching, Lynda Chittenden, Mike Conlon, Laurel Corona, Cathy D'Aoust, Diane Dawson, Peter Elbow, Marie Filardo, Russell Frank, Anita Freedman, Patricia Gatlin, Sue Ellen Gold, Jenee Gossard, James R. Gray, Jim Hahn, Mary K. Healy, Todd Huck, Charrie Hunter, Martha Johnson, Jerry Judd, Sheila Koff, Erline Krebs, Jim Lee, William Lomax, Ken Macrorie, Elizabeth B. Martinez, Nancy McHugh, Carolyn Mendoza, Mindy Moffatt, Paulette Morgan, Barbara Morton, Greta Nagel, Michael O'Brien, Carol Booth Olson, Laurie Opfell, Glenn Patchell, Kathy Pierce, Mark Reardon, Elizabeth Williams Reeves, Charles L. Reichardt, Gabriele Lusser Rico, Judith Sanderson, Charles Schiller, Margaret Serences, Julie Simpson, Dale Sprowl, Susan Starbuck, Carol O. Sweedler-Brown, Irene Thomas, Owen Thomas, Norma Tracy, Mary Turner, Karen Walden, and Sue Rader Willett.

We extend a special thanks to George Nemetz, the Department of Education's consultant in English who recognized how helpful *Practical Ideas* could be to those teachers who are willing to try the suggested approach to teaching writing that is presented in the *Handbook for Planning an Effective Writing Program.* He is the person who first convinced the Department of Education that it should consider publishing *Practical Ideas.* And once James R. Smith, Deputy Superintendent for Curriculum and Instructional Leadership, had an opportunity to review the contents of *Practical Ideas* and to consider its potential for improving the teaching of writing in our schools, he became one of the book's early supporters in the Department of Education. We thank him for that support.

Henia Alony was the administrative assistant for the UCI Writing Project who typed and retyped many of the 525 pages of the original manuscript and who helped maintain the flow of galley proofs from the editorial offices in Sacramento to the 64 authors who contributed material to the 1986 edition of the book. Your help was invaluable, Henia.

As Henia helped in the production of the 1986 edition, Christine Emerson, also with the UCI Writing Project, provided like services during the development of the 1987 edition. We are truly grateful for your help, Chris.

We are also indebted to the following publishers, literary agents, and individuals for granting us permission to use copyrighted material from their publications:

Allyn and Bacon, Inc.: *A Guidebook for Teaching Creative Writing,* by Gene Bradford and Marie Smith, © 1981.

Bay Area Writing Project/National Writing Project: *Showing Writing: A Training Program to Help Students Be Specific in Writing,* by Rebekah Caplan and Catharine Keech, © 1980.

Brandt & Brandt Literary Agents, Inc.: "The Most Dangerous Game," in *Stories,* by Richard Connell, © 1957.

E. P. Dutton and Co., Inc.: *An Introduction to Shakespeare,* by Marchette Chute, © 1951.

Lawrence Erlbaum Associates, Publishers: "How Children Cope with the Cognitive Demands of Writing," in *Writing: Process, Development, and Communication,* by Marlene Scardamalia, © 1981.

Harcourt Brace Jovanovich, Inc.: "Summer Grass," in *Good Morning, America,* by Carl Sandburg, © 1928, 1956; also, *A Special Gift,* by Marcia L. Simon, © 1978.

Houghton Mifflin Company: *The Hobbit,* J. R. R. Tolkien, © 1966.

Los Angeles Times: "1904—The Forgotten Games," in the *Los Angeles Times,* by Grahame L. Jones, © 1984.

Toby Lurie: Poem from *Conversations and Constructions,* by Toby Lurie, © 1978.

Macmillan Education Ltd.: *The Development of Writing Abilities (11-18),* by James Britton and others, © 1975.

National Council of Teachers of English: "Some Techniques for Oral Evaluation," in the *English Journal,* by Michael O'Brien, © 1982.

Oxford University Press, Inc.: *Writing Without Teachers,* by Peter Elbow, © 1973; also *Errors and Expectations: A Guide for the Teacher of Basic Writing,* by Mina P. Shaughnessy, © 1977.

Random House, Inc.: *The Book of Daniel,* by E. L. Doctorow, © 1971.

Charles Scribner's Sons: "Cat in the Rain," in *Short Stories of Ernest Hemingway,* by Ernest Hemingway, © 1938.

Viking Penguin, Inc.: *The Red Pony,* by John Steinbeck, © 1966.

Russell Frank, English and Journalism Teacher in the Walnut Valley Unified School District, was not only one of the contributing authors to this book but he was also the principal photographer for the 1986 edition, and many of his pictures appear in this edition. We are most grateful that he shared so many of his talents in the development of *Practical Ideas.* His photos appear on pages viii, 12, 31—33, 35, 40, 82, 85, 86, 100, 139, 141, 146, 149, 152, 162, 163, 180, and 183.

Barbara Lyter, a photographer with the University of California, Irvine, was the principal photographer for the 1987 edition. We are particularly pleased that she was able to capture on film the enthusiasm that the authors of *Practical Ideas* generated for the hundreds of participants at the "Practical Ideas" conference held at the University of California, Irvine, on October 28 and 29, 1986. Ms. Lyter's photographs from that conference appear on pages iii, ix, 7, 11, 15, 17, 26, 33, 38, 47, 51, 65, 68, 73, 81, 87, 99, 105, 107, 114, 147, 148, 155, 161, 176, 185, 193, 199, and 213.

Like so many associated with the production of this book, Marguerite Wobschall, who is a graphic artist in the Bureau of Publications, also made many contributions to the development of both the 1986 and 1987 editions. In addition to designing the cover and molding the text and the graphics into an attractive format, she went out and took photographs when certain ones were needed to illustrate a particular idea in the text. Her photographs appear on pages 13, 19, 74, 117, 120, and 201. Thank you, Marguerite, for taking such a personal interest in making *Practical Ideas* so graphically appealing.

The photographs provided by David Donnenfield, Howard Koppelman, Jonna Ramey, and Carol Wheeler of the Department of Education's Media Services Unit were used extensively throughout the book, and we are most grateful for their use. They appear on pages 5, 6, 22, 46, 53, 54, 56, 59, 60, 70, 78, 92, 98, 103, 118, 122, 131, 133, 150, 158, 167, 174, 179, 182, 184, 186, 192, 196, 197, and 200.

We also thank Pat Chladek, Education Consultant, for his photographs, which appear on pages 24, 37, 140, 142, 157, 165, 187, 193, 194, and 205.

The other photographers whose work appears in the book follow:

Roy Christian, 137; Leo Cohen, 129; Tom Dunlap, 128; Gary Ferrato, 44, 94; Dennis Hearne, 113; Bob Klingensmith, 135, 136; Kenneth S. Lane, 1, 43; Paul Lee, 96; Kazuhiro Tsuruta, 41; and Ron Zacharias, 2, 4.

We thank all of you for making your photographs available to us.

Finally, we thank all of the staff members of the Bureau of Publications who have taken such a personal interest in the development of *Practical Ideas.* We are most grateful to Janet Lundin for her editorial help on both editions and especially for her painstaking work and that of Ron Zacharias in preparing the index and the list of references that were added to the 1987 edition. Oftentimes, acknowledgments like these do not include the names of those in sales and distribution units who process orders, promote sales, answer inquiries, and put the books in the mail. But we want all of you in the Bureau of Publications who perform the final and very important work in the publishing process to know we love you because you do your work with concern, and you do it so well. Thank you:

Aurora Briseno, Marilyn Butts, Elza Edmonds, Ray Itogawa, Johnnie McRae, Rick Murphy, Don Neumann, Maria Reynoso, Jerry Tribbey, and Jane Wymore.

CAROL BOOTH OLSON
Codirector, UCI Writing Project

THEODORE R. SMITH
Editor in Chief
California State Department of Education

Introduction

The California Writing Project

By James R. Gray
Director, Bay Area Writing Project

The California Writing Project (CWP) is a teacher-teaching-teacher program to improve student writing in California by improving the teaching of writing in California classrooms. Each year nearly 15,000 teachers from all levels of instruction and all regions of the state participate in a variety of summer and school-year programs sponsored by the 19 local writing projects in the statewide CWP network. Each of the projects in the network was established on the staff development model of the Bay Area Writing Project and tied together through a common commitment to a set of key assumptions:

- The universities and the schools must work together as partners in a cooperative effort to solve the writing problems common to both levels. New collegial and nonhierarchical relationships among professors, instructors, and teachers are essential; and the top-down tradition of past university/school programs is no longer acceptable as a staff development model.

- While most teachers in the schools have never been adequately trained to teach writing, some teachers at all levels have learned, out of necessity, how to teach students to write. Also, they have, through trial and error and in the privacy of their own classrooms, developed effective approaches to the teaching of writing. These successful teachers can be identified. They can be brought together through summer institutes and trained to teach other teachers of writing in project-sponsored programs conducted throughout the school year on college campuses and in school districts.

- The best teachers of teachers are other teachers who are believable as consultants, because their ideas and the specific teaching strategies they demonstrate have been developed with real students in real classrooms.

- Teachers of writing must, themselves, write. Teachers need to experience regularly what they are asking of their students, and they need to discover and understand, through their own writing, the process (of writing) they are teaching.

- Real change in classroom practice happens over time. Effective staff development programs are ongoing and systematic—programs that make it possible for teachers to come together regularly throughout their careers to test and evaluate the best practices of other teachers.

- Effective programs to improve student writing should involve teachers from all grade levels and teachers from all content areas. The idea of writing as a means of discovery and as a way of learning is a compelling idea for teachers across the curriculum and across grade levels.

- What is known about the teaching of writing comes not only from research but also from the practice of those who teach writing.

In the summer institutes, which are the best known of the many programs sponsored by the local writing projects, selected teachers are invited to the college campuses as University Fellows and given modest stipends to cover expenses. These teachers demonstrate the specific teaching strategies they have found successful with their own students and, typically, involve the audience of Fellows as students. The presentations are evaluated not only for their effectiveness as approaches to writing but also for their effectiveness as presentations. For many teachers in the institutes, this is the first time in their careers that they have ever been asked to present what they know to another teacher. In addition to making presentations, teachers examine research and key texts in the field of written composition, work with occasional outside guest speakers, and meet regularly in small editing/response groups to share and examine their own manuscripts with one another. The best material is published in an anthology at the close of the institute.

It is an intensive five weeks, but it is only a beginning. Participation in the California Writing Project does not stop with the summer institute; it continues with regular follow-up programs that include monthly meetings that bring together summer Fellows from all past institutes to continue the experience of the summer institute, meetings of the steering committee, meetings to plan local and statewide conferences, and so forth. The most important follow-up programs sponsored by the California Writing Project are the staff development workshops held throughout the school year in school districts near each CWP site. These workshops are conducted by the teachers trained in the summer institutes and usually are held after school in three-hour sessions spaced throughout the year. The best practices identified in the summer institute are presented in the workshops to large numbers of teachers from the areas served by each of the 19 sites. It is in these school district workshops and in the variety of other programs sponsored by the CWP sites that the California Writing Project achieves the ripple effect that now touches teachers in every region of California.

At least two times a year, the directors and co-directors of the 19 CWP sites meet to discuss their various programs and to explore common concerns. It is at these meetings that all of us involved in the writing project movement in California get a sense of

its continuing momentum and ever increasing scope. Most sites now offer several programs beyond the summer institutes and the school year follow-up programs: programs for teachers of limited-language students, programs for teachers of college-bound stu-

dents, and summer programs open to all teachers who wish to participate in a CWP program. Some sites offer special programs for young writers, parents, and administrators. Increasingly, the writing project is asked to conduct writing-across-the-curriculum workshops for whole school faculties. To meet this need, teachers from the various disciplines who use writing as a means of teaching their subjects are participating in the summer institutes in greater and greater numbers. The writing project has also trained teachers in scores of districts throughout California in the techniques of holistic evaluation; as a result, most districts in California now require student writing samples in the proficiency examinations that the Legislature requires all California school districts to conduct.

One outgrowth of the California Writing Project is the publications that have increased in number and variety over the years. Most sites distribute quarterly newsletters to their CWP Fellows, and many publish anthologies of student and teacher writing. Following the lead of the Bay Area Writing Project, still others are producing monographs and disseminating occasional papers on some of the best practices in the teaching of writing that have originated from their respective summer institutes. Reflecting a new thrust of the California Writing Project, the local projects are also sharing the results of teacher-initiated classroom reserarch.

One of the most comprehensive collaborative publication efforts was the development of the California State Department of Education's *Handbook for Planning an Effective Writing Program*. Working cooperatively with personnel from offices of county superintendents of schools and the State Department of Education, representatives from 15 California Writing Project sites contributed their time and expertise to the creation of that document. Accordingly, the *Handbook* reflects the basic tenets of the California Writing Project:

- Writing is a tool for learning because it fosters thinking skills.
- As a learning tool, writing should be encouraged across the curriculum.
- The teacher is a facilitator of the writing/learning process by creating an environment that is conducive to learning; assigning writing is not the same thing as teaching writing.
- Teachers of writing must, themselves, write; good teachers are, themselves, learners.
- Writing, itself, is a process; the act of transforming thought into print involves a nonlinear sequence of creative acts or stages.
- The goal of instruction in writing is to enable students to develop skills in fluency, form, and

correctness; fluency should be stressed first because students must be able to produce text before they can edit it.

The *Handbook for Planning an Effective Writing Program* has reached thousands of teachers in California and throughout the nation; thus, widening the ripple effect that begins at the close of each CWP summer institute. The *Handbook* continues to play an important role in setting forth *what* the essential components of an effective writing program are and *why* the stage-process model of composition is such a valuable tool for teaching and learning. Building on and complementing the efforts of the *Handbook*, the University of California, Irvine/California Writing Project's collection of *Practical Ideas for Teaching Writing as a Process* offers a host of "how to" strategies for implementing the basic tenets of the California Writing Project. Like the summer institutes from which its articles and commentaries spring, this book focuses on what works; the authorities are teachers teaching teachers.

Teachers teaching teachers. That is our formula for success. The California Writing Project has worked because it puts a premium on what is working in the teaching and learning of writing. Its staff development model is not the familiar deficit model that treats teachers as if they were diseased, damaged, and in need of repair. It is a model that celebrates good teaching and enhances the professional status of teachers. Teachers come to these university-based programs not as students but as colleagues, recognized as authorities in classroom practice, who bring with them a source of knowledge about the teaching of writing that is uniquely their own. Their commitment, enthusiasm, and desire to share is the heart of the California Writing Project.

The Handbook for Planning an Effective Writing Program *continues to play an important role in setting forth* what *the essential components of an effective writing program are and* why *the stage-process model of composition is such a valuable tool for teaching and learning.*
JAMES R. GRAY

"We Are All Out-of-Date Scientists":
New Language Research Since You Left School

By Owen Thomas
Professor, English, Linguistics, and Teacher Education,
University of California, Irvine;
and Codirector, UCI Writing Project

In one of S. J. Perelman's books, a character says, "We are all out-of-date scientists." I would like to explain what I think the author meant by that and then to suggest how that meaning relates to teachers of writing.

Mr. Perelman expanded on the statement by saying that our ideas of science are based on the last course we had in a particular science in school. With a very few exceptions, most of us are out-of-date, rather than up-to-date, concerning recent developments in various fields of science. Even scientists are often out-of-date in fields not directly related to their own. Physicists, for example, are often out-of-date in a field such as sociobiology. Organic chemists may well be out-of-date in mathematics. And if this is true for scientists, it is all the more true for most of us who are not working in science every day.

For example, most people assume they have at least some idea of the meaning of infinity. Many people even remember the mathematical symbol for infinity: ∞. But what most people do not know—unless they have kept up with recent developments in mathematics—is that some infinities are larger than other infinities and that there is, in fact, a subbranch of mathematics called the mathematics of infinity.

The point of the preceding example is this: Often, we all sometimes *think* we know a fair amount about a particular subject when, in fact, we are out-of-date. And the fact is that many teachers of writing are out-of-date in some important ways, and I will suggest a few of them. Other contributors to this book will suggest other ways, but none of us knew about these important developments until a few years ago. However, all of us believe that these developments have significant implications for the teaching of composition.

In the next few paragraphs, I will be concerned with two subjects: (1) what young children and adolescents know (in some sense) about language; and (2) what linguists know (in another sense) about language. Finally, I will look briefly at a third subject—namely, what these two kinds of "knowing" imply for the teaching of writing.

Most of the ideas that I am concerned with result from research in the field of psycholinguistics, and particularly in the area of language acquisition. Let us start with one of the most important of these ideas. I will ask a question, and you will believe that you know the answer. Then I will suggest (as gently as possible) that you are out-of-date.

Here is the question: What is the primary function of language?

If you are like most people, you will probably answer, "Communication." Approximately ten years ago, I would have answered the same way. But research during that time has caused me to change my answer. Now I believe the primary function of language is, in a word, survival—and not simply survival in a social sense. (That is, in the sense that, if you do not speak a standard dialect, you would have difficulty surviving in the business world or in some social situations.) I mean survival as the biologists use the term. Consider an analogy with the opposing thumb. Humans have thumbs that can rotate so they "oppose" the fingers. This opposition permits us to grasp things—to hold tools—which has helped us survive by enabling us to develop such things as agriculture. In brief, the opposing thumb enhances the ability of the individual—and the species—to survive in the physical world.

Most researchers now believe that the same thing is true of language. Because we have language, we can name things, express relationships between things, develop concepts of cause and effect, and so on. And all this precedes the use of language in communication with others.

The case of Helen Keller is illustrative here. In the sense that I am now using the term *language,* Helen Keller had language long before she learned to communicate with Anne Sullivan. Miss Keller was, in fact, using her *language* to help her survive. In a loving and supportive way, Miss Sullivan was finally able to help Miss Keller relate this *language* to English. But this fact—the important fact—is that the survival language came first. This helps to explain why people are often apprehensive when we—well-meaning English teachers—try to change their language. (I will return to this subject, briefly, below.)

Once we accept the idea of language as survival, we can more easily accept another, perhaps startling, idea: The acquisition of language is primarily a biological—rather than an intellectual—process. That is, most researchers now believe that the ability to acquire language is passed on through the DNA molecule. There is, in fact, evidence that children as young as 12 hours old have begun the process of acquiring language. Once we accept *this* idea, we can more readily understand several important conclusions that are derived from the idea:

- First, no language is inherently more difficult—more complex—than any other language.

- Second, any child can learn any language as a native language—given the proper circumstances.

- Third, the acquisition of language does not depend, in any way, on formal instruction. Contrary to what many people think, we do not teach language to children. Rather, they learn language biologically and, for the most part, effortlessly.

For the past 15 years, linguists have been trying to describe what it is that children (and adults) know when they know a language. The task is far from over. We have just begun to be able to describe what children "know." Still, what we have learned is, and I use the word with care, *awesome.*

I must proceed slowly here. Actually, I am trying to make two points at once, and both are important:

- First, researchers in language acquisition are convinced that a child entering school has already acquired (biologically) an enormous quantity of linguistic knowledge, particularly syntactic knowledge.

- Second, linguists are still very far away from describing, in any complete way, the precise nature of this knowledge.

As an example of syntactic knowledge, consider one use of *do* in English. There are certain questions, called tag questions, that sometimes require *do* and sometimes do not:

Statement	Related tag question
1. This is interesting.	This is interesting, isn't it?
2. You can swim.	You can swim, can't you?
3. The boy ate the hamburger.	The boy ate the hamburger, didn't he?

The rule for the use of *do, does,* and *did* in such questions is rather complex. It relates to whether the main verb in the statement is a form of *be,* and if it is not, to whether there is an auxiliary verb in the statement. My point, here, is this: Without ever receiving formal instruction in the use of *do,* most five-year-old children know when to use an appropriate form of *do* in a tag question. This is but one example out of thousands that I could cite of a child's syntactic knowledge—hence, my earlier use of the word *awesome.*

The second point is equally important. Although most linguists agree that the amount of knowledge possessed by a child is vast, they do not agree on a description of that knowledge. They do not even agree on such fundamental questions as the basic word order of an English sentence. Some say English is a subject-verb-object (SVO) language. Others say SOV. Still others say VSO.

Both these points relate to the teaching of writing. As a teacher once said to me after I had made the first point (and supported it with considerably more evidence than I have room for here), "Then our job is not to get language *into* the head of a child. Our job is to get it *out*." (The teacher said this to me almost ten years ago. It sums up my point so succinctly that I have been quoting her frequently since then.)

In brief, I believe—and I want to state this as strongly as possible—that any teacher of writing must accept, as fact, the conclusion that school-age children possess an extraordinary wealth of linguistic knowledge. The question, then, is this: How do we get this knowledge "out" in the form of writing?

Much of this book is devoted to suggesting ways of getting the knowledge out, so I will not list these ways here. Rather, I will turn again to the second point.

We know less about the nature of linguistic knowledge—about grammar, if you will—than we do about the structure of the atom. This means, among many other things, that since we do not know the true nature of grammar, we do not know of any way to use grammar when we are teaching children to write. At this point, you may be asking yourself, "But what about parts of speech, what about diagramming, what about defining compound and complex sentences?"

The facts, as briefly as possible, are these. Traditional grammar—that is, of the sort most widely taught in schools today—is an extremely inaccurate description of English. Most people's knowledge of the system of English is as out-of-date as their knowledge of infinity. Moreover, research dating back more than 50 years, and frequently reconfirmed since then, indicates that a knowledge of traditional grammar bears no relation to writing ability. Even more significantly, recent research into brain hemispheres (right and left brains) indicates that the formal study of grammar (a left-brain activity) actually inteferes with writing fluency (principally, right-brain activity).

In summary, we know that most children have linguistic knowledge adequate to the skill of writing, but we do not yet know of any way to use a formal description of this knowledge to help children develop

their writing skills. Some things, however, are clear:

- The starting point in the teaching of writing must be the teacher's belief that children possess the requisite linguistic knowledge.
- Teachers need to use every possible means to give their students confidence in their linguistic knowledge. (Children who believe that they "don't know any grammar" are children who also believe they "can't write.")
- "Getting language out" is a process, and teachers of writing must have an intimate knowledge of this process. The best way of gaining this kind of knowledge is in actual writing.

I have discussed the first two of the preceding points already. The third point requires some comment. In every writing project that comes under the umbrella of the California Writing Project, the Project Fellows spend a considerable amount of time writing and discussing each other's writing. This writing, in fact, is the cornerstone of the project. Usually, at the beginning of a project, the majority of Fellows think the writing segment is only a minor part of the project. The major part, they think, will be the suggestions they receive on how to teach. But by the end of the project, the great majority of Fellows see the writing segment as the single most important part. They have experienced—in a very personal way—both the hardships and the rewards of writing. They know, personally, that writing is seldom fun, seldom easy, and they also know that it can be extremely satisfying.

When they discussed writing before taking part in one of the California Writing Projects, the Project Fellows would talk about dangling modifiers, spelling, subject/verb agreement, and so on—all things that relate to the end product. After the project, they are much more inclined to talk about the process rather than the product of writing. Having shared their writing with other Fellows, they are vastly more sensitive to what a writer's real needs are. Having listened to criticisms—some positive, some negative—of their own writing, they are better able to make helpful criticisms of a student's writing. It is through experiences like these that the Fellows come to appreciate—to experience—the fact that language is more than just communication. Language is associated with our sense of self, and ultimately, with survival.

In summary, in the out-of-date way of teaching writing we once subscribed to, we thought it necessary to put language into students' heads. Actually, the time we spent trying to do that was time we did not spend in real writing, in getting the language out. And it is to the task—and the joy—of teaching real writing that my fellow contributors to this book now ask you to turn.

The Process

Teaching Writing as a Process

By Cathy D'Aoust
Codirector, UCI Writing Project

I was introduced to the concept of writing as a process several years ago at a composition conference at the University of California, Irvine. At that time, I was teaching composition—not very successfully—and found that the idea of writing as a process afforded me a new perspective and had tremendous implications for classroom teaching. I immediately revised my curriculum and began to see my students improve as writers. What I have provided in this essay is a general description of the stages of the writing process and a discussion of the significance of this process for both the teacher and student. Subsequent sections of this book will offer practical ideas for teaching the various stages in the writing process at all levels of the curriculum.

When writers and linguistic researchers describe writing as a process, they are attempting to describe the incredibly complex system of transforming thought into written communication. This description has had a significant impact on the composition teacher whose demand for a product has been replaced by a concern for the series of stages, both focused and unfocused, conscious as well as unconscious, which make up the writing process. It has meant utilizing the stage-process model—prewriting, writing, sharing/responding, revising, editing, and evaluating—as a teaching tool to faciliate student writing. To do so, the composition teacher has had to reassess his or her goals and determine how to marry his or her process as a teacher with that of the student writer to improve the ultimate product.

The stage-process model begins by focusing on *prewriting*. Prewriting activities are designed to stimu-late the flow of ideas before any structured writing begins. Writing arises out of a sense of having something to communicate. Any exercise which stimulates the writer's inner voice to seek verbalization is a prewriting activity. Brainstorming, clustering, debating, freewriting, and fantasizing are a few of the infinite possibilities. Prewriting activities generate ideas; they encourage a free flow of thoughts and help students discover both what they want to say and how to communicate it on paper. In other words, prewriting activities facilitate the planning for both the product and the process.

With a desire to communicate, students move to the next stage, *writing*. They allow their ideas to take shape by putting words to paper. However, the writers may lack any conscious awareness of what they specifically want to communicate. Writing then becomes a discovery on the conscious level. This movement of an idea to the conscious level allows for spontaneity and creativity and must not be impeded by concerns over correctness. Writing is simplified as the writers let go and disappear into the act of writing. As Sondra Perl says in her article, "Understanding Composing" (*College Composition and Communication,* December, 1980), "Writing is a process of coming into being."

Having expressed themselves, the students move to the next stage called *sharing*. Writing can be a very lonely process; some of the difficulty in writing comes from the fact that it is one-way communication. Unlike speech, a writer's words often go untested. The writers use their own reactions to their words for primary feedback. Frequently, writers become so engrossed in what they are saying that it is impossible to distinguish between what they want to say and what they said. Given a chance to share with others, student writers gain a sense of the power of their words to impact others. They gain a sense of audience, a significant trusted other, who will be influenced by the words of the writer. It is not unusual at this phase for writers to discover an incongruity between the purpose and the effect of their writing; writers may have intended to communicate a specific idea but, through the feedback of peers, learn that they did not do so. Then writers are at liberty to revise or possibly reassess their intention.

Besides providing an audience and reactions to the writing, sharing generates enthusiasm about writing. Writers are inspired by effective student models to improve their own communication. Moreover, in *responding* to the writing being shared by others, writers gain a clearer sense of what distinguishes effective from ineffective writing. Once the students have discovered that they *can* write, the instructor can now teach revising and editing skills because the student writers will not only need them but will also request them.

Revising, then, is a *re-viewing* of the writing in light of the feedback. It is a reworking of the composition on both semantic and lexical levels; the writers are concerned not only with the words they have chosen to express their ideas but also with how these words work together. The student writers scratch out, mark over, add, rephrase, and reorder to make their words consistent with the intended meaning. It is a focused and conscious manipulation of words. Changes may be in words, phrases, sentences, paragraphs, or in the total composition.

Revision actually can occur at any time during the writing process because of the recursive nature of the act of composing. Sondra Perl further explains that writing is not simply a linear process but a "forward-moving action that exists by virtue of a backward-moving action." Writers put words to a page and immediately go back to see what they have created. Sondra Perl contends that writers not only go back to bits of discourse but also return to their notion of the topic as well as to the "nonverbalized perceptions that

surround the words." Student writers go backward to discover what they said and move forward to elaborate on it. The impulse to revise could occur at any time.

After addressing meaning, writers focus on correctness. This next stage in the writing process is *editing,* the imposing of correctness. Editing is a focused, deliberate, grammatical concern. The writers continue to rework their papers by adding and deleting and by correcting punctuation, spelling, and grammar. In keeping with the purpose of their work, the writers conform to the standards of written English.

During this altering and refining phase, the teacher will be called on to use his or her linguistic expertise. Appropriately, the composition teacher addresses grammar when it is relevant. Rather than using arbitrary grammar and punctuation exercises, the teacher is able to draw on the students' own writing to illustrate polishing techniques. Within that context, the writers utilize and increase their knowledge of the structure of the language to improve communication.

It is imperative during the focused, more conscious phases of the writing process that students have a clear sense of how their writing will be evaluated and by whom. The teacher and students must be in agreement regarding the standards that will be used for evaluating writing. *Evaluation,* the next stage in the writing process, is simply the final feedback for the student writers and usually comes in the form of a grade. Often, there is a discrepancy between the criteria used by the teacher and the students for evaluation. If a letter grade is a surprise, the writing process is flawed. This generally happens when a teacher sets the standards for evaluation, often with an undue emphasis on correctness, either without adequately communicating the standards to the class or with little or no input from the students.

Dialogue between the teacher and the student writers concerning evaluation also allows the teacher more options. Optimally, the students should be able to assess their own papers. However, if the teacher assesses the writing, the students should have input. One effective technique for this is to have the writers attach statements to their papers in which they give the criteria they would like used in assessing their work. The writers and teacher then have complementary roles in the writing process.

As the teacher facilitates the students' writing process, it becomes apparent that the writing stages overlap and sometimes compete for the students' attention. Student writers do not simply move linearly from procedure to procedure. Their own recursive inner processes dictate the sequence. Rarely do students inhibit themselves while writing from spontaneously editing, revising, and sharing. The stages are ongoing, and with the guidance of the instructor, student writers are able to direct their attention while still acknowledging the demands of their inner processes. (See Figure 1 for an illustration of this conceptual model.)

The result of structuring a composition course around the concept of writing as a process is that student writers come to understand that they have ideas to express, that they can find words to communicate those ideas, that others are interested in what they have to say, and finally that they have or can acquire the expertise to clarify that communication. The teacher facilitates all this and takes satisfaction in watching the writing of students improve. In order to help students discover their individual writing processes, the teacher may have to restructure the classroom and constantly reevaluate his or her role as a writing teacher. The result of this is that the teacher will probably feel better about being a teacher/facilitator of writing primarily because his or her students are becoming much better writers.

Fig. 1. The Writing Process

How Do You *Really* Write?

By Susan Starbuck

**English Teacher, Jordan High School,
Long Beach Unified School District;
and Teacher/Consultant, UCI Writing Project**

Note: The following is a letter I wrote to a colleague at my high school after I attended the 1981 UCI Writing Project's summer institute.

Dear Sheila:

How do you *really* write? I don't mean how do you teach how to write, but how do you actually do it? If this question were your essay assignment, how would you approach it? Would you write an outline? Or would something else happen first? At what point would you develop a thesis? Do you have it developed before the first draft? When do you revise the paper: as you go or after you finish a draft completely? When do you correct the grammar and diction? Even more important, whom do you write for? Who is your audience? What would you say to me that you wouldn't say to another teacher?

The UCI Writing Project came through for me after all, so I've just spent five weeks thinking about these issues. But I haven't been observing the end product of a writing assignment and analyzing what the students can and cannot do. Instead, I have been writing again—getting in touch with the whole scope of writing, not just the expository essays I have been doing for graduate school. In so doing I have "acquired," a key word in the Writing Project, a new view of teaching writing. I understand what we are doing well and why, and I can suggest how we can do it better.

I have been teaching writing in these steps: brainstorm, formulate a thesis, outline, write, rewrite. I present this as a linear process. I tell students that they may abandon their outline in the process of writing or that the rewrite might look very different from the original draft; but I don't think many of them hear me, and now I think I wasn't really sure what I was saying.

The process I just described is very left-brain. Indeed, I do many left-brain functions as I work on a paper. But the truth is I do not get my original ideas from the left brain, as I realized when I listened to

Gabriele Rico, an English and Creative Arts Professor from California State University, San Jose. I definitely use my right-brain integration periodically to sense the whole, constantly moving back and forth in some kind of recursive process between brain functions to shape and order my material.

Personally, I start the writing process with brainstorming to sense the whole pattern, but my experience of brainstorming is not linear just because I jot words in lines on a page. By the time I do an outline, however, my thinking is very linear and left-brain. Yet, long ago, I learned to transcend outlines, to let things happen in some sort of natural way as I wrote, and to ignore or change the outline as I wrote. Furthermore, I figured out that rewriting meant more than changing the words and correcting the grammar; it meant deleting, adding, rearranging, and substituting as much as a page of what I had written or scrapping the entire beginning. Consequently, I am writing this letter in stages that hardly resemble what I teach.

I still haven't been able to form an outline of what I want to say to you because that outline is emerging during the self-discovery of writing. But I know from experience that I will be able to outline this letter when I finish because I have a firmly "acquired" sense of the form of written language.

This summer I learned a more accurate process model to teach to students than I had been using. This model more closely parallels my actual writing process and helps students help each other to "acquire" written language skills through meaningful, social interaction. The model is circular rather than linear and is often recursive in nature. I know through observations of the writing group I participated in that recursiveness, going back to move forward, will begin to happen as a by-product of interaction. The new model looks like this:

And it's all leading to the development of three types of composing skills: fluency, form, and correctness.

I can't wait to get back to the classroom and implement what I've learned. I know that my new perspective on the writing process will definitely influence my teaching. I'm anxious to see how this will affect my students. I'll keep you posted on how things go. In the meantime, why not discover how you really write by writing me back!

Love,

Susan

Interviews—A Good Way to Get Started

By Martha Johnson
Academic Skills Center, San Diego State University;
Codirector, Cooperative Writing Program;
and Teacher/Consultant, San Diego Area Writing Project

Two years ago at the beginning of the semester, I asked students to interview each other and hoped it would help to establish a relaxed atmosphere for writing. Interviewing one another did. It immediately got them talking and writing, and much to my delight, it introduced the writing process as well. I have used this assignment in all my classes with considerable success ever since.

Students are asked to interview someone sitting near them. Each student is given five minutes to ask questions and jot down notes about the other student's background and interests before reversing roles for another five minutes. Then they have 15 minutes to organize a rough draft from their notes. Finally, they read their drafts to their partners for reactions and suggestions so that misconceptions can be corrected and information can be added or deleted. The critical aspect of this partnership is that the listeners are vitally interested in what they are hearing. They do not automatically say, "That's fine," because they are listening to something about themselves.

I end the hour with a few tips for revising what they wrote. I suggest that they focus on something special about the person: hobbies or skills, an unusual background, or future goals. And, of course, if they discovered the other student was making a fortune by growing mushrooms in a closet, it would not hurt to mention that also.

The next day I asked for volunteers to read their papers. There are always a few who will, and they are usually writers of lively papers. The students enjoy hearing about others in the class, and it gives me a chance to comment on the papers' strengths as well as point out how each writer has a sense of style—an individual voice. I conclude by telling the students that in writing about the interview, they have gone through each phase of the writing process: collecting information, organizing ideas, writing, sharing, revising, and editing. They have also learned how important it is to be accurate in their efforts to create a vivid, yet honest, impression of their fellow students.

I have used this assignment with high school students, undergraduates, and with teachers in a graduate seminar, and I have always been pleased by what it accomplishes. It minimizes the dread of writing and feelings of inadequacy. It gets students talking, laughing, and sharing their writing efforts. It is a good way for the teacher to get to know the class and an enjoyable way to introduce the writing process.

Introducing Teachers to the Concept of Writing as a Process

By Sue Rader Willett
English Teacher, Capistrano Valley High School,
Capistrano Unified School District;
and Teacher/Consultant, UCI Writing Project

Practice what you preach! Those few simple words have to be one of the most irritating, guilt-inducing, challenging, hackneyed, and—begrudgingly, I admit—wisest adages I know. They have certainly taunted and guided me through many personal dilemmas, classroom lessons, and, oddly enough, in-service workshops for colleagues, administrators, and lay people.

In fact, I consciously work to practice what we, the teacher/consultants from the UCI Writing Project, enthusiastically preach and teach. Much of our approach to the teaching of writing boils down to five tenets:

1. Teachers of writing should, themselves, write so that they are in touch with their own writing abilities.

2. Students should experience audiences other than the teacher as assessor. Other audiences include self, peer, and teacher as a partner in learning.
3. Peer response groups can lessen the load of correcting papers and yet ensure that the students get ample writing experiences and constant feedback.
4. Students should be involved in the evaluation process.
5. Teachers should stress the written product less and emphasize writing as a process more.

Writing is, indeed, one of the most complex intellectual and emotional processes a person engages in.
SUE RADER WILLETT

Those basic statements of philosophy can easily be translated into an in-service training design.

Planning an in-service training program to introduce the concept of writing as a process is very much like planning any lesson, meeting, or composition. One begins by forming a clear idea of the audience to be addressed and the message to be communicated. Once these two items have been defined, one has to create a procedural plan for presenting the writing process.

I believe that it is imperative to "hook" your audience within the first few seconds of your in-service training workshop, and the easiest and most effective way to do that is to immediately involve them on a very personal level. What is a better way of doing that than writing?

"The Popcorn Reminiscence," which I have used as an opening for in-service training, is a simple exercise in sensory/descriptive and narrative writing. (A little exposition might work itself in here and there, too.) Save the theory and research for later. Begin with an experience, such as the one for "The Popcorn Reminiscence" outlined below:

THE POPCORN REMINISCENCE

1. Planning the experience (to be completed before the in-service training begins):
   a. Assemble the popcorn popper, popcorn, butter, salt, oil (preferable for olfactory impact), serving utensils, and napkins.
   b. Pop or purchase enough prepared popcorn to serve the participants.
   c. Set up your equipment and utensils near a working electrical outlet.

2. Prewriting activity
   a. While the popcorn is popping and the aroma is permeating the entire room, ask the participants to begin clustering the word *popcorn*. Direct them to include any experiences they connect with popcorn.
   b. Serve the popcorn while they cluster. Taste will spark more ideas.
   c. You may wish to use an overhead projector or chalkboard to record (cluster) their words, as shown in Figure 2.

3. Writing activity
   a. Inform the students that they should begin writing when they feel ready and believe they have clustered enough. A prompt might be:

      Write a short personal reminiscence that involves popcorn.

   b. Explain that what they write will be read and evaluated by others for content and any other attributes you wish to include.
   c. Write with them if possible. Many will be nervous, and your openness will help.

4. Postwriting activity
   a. After a few minutes of writing, ask them to finish up and quickly reread for minor editing. Stress that papers are to be read as first and very rough drafts.
   b. Ask each participant to record the last four digits of his or her telephone number at the top of the page and to title the piece.
   c. Conduct a "read around" for evaluation. (See the section on read-around groups, which appears later in the book, for a description of this technique.) Direct the readers to jot down the numbers of the papers they most enjoyed.
   d. After all the papers have been read, ask the participants to share the numbers of the papers they enjoyed. Record the numbers on a chart or chalkboard, and positively reinforce those whose numbers appeared.

5. Establishing closure and directing the participants to take a short break
   a. During the break encourage the participants to discuss the experience they shared.

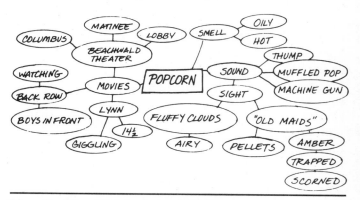

Fig. 2. The Clustering of *Popcorn*

b. You may wish to join in informally or take this time to collect your thoughts or clean up the popcorn area.

After your audience has written and has immersed themselves in the very activity we so quickly demand of our students, they will be open to a fresh view of the complexity of the writing process with all its cognitive and affective variables. Marlene Scardamalia reminds us how complex the task of written composition is:

> "The proposition that it is theoretically impossible to learn to write has the ring of truth," says Peter Elbow [in *Writing Without Teachers*, 1973, page 135]. Too many interdependent skills are involved, and all seem to be prerequisite to one another. To pay conscious attention to handwriting, spelling, punctuation, word choice, syntax, textual connections, purpose, organization, clarity, rhythm, euphony, and reader characteristics would seemingly overload the information processing capacity of the best intellects.[1]

Every practicing writer intuitively knows that. We must reinforce that knowledge and use it wisely. Your audience knows that writing, good writing, is extremely difficult to achieve. Yet, they must be made aware that it can be done in a much less than chaotic, hit-or-miss fashion that many teachers practice—for want of better training and information.

Therefore, it is helpful to explain the writing process at this point in your presentation. It may include these stages:

1. Prewriting: Brainstorming, collecting material, and giving data from which an assignment is written (clustering, lecture, experience, discussion, and so forth).
2. Precomposing: The assignment is given, and a writing plan is formulated (mapping, outlining, and so forth).
3. Writing: Ideas from prewriting and precomposing are developed and given form in verse or prose.
4. Sharing: Writing is shared with others (partner or group) for positive feedback or suggestions for revision.
5. Rewriting: Based on the feedback received in the sharing step, additions and deletions are made on paper.
6. Evaluation: The writing is scored on the basis of a rubric, a list of desirable qualities a paper is measured against (formal or informal).
7. Rewriting and reevaluation: This is an optional step that may be used as many times as necessary.

Remind your audience that writing is a recursive process, and even though we may logically delineate its various stages, they do not occur in a nice, neat, orderly fashion. In fact, they often happen all at once or out of sequence. Writing is, indeed, one of the most complex intellectual and even emotional processes a person engages in, and it draws from the left and right hemispheres of the brain. While the process model outlined above is certainly not a perfect description of the writing activity, it does serve as a very effective teaching design, one that is readily understood by children and adults. (For more information on the process, see the Department of Education's *Handbook for Planning an Effective Writing Program*.)

After discussing the writing process generally and emphasizing the complexity of thought and the stages of the process, you might want to establish that teachers of writing can systematically work to improve writing based on the three goals of fluency, form, and correctness, as defined below:

- Fluency: Authentic voice, facility with words and phrasing, ability to be spontaneous, a "mature" or appropriate vocabulary, a sense of pacing
- Form: Logical development, adequate transition, use of supporting details, variation of sentence structure
- Correctness: Using the conventions of written English (spelling, punctuation, grammar) and departing from them only for a valid reason

We must work to refine and practice the goals of fluency, form, and correctness in our lessons and in our personal writing. I believe it would be safe to assume that these are the same goals even the most respected and prolific writers seek to perfect.

As much as we would like to believe that writing can be perfected, I am not certain that it can be. Certainly, the "greats" come close. Blasphemous as it may sound, consider that William Shakespeare, Alexander Pope, Samuel Johnson, Thomas Hardy, Raymond Chandler, D. H. Lawrence, Ernest Hemingway, Carl Sandburg, Henry David Thoreau, and all the other great writers still needed to refine certain aspects of these goals. And although our students and we writers

---

[1]Marlene Scardamalia, "How Children Cope with the Cognitive Demands of Writing," in *Writing: Process, Development and Communication*, Vol. 2 of *Writing: The Nature, Development, and Teaching of Written Communication*. Edited by Carl H. Frederiksen and Joseph F. Dominic. Hillsdale, N. J.: Lawrence Erlbaum Associates, Publishers, 1981, p. 81. Used by permission of the publisher.

certainly produce works that are far from perfect, we face the same task and the same problems as they did—step by step by step. *Great* writing may be a long way off, but *good* writing could be right around the corner. Just remember, Johnny can and does write with the proper guidance. Your in-service training can make a difference to Johnny's teacher if you plan it with a philosophy in mind, involve your audience as writers, present a systematic approach to teaching, and, of course, *practice what you preach.*

The Demonstration Lesson

By Paulette Morgan
English Teacher, El Monte High School,
El Monte Union High School District;
and Teacher/Consultant, UCI Writing Project

The day before the principal arrives for evaluation is not the best time to begin writing lessons. A few phrases scribbled in a planning book are not adequate either. I used to think I could carry every detail of the lesson in my brain ready to be tapped at a moment's notice, but now I know a better way. The clearest, most specific understanding of the lessons I teach are those spelled out specifically in a format that includes all the details of what is to be taught. Not only do the students understand more clearly what is expected of them, but I also have a firmer grasp of my subject. I also have lessons to trade, to reuse, and to spark new lessons.

The following includes a lesson for the teacher about writing lessons and a lesson for students modeling the lesson for the teachers. Both are based on the concept of writing as a process.

Lesson objective: The teacher will write a lesson that fosters both thinking and writing skills.

1. Prewriting
   a. Construct activities and experiences that lead students to value the writing process and to have confidence in themselves as writers.
   b. Generate ideas that may not be specific to the prompt but that foster higher levels of critical thinking.
   c. Provide for the visual, auditory, kinesthetic, or experiential needs of the students and the thinking and writing skills they are being called on to use.

2. Prompt
   a. Write specific directions for the task.
   b. Tell what is required in terms of fluency, form, and correctness.
   c. Explain what is expected in the content of the final piece of writing.
   d. Remember: The more specific the prompt and the clearer the criteria for evaluation, the better able the student will be to respond appropriately.
   e. Reveal to students the criteria for evaluation. There are to be no secrets or mysteries about how the writing will be judged.

3. Precomposing
   a. Structure activities and experiences to help students generate ideas specific to the prompt.
   b. Include many and various activities.
   c. Aid students in developing a writing plan.
   d. Provide models of what is expected of them.

4. Writing
   a. Allow them time to think.
   b. Stress fluency.
   c. Specify guidelines in precomposing and again in writing to assist students in composing a first draft.
   d. Remove as many constraints and stress factors as possible by providing adequate input in prewriting and precomposing.

5. Sharing
   a. Plan how the students will read and comment on one another's writing.
   b. Provide a list of guide questions and comments to direct students in their responses.
   c. Decide what the role of the teacher will be in the sharing process.

6. Revising
   a. Explain how responses can be used to reassess the quality of the students' own work.
   b. Provide models.
   c. Allow them time to rewrite.

7. Editing
   a. Specify and reinforce the requirements of the correctness from the prompt.

8. Evaluating
   a. Decide on the method to be used to judge the writing.
   b. Specify and reinforce the requirements of the prompt.
   c. Judge and evaluate.

9. Postwriting
   a. Plan what will be done with the writing next (displayed, used as learning tool, shared with another audience).

In the following lesson, "I Am a Scallop," criteria are presented for designing lessons according to the writing process. Use the lesson as a model for developing lessons of your own.

I AM A SCALLOP

Lesson: In this lesson, you will be asked to assume the persona of a creature living in a sea shell and to write a first person narrative. You will need to imagine, illustrate, sequence, and apply research material in order to tell a story.

PREWRITING

Visit a tide pool or marine museum. Experience the land, sea, air, and the total environment with classmates and instructor. Ask questions of, and discuss experiences with, others.

Examine a variety of sea shells. Compare size, color, structure, texture, and appearance.

List the characteristics of one shell you have chosen that distinguishes it from the other shells. Use all five senses.

Draw a picture of the shell you have chosen. Color it as accurately as your skills permit.

PROMPT

Imagine you are a creature living in a seashell. Write a story about a day in your life. Describe yourself and your shell in vivid, colorful language. Describe the area in which you live. Tell about and describe the other creatures and plants that live there. Explain how you get food and what you eat. Illustrate a typical predator and what might happen to you if you became the victim. Demonstrate how you would protect yourself. Make the story informative as well as dramatic, especially when you are protecting yourself.

Criteria for judging the writing will be posted on the board for the period of time you are writing.

The clearest lessons are spelled out specifically in a format that includes all the details of what is to be taught.
PAULETTE MORGAN

PRECOMPOSING

Look up, in an encyclopedia, information about the creature you will be. Read the entry and list specific details about biologic and environmental factors you would be a part of.

Make a list of answers to the following questions for use during your writing:

1. What does your environment look like? What other plants and animals live there?
2. In what areas of the ocean would you live? How far under the surface would you live?
3. What do you eat? How do you get your food? How do you travel around?

4. What do you look like? What size are you? Are you a male or a female? How do you meet others like yourself? How long do you live?
5. What creatures would be likely to eat you? How does such a predator get you out of the shell? How do you protect yourself?

Share lists in response groups. Ask response partners for ideas and information you might add to your list.

WRITING

Write a rough draft of the story following the guidelines of the prompt. Do not be concerned with form or correctness.

SHARING

Use this checklist to respond to writing in your response groups:

1. Is there vivid detail about the creature and its shell? Put a star at the beginning of each sentence that shows detail.
2. Does the writer describe the environment so you can see a picture of it in your mind? Underline sentences that make you picture the scene.
3. Based on what was written, do you fully understand what it is like being this creature? If so, write a positive comment on the paper. If not, write a suggestion about how the writer could make the story more understandable or better.
4. Did the description of the predator and what it might do make you want to avoid it? If so, write "UCK!" at the beginning of the story.
5. Is the story organized so that it reads smoothly and does not jump from one item to another? Does the story have closure? If so, write "SMOOTHIE" at the top. If not, write suggestions that might improve the organization or closure.

REVISING

Write a second draft of the story and incorporate the suggestions and comments made by response partners. Rework and revise the parts that need improvement.

EDITING

Each student must read two other stories for correctness. Your story must be read by two others for correctness. Pay particular attention to spelling, punctuation, sentence structure, and organization.

Write a final copy, double spaced, and in your best handwriting (or typed). Add a title and submit it for evaluation.

EVALUATION

Use the following guide for judging the stories. (This can be done by the teacher, students, or a combination of both.)

5 = Rich in detail and description that makes the reader picture the creature, the shell, its life, and the predator. Story is told in first person with few or minor errors in correctness.

3 = Adequate story, few or bland descriptions, but significant problems with correctness and structure. Consistent point of view in story.

1 = Sketchy details, poor organization, serious problems with structure and correctness. Shifts in point of view.

Talking Students Through the Thinking-Writing Process

By Jerry Judd

**English Teacher, Irvine High School,
Irvine Unified School District;
and Teacher/Consultant, UCI Writing Project**

I have always been a believer in writing with my students, becoming a partner in learning, and engaging in a true dialogue with them about the writing and learning that are occurring in my classroom. To begin this process, I direct students through prewriting activities to help them generate ideas, give them the prompt to guide them, and provide precomposing activities to aid them in translating their thoughts into print. Then the writing begins. At this point, I used to sit at my desk and observe some students writing successfully, some sitting puzzled, not exactly sure what to do next, and others staring at the ceiling, blank page, or at the scrawling hand of the person next to them.

Since I have been exposed to the concept of metacognition, I have become aware of how important it is to model my own thinking and writing process as my students are engaged in the act of composing. *Metacognition,* in its simplest sense, can be defined as thinking about thinking. It is a conscious monitoring of one's own thinking process. It could be the ability to realize that you do not understand something another person just said. It could be paraphrasing aloud what someone has just told you to determine whether he will agree that that is, in fact, exactly what was meant. It could be the realization that someone does not know enough about a particular subject to write effectively about it and needs to gather more information before beginning to write. I have found that one of the most valuable uses of metacognition is as a tool for self-questioning. Rarely, if ever, have students had the opportunity to listen to how a writer thinks during the writing process. My students needed to hear how a writer progressed through the same writing assignments that they were doing.

So, now, when my students are ready to begin writing a draft, I talk them through my own thinking-writing process. I begin by thinking aloud. Those students who are working well are instructed to continue writing and to ignore me. They pause only momentarily as my voice begins; then they go back to their work. Those who are having trouble starting to write focus their attention on me and what I am saying. I admit that at first they look at me and think I am somewhat crazy talking to myself, rambling, talking off the top of my head, and jotting down ideas on the overhead projector. But they get used to this activity rather quickly. There is value in having students see *raw* words scrawled on the page, the first draft being illuminated by the light of the overhead projector.

Here is a partial list of questions to ask yourself when starting this self-talk, self-questioning, metacognitive technique:

What do I want to write about?
What do I know about this subject?
What essential knowledge do I lack about this subject?
What do I want to say about this subject?
How will I organize my piece?
Who is my audience?
What effect do I want to have on my audience?
How do I get from the beginning of this piece to the end?

The only ground rule during this process is that no one can interrupt me or ask questions. I admit, at first, this is a frightening thing to put myself through. Some teachers may want to forego my ground rule and elicit comments and suggestions from the class if they get stuck. It is valuable, though, for teachers to become *stuck* in their thinking. Perhaps this is the best pedagogical tool of all. For it is here that students are able to see the difficulty of the writing process, even for the teacher of writing. "Let's see how he gets himself out of this one," I can almost hear a student think as he leans back in his chair against the back wall.

I go through this self-questioning/thinking aloud process while the students listen, get ideas, and then begin their own drafts. I also do a similar process during the revision and editing stages of the writing process. I do this with my writing as an example and also with students' drafts. Sometimes, students will take my place and sit in the "writer's chair" at the overhead projector and think and write before their classmates.

I have found this technique invaluable in demonstrating to inexperienced writers how a writer thinks through the writing process. This technique brings students in the class in touch with their own problem-solving process and allows them to assess and see what *thinking* must occur before they can write.

For most of the students, they are seeing a new persona they have not encountered in a teacher before. After observing me in this process, my students look at me differently—as a writer, as someone who shares the same frustrations and triumphs as they do. Students often comment that other teachers have told them *what* to write, but I am the first one who has ever shown them *how* to write.

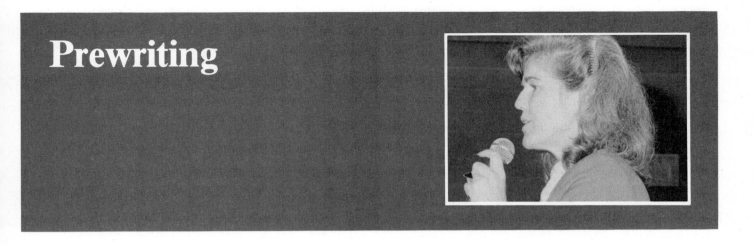

Prewriting

Clustering: A Prewriting Process

By Gabriele Lusser Rico
Associate Professor, English and Creative Arts,
California State University, San Jose

Even after several years of continued experiments with clustering in my classrooms, I remain awed at its simple power, excited by its many applications, surprised at the changes it has wrought in my overall approach to teaching.

The clustering process grew out of my fascination with the findings from brain research of the past 20 years, and it represents a way to involve the talents of the mute right brain in the complex symbolic activity that we call writing. The story of specialized capacities of the two hemispheres of the brain has been told again and again. In this brief space it is enough to say that the left brain has primarily logical, linear, and syntactic capabilities while the right brain has holistic, image-making, and synthetic capabilities.

Clustering is based on the premise that any effective writing effort moves from a whole—no matter how vague or tenuous—to the parts, then back to a more clearly delineated whole. What is of overriding importance for writing is that the talents of both hemispheres of the brain be brought into play in the process. Clustering focuses on that initial whole by fashioning a trial web of knowings from the clusterer's mental storehouse.

What Is It?

Exactly what is clustering? I can define clustering, as a nonlinear brainstorming process that generates ideas, images, and feelings around a stimulus word until a pattern becomes discernible. But the student evaluation of clustering, as shown in Figure 3, presents a clearer, more graphic definition. As this student indicates, clustering makes silent, invisible mental processes visible and manipulable; hence, teachable and utilizable. In short, clustering is a powerful mental tool.

How Does It Work?

How does clustering work? It works, very likely, by blocking the critical censorship of the analytic left brain and by allowing the synthesizing right brain to make flash-like nonlinear connections. A cluster is an expanding universe, and each word is a potential galaxy; each galaxy, in turn, may throw out its own universes. As students cluster around a stimulus word, the encircled words rapidly radiate outward until a sudden shift takes place, a sort of "Aha!" that signals a sudden awareness of that tentative whole which allows students to begin writing.

What Are Appropriate Instructions?

What instructions should you give to begin this prewriting process? I have found the following both appropriate and effective:

1. Tell students that they are going to learn to use a tool that will enable them to write more easily and more powerfully, a tool similar to brainstorming.

2. Encircle a word on the board—for example, energy—and ask students, "What do you think of when you see that word?" Encourage all

responses. Cluster these responses, radiating outward. When they have finished giving their responses, say, "See how many ideas there are floating around in your heads? Now, if you cluster all by yourself, you will have a set of connections as unique to your own mind as your thumbprint is to your thumb."

3. Now ask students to cluster a second word for themselves. Before they begin, tell them that the clustering process should take no more than one to two minutes and that the paragraph they will write should take about eight minutes. Ask them to keep clustering until the "Aha!" shift, signaling that their mind is holding something they can shape into a whole. In writing, the only constraint is that they "come full circle"; i.e., that they do not leave the writing unfinished. Some excellent words are *afraid* or *try* or *help*.

4. After they finish writing, ask students to give a title to what they have written that is suggestive of the whole.

Figure 4 is a cluster and paragraph by a college freshman written on the first day I introduced clustering to the class. Note the quality of wholeness—the completeness of the piece. Note the rather sophisticated stylistic devices, such as repetition and parallel con-

struction, which increasingly become a part of student writing as students continue to cluster. Note also that this ten-minute effort, although complete in itself, has the potential of being developed into a highly focused, longer piece of writing. The organic center is already there.

What Is the Effect of Clustering?

The writer whose cluster and paragraph are reproduced in Figure 4 discovered—even after the first time—that clustering was easy and unthreatening. Since a cluster draws on primary impressions—yet simultaneously on a sense of the overall design—clustering actually generates structure, shaping one thought into a starburst of other thoughts, each somehow related to the whole. That is why clustering so often results in writing that is naturally marked by increased coherence, increased fluency, increased concrete support, and an increased sense of how to expand ideas.

Perhaps the most significant outcome of clustering is its idiosyncratic nature. A stimulus word filtered through the singular experiential grid of each individual clusterer produces a unique constellation. The stimulus (cluster word) *fragments,* for example, produced three widely divergent responses, as shown in Figure 5.

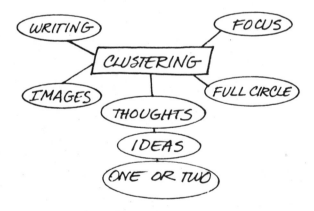

I believe that clustering is a natural process we do unconsciously in our minds. It is more helpful to do it on paper, though. Our mind clusters many ideas and thoughts, but it is unable to sort and sift the ideas into a reasonable order around one main focus. When we cluster on paper, we can visually look at our ideas and choose which ones we want to use. The thoughts in our mind are all piled together, and we see only one or two at a time. On paper, through clustering, we can see all our thoughts at once as a whole.

Fig. 3. An Anonymous Student Evaluation of Clustering

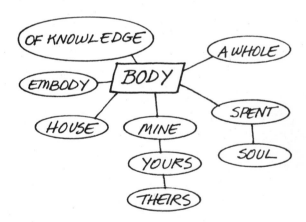

I sometimes wish for a different one—this body that is me. I am inside this scrawny hide that other people react to instead of to the real me. They look at me real funny-like sometimes; maybe they wonder what's inside. So I talk, and they hear what is inside by what I say; perhaps they see what is inside by how I move; or maybe they guess what is inside by what I do. Now, you please talk to me, so I can know something about the you inside your body.

Fig. 4. Paragraph Developed from Clustering *Body*

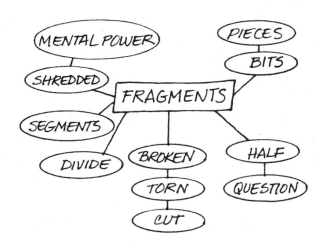

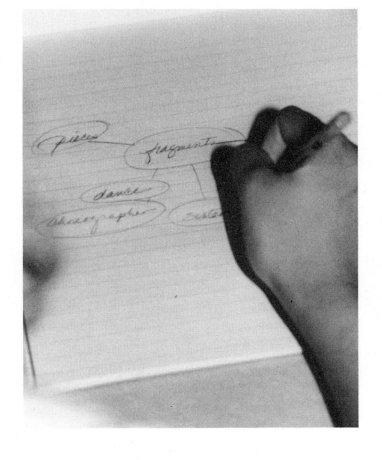

When I think of the word, fragment, *it makes me try to visualize the inside of my head. It just seems as though my mind is always divided, never really coming to a whole. One half wants to do something that the other half doesn't want to do. One seems to be saying, "Come on, let's not go to class; you can do your paper later," while the other side of my mind answers back, "but I have to because I'll be missing out on my learning." These two halves go on and on like that, just bruising the inside of my mind, and, if they continue, they'll probably shred my mind all to pieces.*

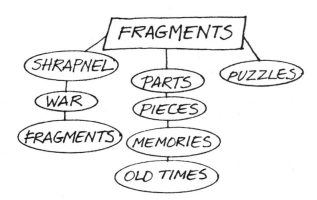

Sometimes, when I'm sitting back, relaxed and reminiscing over old times in my head, small fragments of memories will flash through my mind. They never stay long enough to be recognized by my brain as a complete thought. They seem to stay just long enough to bring back the emotion of the moment, and I will find myself smiling or frowning or wanting to cry. I wish I could grab hold of these pieces of my memory—especially the happy ones—as they fly by the recall part of my brain, but I am happy at least for the glimpses I get.

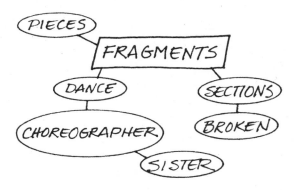

My sister choreographed a dance called "Fragments" last year for the SJSU Arts Department. The reason she named her dance "Fragments" was that the whole dance was made up of bits and pieces of dances. There were about five different movements making up the whole dance. It was as if the entire dance were broken up into five separate themes. Because there was no fixed pattern, the dance really didn't make sense. The dance definitely did not flow together. Well, that was the purpose of her dance—fragments.

Fig. 5. Three Responses to Clustering the Word *Fragments*

In summary, clustering engenders and encourages expressive behavior at all levels of proficiency. As with any useful tool, be it pen or paintbrush, the more it is used, the more natural its use becomes. In my own teaching I have made clustering an integral part of all the writing assignments, long or short, and suggest further that it be introduced as a right-brain tool from the earliest grades onward. The most effective means for getting the *feel* of clustering is to introduce it conjointly with journal writing. Journal writing, long a part of most English curricula with limited success, will take on new dimensions through the focusing power of clustering. As students begin to experience that sense of accomplishment in actually producing a cluster, they discover that they do have something to say after all. They also discover that writing begins to flow on its own if a sense of play is allowed to enter the process. The student's evaluation of clustering in Figure 6 focuses precisely on this play-element of clustering.

Yes, clustering is "fooling around," indeed. Instead of writing as sheer labor, clustering turns writing into something closer to cultivated play. In so doing, such "fooling around" makes contact with our natural right-brain potential for creating connections, for perceiving one idea related to another, and for seeing the world whole.

EDITOR'S NOTE: For further information on clustering, see Gabriele Rico's and Mary Frances Claggett's monograph, *Balancing in the Hemispheres: Brain Research and the Teaching of Writing,* which was published in 1980 by the Bay Area Writing Project, 1615 Tolman Hall, University of California, Berkeley, CA 94720. You will find Dr. Rico's new book, *Writing the Natural Way,* helpful. It was published by J. P. Tarcher, Inc., 9110 Sunset Blvd., Suite 250, Los Angeles, CA 90069; and distributed by Houghton Mifflin Co.

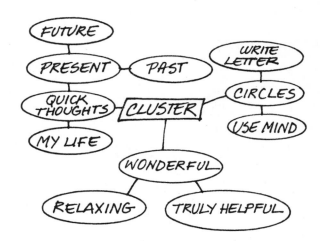

I sat down to work in order to catch up on some journal entries when my mother stood over my shoulder and noticed my clustering. Puzzled, she inquired, "Why are you fooling around making circles when you have work to do?" It seemed a silly idea to her, and it did to me also when I first encountered it. However, I have come to admire my little circles, for it is those circles with words in them that generate thoughts, bring back experiences, and enable me to use my mind to the utmost.

Clustering can be summed up in one word: wonderful. I have learned something that I will carry with me for the rest of my life; that is, I have learned to generate ideas. Thank goodness for those circles.

Fig. 6. A Student's Evaluation of Clustering

Practical Ideas for Using Clustering in the Prewriting Stage

Clustering with Nonreaders/Writers

By Michael Carr
Teacher, Los Alamitos Elementary School,
Los Alamitos Unified School District;
and Teacher/Consultant, UCI Writing Project

Clustering is a method of prewriting that enables the writer to map out all of his or her thoughts on a particular subject and then to choose which ones to use. With nonreaders, clustering can be used for the same purpose. With readers, words are clustered around a central topic, as shown in Figure 7. Non-

readers can experiment with the same technique by using symbols (pictures) to represent the words. In my class we start with a topic, such as being afraid, and then do a group cluster on the board. For example, I

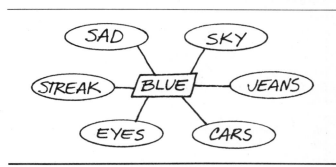

Fig. 7. The Clustering of *Blue*

asked the children to tell me all of the things they were afraid of, and we created a cluster that looked like the one in Figure 8.

Fig. 8. Clustering with Nonreaders

Most of our group clusters had at least 15 items. However, even though the group cluster in Figure 8 is abbreviated in scope, it contains the major topic points. After doing a group cluster, the children then do their own cluster on large sheets of newsprint, using as many or as few items from the group cluster as they wish to. The children also have the option of adding items to their own cluster that were not present on the group cluster. An example of an individual cluster is shown in Figure 9.

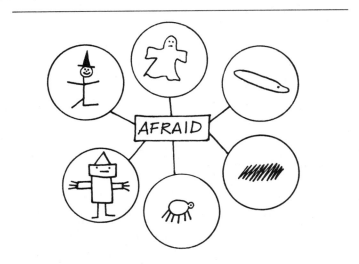

Fig. 9. A Nonreader's Clustering of *Afraid*

From the group cluster the children choose something they wish to write about. Tony, the author of the cluster shown in Figure 9, chose to write about witches. He then did his final drawing on white ditto paper:

Tony dictated, "I am afraid of witches because they might have ghosts." His picture included other elements of things he was afraid of, such as the dark. Note that the children dictate their sentence to me; I write it on paper, and then they copy it.

In clustering with symbols, I have found that children in my class always have something to write, because they do not have to worry about decoding skills that they do not possess. After awhile the children created clusters that included a few words they knew, along with the symbols for those words. By the end of the year, some of the children were able to use all the words in their cluster or a combination of words and symbols. When students are at a point where they can generate three or four sentences, I have them number the word/pictures in their cluster to help them organize their ideas.

The process I use to teach clustering to nonreaders/writers can be described as follows:

1. Introduce the topic and get a few oral responses.
2. Write the topic word on the chalkboard and circle it.
3. Draw all the children's responses to the topic cluster.
4. Have children create their own clusters on large newsprint.
5. Have the children choose those symbols from their clusters that they want to write about and draw the symbols on good paper.
6. Have the children dictate their sentences to you; then have each student copy his or her sentence. (Noncopiers can trace.)
7. Have the children read their papers in a sharing group.

This technique has produced a feeling of "can do" when it comes to writing in my classroom. All the children are able to succeed and begin to see themselves as writers. And, before they know it, they are!

Clustering in First Grade

By Kathy Pierce
Teacher, Horace Mann School,
Anaheim Elementary School District;
and Teacher/Consultant, UCI Writing Project

Clustering is an open-ended, nonlinear form of sorting ideas. It is a visual structuring of concepts, events, and feelings. Once the main focus is chosen or provided, ideas may be generated around it. By clustering on paper, the children can sift and sort their thoughts into a whole. Clustering helps make writing more like the taking of a picture—thereby making writing less frightening.

In the first grade, clustering helps students generate ideas and enables them to relate to something and to write about it. Group clustering is very easy and enjoyable for the children. Using a shared experience—field trips, cooking, special events, or any created situation—students may form a group cluster on the chalkboard. Questions, especially those involving the five senses, will elicit descriptive responses. Children can then form their own sentences from the group cluster. For example, after the children made popcorn, they created the cluster shown in Figure 10.

Individual clustering is also very successful for first graders, especially if you can talk personally with each child. Use questioning to elicit a response as to what the main focus is to be. Additional appropriate questions can generate the images for their clustering, and they can write their own stories from their clusters. After an art project my students formed the cluster shown in Figure 11.

Using journal writing as a daily writing exercise is also a good way to get your students involved in clustering. With pictures, objects, words, or stories as stimuli, you can do the clustering on a chalkboard with the whole group. Then children can generate their own sentences in their journals.

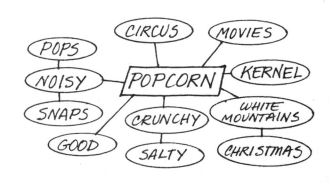

Fig. 10. Clustering of *Popcorn* by First Graders

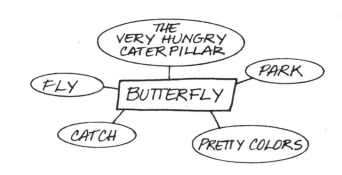

Fig. 11. Clustering of *Butterfly* After an Art Project

Clustering on Circles

By Elizabeth Williams Reeves
Teacher, Pine Middle School,
Los Alamitos Unified School District;
and Teacher/Consultant, UCI Writing Project

Jefferson Newman, one of my fifth grade students when I taught at Los Alamitos Elementary School, generated such marvelous descriptive writing through his clustering that I asked him if I could share it (Figure 12).

What I think is especially interesting about Jefferson's cluster is the way his mind churns out ideas—moving from concrete to abstract, from literal to symbolic. As he writes, the language of his cluster also becomes very rhythmical (almost circular); his form reinforces his content. And it evolved, almost effortlessly, from clustering.

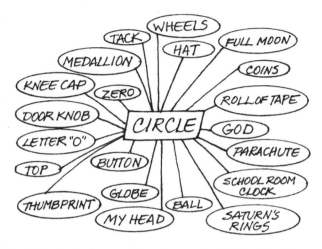

The circle is round and smooth. Coins like dimes and fifty cent pieces are in circles. A circle takes the formation of your knee cap. It is the form of Saturn's rings. The circle is the shape of a medallion glittering in the sun. A circle is like the rings of a bracelet. People get married and have a circle placed on their finger, a wedding ring. A circle shows the significance of how God is infinite. A circle takes the brightness of the full moon. I wear a button almost every day, a circle button. It reminds me of a classroom clock—ticktock, ticktock, ticking time slowly away. A circle is the egg that rests on your table. A circle is the base on which your hair rests. It is the turning of the doorknob, the orbiting of the planets, the parachute springing out as the person leaps out of the airplane. It is the thumbprint of a human being twisted and turned, making the whirls in your thumb. It is the wheel on a bicycle spinning round and round. A circle is a fascinating two-dimensional object.

Fig. 12. Paragraph Developed by Jefferson Newman from Clustering *Circle*

*For me, the initial delight
is in the surprise
of remembering something
I didn't know I knew.*
ROBERT FROST

It Works!

By Elizabeth B. Martinez
English Teacher, Saddleback High School,
Santa Ana Unified School District;
and Teacher/Consultant, UCI Writing Project

Several years ago I attended the annual conference of the California Association of Teachers of English, which was held in San Diego, California. Little did I realize that clustering, a prewriting technique presented at the conference by Gabriele Rico, would have such a powerful and positive impact on me. Not only did it influence my professional and personal life, but it also influenced the lives of my students and colleagues who were later exposed to it.

As I observed Dr. Rico's excellent presentation, I instantly felt that this was exactly what I had been searching for: a simple approach that would involve not just some of my students but rather all my students at any level of writing ability. Needless to say, I could hardly wait to get back to school to try it in my classes.

Daily, my students clustered words and then sentences; later they combined sentences and finally learned to develop a unified paragraph from the original cluster. I soon discovered that clustering could be used to teach almost any facet of an English program. What amazed me the most, however, was the strong response of acceptance with which the students received this technique. After three months of daily practice, I requested an anonymous response to this clustering. I was not surprised. The students overwhelmingly expressed enthusiasm with words of praise and appreciation for this "fun" activity. The one statement that consistently recurred was that the fear of writing had been greatly reduced. The students' attitudes toward writing over the three months had gradually improved. They had become more confident, their assignments were better prepared, and, finally, their grades reflected their success.

In conclusion, I must confess that I was ready to "throw in the towel," so to speak, after repeated years of hit-and-miss failures and successes in the teaching of writing. My personal good fortune of being exposed to clustering revolutionized and revitalized my career. I am now completing my twelfth year at Saddleback High School, and each new group of students that comes through my door receives a shower of clustering experiences. I can enthusiastically say, "I have not given up as a teacher of writing." I feel I am living testimony to the effectiveness and positive results of clustering.

Using Clustering as a Study Skill

By Susan Starbuck
English Teacher, Jordan High School,
Long Beach Unified School District;
and Teacher/Consultant, UCI Writing Project

Because clustering is a holistic process, it is a useful technique for review and study, especially for the essay exam. Through clustering, students can visually chart what they do and do not know, returning to their notes to fill in the blank areas in their charts. In the process they will discover and generate their own key or stimulus words that can be reduced and converted to easily memorized lists. As a result of this thorough review, clustering will build the students' confidence so that they can function well in an exam, even if they have to answer unanticipated questions. There are seven steps for using clustering to study for an essay exam:

1. *Review class materials and identify what is important.* Usually, before an exam, students have some idea of what the teacher has considered most important. Either the teacher designates the important areas during a review session and gives sample questions, or when reviewing their notes, the students identify key words and concepts the teacher has repeated several times. Likewise, the textbook usually contains the repeated key words and concepts in chapter headings and subheadings that reinforce what the teacher has presented. As they review their textbook, students should jot down all the key words and concepts.

2. *Make preliminary clusters.* Using the designated questions and/or the repeated key words and concepts as stimulus centers, the students make clusters to test their comprehension of the material. In some classes, however, the teacher has

not indicated what is important, and the notes the students have taken do not seem to be helpful. Therefore, after identifying what seems to be important, the students may want to do some reflecting by focusing on the class as a whole by using these questions to begin a clustering process: What has been the purpose of the class? What were the recurring themes, characters, and patterns in what we have been reading? The students further cluster each of the ideas that emerge through their master clusters, such as individual books, authors, periods, and so forth. By the time they complete this process, they will have a very good grasp of the dimensions of the class.

3. *Self-check.* When the students finish the clusters, they can go back to the original material in the notes and textbook to do a self-checking and to add any missing pieces to their clusters.

4. *Reduce material to basic clusters and stimulus words.* Because the students are testing their own recall by drawing on the right brain, they will not only be reviewing what they have already assimilated but will also be discovering and creating their own stimulus words. After making their preliminary clusters, the students may cluster again, using their own stimulus words as they focus the material more and more; their goal is

> *Writing should be taught in every class. Clear writing leads to clear thinking; clear thinking is the basis of clear writing. Perhaps more than any other form of communication, writing holds us responsible for our words and ultimately makes us more thoughtful human beings.*
> *ERNEST BOYER*

to reduce both clusters and stimulus words to the simplest possible form. As soon as they have condensed and focused the clusters, they will be able to make simple lists of stimulus words that are important for the exam.

5. *Memorize simplified lists from clusters.* Memorization will ensure that stimulus words are readily available for the exam.

6. *Review final cluster(s) on the morning before the exam.* A last minute review of their stimulus words will give the students confidence that they are knowledgeable about a number of different aspects of the subject.

7. *Cluster around specific test questions.* When they receive their questions at the exam, the students should spend a few minutes making specific clusters that will stimulate their memories and help them organize their thoughts in the terms presented by the question.

Having followed the seven-step process outlined above, the students will have reviewed and made the material so completely their own by translating it into their own words that they will be able to react with some insight to almost any question the teacher asks. On an essay exam the students will be able to construct answers that reveal their knowledge; for more than any other kind of exam, the essay obeys the rule Gabriele Rico quotes from Henry James, "The whole of anything is never told. You can take only what groups together." The students who use clustering will know immediately what "groups" they have available to formulate a good answer.

Propagating Clusters

By Michael O'Brien
English Teacher, Foothill High School,
Tustin Unified School District;
and Teacher/Consultant, UCI Writing Project

Think of them as flowers. Clusters do, after all, resemble flowers whose petals burst forth from the central corolla. Note that clusters do beautifully in both remedial and advanced classes but need to be tended faithfully.

Clusters have been very helpful to me in increasing student fluency. Even after I have done some practice ones on the board, however, some students have had a difficult time getting started on this technique. Be patient. They will become adept at clustering within a few days—a few petals at first, full blooms later on.

Clusters also do well in the "rarefied" atmosphere of the advanced classes. Use them in discussing literature, especially to show comparison and contrast. For example, look at how effectively my classes were able to contrast the two main settings of Shakespeare's *Antony and Cleopatra* (see Figure 13).

Finally, for best results, cultivate clusters faithfully. Use them for your own writing. Ask students to cluster often in a variety of situations. Because we so rarely assign tasks in high school that use the right hemisphere of the brain, students need to be reminded constantly of the clustering method.

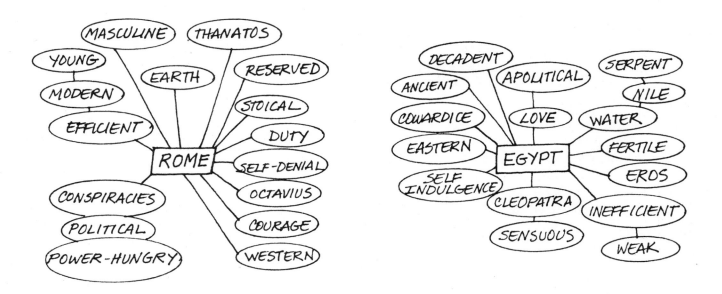

Fig. 13. Contrasting the Main Settings in *Antony and Cleopatra*

Prewriting
in the Elementary School

A Potpourri of Prewriting Ideas
for the Elementary Teacher

By Virginia Baldwin
Teacher, Gifted and Talented Education,
Del Cerro Elementary School, Saddleback Valley Unified School District;
and Teacher/Consultant, UCI Writing Project

The prewriting stage is the main ingredient of the writing process. The writing process can be described as a sort of recipe that brings a composition into being by forming, shaping, combining, or altering ideas initiated in the prewriting stage. A secret formula will not react without its catalyst, just as the writing process will not be successful without the stimulus of the prewriting experience.

Prewriting can be defined as anything that is done prior to composing and that creates motivation, increases conceptual knowledge, builds on to the language bank, stimulates the imagination, or spurs new thinking. The prewriting stage provides the raw materials that will be given shape by the writing process. The writing process is an act of creation.

Children, as prospective writers, especially need to spend time generating, exploring, and experimenting with ideas before they are expected to compose. The prewriting stage affords children the opportunity to generate ideas by exploring prior knowledge or new information, and it gives them time to reach into their bank of language for words to express those ideas. Taking the time to utilize fully this stage of the writing process ensures that children will "have something to say" when they compose. Neglecting prewriting increases the possibility of hearing the plaintive exclamation, "I don't know what to write!"

Fostering the Language Production Process

In order to ensure that children receive the full benefit of the prewriting process, teachers must understand the language production process and how it relates both to generating ideas and planning for the composing process.

The production of language begins when a child reacts to an experience in the environment and begins to think about it (conceptualization) and, in turn, to talk about it (verbalization). During this oral language stage, children begin to compose stories and fantasies while they are at play. This same type of activity may be used in the classroom to move children from oracy toward literacy. The child's stories and fantasies may be written down. Children with this experience will begin to pair speech and print perceptually; then they will gradually transcribe their own sentences and, eventually, complete stories.

Children with much practice in oral composition will progress naturally to nonverbal composition and learn the conventions of written language. It is essential that composing orally precede composing nonverbally. This is a natural sequence in language acquisition and development. Using the oral composition technique allows the child to continue building fluency in language and still learn the art of composing for writing.

Based on this information about language acquisition and production, I have devised a formula for the prewriting stage that can be used prior to composing orally and nonverbally (see figures 14 and 15). This formula can be used by the teacher in eliciting as much language as possible to be used in composing. "Fall Leaves," which follows, is an example of the prewriting formula put to use.

FALL LEAVES

EXPERIENCE

Take the children outdoors to play in the leaves. Encourage children to watch the leaves falling, to smell the leaves, to listen to the leaves moving, to jump in the leaves, to toss the leaves, and so forth.

CONCEPTUALIZATION

Ask questions, such as: What can you do with the leaves? What do the leaves feel like? Why? What do the leaves smell like?

VERBALIZATION

Listen to the children's responses. Encourage each one to express what he or she is thinking and feeling. Praise them for the descriptive words they use.

CONSTRUCTION

Cluster or brainstorm for words and ideas that can be used when writing. This technique can be used to motivate different modes of writing: poetry, stories, an ad for raking leaves, a report on the seasons, or a book about trees. Children reach into their bank of language to express their ideas.

COMPOSING

The children can compose orally, and helpers can transcribe; or they may transcribe for themselves. The children will have ideas to write about because they have been able to act out an experience and talk about it before they were expected to write.

The following examples were developed through the process described above:

Leaves
dusty, crunchy
falling, blowing, flying
trees, branches, colors, sun
laughing, tossing, jumping
funny, happy children.

COMPOSED NONVERBALLY BY A THIRD GRADER

The Fall Leaves

We played in the leaves today. We threw the leaves up in the air and kicked them. We ran and jumped in the leaves. The leaves were crunchy and dry. They were old. It will be winter soon.

COMPOSED ORALLY BY A GROUP OF FIRST GRADERS

The only part of the prewriting formula that I have not discussed fully is construction. This step in the process is where the first shaping of ideas occurs. One of the most effective techniques that I have used for construction is Gabriele Rico's clustering.

Clustering enables children to reach into their language banks and provides a means by which they may crystallize their ideas. It is a very versatile technique and may be used prior to oral or nonverbal composition. It may be used with individuals, small groups, or entire classes. (Clustering is described in depth in the preceding section of this book.)

Finding Ideas for Prewriting

Prewriting will be most effective if you base it on something your children have a prior knowledge about—either through a lesson you conducted in the classroom or an experience they had somewhere else. Children will have more to bring to the writing process if they have had a prior experience with the topic.

Take advantage of school day happenings, such as playing marbles, eating in the cafeteria, or taking a

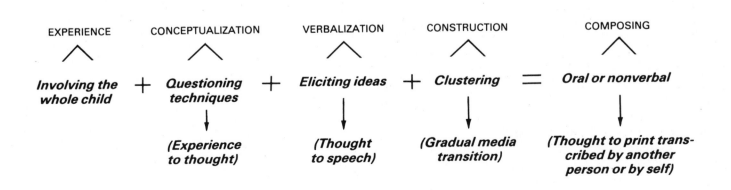

Fig. 14. The Prewriting Formula

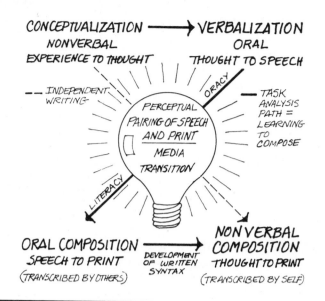

CONCEPTUALIZATION → VERBALIZATION
NONVERBAL — ORAL
EXPERIENCE TO THOUGHT — THOUGHT TO SPEECH

INDEPENDENT WRITING
ORACY
PERCEPTUAL PAIRING OF SPEECH AND PRINT
MEDIA TRANSITION
TASK ANALYSIS PATH = LEARNING TO COMPOSE
LITERACY

ORAL COMPOSITION — NONVERBAL COMPOSITION
SPEECH TO PRINT — THOUGHT TO PRINT
DEVELOPMENT OF WRITTEN SYNTAX
(TRANSCRIBED BY OTHERS) — (TRANSCRIBED BY SELF)

Fig. 15. Graphic Illustration of the Prewriting Formula

spelling test. Special events are always great for prewriting experiences: assemblies, a visit from someone in the community, or a long-awaited holiday. Some of the best prewriting experiences are the spontaneous ones that we sometimes overlook: a windstorm, a stray dog wandering in the school yard, or a classmate who moved away suddenly.

The following are some of my favorite prewriting activities to use in the classroom. Be sure to implement them with the prewriting formula for the most success:

- *Sound Effect Sequence.* This is a good lesson to use with children to show the need for more details in a story. Play a record that contains a series of sound effects for the class. As they listen, ask your students to create a sentence for each sound effect they hear that will tell a story. The sentences can be put on an overhead to show the basic plot line as well as the "gaps" in the story. A group of children can work together to fill in the details.

- *Once There Was a House.* Show or draw a picture of a fantasy house. It could be made out of a shoe, an apple, a mushroom, a tree, or something else that is unusual. Ask the children to imagine who lives there. And ask other probing questions, such as, What do they do? Children may write a short story about the occupants, or they may wish to do a serial story. They will also enjoy creating their own fantasy houses and drawing them.

- *Photo Fun.* You are an Instamatic camera. Each summer your owners take you with them on vacation. Who are your owners? Where do they take you? What do you enjoy taking pictures of? Where is your favorite vacation spot? Why? Photographs may also be brought into the classroom for writing experiences.

- *Comic Dialogue.* Bring in some of your favorite comic books that you have saved, and share a few of them with the children. Talk about the dialogue bubbles and what they mean. Have a large comic "blownup" on butcher paper with blank bubbles. Discuss the pictures and create the dialogue with the group's help. Pass out individual comics with blank bubbles to the children and have them create their own dialogue. This activity can be addicting!

- *Tree for All Seasons.* I have always liked this activity because it offers an opportunity for interdisciplinary teaching. The class adopts one tree on the playground or in a nearby park or neighborhood. The class visits the tree periodically and experiences and records the changes in the tree. If they desire, the children may sit under the tree and write. They may wish to compile a book that is composed of all the activities and writing that the tree has inspired during the year. The book may contain artwork, poetry, reports, stories, photographs, and so forth.

- *Scent and Sentimentality.* Use strong scents, such as strawberry, leather, or pine. Children think of something that the smell reminds them of. Can they remember a time when they smelled this before? What were they doing? Was it a long time ago? Possibilities: a camping trip, a special Christmas, a favorite dessert, or the doctor's office.

- *Mystery Objects.* Show the class an object, such as an antique, an old pair of shoes, or a suitcase covered with travel stickers. Ask them such questions as: Whom do you think this object belongs to? What happened to it? Where has it been?

- *Dream Bus or Fantasy Jet.* Show a picture of a bus or jet and ask the children to imagine that they could go anywhere they wanted to go. Where would they go? How long would they stay? What would they do? What would the trip be like?

Using the Story Formula

The story formula, which is described below, is a versatile teaching tool to use in the classroom writing program to help students generate content and plan for form. It is adaptable for use with students who are just beginning to write narratives as well as with students who are ready to learn the intricacies of short story writing. Beginning students can write a complete story in one class period if they are directed to write two or three sentences for each part of the formula. Another way of using the formula with beginning writers is to take a day or a week to write each part of the story. Specific lessons and models may be presented to help students develop each part fully. More advanced students may use the formula in much the same way as the less advanced students use it, but they should be asked to provide more details. Lessons can be presented to help children use dialogue in their stories. "Showing, not telling" writing may be encouraged for characterization, setting, and problem. Experimenting with alternate voice and a different audience should be encouraged also.

This is the story formula:

1. Write an opening line. You may choose one from a favorite story.
2. Now, choose a main character (MC), and write a description of how your MC looks and acts.
3. Next, describe the setting of the story.
4. Write an episode that creates a problem for the MC. Make something exciting happen to the MC that causes a problem.
5. Describe the problem. How does the MC try to solve it but fails? How does the MC feel about the problem?
6. Now, tell how the problem is solved. Does the MC get help or solve it alone?
7. Now that the problem is solved, write about how your MC feels. What will the MC do to avoid having the same problem again?
8. Reread your story and make up a title for it.
9. Decide what parts of the story would make good illustrations.

Using Books in Prewriting

Children who are avid readers are often the best writers because they have developed a sense of written syntax, are aware of form, and have a good vocabulary. For this reason I like to use books as a prewriting experience. This technique, sometimes called "pattern writing," is a form of emulation. The child takes the pattern and uses it as a springboard for new ideas. I have used the following books to prompt writing in the classroom:

- *I Know What I Like,* by Norma Simon (Niles, Ill.: Albert Whitman & Company, 1971). This is a good book to use when introducing verbs.
- *Sara and the Door,* by Virginia A. Jensen (Reading, Mass.: Addison-Wesley Publishing Co., Inc., 1977). Use this story to prompt writing about a memory from early childhood or about a time that the student felt helpless.
- *If I Were a Cricket,* by Kazue Mizumura (New York: Harper & Row Pubs., Inc., 1973). Children can use the pattern and write what they would do for a human friend if they were an animal, plant, or insect.
- *David Was Mad,* one of the *Kin-der Owl Books* by Bill Martin, Jr. (New York: Holt, Rinehart & Winston, Inc., 1971). This is an excellent book to use when encouraging children to "show and not tell" in their writing.
- *Nothing but a Dog,* by Bobbi Katz (Old Westbury, N.Y.: Feminist Press, 1972). Using the pattern in this book, the children in your class can write about something they have really wanted or wanted to do.
- *The Important Book,* by Margaret W. Brown (New York: Harper & Row Pubs., Inc., 1949). This is a good book to use when introducing paragraph writing. The students will choose a noun and write all the things they think are important about it.
- *Mitzi's Magic Garden,* by Beverley Allinson (Westport, Conn.: Garrard Publishing Co., 1971). Children can write what they would plant in the garden and tell what would result. Imagination will run wild. The illustrations in this book are especially amusing.
- *Janey,* by Charlotte Zolotow (New York: Harper & Row, Pubs., Inc., 1973). This pattern can be used to prompt writing about memories.

Using Puppets, Role Playing, and Story Dolls

Puppets can be used to encourage oral and written expression. Children compose naturally when they play with puppets. They can be given time to play and then be asked to compose something for a dialogue bubble, to tell a story, or to create a play. It is also fun for a group of children to work on plays together in this manner.

Another good approach for a prewriting experience is to have children role-play a situation and record it with a tape recorder. Children can replay the tape and revise it as often as they wish. One person writes down what the group has decided to keep, and the process goes on until their play is finished. This is a particularly useful lesson when you are emphasizing the importance of rewriting a piece until you are satisfied with its contents.

Children love to retell stories with the flip-over dolls that you can purchase in toy stores. They can also make up their own stories with new characters with the story doll. (See Figure 16 for instructions on how to make a story doll.) Have the children use felt scraps, crayons, and so forth to create their characters and then make up a story. The story can be in narrative form or in play form.

Describing the Teacher's Role

If, after reading this section, you feel that the teacher's role in the prewriting stage of the writing process is a complex one, you are right! The teacher must simultaneously initiate the desire to write, induce creative thinking, and help build writing skills. Therefore, you who are teachers must approach your role with a combination of realism and assurance; and, to be successful, you must be well prepared and enthusiastic. It is important to realize that prewriting is often the most painful, the longest, and always the crucial stage of the writing process. You must be assured that there will be results; think of your own prewriting ponderings and deliberations that eventually bring forth writing. Remember that children experience the same apprehensions as you do when faced with the command to create. It is essential that you are prepared with a plan based on the following five points to encourage a successful prewriting experience:

1. Rely on the atmosphere of trust that you have created in your classroom. Children will readily express ideas without fear of ridicule.

2. Base prewriting experiences on something children have a prior knowledge about—either through a lesson you have provided or the experiences they bring to school.

3. Involve the whole child in the prewriting experience. Experiences which stimulate all of the

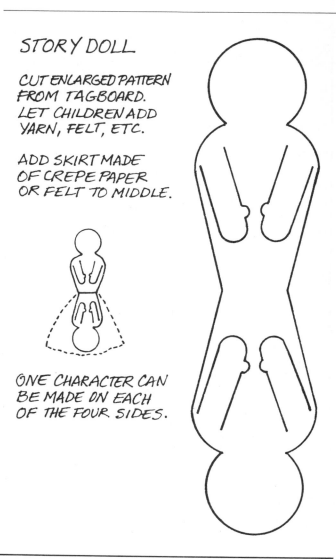

STORY DOLL

CUT ENLARGED PATTERN FROM TAGBOARD. LET CHILDREN ADD YARN, FELT, ETC.

ADD SKIRT MADE OF CREPE PAPER OR FELT TO MIDDLE.

ONE CHARACTER CAN BE MADE ON EACH OF THE FOUR SIDES.

Fig. 16. Instructions for Making a Story Doll

senses have the most potential for prompting ideas.

4. Allow children the time needed to act out and talk out their ideas before you expect them to write or compose.

5. Place the most importance on the ideas which children generate. The most valued writing is based on the worth of its ideas. There is plenty of time later for rewriting and editing for correctness.

Finally, above all else, become enthusiastically involved in the excitement children have when they are generating, thinking about, and creating ideas for writing. Personally, I find the prewriting stage to be the most exhilarating part of the writing process in the elementary classroom. I hope you will feel the same way. Good luck!

Practical Ideas for Prewriting in the Elementary School

Snap, Crackle, Think!

By Laurie Opfell, Sue Rader Willett, and
Julie Simpson
Teacher/Consultants, UCI Writing Project

It is extremely important to provide students of all ages with prewriting activities that will enable them to generate ideas about which to write. With young children, in particular, it is also helpful to tap into concrete experiences so that what they have to say will come relatively easily and, thus, they can focus their attention on how to express it on paper.

The following lesson was designed primarily for special education teachers at the elementary level. Our goal was to demonstrate that younger students, and even students with learning difficulties, are capable of writing papers at the highest levels of critical thinking if they are provided with ample prewriting activities to develop a bank of ideas for writing and careful precomposing strategies for planning and shaping their papers. By precomposing, we mean a type of prewriting in which students focus on the transformation of ideas into written form.

Because of the skill level of the students for whom we were designing the lesson and the potential skepti-

EDITOR'S NOTE: Laurie Opfell is a former English teacher, Irvine High School, Irvine Unified School District; Sue Rader Willett is an English teacher, Capistrano Valley High School, Capistrano Unified School District; and Julie Simpson is an English teacher, Sunny Hills High School, Fullerton Joint Union High School District.

cism of their teachers about what they could accomplish, we felt it was essential to choose a subject that would invite active participation, enthusiasm, and interest in elementary schoolchildren and special education students at all levels and be appealing to teachers as well. So we chose cereal, something we would all have a host of memories, associations, and feelings about. What follows is a sequence of prewriting and precomposing activities that takes students from the knowledge through the evaluation levels of thinking as well as through the various stages of the writing process.

● **Prewriting**

Step 1—Brainstorming. We asked our teacher/students to tell us anything they thought of when they heard the word cereal, and we wrote all of the suggestions on the chalkboard.

Step 2—Categorizing. We passed out copies of a blank grid and asked them to record and organize on the grids the ideas from the chalkboard into basic categories, such as texture, taste, smell, and nutritional value. We also asked them to add any new information that occurred to them. The grid might look something like this:

Texture:			
crunchy			
crispy			
soggy			
lumpy			
Taste:			
sweet, etc.			

Step 3—Experiencing. At this point, we wanted our audience to become involved with their subject matter, so we conducted a taste test of the cereals. As they ate, we asked them to identify the qualities of the cereals by checking the appropriate categories on the grid and adding new information if it was needed. The grid now might look like this:

	Ratings for cereals		
Qualities	Crispies	Charms	Natural
Texture:			
crunchy			
crispy			
soggy			
lumpy			
chewy (hard)			
chewy (soft)			
spongy			

● Precomposing

Step 4—Mapping. In order for the teacher/students to make the transition from checks on a grid to writing about their subjects, we asked them to select their favorite cereal, illustrate it graphically on paper, and then to add in the checked information from the grid where appropriate. We showed them several models; then we asked them to try it on their own. Two examples are included in Figure 17.

Mapping is a right-brain organizational tool which allows creative interpretation of information. We encouraged everyone to add in any new relevant ideas as they created their maps.

Step 5—Presenting the prompt. With a visual plan of organized information to write from, we next presented the group with a series of prompts. They are graduated below from easiest to most difficult. Students can be given the option of choosing their own, or one can be selected for them. All prompts deal with the thinking skills of evaluation:

1. Select your favorite cereal and explain why you like it.
2. Write a paragraph to persuade your mother to buy this cereal.
3. Rank the cereals from best to worst and justify your ranking.
4. Pretending you are the judge of a cereal "taste-off," write your choice for the best cereal and explain why.
5. After tallying the preferences of your classmates, predict which cereal will sell the best and explain why.

Fig. 17. Mapping the Qualities of Cereals

For lower-level students, prompt number 1 might be most appropriate, and a frame could be provided that might look like this:

I like _____ *because*

1. _____

_____. *Also*

2. _____

_____. *Finally,*

3. _____

_____

More advanced students might try prompt number 4 and add setting, character, description, dialogue, and the reaction of the crowd.

● Writing

Step 6—Writing a rough draft. We asked our teacher/students to write a rough draft of prompt number 2 because we felt it was the one they might be likely to try with their students.

● Sharing

Step 7—Providing each other with feedback. Before each writer shared his or her paper with a partner, we pre-

sented a simplified rubric, one that would be suitable for prompt number 2.

After reviewing the rubric, we asked them to look for the specific attributes or the lack of them in the papers and to give each other feedback on positive aspects of the papers as well as possible corrections. Here is the rubric we presented:

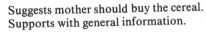

① Strongly persuades and convinces.
Supports with specific information.

② Suggests mother should buy the cereal.
Supports with general information.

③ States personal opinion without being persuasive.
Gives little or no supporting reasons.

Since our primary goal was to demonstrate prewriting and precomposing strategies, we did not take the lesson beyond the first draft. However, classroom use of this lesson should include the revising, editing, and evaluating stages of the composing process. A good motivator would be to award ribbons to each writer.

The teachers who participated in our "Snap, Crackle, Think!" lesson responded enthusiastically to it. We feel a key element in its success is its hands-on quality. Even the most reluctant writers should have something to say after tasting, smelling, touching, and thinking about their subject. More importantly, the prewriting and precomposing activities provide the student with guidance and direction in transforming those thoughts into print.

T he Rock Experience

By Erline S. Krebs
Lecturer, Division of Teacher Education, California State University, Fullerton; and Teacher/Consultant, UCI Writing Project

"The Rock Experience" includes a series of prewriting activities that I have used successfully with elementary students; however, it could easily be adapted to any grade level. I begin this experience by reading to my class *Everybody Needs a Rock* by Byrd Baylor (New York: Charles Scribner's Sons, 1974). This book is about designing individualistic rules for finding "just the right rock for you." After I have read the story to them, the students develop some of their own "rock hunt rules," using the "how to" skills of the practical/informative domain. Then they go outside and survey the school environment for a "rock hunt adventure."

When each student has selected one "special" rock, which takes approximately ten minutes, we return to the classroom and go through the process of getting acquainted with our rocks. In silence each student examines his or her rock, focusing on the senses of smell, sight, sound, taste, and touch. Sometimes, I play soft music in the background; e.g., Johann Pachelbel's "Canon in D." At the end of two minutes, I ring a bell. Each student now selects a partner. One person is designated "A"; and his or her partner, "B." For two minutes, "A" shares with "B" anything about his or her rock; i.e., where and how it was found, description of rock, personality traits of rock. Students are encouraged to use their imagination. "B" listens (no talking whatsoever). The positions are reversed for the next two minutes. I ring a bell at the end of each two-minute segment.

This process is followed by a total group discussion, which may include some of the following "open-ended" questions:

What was this experience like for you?
Were two minutes too long, too short, just right?

"The Rock Experience" has given students practice in discovering, recording, describing, and sharing.
ERLINE S. KREBS

Were you comfortable or uncomfortable sharing?
   In what ways?
Were you comfortable or uncomfortable listening?
   In what ways?
How did you feel about your partner as a listener?
What did you learn about yourself in this process?

Working with the same partners and using one or both rocks, the students move into a brainstorming process in order to develop a *word-bank*. I pass out five 5″ x 7″ cards, each of a different color (yellow, green, orange, blue, pink). One of the partners is designated the recorder. I allow approximately two to three minutes for each segment of this process. Words corresponding to different parts of speech are listed on each card, as follows:

Yellow card: Brainstorm and record all the words that could *describe* (adjectives) your rock(s); e.g., speckled, smooth, sharp, creviced.

Green card: Brainstorm and record all the words that communicate what your rock(s) *can do* (verbs); e.g., roll, skip, fall, hop.

Orange card: Brainstorm and record all the words that communicate *how* your rock(s) *can do it* (adverbs); e.g., slowly, quickly, playfully, listlessly.

Blue card: Brainstorm and record all the phrases that tell *where* your rock(s) *can do it* (prepositional phrases); e.g., under the bridge, over the water, on the sidewalk, in the car.

We discuss the individual lists and, as a group, develop a word-bank for each part of speech on four sheets of butcher paper. I color code each list by using yellow, green, orange, and blue felt-tip pens:

Description of Our Rocks	*What* Our Rocks Can Do	*How* Our Rocks Can Do It	*Where* Our Rocks Can Do It
(List adjectives.)	(List verbs.)	(List adverbs.)	(List prepositional phrases.)

The butcher paper lists are placed on classroom walls.

Now, each pair of students takes out the *pink* card and, together, they create their own magnificent "rock sentence," using all their sentence-combining techniques and skills. I allow approximately five to seven minutes for this process. Of course, these "magic creations" are shared with the whole group.

As a follow-up, the students are usually anxious to set up a Geology Learning Center. In the process of establishing the center, they get opportunities for collecting, conducting research on, and labeling rocks. This may also lead to the following writing activities:

Sensory/descriptive domain: Describing rocks through poetry; e.g., haiku, cinquain, poetic dialogue.

Imaginative/narrative domain: "An Adventure with My Rock" or "My Adventure as a Rock"; i.e., use of visual imagery from the rock's point of view.

Practical/informative domain: Developing a handbook for beginning rock hunters or "Advanced Instructions for the Avid Rock Hunter."

Analytical/expository domain: Developing a position paper; e.g., "The Value of Rocks in the Ecosystem."

There is no doubt that "The Rock Experience" has increased my students' and my own awareness of rocks. At the same time it has given them practice in discovering, recording, describing, sharing, and doing a variety of other prewriting activities. Actually, the *process* of this experience can be used with any item; obviously, it is not limited to rocks. Use your imagination! Have fun!

Developing Fluency Through Poetic Dialogue

By Michael Carr
Teacher, Los Alamitos Elementary School,
Los Alamitos Unified School District;
and Teacher/Consultant, UCI Writing Project

and Erline Krebs
Lecturer, Division of Teacher Education,
California State University, Fullerton;
and Teacher/Consultant, UCI Writing Project

The word is alive
The poem is alive
The poet is alive within his poem
and is speaking to us.
If we wish, we may answer him
by weaving our voices into conversations
which create a new kind of poetic dialogue.
In so doing we come to know the poet
and his poem in a special way
and create poems as a result of this dialogue.

By TOBY LURIE
from *Conversations and Constructions*[1]

[1]Toby Lurie, *Conversations and Constructions.* San Francisco: 1429 Page St., Apt. E, San Francisco, CA 94117, © 1978. Used by permission of the poet.

When introducing elementary school students to poetry, it is not enough to give them a model of a haiku, cinquain, or other poetic form and expect them to write. We have found that our students are fearful of expressing themselves freely through poetry. It is evident that they have many preconceived notions about poetry—that it must rhyme, be easy to memorize, have only so many syllables per line, and so forth—and an overall feeling of "I can't do this."

As with any writing assignment, it is necessary to provide students with prewriting activities. In this case we want them to see that writing poetry can be as easy and comfortable as having a conversation with a friend. That is why we focus on the idea of dialoguing with poetry.

We begin by inviting our students to cluster their thoughts, feelings, and attitudes around the word *poetry,* as in Figure 18.

As a group we take a look at the "cluster" and notice what it is saying. Then we discuss some of the

Fig. 18. Clustering of Thoughts and Feelings Around *Poetry*

myths and fears surrounding poetry. Next, we introduce the concept of dialoguing as a natural way of expressing ourselves, a process we do daily in our conversations with each other. For example, we might say, "Mike, have you noticed the mountains this morning?"

Mike may respond, "You bet. I would love to be skiing right now!" It is as simple as that.

We now have our students respond orally to any line we give them. We tell our students not to "think about" or "figure out" their responses, just express what comes naturally.

Using the same natural process, our students are now invited to participate in a written dialogue. We use Carl Sandburg's "Summer Grass."

SUMMER GRASS[2]

Summer grass aches and whispers.

*It wants something; it calls and sings; it pours
out wishes to the overhead stars.*

*The rain hears; the rain answers; the rain is slow
coming; the rain wets the face of the grass.*

By CARL SANDBURG

As we read a line of the *frame,* each student copies that line of poetry on a piece of paper and then writes his or her response directly underneath. The following is an example of a fifth grade student's (Jennifer's) response:

Summer grass aches and whispers. (*Carl Sandburg's
"Summer Grass"*)
Rain on the grass and wind blowing. (Jennifer)

It wants something:
The baby wants a toy.

it calls and sings;
Birds perching in trees

it pours out wishes
It is raining wishes

to the overhead stars.
Twinkling stars up in the air

The rain hears;
The clouds talk, people hear, the rain falls;

the rain answers;
The clouds listen;

the rain is slow coming;
The rain is very slow, it's sprinkling;

the rain wets the face of the grass.
The grass gets wet, the grass likes water.

By JENNIFER MICHELLE

[2]From *Good Morning, America,* Copyright 1928, 1956, by Carl Sandburg. Reprinted by permission of Harcourt Brace Jovanovich, Inc. (Note: Carl Sandburg's poem will work equally well with students at higher grade levels, as will this entire concept.)

This process allows for a personal involvement with the poem and transforms the experience of poetry from the dull process of analysis and memorization to the intimate relationship of conversation.

Now, the students have an opportunity to share their creations aloud. As we read a line of the frame, a student reads his or her response. We do this with

> **The goal of instruction in writing is to enable students to develop skills in fluency, form, and correctness.**
> *JAMES R. GRAY*

several students on a one-to-one basis, and then we expand the process to include two or more students in order to form a three- or four-person poem. The following is an example of a two-person dialogue with "Summer Grass":

Summer grass aches and whispers. (Carl Sandburg's "Summer Grass")
  Rain on the grass and wind blowing. (Jennifer)
  Summer grass smells good. (Travis)

It wants something:
  The baby wants a toy:
  It is hungry:

it calls and sings;
  birds perching in trees;
  it sings a song;

it pours out wishes
  it is raining wishes
  it pours out your wish

to the overhead stars.
  twinkling stars up in the air.
  looking through a telescope.

The rain hears;
  The clouds talk, people hear, the rain falls;
  People like rain;

the rain answers;
  the clouds listen;
  the rain hears you, the rain listens;

the rain is slow coming;
  the rain is very slow, it's sprinkling;
  it's raining slowly;

the rain wets the face of the grass.
  the grass gets wet, the grass likes water.
  the grass drinks water.

By JENNIFER MICHELLE and TRAVIS BARE

Again, we read Carl Sandburg's frame aloud as Jennifer and Travis read their responses to each line.

As the students experience success and confidence in this process, we now remove the *frame* and intro-

duce the concept of the *silent exchange*. The students select a partner and, together, they participate in a written dialogue with each other. This exercise is done in silence. One student begins and writes a line; the second student responds to that line. They alternate (in silence) until their "poem" is complete. They may illustrate their paper (still in silence) and place it on a bulletin board in the room. Sharing their poem orally with the class adds a special dimension. The following are two examples of the silent exchange done by fifth grade students:

Hot summer sun is shining.
  Everyone is at the beach.
The waves are talking.
  Are they talking to you?
We go home in the dark, cool wind.
  Are you going to stay home?
The wind is blowing.
  The wind is blowing the trees down.
It is very cold and windy,
  So I sit by the fireplace.
The wind blows the fire out,
  So I light the match and stick it in the fireplace.
I want to sleep by the fireplace.
  I dream about going to the beach again.

By ELEANOR VELEZ and SARAH ZAMPOGNA

A nice and pretty flower . . .
  It sits in the grass dripping with water.

The grass is wet and green . . .
  We step on the wet green grass.

Unicorns are nice and magiciful . . .
  Their horns are gold and pretty.

Pegasus is pretty too . . .
  With white shining wings.

Leaves on a tree are brown and orange . . .
  They lie on the ground in autumn.

The trees have many colors . . .
  Nice colors and gold leaves.

By JENNIFER CAMIA and BECKY PENDLETON

We have found that by using the prewriting process of dialoguing as a natural extension of conversation, our students develop greater freedom and confidence in both their oral and written expression. The students "come alive" as they discover their own special "poet within." Now they are ready to dialogue with the self and produce poetry that is uniquely their own.

EDITOR'S NOTE: We especially acknowledge the contributions of Travis Bare, Jennifer Camia, Jennifer Michelle, Becky Pendleton, Eleanor Velez, and Sarah Zampogna, fifth grade students at the Los Alamitos Elementary School.

Pattern Writing with Novels for Adolescents

By Elizabeth Williams Reeves
**Teacher, Pine Middle School,
Los Alamitos Unified School District;
and Teacher/Consultant, UCI Writing Project**

I have found that certain novels provide adolescents with marvelous springboards for writing experiences. Emulating an author's style and content can be quite simple for students if the literature they read is vivid and motivating. For these reasons I have utilized *The Adventures of Tom Sawyer* at the fifth grade level to help my students develop written language skills.

In one section of his novel, Mark Twain creates a conversation between Huck Finn and Tom Sawyer regarding the removal of warts. You may recall the scene. On his way to school, Tom comes upon the "juvenile pariah of the village, Huckleberry Finn," carrying a dead cat, and he asks, "Say—what is dead cats good for, Huck?"

"Good for? Cure warts with," Huck replies. Then Tom tries to convince Huck that "spunk-water" is better, but his curiosity about the use of dead cats to cure warts prompts him to ask Huck about the procedure.

Huck replies that you stand by the grave of an evil person "'long about midnight," wait for the devil to come along to take "that feller away," and then, "you heave your cat after 'em and say, 'Devil follow corpse, cat follow devil, warts follow cat, I'm done with ye!' That'll fetch *any* wart," Huck tells Tom.

After my students have read the passages from *Tom Sawyer*, I guide them, through directed questioning, to develop their own methods of getting rid of warts. Some possible questions the teacher might ask and expected responses from students for this portion of the prewriting phase follow:

1. Where do you need to go to be cured of warts?
   A dark garage . . . up in a plane . . . haunted house . . . a stranger's kitchen . . . a subterranean lake

2. What time would you need to go?
   Any time . . . midnight . . . three in the morning

3. Who or what should you bring with you?
   No one . . . your baby sister . . . a three-eyed frog . . . a ten-foot snake

4. What other materials should you take?
   Pail . . . shovel . . . matches . . . bag . . . book of cures

5. What would you do once you arrived at the appropriate location?
   Varied responses

6. Is there a chant you would need to say?
   "Wart, wart, off you go, where you vanish we'll never know."

Next, students are given an outline that aids them in structuring their writing. The outline for this particular lesson and a sample of the student writing generated from the exercise follow:

OUTLINE FOR THE LESSON

Though many people promote various means of curing warts, I have one sure-fire method: ————————
————————————————————— .

Certain things are essential: —————————
————————————————————— .

First, —————————————————————
Once there, ———————————————————
Next, —————————————————————
Before ————————————————————

SAMPLE OF STUDENT WRITING

Though many people promote various means of curing warts, I have one sure-fire method. Three things are essential: a fat green frog with warts, a bar of soap, and a pond. First, you collect your frog and soap and venture off toward the pond while the sun is high. Once there, expose all your warts to the sun, and begin scrubbing them with the soap. Next, pick up the frog and throw him as far out into the pond as possible. Before he can turn around to look at you, run as fast as you can into the woods. By the time you reach home, your warts should be gone.

Students usually find this kind of patterning experience challenging and fun. It enables me not only to reinforce the literature we are reading with writing but also to teach sequencing and transition skills.

Prewriting
in Different Subjects

Prewriting Assignments Across the Curriculum
Science + English = Success

By Jim Lee
Former English Teacher, Serrano Intermediate School,
Saddleback Valley Unified School District;
and Teacher/Consultant, UCI Writing Project

It has long been a premise of mine that students can benefit greatly from some sort of prewriting activity. No matter what the assigned topic may be, it is to your advantage as a teacher to get your students' thoughts flowing freely. Then the students need to put the thoughts on paper so that they become workable parts that may be pieced together to form the "perfect" paper that most students believe they should be able to write.

The prewriting activity that I have selected to describe for you is one I used in conjunction with a series of science experiments on a well-known backyard mollusk—the snail. My goal was twofold: (1) to integrate scientific observation and experimentation with the teaching of composition; and (2) to provide a concrete experience that would enable my students to grasp the abstract concept of aestivation and its application to backyard mollusks. As you may or may not know, aestivation is a state of physical inactivity (dormancy or hibernation) that snails go into when they are deprived of food and water.

I began this activity by giving every student an aestivating snail and instructed my students to examine their respective snails in terms of color, texture, shape, size, and so forth. Then I asked the students to record their observations in clusters, which provided them with a foundation for eventual sentence and paragraph development. (See Figure 19 for an example of the clustering of observations.)

After clustering their thoughts about the aestivating snail, each student put a drop of water on his or her snail's body and watched as it emerged from its shell. The students then clustered their observations of the snails emerging from aestivation, as illustrated in Figure 19.

The next step in the prewriting activity was to observe snails eating. We gave snails a variety of leaves that were native to the immediate environment (in other words, whatever can be collected during the morning before the afternoon lesson). The students then recorded in a third set of clusters the snails' dietary habits, as shown in the third part of Figure 19.

From this experimental/sensory prewriting activity, the students shared the results of their clustering orally with the rest of the class. I had all of the information that the students volunteered recorded on the chalkboard and categorized under one of three headings: Description, Emergence from Aestivation, Eating Habits. As an example, a class of seventh grade honor students developed the following list of descriptions of aestivating snails:

Basic brown
Coiled like a nautilus shell
Sealed like a tomb
Dead
Tortoise shell color

Bizarre striations
Ribbed texture
Smooth strips with bumps in between
Reminds me of a spinning top
Spirals out like a pinwheel
Intricate pattern fades as it nears the opening
Yellowish tan and dark brown stripes
Looks like a ram's horn from the side
Gross!
Looks like Princess Leah's hair
Has multicolored ribs along the shell
Ribs get farther apart as they move away from the center
Boring
Fragile looking

After a period of sharing observations, the students took the sentence fragments and turned them into simple sentences. Then they shared their sentences, and a lesson on sentence combining evolved from the collected responses, as shown in the following example:

Original Simple Sentences

1. My snail is basically brown.
2. A snail shell is coiled like a nautilus shell.
3. An aestivating snail is sealed like a tomb.
4. An aestivating snail looks dead.
5. A snail is colored like a tortoise.
6. A "backyard mollusk" has bizarre striations on its shell.
7. The intricate pattern on a snail shell fades as it nears the opening.
8. A snail shell is fragile.
9. A snail shell spirals out from the center.
10. A snail has a gold, tan, and dark brown shell.
11. The pattern of a snail is less impressive as it moves toward the opening.

Sentences in Combined Form

1. The snail's coiled shell is fragile.
2. An aestivating snail appears to be dead and is sealed in a fragile tomb made of shell.
3. A snail has a shell with gold, tan, and dark brown striations.
4. A snail has an intricate pattern of gold, tan, and dark brown striations that fade to a basic brown as they approach the opening.

These activities covered the spectrum of experiential, oral, and written prewriting and provided my students with a foundation from which they could write a descriptive, narrative, or expository essay.

The following are examples of prompts that were an outgrowth from our experiments:

1. *Descriptive.* Write an account of a day in the life of a snail. Write from the snail's perspective, and include as much specific detail as possible. Incorporate as much factual data as possible to give added credence to your writing. Use as many sensory/descriptive phrases as possible.

2. *Narrative.* Write a story in which you speculate or fantasize about how the snail got its shell.

3. *Expository.* Suppose that the sun is moving closer to the earth each day. Using the theories of natural selection and survival of the fittest, project what physical changes might occur in the snail as it attempts to cope with its changing environment.

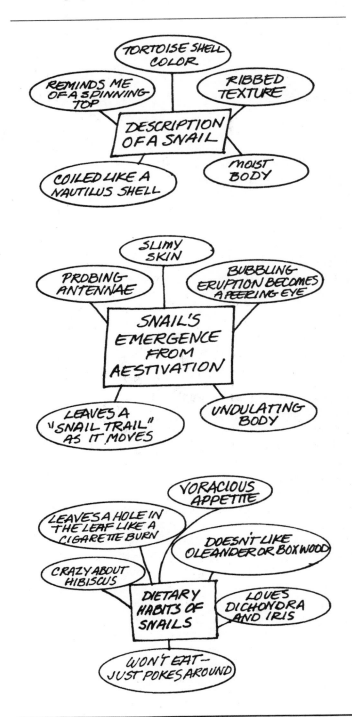

Fig. 19 Clustering the Descriptions and Observations of Snails

As a California Writing Project zealot, I would be remiss if I did not encourage, cajole, and, yes, even beg you to become actively involved in the teaching of composition.

Through the use of prewriting activities and well-designed prompts, you can convince your students that writing, although painful at times, can be exciting, challenging, and rewarding. Once your students understand that good writing is a product of systematically acquired skills and that those skills are learned rather than inherited, they will be much more optimistic about becoming good writers.

Practical Ideas for Prewriting in Different Subjects

A Primary Experience with Snails

By Charrie Hunter
**Teacher, Maple Hill Elementary School,
Walnut Valley Unified School District;
and Teacher/Consultant, UCI Writing Project**

After seeing a demonstration of Jim Lee's "Science + English = Success" lesson at the 1980 UCI Writing Project Summer Institute, I decided to try it with my first and second graders. They had had many previous writing experiences and were well acquainted with the procedure involved. These children were excited about each and every writing assignment they were given and were eagerly awaiting the arrivals of their "surprise" animal!

Before starting the lesson, you will need to assemble the following items: 40 aestivating snails, one rock for each child, one margarine container with water in it for each group of children, one large piece of plastic wrap for each child (12 in. x 12 in. [2.5 cm] or larger), and three different kinds of leaves for each child. Note that some snails have problems waking, so you will need some extra snails. Also, if you must make the snails go into aestivation, placing them in a large paper bag seemed to work, as they need a dry environment to sleep. My snails were crawling all over the place for about two days until I figured out how to keep their environment dry.

Before you pass out the snails, you need to give a little pep talk on this animal; otherwise, the children will be hesitant to touch them. I had acquainted myself with some stories about snails and brought these to share. After stimulating their curiosity with some sample books and illustrations, I handed each child an aestivating snail. Then I wrote the word *snail* on the chalkboard and drew

a circle around it, added the word *aestivating* and explained its meaning.

I instructed each child to examine his or her snail. As we discussed the snails, I asked about the snail's breathing, its color, texture, shape, size, and its unpopularity. As the children volunteered their reactions, I added their words to a group cluster on the board. Then we put a drop of water on each snail to wake each one up and passed out the plastic wrap. I continued the cluster with questions like: Where are its eyes? Can it hear? (Clap hands.) What happens if you touch it? I introduced some new words and talked about each one: *tentacles, feelers,* and *foot.* What is the motion of its foot? (Children let their snails crawl up the plastic wrap as they held it up.)

I passed out the rocks and asked more questions. Will it move over or around a rock? Does it leave a trail? What is the trail like? I passed out the leaves to each child and continued with the discussion and cluster. Where is the snail's mouth? Does it have teeth? What kind of leaves does it like and dislike?

By this time the chalkboard was covered with words, and the children were ready to write. I collected all the snails and equipment and passed out a "shape" book to each child. This book has a construction paper cover and back with several sheets of writing paper inside. The book is fastened at the edge, and then the children cut it out (in this case) in the shape of a snail. The class was then told what the topic of their story was. They were to write a story about a day in the life of a snail. We discussed this topic to generate ideas, and then I wrote the rubric on the board. Every story must include: (1) what the snail looks like; (2) how it moves; (3) what it does in a day; and (4) how your friends feel about the snail.

At this point, I walked around the room and helped those children who needed help. Each child was allowed as much time as he or she needed to complete the story. Some took several days. I do not have children of this age rewrite because I find that rewriting destroys their fluency. I am continually amazed at their desire to achieve perfection without my requiring it. Once the children understood what good handwriting, punctuation, and capitalization were, they used them.

After everyone had completed his or her shape book, we read each story out loud, considered whether the writer had done everything that was in the rubric, and graded the paper accordingly. The children received a smiley face with hair 😊😊 if they had completed all the tasks or a plain smiley face if they had not 😊 . (I always try to make it as positive an experience as possible.)

The children in my class loved this "hands-on" writing experience, and the resulting stories were magnificent. One story was published in its entirety in the district newspaper, along with pictures of my class and an article about the California Writing Project.

Science Search— The Write Way

By Patricia Gatlin
Teacher, Perry Elementary School,
Huntington Beach City Elementary School District;
and Teacher/Consultant, UCI Writing Project

Writing is a great way to stimulate student interest in science because it fits so naturally in the science curriculum. When students complain that science is boring, they are saying that science has no meaning for them; it has nothing to do with their daily lives. If a scientific study is to have meaning, it must relate to something in the students' experiences; it must be a real life application of a scientific concept. Students may not be particularly interested in the composition and movements of the earth until they feel their houses bouncing around on top of shaky ground. But once they have calmed down, they may find that they are asking, "What's going on here?" or "What's causing this?" Now they have a scientific problem—a question that they are itching to answer—that grew from their unique experiences in the environment. Scientific experiments, though memorable and entertaining, achieve additional meaning for students when they have opportunities to write about the experiments and react to what they observe.

Occasionally, every person has scientific problems of some kind that need to be solved. Many of us might consider it handy information to know how long it takes milk to spoil, just in case the refrigerator breaks

> *I believe the primary function of language is, in a word, survival—and not simply survival in a social sense. I mean survival as the biologists use the term.*
> OWEN THOMAS

down. A good way to begin a science course is to make these kinds of problems the basis for the year's science curriculum. The students develop a giant class cluster by identifying every scientific problem that comes to mind. They classify the cluster of questions in categories that become the units of study, and they recognize that it is necessary for the cluster to remain open-ended in order to accommodate incidental scientific questions that may arise throughout the year.

At the beginning of each unit of study, the science class is divided into smaller study groups, with each group selecting from the unit list a problem that it will study. As the students begin scientific experiments to solve their problems, they find that it is essential to keep journals. The journal, which includes a complete account of each stage of the experiments, is the perfect vehicle for practicing different types of writing. The students write daily in their journals and are encouraged to explore all the domains in writing.

Throughout the study, students must observe carefully the characteristics of their experiments. Acute observation is the key ingredient for successful sensory/descriptive writing. A quick glance will not provide adequate details to describe a particular stage of an experiment. Students must be alert to all of the sensory characteristics of the substances used in their experiments. We, their readers, must be able to imagine from the written descriptions the feel, the smell, and the sound, as well as the physical characteristics, of the substances used in the experiments.

The practical/informative mode is the natural style for students to use in reporting the findings of their

experiments. However, the analytical/expository style may be more appropriate if students are asked to persuade other class members that the results of their experiments provide valid answers to their original questions. There are times when providing such proof is truly a reasonable concern. Analytical writing is also appropriate for students' concluding journal entries. At this point, they should reflect on the complete process of the experiment and decide whether or not (1) they solved the original scientific problem; (2) the study triggered additional questions; (3) other questions were answered incidentally during the experiment; (4) some things surprised, pleased, or disturbed them; and (5) they would follow the same procedures to solve the same problem again.

Using the imaginative/narrative style, students can create a story based on the experiment, tracing their observations from the beginning to the end. They may retell the story, changing one of the variables and drawing a new conclusion, or perhaps retell the story from a different point of view. For example, a student might pretend to be the voice of the moldy bread housed within the petri dish.

Students should be encouraged to explore different formats in their journals. They may choose a poetic format, or they may write a short play for puppets or people. The teacher should encourage class members to write in any way that feels comfortable to them at the time. It is important that they feel good about their writing, because they will be sharing a journal entry with the class during their group's presentations given at the close of each unit. For these presentations, each student will share a writing selection that he or she feels is an example of the most interesting or exciting part of the experiment. During these sharing times, the class can get a glimpse of different ways to approach future scientific problems.

> *The production of language begins when a child reacts to an experience in the environment and begins to think about it (conceptualization) and, in turn, to talk about it (verbalization).*
> VIRGINIA BALDWIN

By integrating writing with science, the teacher is providing students with the ideal setting in which to practice decision-making skills, such as identifying cause and effect relationships, drawing conclusions based on evidence, and analyzing possibilities. Writing enables students to extend thinking beyond the basic comprehension level, which is characteristic of questions found in most textbooks. It also links scientific study to the students' outside experiences as they make connections between the principles learned at school and the practicalities of their immediate environments. At the same time, writing about science can appeal to something inside students, as they search for self-understanding and discover their relationships to the universe around them.

Journal Writing Across the Curriculum

By Margaret (Peg) Serences
English Department Chairperson,
Niguel Hills Junior High School,
Capistrano Unified School District;
and Teacher/Consultant, UCI Writing Project

During the first UCI Writing Project in the summer of 1979, using journal writing in the classroom was discussed and demonstrated. Speakers stressed that the goal of using this writing approach was fluency. I was intrigued because I am always anxious to find new ways to encourage students to write. Of the varying forms then mentioned—e.g., diary entry, autobiographical sketch, creative writing exercises, learning aid, and idea collecting—I chose to incorporate the creative writing journal format in my seventh and eighth grade curricula. For three days a week, students were asked to write for ten to fifteen minutes on a topic, which was generally teacher-selected. I found this type of journal writing especially productive when I imposed a time limit, and it provided a prewriting stimulus to get my students writing.

In the English classroom I had students keep their journal entries in a special writing folder. After the writing folder contained several writing samples, the students selected one of their favorites to rewrite and develop into a short composition. Working in groups of four (students were allowed to form their own groups), each student would then read the rewritten composition aloud to the other members of the group. I stressed the importance of "hearing" their own words; this proved an excellent tool for catching sentence fragments and run-on sentences. Next, each student graded each of the four compositions, using the response guide that I provided. Finally, I graded all the papers myself, giving a grade for the compositions and a separate grade for the student's ability to grade someone else's work.

Since I had such good results with journal writing in my classes, I began to wonder how this writing approach would work in other disciplines. As chairperson of the English Department, I encouraged teachers in mathematics, music, physical education, science, and social studies to try weekly or biweekly journal writing projects. I stressed that students could write to discover what they had learned about a subject and that teachers could use their students' journals as a way of determining how effectively they were teaching. Several teachers volunteered to initiate journal writing to see whether it would be a useful learning tool. Here are some student writing samples from other curricular areas:

Physical education: Why I like baseball best of all!

I like baseball because . . . it's fun to *try* to hit the little ball and run around the bases. It's exciting to throw the ball to another player to get the runner out. Baseball is a game of skill. It takes lots of practice to be good. You have to have a good coach too. When you're in a league, you can meet people and make friends, learn things, and have fun. Also, if you have a good team, you can win a trophy. When the season is over, you get to keep the hats and the friends too.

That is why I like baseball.

Music: Compare three selections of music.

After listening to the three pieces of music, I've decided that they all have a beat of some kind. First let me define beat—pulse. But after listening to the third piece, "Sounds," it seems to be different from the others because the first two seemed to use more instruments that flowed into a steady rhythm. They also had a more defined melody and harmony, so it blended together to create music.

Science: What did you learn from dissecting a frog?

Purpose: Mrs. "B" told us to, so we could learn more about the internal parts of a frog.

Observation: On the frog I cut open, I noticed that the skin is almost like rubber. When we cut open the frog, we saw a layer of muscles, which was gross looking. Then we cut that apart and saw a bunch of yellow intestine-looking things. Mrs. "B" told us it was where she produces the eggs, so we had a girl. Her insides are very clear to see. It was a good study.

Conclusion: I think the frog's insides are clear, easy to observe, and neat.

Drama: How do you express emotions on stage?

I make my emotions on stage by thinking I am really that person. I try to really get into it. I remember how people in real life would act. Before I get on stage, I have to make my emotions first. I try not to be me acting like someone else. I try to be them.

Social studies: What was life like in the Colonies?

Life in the Colonies was pretty good because it was easier to get land here, and in Europe it was hard. It was bad for the slaves because they were bought and sold. It turned gloomy in 1763 because England was in debt in the war, and so they started taxing the Colonies. Then the Colonies got mad at England and the Revolutionary War started, and the Colonies won the war.

With the insights gained from journal writing, several teachers, especially in the area of social studies, began to integrate writing in their respective subject areas. I also noticed the use of essay questions as a replacement for the standard multiple-choice examination. It seems to me that the journal writing assigned in other disciplines reinforced and, therefore, strengthened our English program. At the same time, it enabled students to explore what they thought about a given topic in a way that could never be expressed in a fill-in-the-blank or true-false examination.

Guided Imagery in the Social Studies

By Dale Sprowl
English Teacher, Irvine High School,
Irvine Unified School District;
and Teacher/Consultant, UCI Writing Project

A successful method for teaching social studies concepts is guided imagery. It can be used to help students visualize and, thus, internalize different times and places. Writing for secondary social studies classes is generally in the analytical/expository domain, but guided imagery provides students with sensory/descriptive data that involve them personally and give them a foundation for further writing. The technique can also be used to introduce ideas in a unit of study when the culmination of the unit is the writing of an analytical/expository essay.

To teach a concept, such as the impact of technology on humans, I begin with an image of a present, familiar situation. For example, if I were teaching about the industrial revolution and how the invention of machines changed history, I would ask the students to close their eyes and picture themselves in their bathrooms getting ready for school. Then I would ask them to erase any machine from their mental picture. I have them take away their blow dryers, electric toothbrushes or curlers, and the lights in the bathroom. Then I have them move to the bedroom and

erase the stereo and the clothes or furniture that were made in factories. In the living room, I have the students erase the television, video games, and electric lights; in the kitchen, the refrigerator, stove, dishwasher, washer, dryer, and so on. (This image would have to be modified for low socioeconomic students.) After the students have erased appliances, large and small, I ask them to take away the walls and the carpet or floor, because the entire structure is made from machine-made goods. (A colleague of mine uses a similar image to teach about poverty.)

After creating the image, I ask the students to open their eyes, and we discuss how life was more difficult before the industrial revolution. Then I ask them to write about the differences they can see in the life-style before and after the industrial revolution, including the problems that people of that time period had that we do not have and the problems that we have that they did not have. The technique involves students and helps them to learn about the impact of machines on human beings and to consider and evaluate the results of technological change. Similar guided imageries could be used to teach concepts about the results of hunger, genetic engineering, nuclear war, and many other topics.

Mailbags and Miscellany: Writing in History Classes

By Laurel Corona
Director of OASIS,
University of California, San Diego

Most young people enjoy writing when the assignments are enjoyable and when they allow them to use their imaginations, their senses of humor, and their growing sensitivity to the life situations of others. The following two class activities promote this kind of pleasure in writing and allow for creative expression outside the English classroom: mailbags from historical sites and miscellany.

Mailbags from Historical Sites

Mailbags from Historical Sites is a class project, but each student is completely responsible for his or her own part of the mail in the bag and for helping create a mailbag as it might have been filled when it left an important historical site. The mail in the bag should represent the writings of as full a range of people in the community as possible, and the destinations of the letters should be as diverse as possible. The purpose of the assignment is to enable the students to sense the ambiance of another place and time and to feel the past as if they were living in it.

In preparation for creating the mailbag, the students should make a list of the people apt to be in a particular place at a particular time. For example, in a Gold Rush town one might find miners, dance hall girls, preachers and their wives, stable boys, horse thieves, cowboys, teachers, doctors, merchants, and

> *"Then our job is not to get language into the head of a child. Our job is to get it out."*
> A TEACHER QUOTED BY OWEN THOMAS

so on. Each of these would be living a different life in this town and have a different attitude about being there. For the most part, they would not care about or even be aware of being a part of history. They would be concerned primarily with their daily lives. Each of these people would have different reasons for sending mail.

After developing a large list of people in a Gold Rush town and discussing how each might view life there, the students should then project what kinds of letters each might write and to whom. For instance, a preacher's wife might be miserable and write to tell her mother so. The preacher might be inquiring about inexpensive *Bibles*. A horse thief about to be hung might write to bid farewell to his true love. After this part of the project is thoroughly brainstormed, the students should pick which character interests them the most and then write a letter for the bag. The teacher should encourage the students to adopt a writing style, tone, and point of view appropriate to the character they are writing through.

Some creative student might make a bag at home, or one could be fashioned from a paper sack. The most likely way to display the completed project would be to create a montage in the classroom, perhaps with colored string connecting each letter to the bag. Wall space and grade level would, of course, dictate how such a project would be "published."

Miscellany

Miscellany is a class project that is similar to the one featuring mailbags, but more of the work should be done in small groups. Rather than create the finished products that letters represent, in the miscellany activity the students create the debris of an important historical event. For instance, they might imagine what General Ulysses S. Grant's tent looked like after the deciding battle of the Civil War or what his quarters at Appomattox looked like several days later. As a way of comparing and contrasting the two sides in the war, the class might be divided into a group responsible for creating the miscellany of the Union general's side and a group responsible for the Confederate general's miscellany. Miscellany might consist of battle plans, discarded communiques, drafts of speeches, letters to and from home or the President, and so forth. In order to create good, verisimilar debris, the students would have to research the subject thoroughly. Because of this, a project of this sort, if expectations are clearly delineated, makes an excellent alternative to a term paper.

Both of the projects described above can be suited to different grade levels and ability levels and also to different subject matter. Although history students would probably benefit most from such activities, teachers of other subjects might also be able to adapt these ideas for their classes. For example, if a science class is learning about Louis Pasteur, or Pierre and Marie Curie, or Galileo, or if an art class is studying

Vincent van Gogh, or Michelangelo Buonarroti, or Pablo Picasso, the miscellany project might be adapted. Similarly, students of Spanish or any other foreign language might create a town and its inhabitants and create a mailbag from that town.

And, teachers, do not let your students have all the fun. Indulge your own fantasies about dance hall girls or cattle rustlers. Willingness to do your own assignments is the single best way to validate them in your students' eyes.

Just a Few Words on Sentence Combining Across the Curriculum

By William Lomax
English Teacher, Benjamin Franklin High School,
Los Angeles Unified School District

Note: **The following is a sample of my address regarding sentence combining to a group of 32 high school teachers from several subject areas.**

All right, how many of you out there . . . (Is everybody listening?) . . . how many of you have used sentence combining in your classroom in the last, oh, six months? Three, five, six, seven . . . Sir, is your hand up? Okay, eight. That's it? All right, how many of you eight are English teachers? All eight, huh. What about the other, um, 24 of you? What do you teach? History . . . Spanish . . . science . . . government. And how many of you get consistently poor writing from your students? Okay, and how many of you would like to get better writing from your students? It's unanimous again. Well, my friends, let's talk about sentence combining. It may be able to help.

I won't take your time now to go through the research and theory of sentence combining; it's a well-established technique. There are plenty of books available, and it's basically a very simple process. Just ask your local English teacher for a little assistance. I've used sentence combining for several years, and I'm going to describe for you what I think works best.

Sentence combining work should be regular, but never routine. Establish your pattern; then keep it going, but vary it. Have students write the exercises one day; then do them orally the next. Give them as homework, do group work or choral readings, and have competitions between the groups. Use your imagination and sustain a sense of play. Above all, keep at it. After students have learned the basic system, you may spend as little as five minutes a day,

three times a week, on sentence combining. It doesn't take much time, but it should be regular and continuous. There is no goal to sentence combining except better writing, so use it throughout the year. Remember, too, that there are no "wrong" answers in sentence combining, only "better sentence combinations." Help students to see that writing is a process and a skill, not something that is right or wrong.

A single page—five to eight exercises—is enough for one day, once the routine is established, but even that can be varied. I prefer to use at least *two* pages per session. The four basic "signals" used by Frank O'Hare to instruct students (underlining, crossouts, SOMETHING words, and parentheses) are easily learned, but they are addictive.[1] They are harder to unlearn than to learn. That's why I regularly give one page *with* signals and one page *without* signals *from the beginning*. Start students off with signals with something simple, like this:

I drove the car onto the freeway.
I drove the car slowly.

I mean, really simple, right? You won't insult their intelligence, because you'll steadily increase the difficulty of the exercise—never faster, however, than they can do them correctly. You will be surprised, I suspect, at how fast they will progress to more complex exercises, once the signals are learned.

Now, I think the English teachers here are probably familiar with all the different ways sentence combining can be used—to teach vocabulary, sentence structure, grammar, paragraphing, punctuation, literature—all that "stuff" that goes on in an English classroom.[2]

[1]See Frank O'Hare, *Sentence-Combining: Improving Student Writing Without Formal Grammar Instruction.* Urbana, Ill.: National Council of Teachers of English, 1973. Also see Jerry Judd's commentary that appears later in this book.

[2]For further information see William Lomax, "Sentence Combining Across the Curriculum," *California English*, Vol. 16 (November-December, 1980), 18—21.

But what about you other teachers? You're all sitting politely, but the muscles in your cheeks are twitching. You're all asking, what's in it for me, right? What's in it is better writing—for *all* classrooms. Just a few minutes ago, you all said that's what you wanted.

Here's the point: Combining means more than just putting sentences together. It also means *combining form* and *content*. That is, while you're giving your students writing practice, they are simultaneously learning *your* subject matter. You teach history, you say? Then give them an exercise like this:

A man was burned at the stake.
The man was named Giordano Bruno.
He was burned in the year 1600.
He was burned in Rome.

And so on. Now that one is a far cry from the simple little starter we looked at earlier, but it shows where you can go with sentence combining. You science teachers, try this one:

1. Each nerve cell in the body has four major parts.
   One part is the dendrites, which receive messages from other cells.
   One part is the nerve cell body.
   One part is the axon down which the messages pass.
   One part is the synapses, which communicate with other cells.
2. Each axon is surrounded by a sheath of fatty material
   This fatty material is known as myelin.
3. Myelin does three things.
   Myelin insulates axons so nerve messages are not short-circuited.
   Myelin gives the white matter of the brain its appearance.
   Myelin accounts for the large amounts of fatty cholesterol in the brain.

Those are advanced exercises—your early efforts being much simpler—but I think you can see my point: Students are practicing writing while dealing with the subject matter of *your* course.

Let's face it: Writing has, for some reason, been isolated in English classes. Students do learn to write there, but they don't see that what they learn in English is relevant to other classes—simply because we don't expect it of them. Writing should be taught in every classroom where it is used. No, we English teachers still teach writing as intensively as ever; the primary responsibility is still ours. But if you want better writing from your students, you must teach it for the same reason that an English teacher teaches history with Nathaniel Hawthorne's *The Scarlet Letter* and science with Jack London's short story "To Build a Fire." Sentence combining can help you to do just that without taking time from your own subject matter.

Now, before we take a break, there's time for just a couple of questions. Yes, ma'am, sentence combining exercises do take time to prepare, but remember that you design them only once. They're good for the rest of your teaching career. Furthermore, there are plenty of books on the market that you may use instead of creating your own. When you do your own, however—especially you non-English teachers—you can match them to your particular course content. I keep non-consumable class sets of each of my one-page lessons on file in the English office; other teachers can then check them out, use them, and return them for others to use. Students always write exercises on their own paper. Science teachers, get your whole department involved; share the work, and your files will grow quickly. Or ask your English teachers for assistance; they can use your exercises, too. Once your files are established, you'll have a resource that will remain valuable for years to come. And your students will be better writers.

One more word—and this is important—sentence combining is no substitute for a student's original writing. It is just a tool which hones writing ability. Always require students to apply what they learn from sentence combining to their own writing, and give them plenty of opportunity to do that.

Thank you all for your attention. Let's break now before we go to our workshops. Coffee and doughnuts are in the foyer.

Snake in the Grass: An Integrated Approach to Concept Formation

By Carl Babb
Science Teacher, Capistrano Valley High School,
Capistrano Unified School District;
and Instructor, Irvine Valley Community College
and Todd Huck
English Teacher, Thurston Middle School,
Laguna Beach Unified School District;
and Codirector, UCI Writing Project

Picture this:

It is third period. Out on the football field, lined up on the 50-yard line, are ten small groups of students. One member of each group is tensed and ready to run; some are crouched; some are poised like sprinters in a starting position. All are silent, waiting for the signal. Several yards in front of them, the teacher raises the silver whistle to his lips, inhales slowly, hesitates, and blows. Ten students burst across the line, heads down, eyes on the grass, each stopping suddenly and stooping

to snatch a toothpick of red or yellow, blue or green. Now darting a few more steps and taking another plunging stoop, the runners scoop up another toothpick. From the 50-yard line, their teammates scream, cheer, and exhort them to get back across the starting line before the ten-second whistle sounds. All the runners but one cross the line as the whistle shrills. Knowing the rules, the latecomer turns and scatters his gathered toothpicks back across the grassy range in front of his team, while the racers from other teams wrap their collected toothpicks in tape and drop the small bundles into bags held by their teammates.

The formation and retention of concepts are deepened and enriched when students are actively involved in their learning.
TODD HUCK

To the students, this game seems like a cross between a relay race and a treasure hunt, but what they soon discover is that they are experiencing and experimenting with an important scientific concept, the natural phenomenon of protective coloration. Students need no formal prior knowledge about protective coloration to play the game. In fact, it is better if they do not, for the lesson allows students to discover some of the broad dynamics of protective coloration through their own observations and conclusions. As such, this lesson serves as an ideal introduction to this scientific concept.

A large grassy area is needed to conduct the game. Students are divided into roughly ten teams, with approximately three members per team. Teams line up behind a line, leaving at least ten feet between each team. In front of each team, 40 colored toothpicks are randomly distributed in a specified area called a *range*. Each group of toothpicks *must* be made up of ten red, ten yellow, ten green, and ten blue toothpicks. The range should be about ten yards long and three yards wide (see Figure 20). Finally, each team must choose a member to be a *bagger* as well as a racer. The bagger's job is to collect toothpicks gathered during each race, to make sure they are taped together and labeled, and to save them in a bag for use during the next class.

To begin the game, the teacher blows a whistle. The first member of each team has ten seconds to run down the range, picking up as many toothpicks as possible, one toothpick per stoop. When the ten-second whistle blows again, each team member must be back across the starting line; or else he or she must return the collected toothpicks to the range. The players then wrap the gathered toothpicks in a piece of masking tape, label the taped group with the number of the race (Race #1, Race #2, and so forth), and drop the labeled group into the bagger's bag. The procedure of running races and labeling collected toothpicks is repeated until each group member has run three races.

Having played the game, the students are now ready to translate their kinesthetic experience into a carefully considered scientific concept. They will do this, in part, by using writing as a vehicle for discovery. Writing, we know, is not merely a means of recording previously learned information; it is a tool for clarifying and stimulating thinking and for analyzing, interpreting, and speculating about the meaning of gathered data.

Begin the second day's lesson by asking the students to picture this scene:

> **Imagine a large, grassy plain. Among the animals that populate this grassy plain are four distinctly colored varieties of snakes. Some are reddish, some yellow, some blue, and some green. The natural predator that preys on these snakes is a large species of hawk. The hawks fly from mountains near the grassy plain, feeding on those snakes that they can find.**

Now, ask students to cluster for two minutes about the connections they see between the scenario you have just given them and yesterday's game. When the two

minutes are up, take responses from class members about the parallels they have observed and cluster them on the chalkboard. Students are likely to see obvious connections between the game and the scenario, but if they do not go further in their thinking, ask them to do a *quick-write* in which they consider which snakes are likely to get eaten most often and which ones might be least often victims of the hawks. You will probably get a consensus that the red and yellow snakes are more likely to be eaten more often than the blue or green snakes. Whatever their speculations, tell the students that they can check out their hypotheses and draw some conclusions about the factors that affect survival of the snakes by tabulating and analyzing the data they collected in yesterday's game.

Students meet in their teams and are given their bag of toothpicks and tables and data sheets (see Figure 21 for a sample). Students fill in Table 1 by counting the toothpicks gathered in each race and tallying the numbers of each color. Next, students total the number of toothpicks of all colors collected during each race and enter this value in the right-hand column. Table 2 simply helps students summarize and consolidate the data from Table 1.

Students now use their finished data sheets to write individual responses to the following data analysis questions. (An interesting option is to have students

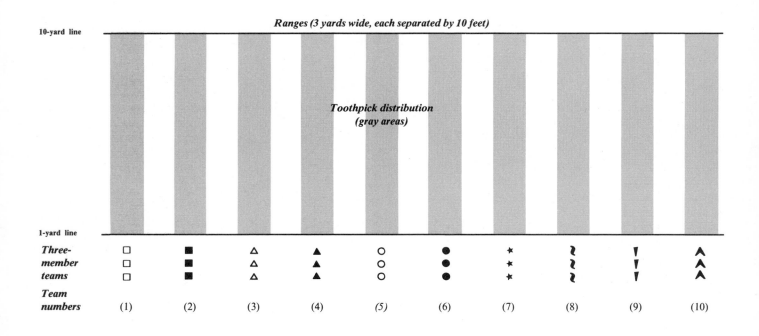

Fig. 20. A Diagram of Team Lines and Ranges

use their data sheets to generate questions of their own to answer before the teacher provides them with the data analysis questions.)

1. Refer to Table 2.
   a. What happens to the numbers of each toothpick color as you go down the chart?
   b. Why do you think this is so?
2. Refer to the right-hand column on Table 2.
   a. Look at the total number of toothpicks picked up over three sets of races. What happens to these numbers?
   b. Why do you suppose that this is so?
3. a. Which color(s) was(were) picked up most frequently?
   b. Draw a conclusion about why this is so.
4. a. Which colors were picked up least frequently?
   b. Why do you think that this is so?
5. As you picked up toothpicks, was it easier to pick them up if they were clustered close together or scattered far apart, or were they both equally easy to pick up?
6. As more and more toothpicks were removed from the grass, how did this affect the numbers you picked up?

When students finish the questions, have the teams meet, discuss their responses, and compile a set of

Choose material proportionate to your powers, you who write, and long consider what your shoulders can carry, what they cannot.

HORACE

answers that reflect their best collaborative thinking. Now, lead a large group discussion about their answers, considering the kinds of thinking they had to do to get their answers. (An optional activity at this point is to draw a blank Table 3 on the chalkboard and collect the numbers and colors of toothpicks gathered for the sets of races from each of the groups to get classwide totals and averages. Students may then conclude whether data from Table 2 or Table 3 are more accurate and why, whether their small sampling of data from Table 2 showed a trend that was supported by data on Table 3, and how the total number of races influences the accuracy of the data.)

Table 1. Toothpicks Collected by One Team Over Nine 10-second Races.
(Each team had three participants.)

Number of race	Number of toothpicks collected, by color				Total toothpicks per race
	Red	Yellow	Green	Blue	
1	//	/	/	/	5
2	/	//	/		4
3	//	//		/	5
....	.....	.....	.....	.....	....
4		/	/	/	3
5	/	/	/	//	5
6	/			/	2
....	.....	.....	.....	.....	....
7	/	/			2
8	/		/		2
9	/		/	/	3

Table 2. Consolidation of Data from Table 1 into Three Divisions

Number of race	Number of toothpicks collected, by color				Total toothpicks collected
	Red	Yellow	Green	Blue	
Races 1—3	5	5	2	2	14
Races 4—6	2	2	2	5	11
Races 7—9	2	2	1	1	6

Table 3. Average Data Collected per Group, Based on Class Average (n = 6)

Number of race	Number of toothpicks collected, by color				Total toothpicks collected
	Red	Yellow	Green	Blue	
Races 1—3	6	7	3	4	20
Races 4—6	4	4	2	4	14
Races 7—9	4	3	1	2	10

Fig. 21. Three Tables of Data on Toothpick Experiment

Participation in the game, speculation about its meaning, compilation of data, collaboration with peers, and interpretation of the assembled information all provide prewriting activities that can lead to a variety of writing experiences in different domains. Here are a few sample prompts based on our snakes and hawks scenario:

Analytical/Expository: The color of a snake may be helpful or harmful to its survival. Analyze and draw conclusions about how the color of a snake affects its chances for survival when it is the prey.

- How does the number of snakes in an area affect their chances for survival? Speculate about how it might be advantageous for animals to travel in groups.
- What can you guess or infer about how the color of a snake might affect its chances for survival when it is a predator?
- How might the data be different if the game were played on a red carpet instead of on grass?
- Based on the data you collected, which group of snakes do you think might first become extinct? Why? Speculate on what colors might be found in a group of snakes in a thousand years.

Practical/Informative. Write a snake survival manual. In the manual tell your snake-reader what it should know in order to survive. What should it know if it is brightly colored? If it is colored so that it blends with its environment? What should it consider when choosing the color and number of traveling companions? Are there times of day when it would be safer for it to feed and be active? Depending on its color, is it better for it to move quickly or to remain still when a predator is around? How might its color affect its search for food?

- Write a script for a television nature documentary that describes and explains the fate of a group of snakes over nine days. Use your data table as the basis of your script.

Imaginative/Narrative. Using diary entries, write an imaginary account of a week in the life of either a brightly colored snake or a snake that blends in with its environment. Consider some of these ideas. What might the snake encounter from day to day? What might it notice about the number and color of other snakes in its area over a period of time? What does it think about and experience because of its color? When does it eat? Why? How does its color affect its ability to get food? Does it travel with other snakes? How does it move when it feels threatened?

Students certainly could learn about the scientific concept of protective coloration through a traditional means, such as a lecture, without going through the rigamarole of this game and its attendant activities. However, the quality of an educational experience and the formation and, especially, the retention of concepts that are embodied in it are deepened and enriched when students are actively involved in their learning, when they have a chance to collaborate and share insights, and when writing is integrated across the curriculum as a learning tool for heightening, refining, and clarifying thinking.

Showing, Not Telling

A Training Program for Student Writers

By Rebekah Caplan
English Teacher, Foothill High School,
Amador Valley Joint High School District;
and Teacher/Consultant, Bay Area Writing Project

Year after year we make student writers cringe with the reminder to be specific. We write in margins next to bracketed passages: *Explain, describe.* We extend arrows over words and under words, we circle words, we draw lines through words, and we accompany our hieroglyphics with captions: "What do you mean? Needs more detail; unclear." When we compose essay questions for examinations, we underline the why or why not at the end of the question twice so that our students will realize the importance of that part of the response. Recently, I talked with one teacher who had designed a rubber stamp which bore the words, GIVE AN EXAMPLE, so that he would not have to scribble the phrase again and again.

The assumption behind the Showing, *not* Telling, Training Program is that most students have not been trained to show what they mean. By training, I do not mean the occasional exercises taken from composition textbooks, nor do I mean the experience gained by writing perhaps eight major essays over the course of a semester. What I mean by training is the performing of a daily mental warm-up, short and rigorous, which is not unlike the training routines of musicians, dancers, and athletes. Six years ago, while teaching

EDITOR'S NOTE: This article is an excerpt from a monograph entitled *Showing Writing: A Training Program to Help Students Be Specific,* coauthored by Rebekah Caplan and Catherine Keech, and reprinted here by permission of the Bay Area Writing Project, 1615 Tolman Hall, University of California, Berkeley, Berkeley, CA 94720. See also *Writers in Training: A Guide to Developing a Composition Program,* by Rebekah Caplan, published by Dale Seymour Publications, P. O. Box 10888, Palo Alto, CA 94303.

reading and composition in a suburban middle school, I realized the important connection between disciplined practice in the arts and the need for it in a writing program. My first students were eighth graders, and not knowing precisely what the junior high school student needed to learn about writing, I experimented for a while.

My Experiment with Eighth Grade Students

For approximately three weeks I assigned my eighth grade students a potpourri of writing exercises and examined their papers carefully for common problems or strengths. I wanted to determine what my students already knew about good writing and how far I might expect to take them. It was not difficult to discover in those first few weeks of my teaching career that although these eighth graders did write with enthusiasm and energy, not many of them wrote with color or sound or texture. In a description of a student's favorite movie, I would read: "It was fantastic because it was so real!" Or the description of a strange person: "He is so weird." Or a description of a friend: "She has the most fantastic personality."

The underlinings proved their earnestness, their sincerity. I attacked these empty descriptions, however, and inscribed in the margins those same suggestions that teachers have used for years. In class I passed out models of rich description—character sketches by John Steinbeck, settings by Mark Twain, abstract ideas by Ray Bradbury. I advised the students, as they scanned the models and glanced back at

51

their own papers, that they needed to be that explicit, that good. That is what writing is all about. I said, "I know that you know what makes a thunderstorm so frightening. I know that you know the same things Mark Twain knew about a thunderstorm. Now what details did he use?" And we would list "the trees swaying" and the sky turning "blue-black" until we had every descriptive word classified on the chalkboard. "And now," I continued, "you describe a beautiful sunset in the same way that Mark Twain described the storm."

The writings from such follow-up assignments were admittedly better; but without the prepping, without fussing and reminding, I could not get students to remember to use specifics naturally. With growing frustration I tried to examine my history as a student writer. I wanted to track down what it had been like for me to write in the eighth grade and what it was like for my students today. I wanted to uncover when it was that I had reached a turning point or gained a sense of discovery about language and expression.

When I tried to recall my own junior high experience, however, I could not remember one assignment, let alone any instruction in writing. What I did remember was signing autograph books and passing notes in class, recording memories in diaries, and signing *slam* books. Those sorts of writings mattered the most. We cared deeply about who was one's friend and who was one's enemy, who was loved, who was hated, who was worthy of secrets, who was not. And as these issues came under judgment, we based our verdict on the degree of someone's good personality. In fact, the supreme compliment paid a friend in an autograph book amounted to "fantastic personality." And it is still so today.

The memory struck me as being significant. The notion that each person has a personality that is separate from looks or dress or wealth is a new thought to the junior high school student. I remember using the same phrase, "a great personality," with fresh, original intentions in diaries and school papers. My friends and I were intrigued by the idea of personality more than any other idea. We were fascinated by people's differences; yet, we could not say exactly what made us like one person and dislike another. Could it be, then, that I was demanding writing that my students were not ready to produce? It seemed crucial to respect their excitement over many of these clichéd discoveries. I had to allow room for naive, exploratory generalizations but, at the same time, challenge them to move beyond simple abstractions and discover what concepts, like personality, were based on—how they derived their meanings from concrete perceptions.

An Examination of My Writing

After examining what motivated my students, I looked at myself as an adult writer. What kinds of things did I strive for? I surely strove for specificity. For years I had kept a journal in which I commented on cycles of personal change. I usually began in a stream-of-consciousness style, listing sensations and noting the details that would explain my perceptions to myself. I wrote often, even if I had nothing to say, in the hope that I would discover something to write about. I believe this ritual of writing regularly developed from my training as a dancer and a pianist. As a young piano student, I practiced daily finger exercises to strengthen manual agility at the keyboard to prepare myself for a Bach concerto. As a young ballerina, I was forced to do leg lifts at the bar for 30 minutes for each lesson; the remaining 15 minutes were devoted to dancing. (How we longed for it to be the other way around!) I notice that beginning artists practice drawing the human body again and again from varying angles, using different materials—charcoals, oils, ink—to capture reality. In the drama classes I attended in college, we began acting lessons with short improvisations that allowed us to experiment with emotions before we rehearsed major scenes for a performance. In all these cases, the learning, the mastering, came more from the practice than from the final presentation.

My Training Program for Student Writers

After drawing these several conclusions about the training of artists, I decided to build into my curriculum a training program for student writers—a program in which I attempted to engrain craft and to make the use of specific detail automatic, habitual, through regular and rigorous practice. I created a writing program that included these coordinating tasks:

1. Practicing daily the expanding of a general statement into a paragraph
2. Applying the difference between *telling* and *showing* in the editing process
3. Practicing specific ways to select and arrange concrete details in developing an idea or structuring an essay

Next, I will describe the initial phase of my training program.

Since students need the discipline of a regular routine to reinforce the use of concrete details in place of, or in support of, their generalizations, I assign a daily homework challenge: I give them what I call a *telling sentence*. They must expand the thought in that sentence into an entire paragraph which shows rather than tells. They take home sentences like these:

The room is vacant.
The jigsaw puzzle was difficult to assemble.
Lunch period is too short.

They bring back descriptive paragraphs—short or long, but always detailed, and focused on demonstrating the thought expressed in the assigned *telling* sentence. I challenge students not to use the original statement in the paragraph at all. I ask them to convince me that a room is empty or a puzzle is hard to assemble without once making that claim directly. The challenge is much like one in charades: They have to get an idea across without telling what it is.

In order to establish the difference between telling and showing, I distribute the following two paragraphs to my students. The first was written by a seventh grader; the second, by novelist E. L. Doctorow. Both passages concern a scene at a bus stop:

Telling:
Each morning I ride the bus to school. I wait along with the other people who ride my bus. Sometimes the bus is late and we get angry. Some guys start fights and stuff just to have something to do. I'm always glad when the bus finally comes.

Showing:
A bus arrived. It discharged its passengers, closed its doors with a hiss, and disappeared over the crest of the hill. Not one of the people waiting at the bus stop had attempted to board. One woman wore a sweater that was too small, a long loose skirt, white sweater socks, and

house slippers. One man was in his undershirt. Another man wore shoes with the toes cut out, a soiled blue serge jacket and brown pants. There was something wrong with these people. They made faces. A mouth smiled at nothing, and unsmiled, smiled and unsmiled. A head shook in vehement denial. Most of them carried brown paper bags rolled tight against their stomachs.[1]

When asked to distinguish the differences between the two paragraphs, most students respond by saying the second paragraph is better because they can picture the scene more easily. They think the people in paragraph two are "weird, poor, and lonely," (all *telling* ideas). But this interpretation comes from the pictures (the students' word), pictures of people wearing torn clothing, carrying brown paper bags instead of lunch boxes, wearing unhappy expressions on their faces. Student writers can easily discern good description. Getting them to write with close detail is not managed as smoothly.

I remind students that the storybooks they read as very young children are filled with colorful illustrations that show the events described on accompanying pages; the writer does not have to describe the lovely red barn with the carved wooden trim, for the picture next to the caption, "The barn was beautiful," reveals that idea. However, in more mature literature, drawings disappear from the pages, and the writer assumes the role of illustrator. Language must be the author's brush and palette. Following such a discussion, I initiate the daily training exercise and explain to students that they will expand one sentence each night from telling to showing during the entire course of the semester.

Below are sample daily sentences. These sentences are given in no particular order and are not necessarily linked by recurring themes. Sometimes students themselves suggest sentences for successive assignments. By choosing generalizations familiar to stu-

---

[1]E. L. Doctorow, *The Book of Daniel.* New York: Random House, Inc., © 1971, p. 5. Used by permission of the publisher.

dents, I increase the likelihood of effective elaboration:

She has a good personality.
The party was fun.
The pizza tasted good.
My parents seemed angry.
The movie was frightening.
The concert was fantastic.
The jocks think they're cool.
I was embarrassed.
My room was a mess.
Foothill students have good school spirit.

The idea of daily writing is, of course, nothing new in itself. I know many teachers who have their students "write for ten minutes" the moment they come to class. My daily writing approach, however, is different in a number of ways. First, many teachers assign topics for elaboration, such as school or family or sports. Although a topic is open-ended and allows more room for creativity, students often spend more time trying to find something to say than they spend in writing the composition. The type of statement I use is similar to the thesis, the controlling sentence of an essay. The generalization supplies the point; the student is given the idea to support. Students are free then to concentrate on experimenting with expressions of that idea. Further, since they are all working on the same idea, they are in a position to compare results—to learn from one another's crafting.

Another departure from other daily writing warm-ups is that this daily writing is done at home. Students must come to class with pieces finished and ready to be evaluated. We do not wait ten minutes while they hastily scribble some sort of solution. I want to give them time—if they will use it—to experiment with and think about what they are trying to do.

Importance of Sharing the Writing

Finally, unlike private journals or some free-writing assignments, the exercises are written to be shared. I use the writings in much the same way that a drama instructor uses improvisation as an instructional technique. The daily sentence expansion becomes a framework for practicing and discovering ways of showing ideas. Just as drama students search for ways of expressing ambition or despair by imagining themselves in real-life situations that would evoke these feelings and discovering ranges of bodily and facial expression, my students arrive at ways of showing "empty rooms" or "difficult puzzles" by experimenting with different kinds of language expression. I instruct them very little, preferring that students find their own solutions. But, finally, although the experimenting at home is free, not judged, the practice includes an important element that parallels instruction in acting: the daily public performance. The students know in advance that some papers will be read to the class for analysis and evaluation. However, they do not know which ones. As their papers might be among those I choose (my selections do not fall into a predicatable pattern), the students are likely to be prepared.

The *performance* or sharing of improvisational or experimental efforts is an important learning experience for the selected performers and their audience. The first ten minutes of every class session, then, is devoted to oral readings, not writing. I choose between five and seven writing samples, which I read aloud to the class, and as a group we evaluate the density of detail. Where did this writer have success with interesting description? Where were his or her details thin? This is the only time I do not comb the papers for errors in grammar, spelling, and usage, for there is not time. Since we respond exclusively to content, students can give full attention to being specific without the pressure of being grammatically perfect.

I grade each paper immediately as the discussion of that paper concludes. Besides assigning an A, B, or C grade, I quickly write a general comment made by the group: "great showing; too telling at the end," "great imagination, but write more." This process takes only a few seconds, and then I move on to the next reading. I record a check in my gradebook for those papers not selected for reading. If students do not turn in writings, they do not receive credit. All papers are recorded and handed back before the end of the period,

giving the students immediate responses and recognition for their work. At the end of the semester, I average the number of grades a student has earned in the series of assignments.

Advantages to Using a Daily Exercise

There are five major advantages to using such a daily training exercise with its follow-up sharing and discussion:

1. *Students write almost every day.* I do not assign sentences on the eve of an examination day, on days major assignments are due, or on holidays.
2. *I am freed from having to grade an entire set of papers each night, yet I provide a daily evaluation.* If a student is disappointed because a particular writing was not selected, I invite him or her to share it with me after class. This tends to happen when the student has written a good paragraph and wants me to enter a grade for this particular one, which I am glad to do. It may also happen when a student is unsure of his or her solution and wants help.
3. *Students who are selected to perform hear useful comments immediately.* They do not have to wait a week to receive responses and constructive criticisms. The other students learn from the process of specifying weaknesses as well as strengths of work and from hearing suggestions given to the performing students by peers and teachers.
4. *Students learn new developmental techniques and linguistic patterns from each other.* Students assimilate new ideas for specificity by regularly hearing other students' writing. In addition, they often internalize the linguistic patterns of other students either consciously or unconsciously. This process is similar to assimilating the speech patterns of a person with a different accent. After close association with this person, we may tune our speech to the inflections of an attractive or entertaining accent. I believe it is often easier for students to learn from other students who write well than from professional writers whose solutions may be out of the students' range.
5. *Students write for a specific audience.* They write with the expectation that classmates may hear their compositions the following day. Therefore, they usually put more effort into their writing than they would have given if the compositions were intended for their private journals or for a teacher's evaluation.

A selection of daily writing samples follows. Two students, a remedial freshman and a college-bound sophomore, show growth and change over a two-week time span. Their writings illustrate two important results of the daily practice:

1. Students write more either because they are finding it easier to generate more writing or because they are working harder on the assignments (or both).
2. Students gain control over a wider range of techniques.

> *The chief purpose of words is to convey thoughts, and unless the wavelengths of the words are right, the receiving apparatus will utterly fail to pick up the thoughts.*
> GEORGE OTIS SMITH

From the daily sentence, *The new students were lonely,* the freshman wrote the following at the beginning of the two-week time period:

> It was the first day of school and there were two new students, Dick and Dan, who had moved over the summer. They were brothers and this was a new city and school which they had come to, and in this school they would have to make friends because neither of them knew anybody or anyone.

As you will note, the freshman's writing is composed entirely of generalities (telling sentences). The writer explains the cause of the loneliness—a new city, new school, absence of old friends—but unless he shows us his new surroundings, unfamiliar faces, and different customs to support those reasons, he will do little to convince us. Perhaps if he could contrast "playing pool with the gang at Old Mike's Pizza Parlor" to the "eyes avoiding his unfamiliar face in the study hall," the reader might appreciate the realities of "new city, new school, new friends." Here is the same freshman student's writing two weeks later; the daily sentence was *The crossword puzzle was difficult to solve:*

> The sixth row down got me stuck. It was plain to tell that this crossword puzzle was rough. The puzzle, as it was, was made for a 12th grade level, and it made me feel as if I was in the 6th grade level. Intellectual words were included, such as "the square root" of 1,091,056 in four digits and others. The next one was a five-letter word for philodendron, which was "plant" to my surprise. I, as a normal person, had a very hard time trying to figure out what an Australian green citrus fruit was with four spaces. Instinctively I gave up the whole game, as it was too frustrating to cope with.

The freshman's selection illustrates his improvement in generating examples. The writer introduces his subject by *telling* that the puzzle was tough, but he immediately proves his claim with a series of illustrations: twelfth grade level versus sixth grade level, intellectual words like square root, unfamiliar plants and fruits that call for specialized knowledge. His writing is more enjoyable to read because of the examples he added. Notice also that his paragraph is longer, but he does not ramble or leave the point.

At the beginning of the two-week period, the sophomore responded to the daily sentence: *The room was vacant,* by writing this:

> The next show didn't start for another hour. As I repositioned the spotlight in the upper balcony, the squeaks of the rusty screws seemed to echo throughout the desolate building. I walked down the aluminum stairs that resounded with the sound of rain beating on a tin roof throughout the auditorium. I then opened the curtains to the large, lonely stage which looked dark and forbidding. As I put up the sets and decorated the stage, I guess it would seem to anyone walking in, that the room was very much alive with color and objects. But to me, even the set and decorated auditorium looked bare.

In the first half of the paragraph, this student carefully constructs detail. Like many students trying to master a skill, he concentrates intensely at first, very mindful of his task. However, there comes a point when, losing his fervor, he reverts to telling. With the sentence, "I then opened the curtains . . .," he abandons his use of specifics, relying instead on vague adjectives like "dark and forbidding," or general nouns such as "color and objects."

Within two weeks, this student increased his observational skills considerably. In addition, he was able to sustain the use of vivid details throughout a much longer piece of writing. With the daily sentence, *The*

roller coaster was the scariest ride at the fair, as a prompt, he wrote:

> As I stood in line, I gazed up at the gigantic steel tracks that looped around three times. The thunderous roar of the roller coaster sounded like a thunder cloud that had sunk into my ears and suddenly exploded. The wild screams of terror shot through me like a bolt of lightning and made my fingers tingle with fear. Soon I heard the roar of the roller coaster cease. As the line started to move forward, I heard the clicking of the turnstile move closer and closer. Finally, I got onto the loading deck and with a shaking hand gave the attendant my ticket.
>
> It seemed like I barely got seated when I felt a jolt which signified the beginning of the ride. While the roller coaster edged up the large track, I kept pulling my seatbelt tighter and tighter until it felt like I was cutting off all circulation from the waist down. At the crest of the hill, I caught a glimpse of the quiet town which lay before me and gave me a feeling of peace and serenity. Suddenly my eyes felt like they were pushed all the way back into my head, and the town had become a blur. All I could see was a mass of steel curving this way and that as the roller coaster turned upside down. I was squeezing the safety bar so tight that my fingers seemed to be embedded in the metal. I could see the landing deck, and I let out a deep breath that had been held inside ever since the first drop. As the roller coaster came to a halt, I felt weak and emotionally drained. When I stepped off onto the deck, I teetered a bit to the left, but caught my balance quickly when I saw my friends waiting for me at the exit gate. I tried to look "normal," while trying to convince them in a weak voice that, "Oh, it was nothing."

Even though he makes general claims—"I felt weak and emotionally drained"—he remembers to support his feeling with specific evidence: "When I stepped off onto the deck, I teetered a bit to the left. . . ." Or, as he tries to look "normal," he proves this with dialogue: "Oh, it was nothing." This student puts himself in the experience every step of the narration. Two weeks earlier, he could not sustain such a practice.

To summarize, the practice of showing, not telling, through daily sentence expansions provides a framework in which students can experiment and discover ways of showing ideas. It is a time for self-exploration in the attempt to attach meaning to experience; it is also a time for increasing fluency and creating a style and voice.

Preparing for Showing, Not Telling, Through Share Days

By Michael Carr
Teacher, Los Alamitos Elementary School,
Los Alamitos Unified School District;
and Teacher/Consultant, UCI Writing Project

Rebekah Caplan's showing, not telling, technique can be taught effectively in kindergarten and first grade. But because many of the students may be non-readers or nonwriters, they will need some oral preparation. *Share Days* make wonderful prewriting experiences for children who are making the transition from speaking to writing.

Essentially, Share Days are an updated version of show and tell. A child brings an object to share to class, but the object must be hidden from view in a bag or box. When it is his or her turn, the child comes to the front of the class, puts the item in our share box, and proceeds to describe it by answering these questions:

What is its shape?
What is its color?
What is its texture?
What is it made of?
What do you do with it?
Who uses it?
What is it like? Can you compare it to anything else?

After the child describes his or her object by answering the questions cited above, selected students get three tries to guess what the item is. See how you do on this example:

The item is round.
The colors are white and gold.
It's hard and smooth.
It's made of rubber.
You throw the item.
People use it.
It's like a flying saucer.

If you guessed a Frisbee, you are right. When the item has been guessed correctly, or all tries have been exhausted, the child can take the item out of the share box to show the class.

Using this process, children in my class are able to construct orally the elements of a showing paragraph by describing rather than telling. This not only increases their oral fluency but also prepares them for writing. Moreover, at the same time that they are getting practice in speaking and, by extension, writing, they are also building problem-solving skills.

Preparing Junior High School Students for Showing, Not Telling

By Marie Filardo
English and ESL Teacher, Serrano Intermediate School,
Saddleback Valley Unified School District;
and Teacher/Consultant, UCI Writing Project

Every September a new wave of students registers for intermediate school all decked out in their designer clothes and speaking a uniform language. Everything is "awesome," "radical," and "mega." Conformity abounds. Unfortunately, the accepted labels in their speech infiltrates their writing, and I know I am in for countless papers filled with stilted, lifeless, abstract images.

As an intermediate school teacher aware of the social impact on writing, my initial step in preparing students for showing, not telling, is to make them aware of the consequences of labeling. In my first assignment I ask my students to write a letter to a friend in which they recall a memorable place, person, or event that they encountered last summer. The following samples indicate the extent to which labeling occurs in their writing:

Dear Kim,
    I remember when we went skin diving at Shaw's Cove. It was rad.

Dear Tom,
    Jim and I went surfing in Laguna. We caught some really gnarly waves.

Dear Michelle,
    My family and I went on the log ride at Knott's Berry Farm. It was awesome.

Dear Collette,
    Friday we all went to Dodger Stadium. We got a bunch of autographs. I wish you could have gone. It was spastic.

Dear Heather,
    Our vacation in Hawaii was mega bucks but we had a blast.

Dear Sandy,

I had the most funnest summer. I went to a friend's house and played so many fun games. I stayed there really late and had the most funnest time.

After collecting the letters, I read them and underline the labeling words. In class the following day, we work in pairs. I ask partners to question what they envision when they hear a labeled word and to jot down specific details of their impressions. During a session of questioning, students realize quickly what was awesome to one student might not have been imagined by the other. In comparing notes, they see that each individual has conjured up a different image of the labeling word. An awesome day at the beach may prove to be a peaceful, lazy day for Tom, while it may mean surfing in 12 feet high waves to John. When individual groups have had sufficient time to review several labeling words, I call the class together and provide a list, such as the following, on which I ask the students to identify words that may be interpreted differently.

Identifying Labels[1]

Instructions: Find every label word in the list below and indicate it by printing "L" beside it.

deafening	green	sexy
threadbare	fantastic	hateful
ugly	malodorous	fabulous
moss-covered	frayed	sturdy
close-cropped	bumpy	great
boring	unlikable	wonderful
awful	immoral	upturned
slow-moving	sharp-featured	awesome
curly	sweaty	bug-eyed
lovely	foul-mouthed	horrible
splotchy	adorable	ragged
capable	timid	purple
blue and white	fetid	right
checked	amazing	exciting
pug-nosed	looming	obese
cautious	wild-eyed	leathery
respectable		

In follow-up lessons we review labeling phrases and labeling paragraphs. In an attempt to have students become cognizant of labeling words in their daily lives, I post a chart on which we record labels as they crop up in daily discussions.

To counteract the unproductive cycle of labeling which permeates both thinking and writing skills, labeling has to be identified as being generic and non-definitive, a statement of opinion rather than fact, subjective rather than objective. Once the students are

---

[1]This is part of a list from Gene Stanford and Marie Smith's *A Guidebook for Teaching Creative Writing*. Newton, Mass.: Allyn & Bacon, Inc., © 1981, p. 4. Used by permission of the publisher.

In more mature literature, drawings disappear from the pages, and the writer assumes the role of illustrator. Language must be the author's brush and palette.
REBEKAH CAPLAN

aware of labels and their effect on writing, we concentrate on replacing labels with words that are less abstract. It becomes our goal to replace a label with concrete images that can easily be perceived by our senses. For example, the awesome log ride at Knott's Berry Farm becomes a slow-ascending, winding, jarring, fast-descending, or splashing ride. This process of replacing labels with concrete, explicit vocabulary focuses the students' attention on the pleasure of communicating more clearly. Indefinite words are transformed into clear images.

Once students are made aware of the pitfalls of labeling, it is necessary to provide them with the skills needed to further the attributes of showing rather than telling. These skills may include:

1. Vocabulary
2. Metaphors and similes
3. Techniques in imagery
4. Sentence structure
5. Paragraph form

From evaluating my students' writing over a period of time, I am convinced that the progression of showing in their writing was directly proportional to the writing skills taught. This fact furthered my sense that it is essential to prepare students for *showing* before assigning descriptive, showing, not telling, paragraphs.

Here is a sample of writing produced after a lesson on the use of similes in replacing labels:

Finding my way to class was like running in a marathon and not knowing where the finish line was. While I was finding my classes, I had a picture in my mind of myself as a mouse quickly running so I wouldn't get stepped on. I felt very relieved at the end of the day, sort of like an experienced adult who has been working at a job for many years. After the second half of the day, I was pretty relaxed and not tense anymore. I had great fun that first day at Serrano. It was like a day at an amusement park.

The following writing sample was generated after a combination of vocabulary, metaphors and similes, and sentence structure skills were taught:

The dark, brown-haired boy came and sat next to me with disdain. When he sat down, he looked as if he was about to throw his books at me with a great deal of strength. As the day went on, my head felt like it was being pounded on while I worried about whether or not he was going to hit me. At lunch he would act very indomitable, like a boulder making its way through other rocks to get his food. Even worse, he acted like his brain was as small as a sunflower seed. He, trying to think, is worse than a pig trying to sing. Sometimes he would try to be funny. None of his jokes were very good. But, you would have to laugh or he would pound you on the head as if you were a nail and he were the hammer. So, if he tells you a joke, for your sake, laugh your head off or he'll knock it off.

Finally, this was a sample of writing taken after all five previously mentioned skills were taught:

My Mother the Worker

Even before the sun rises, my mother does, and she is already busy executing her daily tasks. She begins her day by preparing breakfast for our family. Perfectly browned toast and creamy orange juice greet our taste buds every morning soon after we have awakened. While I am at school, every inch of our house is pampered by her delicate touch. Our floor seems to glitter as if it were gold. The plants in our home are radiant with health. As you get close to them, tiny droplets of water seem to be covering each leaf like a thin skin. Mom takes special care to spray each plant twice a day. After almost seven hours of work, she takes time out of her busy schedule to come and pick me up from school. I hope that someday I can be just like my mother.

My students still would not be caught dead in anything but their designer clothes. And everything they talk about is as awesome as ever. But, in writing, after careful preparation and guidance, they are showing, not telling.

Showing, Not Telling: Setting, Characterization, Conflict

By Laurie Opfell
Former English Teacher, Irvine High School;
Graduate Student, University of Kentucky;
and Teacher/Consultant, UCI Writing Project

After having my students read short stories in an Introduction to Literature class, I decided to ask them to work in pairs to create their own short stories in which they would describe a setting, establish a character, and develop a conflict. My experience with average student writing had led me to expect that the results of this "story" assignment would prove to be the usual fare—somewhat general and flat. Students seemed to have no problems telling a story, but they lacked the ability to add enough details to make the story vivid and exciting. Not surprisingly, the papers that were turned in conformed to my preconceived notions.

After hearing Rebekah Caplan speak at the UCI Writing Project Summer Institute, it struck me that that was exactly what my students were doing—telling a story, not showing or revealing the characters, conflicts, and setting that went with it. I decided that I would have to work *showing, not telling,* into narrative writing the next time my Introduction to Literature class was offered.

At my next opportunity, I told the students that we were going to create the beginning of a short story in several stages:

In step 1, they would create a description of a setting.
In step 2, they would create and describe two major characters.
In step 3, they would write a dialogue between the two characters that would reveal a conflict.
In step 4, they would combine setting, characters, conflict, and dialogue to create the beginning of a short story.

The following are examples of how I worked showing, not telling, into this assignment. In each case, I first give the students a literary model and then a series of directions for creating their own *showing* writing.

- *First Example:* In this section from *Great Expectations,* Charles Dickens could have *told* his readers that this room was full of decay and death. Instead, he *shows* it by writing this:

    From that room, too, the daylight was completely excluded, and it had an airless smell that was oppressive. A fire had been lately kindled in the damp old-fashioned grate, and it was more disposed to go out than to burn up, and the reluctant smoke which hung in the room seemed colder than the clearer air—like our own marsh mist. Certain wintry branches of candles on the high chimney-piece faintly lighted the chamber; or, it would be more expressive to say, faintly troubled its darkness. It was spacious, and I dare say had once been handsome, but every discernible thing in it was covered with dust and mould, and dropping to pieces. The most prominent object was a long table with a tablecloth spread on it, as if a feast had been in preparation when the house and the clocks all stopped together. An epergne or centre-piece of some kind was in the middle of this cloth; it was so heavily overhung with cobwebs that its form was quite undistinguishable; and, as I looked along the yellow expanse out of which I remember its seeming to grow, like a black fungus, I saw speckled-legged spiders with blotchy bodies running home to it, and running out from it, as if some circumstance of the greatest public importance had just transpired in the spider community.

Step 1A *Your assignment:* Look over the list of *telling* titles below and select one (or write one of your own):

The park was deserted.
The room was haunted.
The lot was full of trash.
The beach was peaceful.
The garage was a mess.
The street was crowded.

Objective: Write a one-half to three-fourths page description that vividly *shows* the place the title mentions. Include time of day, colors, mood (emotions drawn out by place), objects in place, smells, temperature, lighting, and sounds.

Step 1B Now, write a setting description for your story. Give it a *telling* title; then *show* it using colors, description of objects, mood, and so forth as you did in the preceding assignment. Use the excerpt from *Great Expectations* as a model.

• *Second Example:* In this section of *The Red Pony,* John Steinbeck could have just *told* his readers that this character was a ranch hand and left it at that. Instead, he makes it obvious by including specific details:

At daybreak Billy Buck emerged from the bunkhouse and stood for a moment on the porch looking up at the sky. He was a broad, bandy-legged little man with a walrus mustache, with square hands, puffed and muscled on the palms. His eyes were a contemplative, watery gray and the hair which protruded from under his Stetson hat was spiky and weathered. Billy was still stuffing his shirt into his blue jeans as he stood on the porch. He unbuckled his belt and tightened it again. The belt showed, by the worn shiny places opposite each hole, the gradual increase of Billy's middle over a period of years. When he had seen to the weather, Billy cleared each nostril by holding its mate closed with his forefinger and blowing fiercely. Then he walked down to the barn, rubbing his hands together.[1]

Step 2A *Your assignment:* Look over the following list of *telling* titles and select one:

He was a spy.
She was an unfriendly nurse.
The man looked old.
The tired girl lay on the couch.
He was an alcoholic.
The lonely man walked away.
He was a construction worker.
The irritated executive shuffled papers.

Objective: Write a one-half to three-fourths page description that vividly *shows* the type of character the title describes. Include type/color of *hair,* *body parts* (hands, legs, and so forth), *facial features* (eyes, mouth, nose), *an attitude* about life, several articles of clothing described in detail, and an *action.*

Step 2B Now, create two characters for your story and describe them carefully. Give your characters *telling* titles; then show them as you did in the preceding assignment. (These characters will later be in conflict with one another.) Keep the way John Steinbeck reveals character in mind as you write.

• *Third Example:* In this section of "Cat in the Rain," Ernest Hemingway uses a dialogue between a man and his wife to reveal the conflicts in their relationship and to show the woman's attitudes about herself and their life-style. Although the author never says directly that George is insensitive or that his wife is lonely and frus-

[1]From *The Red Pony* by John Steinbeck. Copyright 1933, 1937, 1938, by John Steinbeck. Copyright renewed © 1961, 1965, 1966, by John Steinbeck. Reprinted by permission of Viking Penguin, Inc.

trated, it becomes obvious through their conversation.

When the story opens, the couple are staying in an Italian hotel. While looking out the window, the woman notices a cat outside trying to keep out of the rain. After an unsuccessful attempt at going down to rescue it, she returns to their room:

> George was reading again.
>
> She went over and sat in front of the mirror of the dressing table looking at herself with the hand glass. She studied her profile, first one side and then the other. Then she studied the back of her head and her neck.
>
> "Don't you think it would be a good idea if I let my hair grow out?" she asked, looking at her profile again.
>
> George looked up and saw the back of her neck, clipped close like a boy's.
>
> "I like it the way it is."
>
> "I get so tired of it," she said. "I get so tired of looking like a boy."
>
> George shifted his position in the bed. He hadn't looked away from her since she started to speak.
>
> "You look pretty darn nice," he said.
>
> She laid the mirror down on the dresser and went over to the window and looked out. It was getting dark.
>
> "I want to pull my hair back tight and smooth and make a big knot at the back that I can feel," she said. "I want to have a kitty to sit on my lap and purr when I stroke her."
>
> "Yeah?" George said from the bed.
>
> "And I want to eat at a table with my own silver and I want candles. And I want it to be spring and I want to brush my hair out in front of a mirror and I want a kitty and I want some new clothes."
>
> "Oh, shut up and get something to read," George said. He was reading again.
>
> His wife was looking out of the window. It was quite dark now and still raining in the palm trees.
>
> "Anyway, I want a cat," she said. "I want a cat. I want a cat now. If I can't have long hair or any fun, I can have a cat."
>
> George was not listening. He was reading his book.[2]

---

[2]Ernest Hemingway, excerpted from "Cat in the Rain," in *Short Stories of Ernest Hemingway*. Copyright 1938 Ernest Hemingway; copyright renewed © 1966 Mary Hemingway. Reprinted with the permission of Charles Scribner's Sons.

Step 3A *Your assignment:* Look over the list of *telling* titles and select one:

> The brother hated his sister.
> The girl's rudeness angered the teacher.
> The sight of Harry caused Dave to panic.
> The strange behavior of the son worried the parent.
> The scorn of the senior offended the freshman.
> The jock's arrogance frustrated the coach.

Objective: Write a page of dialogue in the form of a conversation between any of the pairs listed above. Although each pair already has a conflict, it will be up to you to reveal it through what they say. In addition, you will want to decide how the characters will show their attitudes toward each other. For example, if you use the brother who hated his sister, his hostility could be revealed through sarcasm, insincere comments, or insults. The sister's attitudes will also need to be revealed. Her responses to him might take the form of surprise, rudeness, or ridicule. Include brief setting information, if necessary, the tone of voice that words are stated in, and words emphasized that will point out emotions.

Step 3B Now, write a dialogue between the two characters you already created for your own story. Reveal their conflict without actually saying what the conflict is; let the reader infer it. Also show the attitudes the characters have toward one another. Give your dialogue a *telling* title.

Step 4 Finally, combine your setting, characters, and their conflict in a three-page beginning of a short story. Introduce the conflict early, because this will be the hook that captures the reader's interest. Be sure that you use ample detail to *show* rather than *tell* what your story is about.

The students wrote their narratives in stages. A writing group edited the rough drafts that had been written in Step 4, and then the students turned in their final drafts and all the prewriting exercises. I found that my students' writing had improved dramatically because of the exposure to showing, not telling. The student writers included far more details and descriptions than I had found in their stories in the past. By revealing or showing the conflict, my students developed a sophistication in their writing that I had never seen before. We read the stories aloud, and an animated class discussion ensued because we inferred and interpreted what the authors wished to reveal through their showing. I also found that working in pairs helped the students make their papers more humorous, creative, and free of errors because the "audience factor" was built in. Showing, not telling, enabled me to raise my expectations, because I learned that if I provide my students with models, training, practice, and feedback, they can attain whatever objectives are set for them.

Integrating Clustering and Showing, Not Telling

By Carol Booth Olson
Codirector, UCI Writing Project

I have good luck with using clustering as a way to introduce and generate ideas about a concept, character, event, or experience and showing, not telling, as an organizational device for logically developing and supporting those ideas in well-detailed, descriptive paragraphs. In a sense, clustering becomes a prewriting activity that culminates in a showing, not telling, writing assignment.

Provided below is an experiential exercise I use to help students enhance descriptive writing skills. The exercise is based on the integration of clustering and showing, not telling.

Lesson Plan for Clustering and Showing, Not Telling, About Blindness

Provide an introduction to descriptive writing prior to this exercise. Activities can include:

- Lecture/discussion on concrete versus abstract diction
- Examination of professional and student models to discover what makes writing vivid
- Presentation of color slides that students respond to with "I see," "I hear," "I smell," "I taste," and "I feel" statements
- Visualization to music

The activities above focus primarily on the visual in descriptive writing. The following exercise enables students to tap their other senses.

Step 1: Orientation

Ask each student in the class to pick a partner. Explain that every class member will have an opportunity to experience blindness as well as to become a guide for a blind person. As you are passing out one blindfold to each pair, ask the students to choose which role—guide or blind person—they prefer to assume first. Once the students have selected their respective roles, the guide should assist his or her partner in putting on the blindfold.

It is the guide's responsibility to lead the blind person out of the classroom and to provide him or her with a sensory experience, which should involve exposure to some or all of the following: smell, texture, taste, the experience of ascending and descending, the feeling of an open space versus a closed-in space, and changing temperatures. No conversation should take place during this excursion. However, students can communicate through body language. After approximately five to ten minutes, the students should stop, switch roles, and continue their walk.

Step 2: Prewriting Exercise

When the students return to the classroom, print the word BLIND on the chalkboard. Ask the students to put this word in the center of a blank piece of paper and cluster in a circle around the stimulus word (in single words and short phrases) all of the images, associations, and feelings that come to mind when they think of being blind. After about five minutes, ask each person to share orally one of his or her cluster words or phrases. As the students volunteer their thoughts, you can ask other students whether they identify with the feelings expressed or whether they have different reactions to add. Record all of these responses in a composite cluster on the board, as in Figure 22.

Step 3: Writing

After the clustering and discussion period, elicit one main idea or feeling about blindness that the group seemed to share. Then create a telling sentence (a general, declarative statement) which expresses that

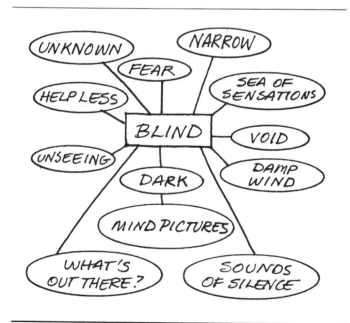

Fig. 22. Clustering of Images and Feelings of Being Blind

idea in a specific context students can illustrate. For example, if the predominant class response to the sensation of blindness was fear of the unknown, you might write a sentence like this on the chalkboard: "The blind woman was terrified of unfamiliar places." Draw the students' attention to this sentence. Ask them if they were to write a paragraph showing a blind woman was terrified of unfamiliar places, what details would they use to:

1. Indicate that the woman was blind.
2. Make it clear that she was in a unfamiliar place.
3. Let the reader know how frightened she was.

Once they have discussed various ways to describe the telling sentence, ask the students to write one or more paragraphs that show how it feels to be a blind person in an unfamiliar place. They can use "The blind woman was terrified of unfamiliar places" as their topic sentence, but encourage them to illustrate this sentence through vivid, sensory details. Allow 20 to 30 minutes for writing.

Step 4: Sharing and Rewriting

Explain to the students that if they have written a vivid, well-detailed descriptive paragraph, they should no longer need their topic sentence. Without the topic sentence, the supporting paragraph should communicate effectively that the blind woman was terrified of unfamiliar places. Ask students to cross out their topic sentence and exchange papers with a friend. Working together, the two should answer the following questions: Does the paragraph communicate the message effectively without the topic sentence? In other words, can it stand alone? If not, what descriptive phrases and sensory details are necessary to show that the blind woman was terrified of unfamiliar places? Provide the class with at least one model of a well-written paper that is rich in showing writing.

Here is an example:

Telling sentence:
The blind woman was terrified of unfamiliar places.

Showing paragraphs:
She cautiously hobbled down the street, her white cane carefully tapping out the steps before her, sensing the ridges and rhythms of each concrete square. She could hear the blaring of midday traffic and the cursing of angry cab drivers and feel the crushing weight of the sound reverberating off tall buildings. Each step was an effort—a venture into the unknown. When would it end? A feeling of nausea welled up in her stomach, and beads of sweat appeared on her brow.

Suddenly, her cane missed a beat, and she stumbled off the curb. Car tires screeched in front of her and obscenities filled the air. An arm reached out to steady her. "Thank you," she mumbled as she collected herself and tried to blend back into the waiting crowd. Clos-

ing . . . it was all closing in. She could feel herself shrinking into the pavement.

"Pardon me, miss," a concerned voice said. "Can I help you across the street?"

Oh, damn, she thought, her chest beginning to tighten as she suppressed the sobs, all I need is for someone to be kind.

He could feel her stiffen as he gripped the back of her elbow and guided her across the street. When they reached the other side, she dismissed him with a "thank you" and appeared to be debating something. Curiously enough, she then reached for the walk button on the streetlight as if to head back in the direction she came from. From a block away, he caught a glimpse of her over his shoulder. Statue-like, she was still standing exactly where he had left her—frozen in indecision.

Allow in-class time for rewriting and a second round of sharing with a partner. Have students polish and edit this draft so that it may be turned in for evaluation.

I like this particular assignment because it starts with a prewriting experience that students can draw on to write about. The clustering exercise that follows is a right-brain activity that helps students express their feelings and generate content. This logically leads into the showing, not telling, lesson where using concrete, sensory detail to create a picture and communicate emotions is stressed. Since descriptive writing is the most concrete writing domain and the easiest for most students to create, the lesson focuses on fluency—getting the language to say what the students mean. Later experiences, such as clustering and showing, not telling, about literary characters, will build a bridge from sensory/descriptive and imaginative/narrative into more analytical/expository writing.

Showing, Not Telling: A Stepping Stone Toward Expository Writing

By Julie Simpson
Sunny Hills High School,
English Teacher, Fullerton Union High School District;
and Teacher/Consultant, UCI Writing Project

In his office in the English Department at the University of California, Irvine, Owen Thomas has a Japanese watercolor of stepping stones leading across a pond, and he is fond of pointing out that the writing process is analogous to that picture. In order to convey the intended message, a writer must carefully place his or her informational or symbolic stepping stones to guide the reader to comprehend the meaning. The same can be said for the process of teaching writing: The teacher must provide a sequence of writing activities that bridge the different domains of writing.

I use Rebekah Caplan's idea of showing, not telling, as an initial stepping stone from one writing mode to another and over to the path of exposition. With Harper Lee's novel, *To Kill a Mockingbird,* as the stimulus, I lead my freshman class from the *what* of description to the *how* of narration and toward the *why* of exposition. Along the way, we develop showing paragraphs into showing essays by means of telling sentences expanded into telling frames. All this is done as prewriting exercises that help students incorporate specific detail into expository writing.

> *Students learn to write by writing. Guidance in the writing process and discussion of the student's own work should be the central means of writing instruction.*
> COMMISSION ON COMPOSITION
> OF THE NATIONAL COUNCIL OF
> TEACHERS OF ENGLISH

We begin by describing places and people, using models from *To Kill a Mockingbird.* In the novel Harper Lee writes wonderful showing descriptions:

Of her setting—"Maycomb was an old town, but it was a tired old town when I first knew it." (p. 11)
Of Boo's rumored activities—"Inside the house lived a malevolent phantom." (p. 15)
Of Dill's appearance—"Dill was a curiosity." (p. 13)
Of Mrs. Dubose—"She was horrible." (p. 115).[1]

We discuss what makes Harper Lee's descriptions so vivid and write our own parallel paragraphs from personal experiences. Here is student Juli Hara's description of a "curiosity":

The child wore a pink checkered frock with white cuffs and collar. Her white knee socks dropped around her ankles, and her shiny black patent leather shoes reflected the Barbie lunch box in her right hand. Her pixie-like face was generously covered with copper freckles, and her bright eyes, framed by long blonde lashes, sparkled in the sunlight. Her long, flaxen hair was plaited into two thick braids that swung softly to and fro as the child twisted at the waist in a gesture of impatience.

When the students have achieved this kind of control, I move them to narration. We still use the book for inspiration, but now I create the telling sentences,

[1]Harper Lee, *To Kill a Mockingbird.* Philadelphia: J. B. Lippincott Company, 1960.

and we include the telling statement as the opening of the paragraph.

Since writing about literature is more difficult than writing from experience, we tread carefully. I begin with narrative frames to help students see how to include the *what* of description in with the *how* of narration. For example:

Jem risked his life to avoid a lie. He had lost his pants when he and ——————————————— Mr. Radley had seen them and ——————————— . As they ran, ———————————————————— . Jem knew he would be in trouble if ———————— . So he lied and said ————————————————— . Then, to avoid being caught in the lie, he had to ——— . Scout tried to —————————————————— but ——————————————————————— . Late that night, Jem ———————————————— .

From this explicit frame, we move to an expanded version:

Scout's innocence broke up the mob. (*Describe the scene at the jail.*) ————————————————

————————————————————————————

In the midst of this angry mob, Scout recognized Walter Cunningham's father. Wanting to break the silence, she tried to be polite. (*Summarize what she said, how the father reacted, and what the mob did.*) ————————— .

————————————————————————————

When the students begin to feel comfortable with the narrative step, we move into independent writing and frame summaries from the plot with personal experiences. "Scout learned there is a time and place for everything" asks students to recount the incident when Scout insulted young Walter Cunningham at the dinner table. To parallel that, we might use, "I can remember learning the same thing." Another narrative-telling duo includes:

"They never listen to my side." (*Tell about a time when you broke a rule for a perfectly good reason, but were not allowed to explain.*)

PAIRED WITH

"Uncle Jack wouldn't listen to Scout's side." (*Narrate the fight with Cousin Francis.*)

This kind of narration from telling sentences is just a skip away from the expository side of the pond. But to secure footage, we pause at a mid-step. We analyze the functions of the frames I have been writing for the class, as well as the function of a telling sentence. To the later narrations, we write our own frames. For instance, when we get to the trial section of Harper Lee's novel, I give this pair of starters: "Mayella false-

ly accused Tom Robinson of rape." "But Tom is innocent." To these shorter sentences, students merely narrate the separate versions of the crime. After they have written the two showing narrations, we begin to discuss why Mayella lies. In one of my classes, we came up with the following:

> Mayella is poor white trash. The only people beneath her and her family on the social scale are the blacks. Once, out of her extreme loneliness, Mayella makes a pass at Tom Robinson, a black man. When her father catches her and beats her, she has to make Tom look bad.

We place this paragraph at the beginning of two other good student *showing* paragraphs[2] and read it as a whole essay:

> Mayella is poor white trash. The only people beneath her and her family on the social scale are the blacks. Once, out of her extreme loneliness, Mayella makes a pass at Tom Robinson, a black man. When her father catches her and beats her, she has to make Tom look bad.
>
> Mayella accuses Tom of rape. Wanting to support her father's testimony, she tells the jury her story of what happened. Mayella had asked Tom inside the fence to chop up an old chifforobe for kindling. When she went inside the house to get his nickel pay, he followed her. As she turned around, he was on her. He got her around the neck, beat her, and left marks and bruises on her right side. "He caught me and choked me and took advantage of me," Mayella testifies in a flood of tears. Even though she says she passed out for a while, she remembers that she "fought him tooth and nail." Atticus shows Mayella

---

[2](*NOTE:* The first paragraph was written by Laura Turner; and the second, by Jonathan Reinstein.)

that Tom is crippled in his left arm and could not have attacked her, but she continues her story. She says she ducked his right-fisted blow. "It glanced, that's what it did." And when Atticus asks her if she had not screamed until she had seen her father in the window, she still maintains Tom's guilt. He "took advantage of me an' if you . . . don't wanta do nothin' about it, then you're all yellow stinkin' cowards, stinkin' cowards, the lot of you."

> But Tom is clearly innocent. His story is that he has been doing chores for Miss Mayella for over a year, "choppin' kindlin', totin' water for her." She often called him into the yard to help her. On the evening in question, Miss Mayella had asked him into the house to fix a door that was off its hinges. But when he went inside, the door was fine. And Tom noticed that none of the seven brothers and sisters were around. As she shut the door behind them, Mayella asked him to reach a box down from a cupboard. He stood on a chair to reach. In the process, Miss Mayella grabbed him around the legs and scared him so that he turned the chair over as he hopped down. Then she hugged him, kissed him, and demanded that he kiss her back. Tom resisted without being harmful to Mayella, and ran away before he could be dealt with by Mr. Ewell, who had appeared at the window. Even though he had done nothing wrong, Tom was scared. "It weren't safe for any nigger to be in a fix like that." He was "scared I'd hafta face up to what I didn't do."

After reviewing what we had developed, we decided that the account clearly needed a conclusion; so we created a brief, closing paragraph:

> Unfortunately, in the racist community of Maycomb, all the facts in the world wouldn't allow a jury to support a black man against a white woman. So innocent Tom is found guilty.

By creating their own frame for their showing writing, the students have stepped onto the path of expository writing. We discuss again how description shows *what*, narration explains *how*, and exposition interprets *why*. The process of expository writing requires the use of the showing writing to explain and back it up.

The final assignment is designed to reinforce the students' awareness of the expository form. In the assignment, the students choose between two tasks. They examine either Harper Lee's definition of courage or her explanation of why it is a sin to kill a mockingbird. They write their own frame, beginning with her idea as the main (thesis) telling statement, and add supporting telling sentences for each person they will discuss in the paper (e.g., three mockingbirds or three degrees of courage). By adding a showing narrative summary of episodes to their supporting statements, they create with their first full essay, an essay that integrates descriptive, narrative, and expository writing and that shows as well as tells.

Writing About Literature with Showing, Not Telling

By William Burns

English Teacher, Sonora High School,
Fullerton Union High School District;
and Teacher/Consultant, UCI Writing Project

One of the strengths of a great idea is its ability to be applied in a variety of conditions, to meet different needs, and to solve a problem in different environments. Rebekah Caplan's articulate and practical application of showing, not telling, to teaching writing is one of those great ideas. It works with elementary, middle school, high school, and college students. It works in all of the domains: sensory/descriptive, imaginative/narrative, practical/informative, and analytical/expository. After hearing Rebekah's presentation at the University of California, Irvine's (UCI) Summer Writing Project, I knew I had been given a powerful tool. But at that time, I did not recognize just how powerful and versatile this idea could be.

As the new school year started, I was eager and ready, armed with a myriad of writing strategies. My students would learn to be explicit, specific, and concrete, giving details and examples wherever necessary. I used some of Rebekah's sample sentences, found others from the students' own writing, and made up my own. Students began to use more and more specific details to expand the rather lifeless opening sentences I gave them: "My sister is a brat"; "Math is hard (*or* easy)"; "The sand at the beach felt good."

After a while, they asked whether they could move the sentences to other places in the paragraphs. "Yes," I said. Then I asked them whether they knew what else these sentences might be called. And as I had hoped, one student said they were like "topic sentences."

I used to give several lessons about what topic sentences were and what they did; and now, without any such contrivances of mine, they knew what a topic sentence did and that it could be moved around in a paragraph. It was not too long afterwards that a student complained about the "dull, boring" sentences she had been given and asked whether she could omit the telling sentence. "It messes up my writing." Who was I to argue with creative insight?

As the semester progressed and we began a short story unit, I continued the showing, not telling, assignments, but only occasionally. I knew better than to wear out a good thing. One day, after reading the short story, "The Fifty-First Dragon," I gave them this sentence: "The dragon's countenance was hideous."

"What's *countenance* mean?" was the sudden chorus. "Look it up," I told them. And they did.

The next day, their descriptions about the dragon were wonderful, and everyone knew what *countenance* meant. A little flicker of insight entered my mind. I could teach vocabulary with these sentences, and the students would have to do all the work! They soon had showing, not telling, sentences that had such words as *pugnacious, sagacity,* and *lithe.* And some of their writing changed in tone, depending on the words I gave them. I even tried to see what they would do with a much more sophisticated sentence: T. S. Eliot's "April is the cruellest month." Their responses certainly were creative, and several expanded the sentence in much the same way as Mr. Eliot meant. At this point, I should have recognized the potential of showing, not telling, sentences as a way of exploring literature; but I did not. I needed more time.

Later in the year my ninth grade class began the study of John Steinbeck's *Of Mice and Men.* I was ready with discussion questions, quizzes, reading assignments, group activities, and the final essay question. I planned to review and use the ideas of setting, plot, character, writing techniques, and theme as we explored the novel. And I knew I wanted the students to do some writing to help them better understand John Steinbeck's story and characters. We had recently completed some journal writing in a poetry unit, so I was looking for a different way to

get them to write. I thought of showing, not telling. Could I make up some sentences from the book similar to the few I had taken from the short stories? As I wrote some samples, I realized I could group them according to setting, plot, character, and so forth. Here are a few examples:

It was peaceful in the woods along the Salinas River.
The bunkhouse was obviously a place where men lived.
Lenny was different.
George and Lenny had a dream.
Curly and his wife had a different relationship from the one George and Lenny had.
George's and Lenny's relationship was like that of Candy and his dog.

As the first few assignments came in, I knew I was on to something. The students were reading the book more closely in order to *answer* the telling sentence. I told them they could use John Steinbeck's words, but they would have to organize them to provide the transitions and closings. They were using examples from the text to clarify what the general telling sentence said. I have always struggled to get students to use examples from their reading to support their generalizations. Now they were doing it without a lot of lecturing or cajoling on my part. And I discovered another benefit. I no longer needed to give those little reading quizzes that I used to give to make sure students were doing their readings. The compositions were taking care of that, too. When we completed our study of the novel with a more comprehensive essay, students wrote with better support than they had before, pulling examples from topics they had previously developed.

I was pleased with the improvement in my students' writing as a result of showing, not telling, but something was still bothering me. I was doing a lot of the hard thinking for the students. I was creating the telling sentences; I was organizing them around topics and techniques; I was doing much of the analysis. I knew that my ultimate goal would be for them to create such telling sentences, since not only was it important for them to find specifics to support the generalizations, but also it was important for them to be able to work the other way and arrive at more sophisticated generalizations based on seemingly unconnected details found in their reading.

Our concluding literature assignment for the ninth grade was *Romeo and Juliet*. I wanted students to have fun with the play, explore the language, read passages, act out parts, watch a film of the play, and generally have a good time, yet still pay attention to its literary content and ideas. We were not going to write during our reading of the play, but a final essay would be required.

As I looked over the various essay topics I had developed and collected from years past and as I thought about all the showing, not telling, my students had done during the year, I realized this was a perfect time to see whether they could come up with their own telling sentences. After all, if the sentences were

> *Devise, wit; write, pen; for I am for whole volumes in folio.*
> WILLIAM SHAKESPEARE

any good, I could use them some other time. And if the students had learned anything from their practice, their telling sentences ought to be good summaries of what they were learning from the play. I asked each student to turn in ten telling sentences, organized in the following manner: two setting sentences, two plot sentences, five character sentences, one theme sentence, and one writing technique sentence. The results exceeded my expectations. Here are some of the students' sentences:

Verona is full of love and hate.
The apothecary's shop, where Romeo buys poison, is a dirty, rundown place.
Romeo is a "fortune's fool."
Tybalt is full of mischief.
The relationship between Romeo and Friar Laurence was similar yet different from the relationship between Juliet and the Nurse.
Despite their bitter hatred of each other, the Capulets and the Montagues were very much alike.
Feuds seem to destroy the most innocent ones.
Those who act in moderation have a better chance at survival.

I could tell quite a bit about a student's understanding of the play from the telling sentences. I put a check mark by one of them and told the student to write an essay elaborating on that sentence. In this same manner, I chose sentences that would give students a challenge but would be within their level of skill.

I am just beginning to discover how to use telling sentences to help students be more explicit, to help their reading, and to enhance their understanding of both reading and writing. They are writing more and I am reading less. Now students are not limited to writing a number of assignments based on how many papers I can read. That is a good start that I gained from a great idea: showing, not telling. Isn't it curious how simple concepts turn out to be so subtle?

Showing, Not Telling, About *The Canterbury Tales*

By Sue Ellen Gold

English Teacher, Irvine High School,
Irvine Unified School District;
and Teacher/Consultant, UCI Writing Project

Just three weeks into my first semester as a high school English teacher, I knew I was in trouble. I was teaching Chaucer's *The Canterbury Tales* to a group of bright, reasonably motivated students who worked hard, listened well, laughed at the correct times, and understood almost nothing. Left on their own with the text, they floundered in the 600-year stylistic gap. Because I knew my students were caught up in the twentieth century visual world of television, movies, and video, I decided to develop a lesson that would draw on their innate abilities to visualize. To do so, I used Rebekah Caplan's showing, not telling, process.

Now, when I teach the *Canterbury Tales,* one of my first goals is to move my students past what I call the "text as God" plateau, the point at which they revere the text, not because they understand or appreciate it, but precisely because they do not. To do this, I begin

> *Noght o word spak he moore than was neede,*
> *And that was seyd in forme and reverence,*
> *And short and quyk and ful of*
> *hy sentence.*
>
> GEOFFREY CHAUCER

by reading a few lines at a time out loud and then questioning, "What does this mean? Do you like that? Is this the sort of person you would like to invite home for dinner?" When the students are prodded to think of the characters outside the fourteenth century context, they are soon able to drop their Chaucer-induced awe and get on with the job of enjoying and even understanding the text.

This comfortable teacher-read/student-answer pattern usually lasts through the first seven or eight characters. At this point, I step out of the presentation mode and arrange the class in groups of three or four. The students maintain these groups for the remainder of the unit. These groups are assigned a portion of the remaining characters, and they are expected to answer the following questions for each:

1. Who is the character?
2. What is his or her occupation or station?
3. Describe his or her appearance?

4. Does he or she say anything?
5. Does your group like or dislike the character? Why?
6. Choose five of your own adjectives to describe the character.

These groups then take turns presenting their findings orally to the class and guiding the class discussion.

The next step helps prepare the students to begin using their visual arsenal. Each group is reassigned several characters and, drawing on the class discussions, develops *telling* sentences for each; for example: "The Squire was young and vain"; "The Summoner's appearance was something to behold"; "The Miller was belligerent." After the class shares the sentences, each student picks one to develop into a *showing* paragraph.

At this point, the class is ready to categorize the pilgrims, and we spend a lively session debating which characters are good, which are bad, and which are absolutely horrible.

Most students have, by this time, been convinced that Chaucer *is* accessible, and they are ready for the prompt. They are asked to assume the guise of a fourteenth century traveler who happens to arrive at the Tabard Inn on the same evening as the pilgrims. During the course of the night, they will somehow encounter at least three of the group who will, through conversation, action, and appearance, reveal their true personalities. The narrator is also expected to describe the town, inn, and social atmosphere and to develop a narrative thread that holds it all together.

The next week is spent doing short precomposing assignments, both during and outside the class time. I bring in costume books and posters, and the students brainstorm their ideas about appropriate fourteenth century clothing. I often have to guide them on the details, as well as explain that polyester and rayon made their debut much later.

The class also discusses the varied possibilities for the Tabard Inn itself. These have ranged from dirt floors with chickens underfoot to elaborate taverns with extensive, highbrow clientele. Here are two showing paragraphs from a student's paper which introduce the reader to the Tabard:

As I got off my horse, I began to hear voices and laughter coming from inside the Inn. While I was tethering my horse, I looked up at the starry sky, which had the appearance of black velvet with pearls carelessly cast upon it. Glancing back at the Inn, I noticed that the doors were open and this made me feel welcome. As I walked into the building, I saw that each of the doors was engraved with *The Tabard.*

On this particular night, The Tabard was packed with people, making it seem small, despite its large size. Once my eyes adjusted to the light emitted by the burning torches and glowing candles, I bought a mug of ale, found a table, and stepped on a roaming chicken in the process of doing so. While drinking my ale, I finally took time to look around. The Tabard itself seemed fairly new with its stone walls and ceilings. There were many wooden tables to sit at, each one adorned with candles. While some people were sitting on benches, others used empty boxes and ale kegs as furniture. To my right, in the center of the room, there was a large, circular, stone fire pit with black, charred scraps of wood in it. No fire tonight, I thought to myself. It's too warm tonight.

When the students think of the characters outside the fourteenth century context, they drop their Chaucer-induced awe and enjoy and even understand the text.
SUE ELLEN GOLD

After the students have visualized the setting in which their encounter will take place, each one is ready to chose the three pilgrims he or she wants to encounter. I suggest one from each category—"the good," "the bad," and the "absolutely horrible." After the students have decided, I spend time discussing how visual and aural clues such as dress, speech, and mannerisms can help build a character. Since Chaucer gives relatively few details of this sort, the students are challenged to pick out the specifics Chaucer does give and then to generate additional ideas on their own. As a class, we practice filling out the following chart on some of the less popular characters; then each student completes the same task for his or her three pilgrims:

Pilgrim

Clothing
   Color _____
   Type _____
   Accessories _____
Personality
   Speech habits _____
   Visual mannerisms _____
Activities he or she likes to do _____
_____

After the students have completed the previous step, I ask them to practice writing a plot with their groups. To accomplish this activity, I randomly choose three characters; and each group role-plays potential situations that could bring the three characters together. I warn the students to pay particular attention to what they know of the characters and how they might react in various situations. Obviously, there are innumerable possibilities. An example from one tenth grade group included the following:

Wife of Bath
Knight
Pardonner

Wife falls over one of the Prioress's dogs. The Knight comes to her aid by removing the dog and helping her up. The Pardonner rushes over to her, offering some relic to help her heal her bruised elbow. She shakes him off, scoffing at his high voice. She turns to confide to the narrator that she dislikes the Pardonner's greasy, lanky hair.

The same types of activities are conducted to develop dialogue. At this point, I find it appropriate to discuss correct punctuation and the misuse of slang.

Each student is now set free to develop his or her own setting, characters, plot, dialogue, and tone. With additional group assistance on revising and editing, each student is capable of completing a well-written, cohesive narrative. Because this unit draws so heavily on the showing, not telling, technique, the students are able to use their tremendous potential to visualize and then fluently describe Chaucer's world. Their success in this effort ensures their future enjoyment of Chaucer, and I am always excited to read the papers and see what new details these modern teenagers add to the fourteenth century text.

Writing

Developing a Sense of Audience, or Who Am I Really Writing This Paper For?

By Mary K. Healy
Codirector, Bay Area Writing Project

Simply stated, having a developed sense of audience on the student writers' part means that as they write, they have images of the intended readers of their writing flickering—consciously or unconsciously—around in the background. To the degree that these images are sharply delineated in the writers' minds, student writers will select details and develop their pieces of writing, anxious always that their known readers' expectations be fulfilled.

Students who have developed beyond the point where writing is more of an exercise in physical dexterity than an exercise in composing thoughts on a piece of paper can tell what their teachers will look for when reading and evaluating their papers. For some teachers, neatness really counts—no ink blots or crumpled papers are allowed. For others, mechanical accuracy is primary—periods where they belong, capital letters signaling sentence beginnings, and commas accurately placed and not scattered like confetti to make an interesting, albeit illogical, design. To still other teachers, what counts is what happened from the first to the last draft—what changes were made, what tightening and expanding, what diction—in sum, what evidence there is of a mind at work revising, reseeing. There are a legion of other teachers' priorities—from sophisticated vocabulary choices and

syntax to the students' adherence to injunctions, such as never starting a sentence with the word *and*. Whatever the constructs may be through which the teacher views the students' papers, it is certain that the students will understand what they are as soon as enough marked writing has been returned. And the students will know the real nature of their audience—and be fairly accurate in describing the teacher's values—regardless of how the teacher describes orally what he or she values. Students can do this because they make their generalizations about what is important to the teacher on the basis of hard evidence: the grades and final comments they get on their papers.

The task of developing a sense of audience is, in fact, a misnomer. After a few years in school, student writers already have a sense of audience, even though they might look at you blankly and mumble something like, "We don't do that in here," if asked for which audience they are writing. A more accurate description of the task for the thoughtful teacher of writing might be described as expanding the students' sense of audience to encompass a wider range of responsive readers. And a major step in this expansion is simply to provide audiences for the students' writing beyond that of a conscientious proofreader and evaluator.

In the landmark study *The Development of Writing Abilities (11—18)*, James Britton and his colleagues in England outlined a broad spectrum of the possible audiences that students might meet in the writing situations in their schools. In their research sample

EDITOR'S NOTE: For further information on the concept of audience in writing, see Mary K. Healy's monograph, *Using Student Writing Response Groups in the Classroom,* which was published by the Bay Area Writing Project, Education Business Office, 1615 Tolman Hall, University of California, Berkeley, CA 94720.

Mr. Britton and his colleagues used this range of audiences as one of the characteristics by which they categorized over 2,000 student papers from subjects across the curriculum. As the researchers put it, ". . . one important dimension of development in writing ability is the growth of a sense of audience, the growth of the ability to make adjustments and choices in writing which take account of the audience for whom the writing is intended."[1] The main categories which the researchers used and the percent of papers falling in each category are shown in the accompanying table, which is reproduced here from *The Development of Writing Abilities (11—18)*.

It is evident from the research James Britton and his colleagues conducted that the ever-present audience for the writing done in most classrooms is the teacher-as-examiner. This audience can make itself manifest in many ways: a single letter grade for overall quality; split letter grades, one each for content and mechanics; a written critique of the piece, outlining the strengths and weaknesses of the style, organization, structure, or mechanics; a written response to the piece, featuring the reader's involvement with the content and raising questions of clarity and development. However, in all of these instances, the emphasis is still on the evaluation of a final product.

Just as writing for an audience of teacher-as-examiner is the most prevalent in schools today, writing for self is the least prevalent. Yet the self as audience is crucial to young writers' development, because it allows students to discover how the act of writing can be functional for them in the day-to-day life of the school. Keeping logs or journals of reactions to class events, to books or films or TV programs, and to chapters in a textbook can be a valuable first step in making personal sense of new information. Writing to work out new ideas, to raise questions, and to find out what one understands enables students to see that writing can be of direct benefit to them both in their initial development of a new subject matter and as preparation for the more formal, extensive writing required in their courses. Because students have an extended record of their own emerging opinions and understandings, they have themselves as resources when it comes to developing and shaping an essay or a final report. The teacher can encourage this type of writing by providing models of subject matter journals or logs, by setting aside class time for this writing, by allowing credit toward the final grade for completion of such writing, and by allowing students to keep their logs handy during the writing of tests or essays in class.

[1]Reprinted, by permission, from James Britton and others, *The Development of Writing Abilities (11—18)*. (Schools Council Research Studies) Basingstoke, Hampshire: Macmillan Education Ltd., 1975, p. 58.

> *A poem . . . begins as a lump in the throat, a sense of wrong, a homesickness, a lovesickness . . . It finds the thought, and the thought finds the words.*
> ROBERT FROST

One of the next steps a teacher may take to expand student writers' sense of audience beyond that of writing for teacher-as-examiner or for the self is to begin to respond to the students' writing at stages earlier than the final draft. This response can take the form of comments written on a first draft, which provide the writer with a sense of a real reader's initial reaction. These comments may be questions: "How old were you when this happened?" "What did the room look like?" "How did she feel when you said that?" These questions indicate to the writer that the reader is interested in what is going on and wants more information. Or the comments may take the form of an anecdotal response: "The same thing happened to me when I was in high school." "I remember being terrified of water also." Such comments let the writer know that the reader has made a connection with the piece, and the feedback is very important. Another form these comments might take is that of responsive coaching: "Why not leave out the parts about the journey to camp and concentrate on that frightening first night?" "I need more specific details here about conditions in the camp to understand how the rebellion started." All of these responses and their thousands of variations serve to enable the writer to visualize better the effect of the words on a reader. Giving

Table 11 Distribution of audience categories*

(n = 2,104)

Categories	Percent
Child to self	0.5
Child to trusted adult	1.6
Teacher-learner dialogue	38.8
Pupil to teacher, particular relationship	1.0
Pupil to examiner	48.7
Expert to known laymen	0.0
Child to peer group	0.1
Group member to working group	0.2
Writer to his readers	1.8
Child to trusted adult/teacher-learner dialogue	0.6
Teacher-learner dialogue/pupil to examiner	4.0
Teacher-learner dialogue/writer to his readers	1.0
Miscellaneous	1.7

*This table is reproduced here, by permission, from James Britton and others, *The Development of Writing Abilities (11—18)*, (Schools Council Research Studies, Macmillan Education, Ltd., 1975), p. 130.

such responses on early drafts allows the writer to make revisions—to work on the piece in progress, not after the writing has been completed, polished, and handed in.

Responses from the teacher like those mentioned above might be classified in James Britton's audience terminology as teacher as "trusted adult" or as "partner in dialogue." Either audience is certainly necessary before the teacher assumes the traditional role of examiner.

Beyond the variations of teacher as audience, many others can profitably be addressed in classroom writing. Students can write for their peers—either fellow students in their classes or those in other classes or other schools. The key point here is that this writing be genuinely addressed to an audience that will, indeed, read and respond to the writing. Only through this genuine response, with all the attendant confusions and misunderstandings, can a real sense of audience develop. For example, juniors in high school can write to incoming freshmen and describe the school and offer suggestions on how to succeed. In this case, it is crucial that real incoming freshmen read those letters and write back. The whole point is lost if the teacher asks the juniors to write as if they were writing to incoming freshmen and then reads and evaluates the papers herself. For in that case what the teacher has done is set up a double image; the real teacher audience is superimposed on the "imaginary" freshman audience, and the writer's job then becomes doubly difficult. For the sake of an evaluation, the student must imagine what the teacher thinks one should say to incoming freshmen and how the teacher would like it said. It is not surprising that writing of this kind often sounds strained and false; it is almost

inevitable when students are placed in an artificial situation in which they are asked to satisfy two different audiences at once. And in addition to the double image difficulty, the student is being asked to perform, in James Britton's words, a "dummy run," a practice exercise instead of a piece of real communication.

There is little reason for relying completely on "dummy runs" when there are so many genuine situations that call for real writing. What follows is a listing of possible contexts in which students can write for audiences beyond the classroom teacher:

- *Writing for Other Students*
  1. An exchange of letters between classes. The topic may be a book both classes have read, a film they have both seen, or a reaction to some contemporary issue.
  2. An exchange between classes of profiles written about people in the community. This exchange could take place before the final drafts were written so the revisions could incorporate the readers' questions.
  3. Notes written to absent classmates explaining what went on in class so the students will come back prepared.
  4. Booklets or stories written for younger children and "tried out" on them by the writers in the younger children's classroom.

- *Writing for People in the Outside World*
  1. Letters written to authors of works read in class, in which the students discuss points that had arisen during class discussion. Similar letters can be written to film writers or directors.
  2. Actual letters of application for part-time jobs.
  3. Letters to the editor of local newspapers or magazines in which the student writers discuss topics of interest to students.
  4. Oral histories, transcribed and shaped by the students and presented in a booklet for distribution or purchase through some community organization.
  5. Stories, poems, or essays for the school literary magazine.
  6. Argumentative or persuasive essays on contemporary topics sent to a local political or civic organization.
  7. Entries written for writing contests of any kind.

These are only a few of the many possible audiences for students' writing. All of them demand that the writers think about their audience's uniqueness and shape their writing accordingly. The teacher can be of enormous assistance here by showing students how to analyze whom they are writing for. This can be done either by giving exercises in the whole class in which the general characteristics of a known audience are listed on the chalkboard or by asking specific questions about the intended audience of each student who is already working on an initial draft. Questions such as, "How much does your audience know about the subject?" or "How formal do you think you have to be in word choice?" subtly remind students that there is no one way to write anything. Rather, the craft of writing demands that students pick the best way in this particular case for this particular audience. And, over time, with thoughtful nurturing from responsive teachers, this sense of an audience's needs will become automatic—as automatic, we hope, as beginning a sentence with a capital letter and ending it, eventually, with a period or a question mark or an exclamation point!

Practical Ideas for Developing a Sense of Audience

An Exercise to Introduce the Concept of Audience to Students and Teachers

By Lynda Chittenden
Teacher, Old Mill School,
Mill Valley Elementary School District;
and Teacher/Consultant, Bay Area Writing Project

The following is a guided fantasy that successfully communicates the concept of audience. Many teachers have used this exercise both in in-service workshops and in the classroom.

First, ask your group to take out a scrap of paper. Tell them this writing will not be turned in or shared without each writer's approval. Ask each member of the group to select a place where, right now, he or she would rather be. Even the most dedicated teacher or student has a fantasy place that he or she periodically escapes to. Ask all members of the group to close their eyes and imagine themselves in their fantasy land.

Pause awhile; then, speaking slowly, ask the members of the group to visualize themselves in their fantasy lands. What is their position? Are they standing, sitting, lying down? After a few moments, ask them to be receptive to the tactile sensations that are part of being there. What is the weather like? What smells might they also be aware of? What are the sounds that are very much a part of this place? Allow a few more moments for each individual's fantasy to grow.

Encouraging them to imagine and believe that they are compulsive recorders who wish to capture this moment so as to be able to relive it later, ask them to begin a diary that will do just that. (See a sample in paragraph number 1 that follows.)

After four to five minutes, state that you know this piece is unfinished, but skipping a few lines and, remaining in this place, ask them to begin a letter to Mom, or some other loved one, in which they tell the person about this place. (See paragraph number 2.)

After three to four minutes, acknowledge that this letter is also unfinished but, skipping down a few more lines, ask them to begin writing a memo to their principal or superintendent in which they request funds to subsidize their being in this place and which justifies the released time necessary for them to be there. (See paragraph number 3.)

At the end of three to four minutes, ask for volunteers to share the results of their guided excursion to a special place and to talk about what they noticed in their own writing as they did this exercise. Participants are often surprised to discover how much impact audience has on style. When writing for themselves (paragraph number 1), they tend to be very descriptive and detailed. Concentrating on sense im-

For teachers and students alike, the guided imagery exercise is an experiential introduction to the concept of audience.
LYNDA CHITTENDEN

pressions, they, in effect, paint pictures of their memories with words. Many of them become so absorbed in writing that when you call them to a halt and switch audiences, they get slightly annoyed. In paragraph number 2, addressed to Mom or a friend, they often assume a more conversational tone and do much more telling than showing. Sentence length is reduced as rich detailed descriptions are omitted from the writing. Finally, in paragraph number 3, the letter to the principal, they become very formal, and the "voice" in the writing is much more distant. Much less is likely to be written during this part of the exercise because the audience sometimes can inhibit fluency. A sample of an unedited exercise that a UCI Writing

Project teacher shared with the group will illustrate these general points:

1. A moss green sea turtle glides lazily by, and a huge rainbow striped parrot fish in hues of lime green, turquoise, and tangerine slowly weaves its way through the filtered light. I can hear my breathing through the snorkle as I float upon the surface of the salty ocean, my back broiling in the sun and turning a deep shade of crimson. I must appear to the inhabitants of this estuary an ungainly creature—lumbering about in the tranquil waters of Xel Ha. How pleasant it is to float weightlessly in their watery kingdom.

2. Dear Mom:

   Michael and I took a trip to a natural aquarium of sorts called Xel Ha today that was truly fantastic! This is an estuary where the river meets the Caribbean. The whole area is enclosed by a coral reef that keeps the sharks out—thank goodness. Anyway, we went snorkling and saw some of the most amazing fish. The colors were just fantastic! One fish I saw was all the colors of the rainbow. Orange wasn't orange but tangerine. It was really unbelievable.

3. To: Dr. Barrow

   I have enjoyed my vacation in Cancun immensely and see many possibilities for offering a unit of study on this area. I'd like to stay on a bit longer to investigate all the educational possibilities further. I'm sure I could design a class that would benefit my students. I'm planning to take many slides for illustrated lectures on: the natural aquarium at Xel Ha, the Mayan ruins at Tulume, the windy island of Isle Mujeres, etc. I hope you'll be as excited about my idea as I am . . . .

For teachers and students alike, the guided imagery exercise is an experiential introduction to the concept of audience. It makes what could be just an abstract idea tangible and concrete and creates a positive awareness of audience in future writing assignments.

Writing for a Live Audience

By Anita Freedman
Teacher, Fairhaven Elementary School,
Orange Unified School District;
and Teacher/Consultant, UCI Writing Project

One easy way to provide a live audience for your class is to have your students write for children in the lower grades. I begin to help generate ideas for writing by showing the class my "Mouse Collection." I have a large box filled with discarded story display figures: mice outfitted to play tennis, baseball, or golf; to play cards; to clean house; or to stitch up the American flag. I take out one figure and we discuss possible stories about it, stories which younger children would enjoy. "What could we name him?" "Think of a problem he might have." "How could he solve it?" I write their suggestions on the chalkboard, and from them, we develop a story.

Then everyone gets a chance to pick out a mouse. I have several duplicates, so there are no hassles. As the students write their stories, I walk around the room, making suggestions, serving as a word bank for those who need a walking dictionary, and offering story ideas for those students who get stuck.

When the stories are finished, I use either whole-class or small-group evaluations. Generally, I stay out of the discussion and let the class decide whether or not the stories meet the criteria of sustaining interest, clarity, and appropriateness for the chosen grade level. They may ask such questions as these: Is it interesting? Is it clear? Who would enjoy it? My students do a truly fine job of evaluating, and they give succinct comments. I have heard them dismiss wandering writers with, "That's too long for little kids." They motivate the author to go back and tighten his or her efforts. Sometimes boys are told, "That's too scary," so they omit the dripping blood.

Peer groups are also efficient at assigning papers to the correct grade level: "Kindergartners'd love that." "Yours is kinda grown-up; you'd better send it to the third grade."

After the stories are written and evaluated, we set up a schedule for each student to read his or her story and to show his or her mouse to children in a lower grade. Teachers of the primary grades will welcome this when it is arranged in advance. Even though our school is very small, my 30 or more children are all given this opportunity to read their work to small groups. As a special reward, I let my authors display their figures on their desks for the rest of the day.

Everyone basks in the obvious approval of the audience. Some receive letters! It is always a huge success, and I see a great improvement in my students' ability to put words on paper and to structure a story.

Pen Pal Clubs

By Virginia Baldwin
GATE Teacher, Del Cerro Elementary School
Saddleback Valley Unified School District;
and Teacher/Consultant, UCI Writing Project

Starting a pen pal club at your school or in your classroom is a great way of changing the audience for your children, promoting writing in the practical/informative domain, and for opening the door for writing across the curriculum.

The International Friendship League sponsors a pen pal program, which is designed for students of all ages. Educators in over 100 countries cooperate with the League in its program of matching "pen friends" of like ages and similar interests. To get pen pals, students submit an application and a registration fee of $3 (or $5 for those over nineteen years of age) to the International Friendship League. On the application the League asks for each student's name, address, sex, age, and hobbies and special interests. The students may also specify the part of the world in which they would like a pen pal, but the League prefers "to have the privilege of selecting the country." For information on the program, write to the International Friendship League, Inc., 55 Mount Vernon Street, Boston, MA 02108; or phone (617) 523-4273.

Once the letters start arriving, post a map in the classroom. Use map pins and string to indicate where each student has a pen pal. Children can keep a scrapbook of the letters and small items (stamps, menus, napkins, postcards, photos, artwork, recipes) that they have exchanged with their pen pal.

You may also wish to have students research the state or country of the pen pal. They may write a saturation report, learn songs from the country or state, order travel brochures, and locate and display books that pertain to their pen pal's home. The possibilities are endless.

You might have one of your students who has artistic talent design special stationery, which can be duplicated, or you may wish to have each student design his or her own stationery. This is a great motivation for writing more letters.

Writing to "Dear Abby"

By Karen Walden
Teacher, Sunkist School,
Anaheim Elementary School District;
and Teacher/Consultant, UCI Writing Project

I became uncomfortable and almost indifferent about using textbooks as the sole source for the written communication of ideas to students in my classroom last year. Daily, I felt the nearly impossible struggle of making appropriate, meaningful connections with those remote, impersonal messages found in textbook selections. That material written from writer to unknown audience caused such a feeling of indirect involvement in me and in my students that it became more and more difficult to justify basing my lessons on the textbook selections.

One day I brought a newspaper into the classroom. I hoped that the fact that the paper had been published that day would make the nature and the purpose for the writing more immediate. As we reviewed and discussed the various sections in the newspaper, students began to demonstrate increased interest in the writing. Those articles to a then known audience began to take on meaning.

As we extended our exploration of the newspaper, the children discovered a column that elicited an even more personal response—Dear Abby. Their enthusiasm prompted my weekly initiation of role playing in the class. For the next few weeks, I decided to become a Dear Abby of sorts, providing my students with a new audience to write to. They wrote small, anonymous messages on folded pieces of paper and placed them in a collection box. I then attempted to provide suitable answers to real problems. Each Monday morning eager faces lined up outside the door to receive a handout of questions and responses for our "Dear Abby" session. I was truly pleased with the trust that began to develop.

In the weeks that followed, students offered additional comments to my responses, oftentimes posing solutions far more appropriate than mine. Thus, I began gradually to relinquish my role to secretly chosen "Abbys" or "Alberts" and to reassume my previous capacity as full-time teacher. What a success! Additional questionmakers began to emerge in the class. Students felt less inhibited about identifying themselves when they wanted or needed answers. The range of topics began to broaden. We discussed the validity of school rules, difficult relationships with siblings, inadequate allowances, the effects of drugs and smoking, consequences of shoplifting, and pending love affairs—just to mention a few. As our chosen expert responded to a particular problem, classmates listened attentively. They displayed unquestionable tolerance of her or his opinions. Differing points of view were both respected and appreciated. Our expert's literary skills in actual interpretation and editing also naturally emerged, as some of the written questions required revising for clarity.

The experience in writing to a real audience was most rewarding. It provided not only motivation for written communication but also fostered meaningful relationships among class members.

I Think We Need to Write a Substitute's Manual

By Lynda Chittenden
Teacher, Old Mill School,
Mill Valley Elementary School District;
and Teacher/Consultant, Bay Area Writing Project

The self-contained elementary school classroom provides many opportunities for children to write to a real audience and for a specific purpose: a job description book that specifies exactly how each clean-up job must be performed at the end of the day or a list of adopted rules for those physical education games that are a continual source of argument.

Early in the school year, I plot to create in my fifth grade classroom the circumstances that result in a wildly successful project. I am rarely absent in September. However, on the first rainy day in October, I take a planned day off and spend it in bed reading a trashy novel. On returning to class the next day, I am assaulted by a predictable barrage of complaints: "Don't you *ever* get that terrible person again!" "She wouldn't even let us read at the rug!" "I only missed three problems, but she made me do the whole page over."

I listen to these laments with great seriousness, which encourages even more verbalized outrage. With furrowed brow and in a concerned voice, I say, "This is terrible. Our class is so special and different that it must be very difficult for a stranger to try to understand how we work. I think we need to write a substitute's manual!"

With that prewriting exercise accomplished, we get to work. First, we brainstorm all the necessary ingredients for such a book. From that we write on the chalkboard a list that will become the manual's contents: the class meeting, the day's schedule, the class

standards, terrible tasks, learning logs, math time, writing groups, group response, literature, physical education, clean-up, and so forth.

Last year, instead of the experienced authoritarian matron, the class had as its first substitute a young person who allowed herself to be completely overwhelmed by a majority of rowdy boys. The next day when we were brainstorming, someone made the appropriate suggestion that we also include a chapter of advice. We did:

1. You must expect some persons to change their names at roll call, and sometimes drop pencils at math time, *but* don't let that offend you.
2. At the class meeting, if the class is out of hand, don't leave the chairperson to do all the work. Help the chairperson contain the class!
3. When you come in the room, you should expect everyone seated at the rug unless people are turning in homework.

This year, we began the Substitute's Manual with some more direct talk about expectations:

We expect you to be patient with us and we'll try to be patient with you. Sometimes things that seem easy for you are hard for us, and we don't want a lecture about how simple it is. We expect you to be a teacher, not a parent or friend. You should expect us to do our best work, although sometimes we forget and fool around.

Once we agree that we have thought of everything a substitute teacher needs to know about our class, we decide who will write what. Knowing that the best writers always volunteer first, I start with the most important beginning chapters of the book. "Who wants to do expectations?" The two or three students

> *The self as audience is crucial to young writers' development.*
> MARY K. HEALY

who raise their hands get that assignment. "Who wants to write the advice section?" Those with raised hands then have their assignment. If at the end of the list, some students do not have assignments, they may do the illustrations; for example, a picture of a boy out picking up trash in the yard—a "terrible task" consequence of breaking a class standard.

Once the first drafts are completed, the students meet in their writing groups to determine what must be done to make these important pieces of writing clear and completely understandable to a substitute teacher. The final drafts are then written and handed to a small committee that puts them together, numbers the pages, prepares the contents page, and binds the manual with a front and back cover.

When the manual is completed, we have much more than an aid for the next substitute teacher. Through a seemingly subtle process, the necessary structure and expectations of the class have been clarified for everyone.

Providing an Audience for ESL Students and a Reason to Write

By Carolyn Mendoza
ESL Teacher/Reading Department Chair,
Santa Ana High School,
Santa Ana Unified School District;
and Teacher/Consultant, UCI Writing Project

English-as-second-language (ESL) students have a wealth of experiences to share with native English speakers. One of the most interesting and most immediate experiences they can draw on and translate into a narrative is the story of their departure or their parents' departure from their homeland and their journey to the United States.

At the prewriting stage, we have a discussion about these students' experiences. Many of them have traveled extensively, seen other parts of the world, lived in cultures with different customs, and so forth. I point out to the ESL students that many Americans would love to meet and talk with them and find out where they came from because most Americans have little information about their country's most recent immigrants.

As a prewriting exercise, I tell the students that a whole book has been written about immigrants traveling to the United States; their experiences are also worth sharing. I then read a selection from *American Dreams: Lost and Found*, by Studs Terkel.[1] It is an account of Dora Rosenzweig, a Russian immigrant. Dora's story becomes the model for my students' own narrative.

After I read this excerpt from *American Dreams*, we discuss what Dora said and identify what we think would be interesting to United States citizens. Before we begin to write, I ask for the students' input about what should be discussed in the narrative in sequential order, and I write their suggestions on the chalkboard. For instance, we begin asking questions that we believe people would most like to have answered:

1. How long ago did this event take place?
2. How did you learn that you would be moving?
3. What was your life like before you left?

4. How did you actually escape/move?
5. Whom did you travel with?
6. What was your travel experience like?
7. Were there any problems or exciting experiences?

Next, I tell the students to write only what they feel comfortable with sharing and to give as accurate an account as they can so that their audience can picture their experiences. I also tell them that only I will know the authors' true identities. To provide some structure for their reminiscences, I ask the students to write about their family life first, followed by their traveling and immigration experiences, and finally how they feel about life in the United States.

Because my students already have a wealth of memories to tap in telling their stories, they can focus less on what they want to say and put their energy into how they will say it. Providing an interested audience for them—a classmate at school, new neighbor, supportive teacher—and a topic they have deep feelings about motivates them to communicate as clearly and descriptively as they are able. Once they relate their experiences on paper in this new language, they can read them aloud in small groups or work individually with the teacher to make any necessary corrections. A sample of one of my student's papers follows:

(NOTE: This is an unedited first draft. The writer was at the 2.0—4.0 reading level. I would recommend this assignment only for ESL students whose English proficiency is at the second through fourth grade level or above and whose reading proficiency is equal to or better than second through the fourth grade.)

MOVING

It has been two years since this happened two years-seven hundred thirty days in a rather long time. In fact, for most people, things that happened two years ago would have faded out from their memories. But I can still remember things that happened to me two years ago so well, so clearly. Of course, it did not mean that I have a better memory, but it is because of things themselves that were big enough to change my whole life and that I can never forget.

It was an early cold morning in March of 1979 when I was waken up by my mother to prepare my luggage. I was leaving home, taking a journey that no one would know how long, how far and how dangerous to look for freedom. Since this would were formed, so many people had struggle, killed one another for the sake of freedom. What an abstract noun. it was, and now, for the sake of it, I was leaving my lovely home, my lovely folks for an unknow day to return. Thinking of this, tears filled my eyes, and the past came to my mind.

Before the communists take over of South Vietnam in April 1975 my father own a prospersons factory, making and sometimes exporting picture frames to the United States. Everything was going on so well that didn't need to worry about our living, we didn't even need to worry about the borring war that had been lasted for so long

[1]Studs Terkel, *American Dreams: Lost and Found.* New York: Pantheon Books, 1980.

time. Everything seemed so brilliant. However, thing were changed greatly after the communits came to the South from the North. Private commerce, industries were prohibitt doing things in one's own way was no move allowed. wearing fashioned dresses was warned by the Communists. In short there was no more individual freedom, no more human right. More seriously, food was not enough for the people, medicines were stopped to import. No food no medicines the whole country was put into a terrible condition. Consequently people began to seek ways to saves lives. The most common way was to flue the poor country by boats. Boat people were produced acodingly. The misseries of "Boat people" had been heard for so long. They might lost their lives on their ways of escape, they might meet the Thailand pirates and be robbed or killed by then on their way to look for freedom they might be.

Now, soon it came to my turn to be a "Boat people". I wonder it was worth while or not. For this fleeing the country, my family had paid ten ounces to communist government (approximately 4000 US. dollar by that time). and the priceless parting of family. (For some reasons, beside my brother and I, the rest my family had to stay in Saigon, temporarily I wished). Furthermore we didn't know when this escape would be sucussful or not. We might lost our lives if it failed.

At five o'clock, my brother and I came to the bus station to wait for the bus that would bring us down to Bac Lieu, a southern province in Vietnam and the boat that we was going to embark was suppose to park there.

Finally we came to Bak Lieu and then trans ferry to Camau the southern most port. It has about twelve o'clock mid night when we boarded on the boat names Phuoc An-meaning happiness and safety. From that moment on, I had left my Mom, my dad, and my yougest brother my ralatives, my friends, my country, my everythings!

The boat was a little old and fragile boat. It's unbelievable, a boat of 25 yards long and 10 yards wide carrying more than three hundred fifty people. It was really crowded on the boat. people were jammed together like sardines.

the boat began to sail for our supposed destination Malaysia at about one o'clock. The first day of our journey was uneventful. The sea was as calm as the mirror, therefore, it did not seem much trouble in our trip so far. However, in the second day when the unexperienced captain declared that we had lost our way after reading at the international water-way. It's hard to imagine how it was like to lose one's way in the ocean. It was dangerous to sail without knowing wehere one was going. Misfortune never came singly. At noon time, we saw three ships were approaching us, we thought they might be our saviour. Unfortunately they were not saviors but killers. They were the barbarous Pirate of Thailand. When their ships came close to our little boat, about ten of them just jumped over our boat with blunt lornibes axes and began their search for valuables. Of course, by the means of robbing. After a few hours searching, these beastly pirates finally left with bags of watches, golds, dollars,

etc. In fact, we were lucky that we were not killed by them. and the women on the boat were not raped by them. This had to be God's help.

The next day, Good luck came to us, we metanother boat which was on it way to Malaysia too. with the gruidernce of this boat, we were came to the region of Malaysia. When were hanging around there, a Malaysian naval ship appeared and the soldiers ordered us that we could not land on the Malaysian territory, but they hinted us that if our boat could bribe them with a cartain amount of money, they might help us.

After satisfying their demand, we were at last allowed to land on an island names Panang of Malaysia. This was the fourth night of our journey. And these four days journey were at last ended.

After living in the small island of Panang for a week, we were transferred to the famous refugee Camp Bidong where thousand of refugees were get there.

Thus our new living as refugees began. In Bidong, we received such as rice, canned food, and water from the United Nation High Commissioner for Refugees. Meanwhile, we were to make procedures so that we could be resettled down in a third country.

Fortunately, our application for resettlement in the U.S. was accepted by the U.S. Governement. Consequently, we came to the United States in August 1979 after four months living in Malaysia.

From Vietnam to Malaysia, and from Malaysia to the U.S. it was really big move in my life, it was no wonder it had rooted in my memories.

Diem

May 1, 1981

Although Diem's story is clearly deficient in its correctness, it is one of the most fluent pieces of writing that she produced all semester. Because she had an important story to tell and an audience to write to, she truly searched her memory (and the dictionary) to find the English words to convey the dramatic events of her flight from Vietnam. Her story and the many others like it by her classmates are starting points—a way to make writing in English meaningful for ESL students.

Learning Logs

By Mindy Moffatt

English Teacher, Walker Junior High School,
Anaheim Union High School District;
and Teacher/Consultant, UCI Writing Project

If your students could *freewrite* (à la Peter Elbow) about what they had gleaned during the school day, what do you imagine they would write? As a junior high school teacher, I also wondered. What would their perceptions of the day be? The idea of writing in a learning log intrigued me enough to try it.

Starting from the first day of the school year and every day thereafter, students were instructed to write during the last ten minutes "about the day" and to date each entry. Students earned credit for each day's notation. I collected their logs once a week, staggering the collection day so that I would have 30 logs a day to review instead of 180 a week. Each class period had a regular day of the week when the logs were due. I was surprised that reviewing each day's logs took only 20 to 30 minutes, depending on how many quick comments I wrote.

Imagine my reaction when I read Pam's log of the first week:

9/9/85: I'm in English class right now (unfortunately). The teacher wants us to write this stupid, dumb, and absolutely boring paragraph. Well, anyway, I'm going to learn in this class—but I also have to because the teacher will probably yell my brains out if I just sit here. I hate this class. I really think it's stupid because it's not like I'm going to grow up and tell my kids to do this.

I hadn't quite prepared myself for such an honest reflection. But I persevered through her accounts:

9/10/85: Well, today I'm in English again! No—I don't want to be but have to be! Well, today we were supposed to be doing a talk about the stupid paper I wrote about yesterday, but the teacher sent me and Michelle out of class because we didn't have the paper, and it was in our locker and she wouldn't let us go get it. This is boring!

9/11/85: Today we got together in groups and discussed things about ourselves. I met some people today that are in our group. I guess it's gonna be cool. Three more minutes until the bell. I have to go home! I'm dying of starvation. I'm getting pretty proud of myself because today I made a friend that was my worst enemy for two years. Bye Bye.

9/12/85: Well, I've got three minutes to tell you everything I have to. I feel fine about my writing. My writing makes me feel good because I write down what I feel, think, and believe, so if people don't like it, that's ok, because it's me and they don't have to be me.

9/13/85: We write in the learning logs so we can write down what we feel, think, and believe. I like the learning logs because we can write down what we want to. There's nothing really I don't like about learning logs.

Reading Pam's account of her first week in the eighth grade made me believe in both the cognitive and affective values of learning logs. This activity provides insight for a teacher to keep in touch with the development of students. I enjoyed writing supportive, positive comments to students: "I feel this way, too!" "I'm impressed!" "Thanks for sharing this."

The students were anxious to get their logs back; not only did they look for my remarks, but also they reread their entries to see what they had written the week before. With some junior high students, it often seemed as if a lifetime had passed during the week. They remembered the captured moments, the exercises in class, and the trials and tribulations that they had survived.

Learning logs provide insight for a teacher to keep in touch with the development of students.

MINDY MOFFATT

After the first week, when students began to trust writing in their logs, I gave them more specific prompts:

Write first about everything you did in class; then tell your reactions and feelings about the activities.

We had read-around groups that helped us with our paper in punctuation and spelling. If I didn't have them, I'd be lost like a needle in a haystack. *Greg Hughes*

I got a good start on my draft about Renee. Debbie really gave me some great suggestions on how to spice up my draft. *Kevin Donovan*

This was interesting to have other people besides teachers tell you honestly what they think about your writing. . . . I learned how to help other people without giving away the answer. *Heather White*

Today we proofread each of our papers. It was kind of fun reading other people's papers and correcting them. *Nico Dourbetas*

Today we started to proofread other students' material. I think that it helps me as much as the student I proofread for. *Russell Clark*

I had fun working on my paper today. We talked about it and discussed what I could do to fix it. *Eric Degenhart*

The class got noisy and Ms. Moffatt almost gave the whole class a detention. *Eric Degenhart*

Today, We Noticed things that were
    very Interesting and
    very Different. I
      Learned that
    people Live and
      Listen according to
    their Lifestyles and sometimes
    their Status. *Chris May*

What is something you want to know more about?

I like writing. I would like to learn more about science fiction writing. *Brady White*

I'm a person who is especially interested in new ideas and would like to learn. *Deborah Wissink*

I knew within a week where certain students needed my assistance; I did not have to wait until later in the quarter to discover that someone was having trouble.

What do you like about our class?

I do like working in groups because they give opinions and help you with what you are doing. *Sheila Nora*

It makes me feel good when I think of something to write. . . . I like it because it lets my mind do the writing. *Sean Ciechomski*

I like learning logs because you can tell the teacher how you feel about things. *Jason Bumcrot*

It's fun writing in learning logs because you search for and gather your thoughts in a short period of time. *Russell Clark*

What don't you like about learning logs or our class?

Sometimes I don't like learning logs because there is either nothing to write about or not enough time. *Rex Huang*

I don't like the learning logs but as long as we have to do them, I might as well try and make it fun. *Anthony Lawson*

If your parents had been watching this class through a one-way mirror, what would they have seen? Explain to them what you were doing.

If my parents were here . . . they would have seen us in groups talking and commenting about each other's papers which makes it look like we were passing notes or something. *Rex Huang*

If my mom or dad were observing our class today, they'd be pleased cuz we got a lot of work done . . . I'm proud of myself, and I'm sure my parents would be too! *Stefanie Takii*

If my parents were observing this class, they would infer that we were a rowdy, unsupervised, uncontrolled class, but in a way independent because even though we were talking a lot, we were also working at the same time. *Michael Lietzow*

I was learning a great deal about my students' learning processes. Their feelings were validated when I discussed their responses with the whole class. For example, Chris May wrote, "My writing makes me feel good in a way that everybody in the class will probably respect me for it."

When I shared an insight from a log, the students' learning became more personalized, and my teaching became more focused.

Reading their learning logs was an activity I looked forward to, especially after a difficult day. The students' entries were all I needed to remind me of my reasons for becoming a teacher. "This is Ms. Moffatt's learning class," wrote Tashawna Donaldson.

"It gives us a chance to use our brains," said Chuck White. I felt that I had time to adjust my goals and plans so that I could continue to teach students, not just content.

So many enlightening responses appeared in the logs that I made a bulletin board of their disclosures. I noted particularly valuable phrases, allowing students to edit their "freewrite" comments for display. Students valued the log entries more when this postwriting step was added. "I want one of my quotes to go on the board, but I can't think of anything good enough to write," noted Tod Grossman.

Parents also appreciated the learning logs. They were pleased and entertained to see such insight from the students. During conferences with parents the logs became a concrete basis for them to understand a student's perspective regarding goals and expectations of the class. Parents saw that students were learning how to learn, and I was rewarded when parents expressed that they wished their English classes had been like this. They valued the writing and supported the effort.

Students were not the only writers at the end of the class period. I joined them by writing in my own log and allowed them to read my entries. Through this sharing of my own trials and tribulations, I found myself facing the same challenge as they—trusting one's audience. Having ten minutes of "quiet writing time" at the end of each class was immensely therapeutic, especially in a junior high schedule of seven daily periods. We were all more prepared to meet the challenges of our next classes after such closure.

Regardless of the subject matter or the ability levels of students, spending the last few minutes of class writing learning logs allows teachers and students to harvest memories, trust, smiles, and knowledge. As Stefanie Hill explained, "It kind of makes me feel good to know that I'm helping people with using my knowledge and putting it together with theirs to make our writing better." We are learning how to learn with logs.

Domains of Writing

Teaching the Domains of Writing

By Nancy McHugh
Director, Writing Competencies,
Los Angeles Unified School District

Dividing the "universe of discourse" into domains is not new. Traditionally, there have been at least three domains in the curriculum: descriptive, narrative, and expository writing. However, until recently the widespread practice had been for teachers in the elementary grades to concentrate on *creative* writing (mainly imaginative/narrative writing) and for teachers in the secondary grades to emphasize expository writing almost to the exclusion of other domains.

The Los Angeles Unified School District reintroduced the broad concept of domains in writing in 1976 when it printed and distributed a description of its composition program and suggested four domains: sensory/descriptive, imaginative/narrative, practical/informative, and analytical/expository. Several theories were behind this move. One was that students do better in one domain than in another; therefore, the curriculum should have balance to provide equal opportunity for success for all students, regardless of their abilities, and plans for careers or continuing education. Another theory was that, although the domains are not totally discrete (indeed, they often blend one into the other), each has a place in writing/thinking development; and all are necessary for competent writing. With the most difficult expository task, a person probably uses all four domains to develop a theme. Another theory for using the four domains was that, although any mode can probably be used in any domain (poem as description, as narrative, as information, as analysis), working in separate domains encourages the teacher to use a wide variety

of modes and audiences. A teacher may plan lessons exclusive to one domain at a time (a domain as a unit) and explore the variety of modes within that domain (sensory/descriptive domain: journal entries, tone poems, informal essays, letters, monologues, and so forth); or a teacher may choose to work with a theme or an experience and move from domain to domain and mode to mode crafting communication for a variety of audiences and purposes. Preplanning is essential, even though the teacher may choose to follow up an in-class lead and deviate from the plans occasionally.

Description of the Four Domains of Writing

The four domains are categories for defining somewhat exclusive purposes of writing. Part of writing competence is having a clear concept of the intent for the writing, including audience, and being able to organize in the mode (form) that best fits that intention. In the early grades, the teacher may want to select the mode best suited for the domain and writing task. In the upper grades, the teacher may want to encourage students to select the mode that seems most reasonable, perhaps providing a variety from which to

> *Writing to me is a voyage, an odyssey, a discovery, because I'm never certain of precisely what I will find.*
> *GABRIEL FIELDING*

choose. For example, after a prewriting exercise of listening to a record, the students may want to express their feelings about the experience. They will be using the sensory/descriptive domain. The students may be assigned a word poem or a paragraph, or they may be asked to express their feelings, and a number of ways might be suggested: Dear Diary, a word poem, haiku, a letter to a friend, and so forth.

The easiest of the four domains in writing is sensory/descriptive because it deals with the concrete. In this domain a student tries to present a picture in words, one so vivid that the reader or listener can recapture many of the same perceptions and feelings that the writer has had. The writer draws on all the senses to capture this picture of a person, place, or object. In this domain student writers must focus and sharpen their powers of perception and ability to choose precise words.

A second domain is imaginative/narrative (creative) writing in which the writer's main intent is to tell a story—sometimes real, sometimes imaginary. The forms may range widely, but the main idea is to tell what happens. In this domain student writers build on the first domain in that they must put descriptive detail into a time/order frame. Students learn ordering, transition, balance, suspense, climax, beginnings, and endings. This domain requires students to become more adept in using verb forms.

In the third domain, practical/informative, students are required to provide clear information; often the writing in this domain takes the form of what might be considered social and business correspondence; for example, letters, memorandums, directions, and notes. The main intent is for the writer to

present information without much analysis or explanation. Working in this domain, students learn to give attention to detail, accuracy, clarity and appropriateness of tone, and mastery of forms like the letter.

A fourth domain is analytical/expository, which is the most difficult because it is the most abstract. In this domain the intention is to analyze, explain, persuade, and influence. The writers tell why and how about a subject. They borrow from the other three domains to make their points, and they emphasize organization and development.

Intent and Suggested Modes of Each Domain

The following chart identifies the intent of each domain and suggests possible modes of writing within the domains:

I. SENSORY/DESCRIPTIVE

Intent: to describe in vivid sensory detail; to express individual feelings

Possible modes:
    Journal entry
    Diary entry
    Personal letter
    Personal essay
    Poem (haiku, diamante[1], cinquain, catalogue, prose poem, acrostic, and many others)
    Monologue
    Dialogue
    Advertising copy
    Character sketches

II. IMAGINATIVE/NARRATIVE

Intent: to tell what happens, real or imaginary; to put in a time sequence

Possible modes:
    Anecdotes
    Limericks
    Diary entries (fictional and real)
    Captions to cartoons, pictures
    Dialogues
    Monologues
    Scripts
    Capsule stories (outline for plot or reconstruction of a cartoon strip)
    Biographical and autobiographical sketches
    Vignettes
    Short stories
    Folk tales
    Myths
    Allegories
    Ballads and other poetic forms (story emphasis)

---

[1] A diamante is a seven-line poem written in the shape of a diamond. The form of the poem is as follows: one noun, two adjectives, three participles, four words that form a phrase, three participles, two adjectives, and one noun.

III. PRACTICAL/INFORMATIVE

Intent: to present basic information clearly

Possible modes:

Postcard message
Friendly notes of various kinds (invitation, thank you, acknowledgment of gift, and so forth)
Lecture/class notes
Memorandum
Directions/steps in a process
Self-evaluation statements
Commercials
News report
Accident report
Business letters (complaint, order, request for information, and so forth)
Application
Summary
Precis
Scientific abstract
Encyclopedia paragraphs

IV. ANALYTICAL/EXPOSITORY

Intent: to explain, analyze, persuade

Possible modes:

Single paragraph/topic sentence plus support
Editorial
Little theme (three paragraphs)
Letter to editor
Speech
Dialogue to persuade
Reviews and reports
Poems (to persuade or analyze, make analogies)
Multiparagraph themes (describe/conclude; narrate/conclude; analyze/conclude; analyze/persuade; define, classify, defend a judgment, interpret literature)
Library/research paper

Note that the same prewriting experience may be used as the stimulus for a variety of exercises in the domains. For example, after popping corn, one may describe in a variety of modes, explain the process, write advertisements, explain popcorn's origin in a folk tale, analyze the various uses of popcorn, or attack or defend it as a food.

A Plan to Introduce the Domains of Writing

Depending on your students' needs and the objectives of your course, you may want to spend from a few days to several weeks on each of the four domains. Provided below is a five-day plan to introduce the domains of writing to your students:

Objectives: Students will be able to awaken their senses, use clustering to elicit language, produce metaphoric description, create poetic forms, fashion commercials/advertisements, form interview questions, vary sentences, write exposition.

> *We do not write in order to be understood; we write in order to understand.*
> C. DAY LEWIS

Materials and equipment: Popcorn or other suitable sense stimulus, paper and pen, chalkboard, overhead projector.

Prewriting: Popcorn (if possible, popped in class) is sampled by students who examine it minutely and cluster all of their responses. Students share clusters (in groups, orally, on chalkboard). These experiences and ideas form the basis for later writing. (For more suggestions on using popcorn in a prewriting exercise, see Sue Rader Willett's practical idea, which appears in "The Process" section of this book, and the section of the book entitled "Clustering: A Prewriting Process.")

Composing skills: Students write two or three of their cluster ideas in complete sentences and check each other's work. The teacher shows them how to transform these sentences into metaphoric statements: The popcorn is white = The popcorn is as white as cotton puffs. The teacher also reviews the form for a diamante or cinquain. Subsequent to later assignments, the teacher reviews the format and special rules for a commercial or advertisement, a descriptive essay, an interview, and an expository essay.

Writing Task I: (Differentiated) Choose one or more of the following to try:

1. Write another of your cluster ideas as a metaphoric statement.
2. Write several of your ideas in metaphoric statements, and put them together to form a catalogue poem.
3. Write a cinquain or diamante, including one of your metaphors in it.

Editing and evaluation: Students share their work in pairs or small groups, making suggestions for revision or corrections. The focus is on "help" and "appreciation," not "criticism."

Extension activities[2]: (To be used over the next three or four days, depending on the nature of the class):

Sensory/Descriptive

1. In small groups, read several poems, especially visual ones (e.g., Robert Frost's "Stopping by Woods on a Snowy Evening," Theodore Roethke's "My Papa's Waltz"). Cluster or draw the visual images in the poems and share in pairs or small groups. Cluster the ideas that the poet is trying to present through these images. Share your concepts in groups. Write a brief explication of the poem that you like best. (Draw scenes.)

---

[2]These activities were based on ideas provided by Kathy Schultheis, Cadre II, Writing Competence Project, Carver Junior High School, Los Angeles Unified School District.

Sensory/Descriptive

2. Expand your original clustered ideas into a sensory/descriptive essay. You may put it in the form of a diary entry or journal if you wish. Try to involve as many senses as possible in your description. Try to include a few metaphors as well. Cluster again if you need to do so.

NOTE: The teacher may present a sentence combining exercise as a composing skill prior to this exercise or the next.

3. Examine or revise your cluster on popcorn to gather data for a commercial or advertisement. Name your product (e.g., Happy Hour Popcorn) and do one or more of the following:
   a. Create a one-sentence slogan for the product.
   b. Create an advertisement by giving your slogan and two other sentences which follow up on the ideas.
   c. Expand your advertisement to a full-page or a commercial. Add description and selling points. Create a dialogue or skit if you wish.

Students may present their advertisements or commercials complete with props.

Practical/Informative

4. With a partner, create a series of questions (five to eight) that you could ask an adult and that would elicit some good ideas and memories. Example: Do you remember an early encounter with popcorn? Interview three adults about their memories, feelings, and ideas about popcorn. You may want to revise your questions after you ask them once.

Write a paper from the information you collected in your interview, and share the results with the class.

Analytical/Expository

Write an expository essay on one of the following: uses of popcorn, changes in the way popcorn is used today and 20 years ago, popcorn as a common bond between generations, values that popcorn offers. (Choose your own topic if you prefer.)

Writing Assignments in Each Domain

The following are descriptions of writing assignments that are specifically focused on each of the four domains. You may use these as points of departure to develop your own lesson plans.

I. SENSORY/DESCRIPTIVE DOMAIN
OBSERVING AND ORGANIZING DETAILS

OBJECTIVES

1. Students will be able to sharpen their senses and deepen their sensitivities to sensory impressions.
2. Students will be able to write vivid, specific, creative sentences.
3. Students will be able to use figurative language.
4. Students will be able to write effective, coherent, organized descriptions.

MATERIALS

1. Holiday cards
2. Paintings or photographs

PREWRITING ACTIVITIES

1. The teacher will present several greeting cards and ask each student to select a card.
2. The students will look carefully at the picture on their cards and concentrate on remembering as many details as they can.
3. Each student will cluster as many details of his or her picture as possible in one minute without looking at the picture.
4. The students will write titles for their pictures based on the details they have created.
5. The teacher will help students to state in a sentence the main impression that they received from the picture and ask them to develop it with the specific details from the cluster.

COMPOSING SKILLS

1. Make use of descriptive words. Describe sensations of feeling, hearing, seeing, smelling, or tasting.

   Copy each adjective and after each write at least one noun that completes a picture.

   Example: *Blazing fire, blazing furnace, blazing sun*

bitter	dazzling	roaring	sharp
buzzing	gritty	rough	tart
clanging	moist	rushing	whizzing

2. Use words as nouns and adjectives. Write one sentence using the word as a noun and another as an adjective.

   Example: Flower

   Noun—My favorite *flower* is the lilac.

   Adjective—Dad exhibits lilacs in the *flower* show.

fruit	house	guest	tree	egg
silver	winter	song	program	dress

3. Make a comparison: Compare things which are not really alike, recognizing one similarity between two basically unlike objects or ideas.
   a. Students will work in small groups of three or four. They will examine all the cards and identify at least a major impression and the details which evoke it for each card.
   b. The cards will be circulated until each group gets a new set to work with.
   c. As students view cards, they will respond by pointing out similarities they see between the object illustrated and something else.
   d. Students write a simile or metaphor about a holiday card.

4. Review elements of complete sentences.

WRITING TASK

Write an interesting paragraph in which you discuss your painting or photograph in close detail. Try to make the reader (your audience is a pen pal) see your painting or picture as vividly as possible and feel what you feel for it. You should write complete sentences and also vary your sentence structure to create interest.

EDITING PLANS

Students exchange papers and read them aloud in small groups. They will make needed corrections.

EVALUATION

Teacher selects examples and duplicates them. Students are to underline the phrase(s) expressing the main impression in each paragraph and to discuss whether or not there are enough supporting details and whether any of the details do not support the main idea.

EXTENSION ACTIVITIES

Students create their own greeting cards and write a poem based on their experience with sensory impressions: haiku, acrostic verse, or starters.

II. IMAGINATIVE/NARRATIVE DOMAIN
POINT OF VIEW

OBJECTIVE

Students will be able to narrate an imaginary experience using the voice of a person.

MATERIALS

Chapter Three in John Steinbeck's *The Grapes of Wrath,* a chapter devoted entirely to a turtle that makes a torturous crossing of a main highway, during which it is flipped like tiddledywinks after a pickup truck runs over the edge of its shell

PREWRITING ACTIVITIES

1. Using cartoons, pictures, poems, and so forth about turtles, make observations and discuss turtles.
2. Read orally Chapter Three of *The Grapes of Wrath.*
3. Discuss the changes that would have to be made in the story if it were told from a different point of view; e.g., the turtle's.
4. Discuss possible points of view.

WRITING TASK/COMPOSING SKILLS

First, choose one of the following to cross a highway as the turtle had to do:

blind man	chicken	snake
puppy	child	boy scout and old lady
drunk	tarantula	a person or animal of your choosing

Then choose one of the following to come down the highway and confront the one you chose above:

Hell's Angels	pickup truck
Marine Corps Band	A group or vehicle of
moving van	your choosing

Then, using the voice of one of the participants, describe the trip across the highway.

EXTENSION ACTIVITIES/EVALUATION

With sound effects record the good papers on tape.

EVALUATION

Teacher reads final drafts holistically. (See the "Evaluation" section of this book for a discussion of holistic scoring.)

EXTENSION ACTIVITIES

Those who wish may read their stories to the entire class.

III. PRACTICAL/INFORMATIVE DOMAIN
BALLOON EXPERIMENT

OBJECTIVES

1. Students will be able to address postcards.
2. Students will be able to write simple, clear, and concise directions.
3. Students will be able to use map and measuring skills.
4. Students will be able to draw logical conclusions from given facts.
5. Students will experience a "space" launching.

MATERIALS
1. Postcards, pens, stamps
2. Maps of California
3. Balloons (ordinary rubber balloons), string
4. Helium

PREWRITING ACTIVITIES
1. Class discusses space launchings, lighter-than-air aircraft, the properties of gases, and the properties of helium.
2. Students are each assigned to bring to school a postcard and stamp. Further, they are told that if they fulfill the assignment, a surprise will await them.
3. At the next class meeting, the surprise, the balloon experiment, is revealed and discussed.

COMPOSING SKILLS
1. The teacher presents instructions on how to address a postcard.
2. The teacher reviews sentence and paragraph structure.
3. The teacher reviews the development of a paragraph by successive steps.
4. The teacher reviews the necessity to write clear and complete sentences.
5. The teacher stresses the necessity to use correct forms in addressing and writing postcards.

WRITING TASK
Write your address in the proper space on the postcard, and put a postage stamp on the card. Using an appropriate salutation, write a message on the postcard to the person who will find it. In your message, tell this person that you are doing an experiment for your physical science class; therefore, you are requesting that this person first write on the postcard the names of the city and cross streets where the postcard was found and, secondly, to drop the postcard in the nearest mailbox. Use an appropriate complimentary close and sign your name.

EDITING PLANS
Teacher will edit the rough drafts of the messages (before the messages are written on the postcards).

EVALUATION
Using a rubric, the student and then the teacher will evaluate the completed postcard. (See the "Evaluation" section of this book for suggestions.)

EXTENSION ACTIVITIES
Punch holes in the postcards and fill the balloons with helium. Then attach two or three helium-filled balloons to the postcards. A month later, most of the postcards should have been returned, depending on climatic factors. Then compile a list of the places where the postcards were found. The students are assigned to locate these places on the map, to measure the distance each balloon traveled, and perhaps to write a complete report of the experiment.

IV. ANALYTICAL/EXPOSITORY DOMAIN
A LETTER TO THROCKMORTON
(U. S. History)

OBJECTIVES
1. Students will be able to formulate explanations and a rationale for the American Revolution.
2. Students will be able to organize a friendly letter.
3. Students will be able to develop logical sequence in written arguments.
4. Students will be able to analyze historic events from the perspective of the eighteenth century.

MATERIALS
1. Any good U. S. history textbook
2. Copy of fictitious letter from a former teenage classmate in England

PREWRITING ACTIVITIES
With readings, discussions, and lectures, the teacher and students explore in depth the causes and events of the Revolutionary War period.

COMPOSING SKILLS
The teacher and students review the form for a friendly letter.

Pretend you are a young person in the colonies about 1776, just after the Declaration of Independence was issued. You still remember your good friend, Throckmorton Algire, with whom you went to school in London before you and your parents came to the New World. Throckmorton has written to you that he is surprised that the colonies are now in open rebellion against King George; Throckmorton is sure it is treason. And he is confused about the reasons why such a rebellion developed. In a recent letter to you, he asked you these questions: "Do you think such a treasonous thing as the Declaration of Independence is defensible?" and "Who will win this war?"

Read Throckmorton's letter carefully and write back to him.

Keep in mind that Throckmorton gets news from a great distance, and his letter indicates that almost everyone in England thinks of the "patriots" as traitors. You will need to explain carefully and logically how the current rebellion developed. You should include facts and your own opinion to help your friend understand both the sequence of events and the prevailing colonial spirit.

EDITING PLANS

Students may check each other's letters for facts, tone, and letter form.

EVALUATION

Teacher develops a rubric for correctness of letter form, logicalness and completeness of both facts and concepts, and perception of the prevailing sentiments of eighteenth century America.

EXTENSION ACTIVITIES

Without identifying writers, teacher chooses especially effective and ineffective letters and reads them to the class (ineffective first). Then the class votes on whether or not their views would have been changed if they had been Throckmorton. If possible, the teacher should read letters from a different class to avoid embarrassment of authors.

Providing students with practice in all four domains of writing will enable them to hone specific writing skills (use of concrete diction and figurative language, sequencing, transition, construction of a logical argument, and so forth) and make them aware of their options as writers. Then in the future the students can consciously integrate elements from the different domains to suit their purpose and audience.

Practical Ideas for Teaching the Domains of Writing

MARY TURNER AND RICH BLOUGH

Specific Activities for Teaching the Domains of Writing in the Elementary Grades

By Mary Turner
Principal, Rolling Hills Elementary School,
Fullerton Elementary School District;
and Teacher/Consultant, UCI Writing Project
and
Rich Blough
Principal, Fern Drive Elementary School,
Fullerton Elementary School District

We developed the following continuum of writing activities to make the domains of writing meaningful to elementary classroom teachers. Using the Los Angeles Unified School District's model as a point of reference, we created a graduated list of specific examples of writing skills for each of the domains, kindergarten through grade six. We found that a detailed sequence of this kind encouraged teachers to include lessons in all of the domains rather than to concentrate on one or two modes of expression.

Activities for Kindergarteners in the Domains of Writing

Sensory/Descriptive	Imaginative/Narrative	Practical/Informative	Analytical/Expository
• Tells about experiences in the five sensory areas of seeing, hearing, tasting, touching, and smelling • Uses words to describe colors • Uses words to describe shapes and sizes • Begins to use words that describe people and animals and their characteristics • Begins to use language to identify sounds and noises • Begins to use language to designate location	• Begins to identify and participate orally in simple nursery rhymes, chants, limericks, and jingles • Begins to dictate stories • Begins to create fanciful characters • Begins to tell stories in own words • Begins to create simple stories • Begins to create imaginary animals	• Dictates notes • Dictates simple stories about experiences • Dictates signs, labels, and captions • Dictates invitations • Dictates greetings • Identifies own name	• Begins to tell about a series of pictures • Begins to summarize a story • Begins to explain an incident or event

Activities for First Graders in the Domains of Writing

Sensory/Descriptive	Imaginative/Narrative	Practical/Informative	Analytical/Expository
• Uses descriptive language to tell about experiences and impressions for each of the five senses: seeing, hearing, tasting, touching, and smelling • Uses specific language relating to colors • Uses specific language to describe sizes and shapes • Begins to use language of comparison • Uses specific words to describe people and animals, their characteristics, and their actions • Uses language that describes sounds and noises • Uses language to designate location	• Begins to identify and to create simple rhymes, chants, limericks, and jingles • Begins to dictate and write experiences and stories • Begins to dictate and write words for simple songs • Begins to create characters, lifelike or fanciful, and to dictate or write stories about them • Begins to dictate endings for stories • Begins to dictate and write original stories • Begins to describe imaginary animals • Begins to use personification in dictating or writing a story	• Writes letters of the alphabet • Begins to dictate and write own name • Begins to write simple notes • Begins to write invitations • Begins to write signs, labels, and captions • Begins to dictate and write friendly letters, using simplified letter format • Begins to dictate and write simple greetings • Begins to write one or two facts about an event or special interest	• Begins to organize a series of pictures in sequence • Begins to organize a series of sentences in a logical sequence • Begins to categorize items • Begins to collect information • Begins to summarize a story in appropriate sequence • Becomes aware of and begins to use a variety of sentence types or patterns in dictating and beginning writing • Begins to write one- and two-sentence accounts of an experience

Activities for Second Graders in the Domains of Writing

Sensory/Descriptive	Imaginative/Narrative	Practical/Informative	Analytical/Expository
• Expands use of specific words that relate to the sensory impressions	• Writes endings for stories	• Writes own name and the names of others in manuscript letter forms	• Writes one or more sentences about a picture or series of pictures
• Expands use of language relating to colors	• Writes simple summary of story heard	• Writes simple notes	• Sorts and lists items in two categories
• Expands use of words in describing sizes and shapes	• Writes new endings for familiar stories	• Writes invitations	• Collects and organizes information
• Increases use of vocabulary in describing location	• Writes about imaginary animals, people, and objects	• Writes signs, labels, and phrases for captions	• Summarizes a story in sequence
• Expands use of comparative language	• Begins to use personification in writing original stories	• Writes simple friendly letters and greetings	• Uses more than one kind of sentence in writing about an event or experience
• Uses language of contrasts	• Dictates and writes new endings for limericks and poems	• Writes lists	• Writes two or more sentences about a single idea, event, or experience
• Expands use of language to describe people and animals, their characteristics, and their actions		• Writes one or more facts about an event or area of interest	

Activities for Third Graders in the Domains of Writing

Sensory/Descriptive	Imaginative/Narrative	Practical/Informative	Analytical/Expository
• Writes about experiences and impressions in the areas of each of the five senses	• Writes simple rhymes	• Writes invitations and greetings	• Writes about events in sequence of ideas
• Uses specific language to describe colors and shades of colors	• Writes new endings for limericks, poems, and chants	• Writes signs, labels, and sentences for captions	• Begins to write articles for class newspaper
• Uses specific language to describe sizes and shapes in writing	• Begins to write haiku and other forms of poetry	• Writes titles for stories	• Begins to collect facts on a selected topic and writes an explanation using them
• Continues to expand use of comparative language	• Writes original fairy tales and tall tales	• Writes personal letters and notes	• Begins to select and use exact words in writing a description
• Expands use of contrastive language	• Begins to keep a class diary	• Writes addresses and return addresses on envelopes and postcards	• Begins to write simple dialogues about events
• Selects and uses words to describe emotions	• Begins to keep a personal diary	• Begins to write reports	• Begins to write simple explanations
	• Rewrites in own words fairy tales, tall tales, myths, fables, and folktales	• Records telephone messages	• Begins to use outline form in writing explanations
	• Composes original fairy tales, fables, and tall tales	• Fills in application for library card	• Begins to use paragraphs in writing when interpreting a sequence of pictures, explaining a picture, and describing a happening
	• Writes simple lyrics for songs	• Begins to prepare book reviews	
	• Adds episodes to stories	• Begins to chart information	
	• Begins to write short plays	• Prepares group reports	
	• Writes a new plot for a familiar story		
	• Lists things that objects would say if they could talk		

Activities for Fourth Graders in the Domains of Writing

Sensory/Descriptive	Imaginative/Narrative	Practical/Informative	Analytical/Expository
• Expands use of vocabulary relating to sensory impressions	• Creates and writes rhymes	• Writes friendly letters	• Writes an account of an experience or event in sequence
• Expands use of language relating to colors and shades of colors	• Writes original riddles, limericks, and chants	• Writes simple business letters	• Arranges a series of facts and writes them in chronological order
• Expands use of language relating to sizes and shapes	• Writes haiku and other forms of poetry	• Writes original invitations and greetings	• Selects and uses specific words in writing a description or explanation
• Adds to vocabulary of contrastive language	• Composes and writes original myths and legends	• Writes addresses and return addresses on envelopes and postcards	• Writes an account of an event from a simple outline
• Begins to write personal sketches	• Writes puppet plays and vignettes	• Writes short reports	• Writes simple explanations
• Selects and creates specific words to describe emotions	• Writes original stories	• Records telephone messages containing one or more facts	• Uses outline as basis for writing explanation
	• Writes original lyrics for known songs	• Charts information	• Develops and writes a paragraph as a unit with a main idea and supporting facts
	• Creates new names for known things	• Writes simple news articles of one or more sentences	• Begins to expand ideas in written form
		• Fills in various forms, such as library card application and front of test answer sheet	
		• Writes sentences for news items on bulletin board	
		• Writes individual report	

Activities for Fifth Graders in the Domains of Writing

Sensory/Descriptive	Imaginative/Narrative	Practical/Informative	Analytical/Expository
• Creates sensory images through word choices	• Creates and writes rhymes in more than one pattern	• Writes friendly letters of more than one paragraph	• Writes a paragraph account of a sequence of events
• Creates language relating to colors and shades of colors	• Writes original riddles, limericks, chants, and poems	• Writes business letters	• Writes directions with increasing precision in selection of vocabulary
• Creates language relating to sizes and shapes	• Writes haiku, cinquains, and other forms of poetry	• Writes invitations, greetings, acceptances, thank-you notes, and congratulations	• Selects and uses exact words in writing an explanation or description
• Extends use of vocabulary of contrast	• Begins to write ballads	• Takes and records telephone messages	• Uses transition words, phrases, and sentences
• Writes personal sketches	• Begins to write a log	• Writes directions and recipes	• Uses outline as basis for writing
• Begins to write biographies and autobiographies	• Writes simple dialogue	• Records and organizes notes	• Expands ideas
• Identifies, selects, and uses synonyms, antonyms, homonyms, and homographs	• Writes simple short plays and vignettes	• Writes reports based on interviews	• Develops and writes one or more paragraphs as units, each paragraph having a main idea
	• Continues to write original myths and legends	• Writes more than one kind of newspaper article	
	• Writes interpretations of old sayings	• Fills in various forms	
	• Writes original songs	• Writes reports based on reading and on spoken reports by others	
	• Expands known stories	• Writes simple announcements and explanations	
	• Writes original stories		
	• Writes poems about historical events and others based on scientific topics		

Activities for Sixth Graders in the Domains of Writing

Sensory/Descriptive	Imaginative/Narrative	Practical/Informative	Analytical/Expository
• Writes personal sketches • Writes to express feelings and actions • Writes personal essays • Creates sensory images through choice of words • Writes and creates images through use of language comparisons of many kinds of things • Writes factual descriptions in imaginative ways using descriptive and specific language • Writes descriptions of characters • Uses and writes with synonyms, antonyms, homographs, and words with multiple meaning • Creates word pictures through choices of words	• Writes rhymes in a variety of patterns • Increases ability to write original riddles, limericks, chants, and poems • Writes short stories • Writes biographies • Writes an autobiography • Writes various kinds of poetry • Writes ballads • Writes and keeps a diary • Writes and keeps a log • Creates and writes original dialogue • Creates and writes plays and vignettes • Creates and writes original folktales and tall tales • Creates and writes original myths, and legends • Writes conversations • Writes new twists for old sayings • Writes interpretations of figurative language • Writes continuing stories • Writes original scripts for films and filmstrips • Rewrites stories into scripts for films and filmstrips • Writes poetry and stories on historical and scientific topics	• Writes friendly letters using greeting, body, and closing • Writes business letters using proper format • Writes invitations, acceptances, thank-you notes, and letters of congratulations • Writes messages on a postcard • Addresses envelopes and postcards appropriately • Records telephone messages with exact facts • Writes directions, recipes, and steps in making a product • Takes and organizes notes • Makes lists • Writes announcements and explanations • Writes reports based on facts • Writes reports based on spoken reports, interviews, and readings • Writes a variety of news articles • Writes telegrams • Writes comparisons • Writes opinion based on facts • Writes concise titles and captions • Writes simple original commercials for original products or existing products for television time slots • Writes news stories and headlines • Composes original advertisements • Writes weather reports • Writes editorials • Uses reference sources, including bibliographies	• Writes more than one paragraph in an account of an event or experience, a description of a favorite food or sport, or an explanation of how something works • Expands use of transition words, phrases, and sentences in writing an explanation • Uses supporting facts in writing a report • Takes notes, organizes them, and expands them for a report • Uses outline form in writing • Writes opinion supporting a point of view • Writes summaries • Writes comparisons to clarify meaning • Writes contrasts in sentences and paragraphs • Develops ideas in depth

Using Visual Stimuli to Motivate Reluctant Writers and to Foster Descriptive Writing Skills

By Sue Rader Willett
English Teacher, Capistrano Valley High School; and Teacher/Consultant, UCI Writing Project

Motivating reluctant students to write is one of the toughest challenges facing any teacher. Often we blame the problem on previous instructors, poor self-images, television, inadequate funding, boring textbooks, and (sometimes) ourselves. The problem seems to be perennial, but it is not without its solutions. I have found that using concrete visual stimuli in writing assignments seems to motivate and stimulate students to begin writing.

The following lesson on beginning descriptive writing works well with students of wide ranging abilities and grade levels. I have employed it with great success in seventh through twelfth grade English classes, but I foresee no difficulty in adapting it for students in the primary and upper elementary grades.

LESSON: I SEE, I HEAR, I SMELL, I FEEL, I TASTE

Supplies needed: Slide projector, screen, slides of interest to students. (I have used slides of scenic vacation spots, local places of interest, common neighborhood and household scenes, master artworks, and historical sites. Many can be purchased at parks, museums, or through publications such as *Arizona Highways.*[1])

Set the stage: Explain to your students that they will become sensory guides to their classmates, and it is their responsibility to construct vivid images for each other. Emphasize the importance of using an accurate vocabulary that focuses on the senses. To help my students, I

---
[1]*Arizona Highways* is published monthly by the Arizona Department of Transportation, 2039 West Lewis Avenue, Phoenix, AZ 85009.

have planned vocabulary lessons of sensory/descriptive words. For example, I have shown my students a box of 64 crayons to remind them of the variations in shade and intensity of color. They often forget about magenta, teal blue, and chartreuse.

Take a quiet moment to tune the students into their present environment. Have them stop to listen to all the different sounds in the room, feel the temperature, look carefully at the carpet, and so forth. When you feel the class is ready to begin the exercise, turn out the lights and project the first slide on a screen that all can see.

Slide one: Ask for volunteers to describe the scene in front of them as if they were there. One at a time, students will begin to explain what they sense by prefacing their statements with, "I see . . . , I hear . . . , I smell . . . , I feel . . . , I taste . . . ." (You may wish to omit the sense of taste, but do not ignore it completely for later assignments.)

Give immediate positive reinforcement to those who use specific and vivid language to create the scene. Tell them exactly what you find effective: "The word *mahogany* describes accurately the color of the leather saddle . . . I get a strong feeling of the sun warming your shoulders . . . ."

When you and your students believe you are ready to proceed, ask for a few (two to five) imagery guides to continue looking at the screen while the others put their heads on their desks and cover their eyes.

> *Part of writing competence is having a clear concept of the intent for the writing, including audience, and being able to organize in the mode (form) that best fits that intention.*
> NANCY McHUGH

Slide two: Project another slide on the screen, and ask the guides to begin constructing the scene for the other "blind" class members. One by one, the guides tell the others exactly what they see, hear, smell, feel, and taste. It is important to keep the comments quickly paced to increase interest and motivation.

The "blind" students may then ask the guides questions for more specific information: "How close is the tree to the rock? What shade of blue is the sky? What else would I hear?" Stop the students from asking questions when you believe sufficient descriptions have been provided.

All the students may then look up to see the slide. Ask the students if they had imagined the scene as it really appears and, if not, what did they see differently and why? Emphasize the strengths of the descriptions of the student guides but also tactfully suggest how they could have improved their descriptions. This is the natural time to discuss descriptive techniques that lead to effective writing.

You may wish to reinforce the following:

1. Organization, order, unifying factors
   a. Top to bottom and bottom to top
   b. Side to side
   c. Diagonally
   d. Out to focal point or in to focal point
   e. Tracing the light source
   f. Near to far or far to near

2. Word choice
   a. Vividness
   b. Accuracy

3. Comparison and contrast
   a. Metaphor
   b. Simile

4. Originality
   a. Avoiding clichés
   b. Using a fresh approach
   c. Creating an apt mood or impression

5. Full sensory involvement
   a. Sight (shape, light, color, texture)
   b. Sound (pitch, volume, intensity, rate)
   c. Taste (sweet or sour, texture, temperature)
   d. Touch (texture, temperature, weight)
   e. Smell (often linked to taste)

Continue the oral practice until the students are confident with their skills and are ready to stop. (Do not "slide" them to death!)

Begin to write: Ease into the writing practice by assigning students to write individual phrases or sentences rather than to say them aloud to the class. After the majority of the students finish writing their descriptions, encourage them to share their best sentences with the class. Continue to reinforce good techniques.

Variations of this exercise may include clustering or making lists of words or phrases. Homework may involve continuing the writing practice by having students use magazine pictures or snapshots as motivators.

This practice is designed to lead your student writers into developing effective paragraphs and compositions. Longer papers may be developed, with entire paragraphs unified by one of the five senses. The writing may also be integrated into assignments of narration, saturation reporting, journal writing, impression cataloguing, poetry, expository essays, letter writing, speech writing, and so forth.

As you begin to motivate your students to write by using slides and photographs as motivators, you will develop your own techniques to charm that reluctant writer into action. Then, believe it or not, one day you may even hear, "May we do some more of that fun writing today?"

Guided Imagery in the Sensory/Descriptive and Imaginative/Narrative Domains

By Dale Sprowl
English Teacher, Irvine High School,
Irvine Unified School District;
and Teacher/Consultant, UCI Writing Project

Guided imagery, a technique that enables students to tap their creative imagination and visual thinking skills, motivates students to write fluently in the sensory/descriptive and imaginative/narrative domains. "A Walk Through the Forest" is an exercise in guided imagery that I have used with students in a ninth grade basic level class, and it is outlined below. However, the lesson could be adapted to any other grade or ability level. The role of the teacher in this exercise is as a guide to help students create pictures in their minds. Once they have formulated these mental images, it is easy for them to translate the images into descriptive or narrative passages.

A WALK THROUGH THE FOREST

Day 1—Prewriting exercise: Turn off the lights and ask the students to close their eyes and relax. Read the following story slowly, pausing between sentences, to give the students time to develop images. Take 10—15 minutes for this.

> Picture yourself in a forest. You are walking through the forest on a path. As you walk, you see a person. You exchange glances with the person, but then the person leaves. You continue walking and you come to a body of water. You cross the body of water. You begin walking on the path again. Soon, you find a cup. You pick it up, look closely at it, and put it down. You continue walking until the path leads you to a fence. On the other side of the fence, you see a house. You go through the fence and into the house. Inside is a table. Something is on the table. As you are looking at it, you see the person you met in the forest.

As you are relating this story, you may want to add questions such as, "What does the forest smell like?" or "What is the weather like?" or "What is the texture of the water like?" Try not to limit the students' images by using only *he* for the person or by adding a handle to the cup. If it is left open to the student, he or she will be able to create a more vivid picture.

After telling your students the story, turn on the lights and ask them to share what they saw on their walks through the forest. Be sure to ask for specific descriptions of items—such as the cup, the house, the table—and list on the chalkboard the various perceptions your students had. Then ask them to retrace their journey in writing. Allow 20—30 minutes for this exercise.

Day 2—Read three to five papers aloud and ask the class to discuss the techniques the writers used to convey the pictures in their minds. Reinforce sensory details, similes, metaphors, alliteration, or fine word choice. If the students were vague in their writing ("I saw a body of water."), elicit and list on the chalkboard possible bodies of water. Then ask specific questions about size, color, texture, surroundings, and so forth. Have the students reread their drafts and clarify hazy images.

Day 3—Read three to five more stories aloud and discuss them as you did on day 2. Ask the students to extend their stories by adding dialogue. Discuss natural places for dialogue to fit in the story. If necessary, teach dialogue form. Continue writing.

Day 4—Break down into peer response groups. Each person reads his or her paper to the group. Then each person in the group makes three positive comments about how the writer conveyed the images ("I like the way you used detail to . . . ." or "One phrase I liked in your paper was . . . ."), and each person makes one helpful suggestion ("One part that was hard for me to visualize was . . . .").

Rewrite according to the comments. Make sure all items mentioned in the story are described in detail and in sequence.

Day 5—Papers are due. Read three to five papers orally. Discuss vividness of detail, sequence of events, and liter-

ary terms that apply (plot, character, conflict, setting, point of view, and theme).

"A Walk Through the Forest" is just one of many guided imagery exercises that can be used to stimulate fluency and enhance both descriptive and narrative writing skills. Try this particular prewriting experience as a trial case, and then develop your own guided imagery frames to suit the objectives of your class.

Sequencing to Music: The Narrative Domain

By Mike Conlon
English Teacher, San Clemente High School,
Capistrano Unified School District;
and Teacher/Consultant, UCI Writing Project

Whether we approve or not, music has become the "message" from our students' point of view. For them, shopping in the mall, tanning at the beach, riding in a car, working, studying, and even writing have one common element—a constant musical accompaniment. Rather than fight their system, I believe it is both appropriate and essential to tap these airwaves and thus achieve our purpose as instructors and "muses" of writing. Music, I have found, not only unleashes an inner realm of unlimited fantasy but also provides the student with a quasi-meditative audio sensation that allows him or her to focus on the task at hand while quickly discarding any other present or impending distractions.

With this in mind, I set about teaching my students the basic aspects of *sequencing* within the narrative domain of writing by simply reading to them a short story framework (with six sections missing), accompanied by appropriate mood music. With the proper procedure, an adequate sound system, and a dramatic reading of the framework and "prompt" questions, magical things occur on paper. The five-step procedure I have used follows:

- *Step 1.* Inform students that you will be reading a story to them with parts missing, and each of them will be asked to supply the missing segments. Tell them which of the six parts they will be responsible for after they have heard all of the piece read once. They should listen for the missing sections as well as to the suggestions as to what might appear in these spots.

- *Step 2.* With lights out or with the students' eyes closed, start the music, and after the mood of the piece is established, slowly begin reading "The Mysterious Journey" (included below). On arriving at an omitted section, read the prompt-type questions and suggest possibilities for the section. Then allow students time to imagine how they might complete the missing piece. Continue until you are finished.

> *Writing and rewriting are a constant search for what one is saying.*
> JOHN UPDIKE

For this particular writing-to-music exercise, I use Igor Stravinsky's *Le Sacre du Printemps (The Rite of Spring).*

THE MYSTERIOUS JOURNEY

John inched the car along the gravelly road through the fog in search of a place where he could stop and rest and resume his lengthy drive up the coast in the morning. Drowsy-eyed, he continued to direct the car toward the ever-growing light which, seconds before, had pierced through the fog like a star in the dark wilderness. When John reached the crest of the hill, the light that was beckoning him forward now mingled with his headlights and illuminated a house which seemingly drifted in the fog, not 50 feet from where John now got out of the car. As he approached the house, John noticed . . .

(MISSING SECTION ONE—Describe the house and surrounding area. What did John notice? How much of the house could John see through the fog? What was the surrounding area like? Were there trees, swamps, animals, shadows, noises . . . ? What details of the house did John notice as he walked up the path?)

The old wood creaked with each footstep as John ascended the steps toward the guiding porch light. The wind had picked up, blowing the fog silently across the moonlight which shone down on the house. As he reached out to knock on the door, he became aware of his heart pounding, just is it had that late October night when . . .

(MISSING SECTION TWO—Flashback. What happened that October night when John's heart was pounding? Was it at Halloween or some other time? What thoughts of this past event raced through his mind as he knocked on the door?)

The second knock was answered by a feeble, "Come in." John slowly opened the door and moved toward a weaker light flickering from a room through the doorway to the left. John carefully crept over to the doorway and looked in, seeing . . .

(MISSING SECTION THREE—Describe the room. Picture this room. What details could John make out? What type of furniture was there? What type of floor covering? What was on the walls? . . . the ceiling? Did his mind exaggerate any details?)

Within this room sat what appeared to be an elderly lady in a rocking chair, her back to the doorway, seemingly content to stare out her picture window into the drifting fog. As John approached her, he noticed . . .

(MISSING SECTION FOUR—Describe the old lady. How do you picture this old lady, the clothes she was wearing, the texture of her face and hands, the state of mind she seemed to be in as John approached her? Does she make any noises? Does John move closer to get a better look?)

"Good evening, young man," she said, and John . . .

(MISSING SECTION FIVE—Dialogue and action. What did John do? Why did he enter the house in the first place? What was his purpose? Do they speak? What surprises occur? Something did happen to cause John to react the way he did . . .)

He stumbled down the walkway to his car. He veered out onto the main road, racing toward the city nearly two hours away. He thought ahead to the . . .

(MISSING SECTION SIX—Conclusive action. What was he thinking ahead to? Why was he making the drive in the first place? Is there someone or something awaiting him? Finally, what happens to John on that foggy road, racing toward the city? Something did happen, because . . .)

. . . They had not been expecting him to arrive anyway.

- *Step 3.* When you are finished reading, distribute to each student the framework and prompt question sheet, with his or her specific section marked for completion. Then reread the entire piece, with each student brainstorming when his or her particular section arrives.

- *Step 4.* Divide students into groups, with at least two groups for each missing section (three maximum), such as groups 1A, 1B, 2A, 2B, and so forth. The task of the group is to combine the ideas of the individual members into a unified piece of between one-half and one page in length, which connects the frame for the story smoothly and appropriately.

- *Step 5.* A group leader, spokesperson, secretary, or volunteer is identified and given the task of reading the group selection from his or her desk or at the front of the class (with teacher and five other orators, it is less threatening). The music is replayed, and the teacher resumes narration; then the students supply the missing pieces—first the "A" groups, then the "B" groups.

The most effective means of teaching sequencing for me is to type up all of the missing sections submitted by the groups and then to distribute copies to the class. We then go through the framework, section by section, and determine which entry works best and why. Obviously, the choices for sections one and two will affect the later selections. The creation of continuity is one of the purposes of the exercise.

More often than not, frustrated or inspired students relish the opportunity to write a missing section (sometimes all sections) on their own and to develop a true cohesiveness in the piece. I offer this opportunity as extra credit.

After completing another similar assignment, including a framework, prompt-type questions, and music, the students are soon able to construct their own stories without a framework. They need only be provided with evocative music and a hypothetical situation to start; for example, *La Mer* by Claude Debussy or music by a popular musical group and the hypothetical situation of a surfer at the beach at dawn.

Finally, as a project, students are invited to choose their own music and submit an accompanying scenario of setting and action that corresponds to the variations in the music.

How to Carve a Pumpkin— A Writing Exercise in the Practical/Informative Domain

By Michael Carr
Teacher, Los Alamitos Elementary School,
Los Alamitos Unified School District;
and Teacher/Consultant, UCI Writing Project

Holidays can serve as a springboard to a wealth of activities in all of the domains of writing. In my classroom (kindergarten and grade one), Halloween provides a great opportunity to introduce practical/informative writing in which the objective is to present information clearly, systematically, and sequentially.

For this lesson, I brought to class two pumpkins and a knife and proceeded to discuss "How to Carve a

Pumpkin" with my 25 children. I asked the class what we needed to do first and, after much discussion, we decided we needed a pumpkin. Since most of my class consists of nonreaders, we used symbols to represent the words and later added the words. Following their directions, I put the sequence given below on the chalkboard:

1. Get a
2. Get a [saw] to draw with
3. Draw [triangles]
4. Draw a [triangle]
5. Draw a [mouth]
6. Get a [knife]
7. Cut out a [lid]
8. Take out the [seeds]
9. Cut out the [triangles]
10. Cut out a [triangle]
11. Cut out a [mouth]
12. Put on the [lid]
13. Cook the [seeds] [1]
14. Happy Halloween!

Then, to verify the accurateness of our sequence, I demonstrated each step on our class pumpkin.

After printing the process on the chalkboard and carving a model Halloween pumpkin, I transferred the data to packets of 14 pages of ditto masters—one for each step—leaving room for the children to draw pictures to illustrate the directions. When all the children had completed their booklets, they were able to follow their own directions and carve a pumpkin at home.

The main objective for me in this writing exercise was to give the children a problem-solving activity that involved group discussion, sequencing, clarity, and fun! In addition, they learned the words that corresponded to their pumpkin-carving symbols.

[1]Recipe for parents:
1. Wash and salt seeds.
2. Cook for an hour to an hour and a half at 250° F.
3. Turn seeds over (at halfway point).

How to Do "How To"

By Greta Nagel
Teacher, Rio Vista Elementary School,
Placentia Unified School District;
and Teacher/Consultant, UCI Writing Project

Students in our classes ride across campus on horses, set up model trains that whiz around the classroom, encourage dogs to do tricks, and cast trout flies across the basketball court. They cook and serve fancy hors d'oeuvres, set up mock theaters and roller coaster rides, and toss bowling balls across the carpet. They do these and many more things as part of the "How To" project.

"How To" is a unit of research and practical/informative written/oral work that is based on the students' hobbies. Each student does work that is related to his or her favorite hobby during eight to ten weeks of language class time. The project has four phases: (1) the basic written report; (2) the oral report and hobby fair; (3) extra written activities; and (4) follow-up activities.

My colleague Terry Kristiansen and I designed the "How To" activities in 1973 for students in grades four through eight. That year, the project won the "Promising Practices Award" that was offered by our school district, the Placentia Unified School District. Over the years, students have worked on "How To" in our classes and in classes of other district teachers who like the idea. Former students return years later and talk about the hard work and the fun that they had. High school teachers have mentioned that they are able to adapt "How To" ideas to their students' needs. It has been, indeed, a promising practice.

Tips on the "How To" Project

In order for the activities of the lengthy project to be effective, we believe these tips should help:

1. Work on the unit during a time when students have already had some introduction to research tasks and to various types of writing. Otherwise, plan to do a great amount of intermittent modeling and practice as you proceed through the activities.

2. At least two weeks prior to starting the unit, announce that each student needs to choose a hobby. (Note: We have always allowed students to think of sports as a hobby.) Not only does this allow students to form a mind-set, but it also permits you to check on the appropriateness of the topic and the availability of the materials. A topic like "How to Collect Smurfs" is difficult to research and hard to demonstrate. It is probably best left alone. A topic like "How to Collect

Baseball Cards" can, on the other hand, be researched well if prior contacts are made with stores and organizations. Giving a two-week notice can also provide students with time to locate other people who practice the hobby and who can serve as valuable research aides.

3. We always provide at least one piece of research material for each student. He or she must obtain two or more additional resources. The public libraries (children's sections) have been very accommodating in lending groups of books on special teacher loans, mainly because the choices are so varied and the supply of any one type of book will not be exhausted.

4. Plan to model activities for your students; show clearly the expectations that you have for their work. Terry Kristiansen and I share the hobby of cross-country skiing. We both brought in our outfits and equipment, and we demonstrated how we would write and do the various activities related to our hobby. We also designed posters (related to x-c skiing) that helped remind students of the basic sections of the report. We used these posters to decorate the classroom walls during the duration of "How To" work.

5. Do not forget to ask students whether or not you may save drafts of their work, samples of both the good and the average. They serve as excellent models for future classes.

6. Another tip is to set up a workable management system for handling the large volume of rough and final drafts that will come your way. Evaluate as you go along; do not wait until the end of the project. The threat of misplacing papers led me to set up a system of mailing envelopes. One envelope per activity is labeled and has a class list grid stapled to the front. Papers are checked in, and scores are recorded on the fronts of the envelopes, not in a separate grade book. At the end of the unit, I glue two sheets together, matching class list entries, and I have a complete permanent record.

7. A final tip: Keep a camera handy. The nature of this project makes it highly motivating; it is tied to students' senses of relevancy. They are proud to share their expertise in subjects usually not touched by the school's curriculum, and they are interested in one another's hobbies. They also enjoy bringing in their equipment and products for their oral reports and for the hobby fair. Snapshots and slides enhance those special moments—the boy with his king snake wrapped around his neck, the girl rollerskating backward across the classroom linoleum, the boy on his dirt bike by the chalkboard. Admittedly, excitement about the "fun" times helps students to plow through the great amount of writing. A spoonful of sugar . . . .

The Written Report

The first phase of the project, the written report, requires skills in research, notetaking, outlining, and the writing of rough and final drafts. There are six segments in the written report. For fifth and sixth graders, the usual lengths produced have been:

1. *History*—one or two handwritten pages: a narrative.

2. *Steps*—five to ten pages: Lists and drawings form just a part of a narrative piece that explains in great detail how to learn and do the hobby.

3. *Famous person*—one or two pages: a narrative about a person or animal that is related to the hobby. Some students have written about persons with an obvious tie-in to their hobby: Charles Schulz, Jesse Owens, Ringo Starr, and Margaret Bourke-White (photography). Others have used persons with an indirect relationship: Benjamin Franklin (philatelist), Teddy Roosevelt (stuffed animals), and Elizabeth Taylor (horses). Research strategies have sometimes included writing to famous people.

4. *Powers and pitfalls*—one or two pages: a narrative or a sentence chart that notes the good aspects and rewards of the hobby as opposed to the things that can go wrong, the dangers, and the costs. In this segment the student writer explains how to avoid or overcome the pitfalls.

5. *Interesting experience*—one or two pages: a personal account of an experience with the hobby, such as "The First Time I Rode Colossus," "My First Tornado," "The Day I Won the Third Grade Art Contest," or "A Bad Luck Day Trading Baseball Cards."

6. *Interview*—two to five (or more) pages following a narrative, then question and answer format (a la "Q & A" in the *Los Angeles Times's* magazine, *Home*): Students seek face-to-face contacts with neighbors, shop owners, or local instructors. Telephone contacts are allowed when it is not possible for the students to meet a "local authority." Students often use tape recorders but are nevertheless expected to do written versions.

Oral Report and Hobby Fair

Once the written reports are completed, oral reports are scheduled and students are allowed 15-minute time slots in which to tell about and demonstrate their hobbies. We have their fellow students complete evaluation score cards at the end of each report, noting points for each of the segments: (1) catchy opening;

(2) how to; (3) audiovisuals; (4) eye contact; (5) loudness; and (6) appropriate time. Each speaker is expected to start with a "catchy" opening. Some examples are:

"I have a real catchy hobby." (fishing)
"This hobby will keep you in stitches." (sewing)
"My hobby is a real hit." (baseball)

Mini-demonstrations are also required. Students show how to hinge stamps for album placement, to tie flies, and to do knots for macrame pieces. They also show how to do ski turns, to fix a bicycle chain, and to sink a difficult putt.

When the class finishes giving oral reports, we hold a hobby fair and invite parents and other students to come. All class members set up booths where they display equipment and give minitalks to passersby during "milling" time. Several chosen speakers give their full oral reports at designated times. (Peer selection of honored speakers seems to work well.) If the room is large, several speakers may talk at once to their own audiences clustered near them. It is possible for two, or even three, shifts of speakers to talk, with their report times alternated with milling time for fair visitors. All students display their written reports.

Extra Written Activities

The extra activities are all creative in nature. Students enjoy these tasks and come up with delightful results. They write new words to old tunes ("Art of My Heart"). Using magazine advertisements, they practice the ploys of advertising copy and format ("Strong, adventuresome people collect stamps."). With graphs and lists, students present and analyze the results of popularity surveys and questionnaires ("From these five choices, more people selected rollerskating."). Complete with costumes and props, students entice new hobbyists from their "television studio" ("You'll just love learning to cook!"). With poems, often humorous, they proclaim positive and negative aspects of hobbies ("Breathing, panting, gasping along"). Using home movies, the students show the details of "How To" ("Here's my dad guarding our basketball net."). Through an original piano solo, a student musician expresses the joy of playing the piano.

Follow-up Activities as Final Phase

Once the students' notebooks are compiled, one last phase of the project is possible. The follow-up activities are evaluative and analytical tasks that require the students to take a close look at the practical/informative "How To" experience. As they look back, students are pleased to have polished their skills in oral/written expression as they polished their skills with their hobbies.

Teaching Practical/Informative Writing Through Novels

By Elizabeth Williams Reeves
Teacher, Pine Middle School,
Los Alamitos Unified School District;
and Teacher/Consultant, UCI Writing Project

Novels for adolescents provide excellent vehicles for teaching writing in a variety of domains. Characterizations and settings lend themselves to sensory/descriptive writing; story plot and embellishments and adaptations of a plot are appropriate for imaginative/narrative writing; analyses of characters and authors' style and content are suitable for analytical/expository writing. Because it is often viewed as a somewhat mundane, uncreative domain, practical/informative writing is frequently ignored. But the content of a novel often provides motivational material for practical/informative writing.

One practical/informative lesson that I have particularly enjoyed is based on a portion of *The Hobbit* that describes a barrel ride. In it, Bilbo, the hobbit, and his dwarf friends ride down a river in barrels in an attempt to escape from the Wood-elves:

> . . . first one barrel and then another rumbled to the dark opening and was pushed over into the cold water some feet below. Some were barrels really empty, some were tubs neatly packed with a dwarf each; but down they all went, one after another, with many a clash and a bump, thudding on top of ones below, smacking into the water, jostling against the walls of the tunnel, knocking into one another, and bobbing away down the current.[1]

After students have read the complete section of *The Hobbit* in which this account appears, I ask them to write practical/informative instructions to a novice on how to go barrel riding. During prewriting, discussion questions should focus on the sequence of steps needed to ride in a barrel. For example, I ask the students to consider what would be the first thing to tell a person who is about to go barrel riding—then the second, the third, and so forth. I stress that their instructions must be clear and well-organized so that the reader can follow them easily.

Practical/informative writing developed through the use of novels can be most inventive. An example of a fifth grader's description of the barrel ride follows:

> If you are going to ride a barrel down a river, you must take certain steps. First, find a barrel big enough

for you. Empty out contents, if any. Then wash the smell out. Lift or cut the lid off the barrel. Then cut air holes on top of the barrel—about seven holes an inch wide. Now, get inside the barrel. Have someone help you get packed with straw or anything soft. Brace yourself. You might get bumped a little. Put the lid back on. Someone will push you off into a river or stream. Don't panic. Stay calm. Don't rock too much, and keep your air holes up. Last, but not least, wait for someone to get you out.

This barrel riding exercise not only reinforces the sequencing skills necessary for "how to" writing but also enhances critical thinking ability. In order to write precise barrel riding instructions, the students must read and evaluate the text carefully, determine which details are essential, organize those details or steps, and compose an account that incorporates what they know of barrel riding with what they surmise a rider would need to know. In addition, because they are writing for a person who is about to embark on a barrel ride, their sense of audience is strengthened.

Novels for adolescents provide excellent vehicles for teaching writing in a variety of domains.
ELIZABETH WILLIAMS REEVES

The Bumper Sticker Approach to the Topic Sentence for Opinion Writing

By Trudy J. Beck
English Teacher, El Toro High School,
Saddleback Valley Unified School District;
and Teacher/Consultant, UCI Writing Project

In one of those do-or-die attempts to introduce the topic sentence and to retain my own sense of humor in the process, I decided to try using bumper stickers as a point of departure for the topic sentence in an opinion paragraph. I almost discarded the notion because of the potential for obscenity, but the advantages seemed to outweigh the possible problem, so I gave it a trial run. Of course, I had to revise and reorganize my plan after that first try, but it was worth the risk. The bumper sticker approach to the topic sentence for opinion writing works.

I use several variations of this lesson. The two I offer here are the foundation lessons, and their sequencing is important. Phase I does not involve any

---

[1]From *The Hobbit* (p. 177) by J. R. R. Tolkien. Copyright © 1966 by J. R. R. Tolkien. Reprinted by permission of Houghton Mifflin Company.

actual writing of sayings, just responding to the samples. In Phase II students write their own bumper stickers.

First of all, I have students bring to class examples of bumper stickers or slogans and aphorisms. These must meet my rules for what is or is not acceptable. Anything obscene or even cutely obscene is prohibited, and each saying must offer an opinion in sentence form or a form easily converted to a sentence. I begin the lesson by walking around the classroom and reading some of the bumper stickers aloud. This gives me a chance to select examples of some of the ingredients I want to discuss. I point out the following: tone, audience, ambiguity, purpose, attitude, audience response, direction, theme, point of view, and the different types of development to which the various topics and statements lend themselves.

Using their own samples, students then try to anticipate the questions that their sayings might evoke from an audience. The "No nukes is good nukes" sticker might elicit these questions:

What does *nukes* mean?
Why the play on words with *nukes* and *news*?
Why shouldn't we have nuclear weapons?
Why shouldn't we use nuclear energy?
What would nuclear disaster mean to me?

After the students have composed their questions, I collect the bumper stickers, and I make certain that the owner's name is on the back of each sticker. (Use index cards if stickers are not available.) I then redistribute the stickers to other students and ask them to write one paragraph in support of the position indicated by the new saying. Writing may be either serious or humorous. I usually time the writing and allow 15—20 minutes for the exercise.

At this point, I divide the class into groups of four and ask them to compare each of their paragraphs in support of a particular slogan with the questions developed by the student who brought in that sticker. As a group, they decide whether the questions have been adequately answered, whether those not covered need to be covered, and whether the paragraphs are still effective in spite of having neglected to answer the questions written by the original contributor. (This does happen occasionally. But it is all right, and it might just signal a different problem that may need your attention.) The authors record comments and suggestions about their paragraphs, make suitable corrections, and rewrite.

In Phase II the bumper stickers can be used to reinforce the writing of concise topic sentences. The students select a controversy or other suitable topic for creating their own sayings. I recommend prewriting activities here, specifically modeling and group writing first. We discuss puns, deliberate ambiguity, the double

entendre, malapropisms, and spoonerisms. I emphasize the necessity of getting tone, audience, purpose, attitude, and topic into a brief, on-target statement that is not mechanical.

Once the students begin writing their own bumper stickers, I encourage them to share the sayings with their neighbors. When the statements are smooth enough, the students then write accompanying paragraphs of support. Student partners identify the unanswered questions that they believe need to be addressed, and the paragraphs are rewritten. We then evaluate the finished products via a holistic read-around. (See the section of this book entitled "Read-Around Groups for Sharing/Responding" for a discussion of this technique.) The best examples are placed on the wall of the classroom. Because I have a window that faces the hall, each day one bumper sticker and its supporting paragraph are displayed in the window for the students to read as they pass by.

My greatest satisfaction in using the bumper sticker approach comes from the fact that this method gives focus and direction to topic sentences and, in turn, to the paragraphs that accompany them. Besides, it is fun. This lesson is not intimidating, yet it can be used to span a wide range of abilities, interests, and motivational levels. It keeps the students' interest high and promotes good student interaction. It is clear, to the point, and easy to model—but challenging. This is a nice way to provide the opportunity for the student who is so inclined to "test the water" in writing humor without making humor a major focal point of the assignment. Finally, I have witnessed an increased retention of the skills in writing topic sentences and a change in the quality of topic sentences because, by its very nature, the bumper sticker approach limits the excess verbiage that often accompanies unskilled opinion writing.

Welcome to the New World!

By Laurie Opfell

Former English Teacher, Irvine High School; Teaching Assistant, English Department, University of Kentucky; and Teacher/Consultant, UCI Writing Project

I have had remarkable success in my eighth grade English class with my "Welcome to the New World" assignment, which is outlined below. This project taps each of the four domains of writing, reinforces peer group interaction, and integrates writing, speaking, and drawing activities. It also enables me to introduce relevant works of literature, such as Jonathan Swift's *Gulliver's Travels*, William Golding's *Lord of the Flies*, and so forth. The enthusiasm generated by the assignment has been extremely high, and the level of cooperation in the classroom has improved greatly. I give my students the following instructions for the lesson:

Welcome to the New World. In the next few weeks you will be involved in creating your own utopia or "imaginary or ideal world." You will be graded on the completeness of two individual assignments, all group assignments, and the quality of your work. However, the most important aspect of the grade will be how you combine imagination, creativity, and innovation with the basic requirements. The objective of the project is for you to clarify and use your values, wishes, ideals, knowledge, and talents to create a personal and group statement about what you want and hope for in life.

The assignments described below are for each person in the group to do. They will be assigned over many days:

Assignment 1

A. Although you are extremely wealthy, you and your friends are tired of the rat race and decide to get away. You decide to buy an island, but before seeing the real estate agent you each:
   1. Write down a preferred location.
   2. List four to six things you want your island to include; for example, beaches, mountains, and so forth.

B. Now, compare your lists and decide on a group location and a list that includes everyone's desired features.

C. You are now ready to see your agent. She has just the place and shows you some slides.
   1. Sketch out a few practice shapes for a map of your island, decide on one (or a combination), and draw the outline on a large sheet of paper.
   2. Now divide your island into equal portions so each group member has a section.

3. Agree on a symbol for each of the features on your group's list; for example, mountains ⋀⋀, lakes ﹏, beaches ⌒⌒, and so forth. Each person is responsible for filling in his or her section with the features that are appealing.
4. Be sure you also include a scale of miles, directions, symbols for roads, cities (if there are any), rivers, and so forth.
5. Decide how all major services (mechanics, food supply, health care, and so forth) will be handled, and set up a location for them.

Now, go back over what you have noted and write it into a well-organized, descriptive one to one and one-half page piece. Share it with at least two people in your group, and get some suggestions for revision before you write your final draft.

> *Have something to say, and say it as clearly as you can. That is the only secret of style.*
> MATTHEW ARNOLD

Assignment 2

A. You now need to decide on the values that will be the controlling ideals of your island's government. Make a list:
   1. Helpfulness?
   2. Equal power?
   3. Freedom?
   4.
   5.
   6.
   7.

B. Now, share your list with your group members. As you read it to them, explain why you think each item is important. Make a group list of everything you all agree on.

Assignment 3

Since you have unlimited money, you need to start thinking about the home you will build. Take about 15 minutes to brainstorm, and then start writing about your ideal home. What would it look like? How many rooms? What type of furniture? Colors? Building materials? View? Landscaping?

Now, go back over what you have sketched and write it into a well-organized, descriptive one to one and one-half page piece. Share it with at least two people in your group, and get some suggestions for revision before you write your final draft.

The next assignments are individual. You must select any two of the options listed below, all of which involve some critical thinking and creative writing:

1. Constitution. Write up your group's values or rules of living into some sort of document. (Look at the U.S. Bill of Rights for an example.) Make it beautiful, official looking, and one to one and one-half pages long. Include a statement of your philosophy.

2. *Architecture.* What types of design are likely to be seen on your island? Do they stand out? Blend in with the environment? Are they energy self-sufficient? Beautiful? Modern? Old fashioned? Draw four or five different buildings, and write a paragraph explaining each structure's best features.

> *Now the first merit which attracts in the pages of a good writer is the apt choice and contrast of the words employed.*
> ROBERT LOUIS STEVENSON

3. *Clothing.* How do people dress on your island? Design four or five possible outfits that adapt to the environment. Make them as crazy, practical, or comfortable as you want. Draw a picture of each one and write a paragraph explaining it.

4. *Foods.* What are the island's staples? Interview all persons and get a list of their ten favorite foods. Design a restaurant menu that features everybody's favorite foods. Describe the foods and illustrate the menu with magazine pictures. (You might want to think up some original specialties.)

5. *Recreation.* What are the major forms of recreation? Interview all persons and find out what they want included. Then design a park that includes each item. Try to come up with at least three original sports or ideas that can be enjoyed only on your island. Illustrate and explain the new sports, and draw a picture of the park on a separate sheet of construction paper.

6. *Flora.* Your island is the home of many different plants, but in addition to the usual varieties, you have several exotic types of trees and flowers. Illustrate and describe three of them, and also include your island's environmental protection policy.

7. *Fauna.* Your island includes some well-known animals as well as a few that have yet to be discovered. Describe four or five of these rare species and write a paragraph explaining each one.

8. *Travel agent.* You are in charge of designing a brochure that advertises your island. Include a small map that mentions important or beautiful places, and add photographs from magazines accompanied by flowing descriptions. Make it the ⬚⬚⬚ fold-out kind. Neatness and layout are very important.

9. *Culture director.* What do the people on your island do to improve their lives? Interview the members of your group to discover their educational and artistic pursuits. Design and illustrate a cultural center and make a program of activities; for example, theater, movies, music, mime, computers, science, and so forth.

10. *Production manager.* On the final day of the project, you will present your island to the rest of the class. There will be only one chance to do this, so only responsible persons need apply. You will need:
    a. A specific knowledge of all important aspects of the island
    b. Good speaking ability
    c. Slides or visuals to use for illustrations
    d. Two or three music selections to play as background music

    Write a five to ten minute presentation that coordinates all of the above. Consult the clothes designer and wear a suggested outfit. You will be graded on your organization and how well you capture our interest.

11. *Editor.* The group grade depends on you because you will compile all of the individual articles into a guide to your island. Proofread the articles for errors in correctness. Everyone should hand his or her rough draft in to you. Underline spelling, punctuation, and grammatical errors. Pay special attention to sentence structure. If you have any doubts about fragments or run-on sentences, consult with me or a parent. Return the edited drafts to their authors for correction. Final drafts must be written neatly in ink or typed and must be done on your own time. As the editor, you are in charge of collecting the articles, compiling all of the them in a folder, and preparing a table of contents.

Congratulations on the creation of your own personal utopia.

Exploring the New Domains with an Extraterrestrial

By Todd Huck
Teacher, Thurston Middle School,
Laguna Beach Unified School District;
and Codirector, UCI Writing Project

For several years now students in my classes have been sharpening their sensory/descriptive skills by creating vivid, precise word pictures of outer space creatures. As part of the assignment, they have shared their otherworldly visions with their classmates, who have provided feedback, both in words and in pictures, as to the clarity and precision of their depictions. The writers, in turn, have used the feedback to tighten and clarify their written descriptions. It has proved to be one of those no-lose assignments. The students enjoy both the writing and the artwork involved. (Never once has a student said to me, "I'm sorry. I just can't write about a space creature.") I have been happy not only because the students have responded well to the assignment but also because it has addressed an important writing issue on my instructional agenda: the need for students to revise their papers for greater specificity and clarity. Nonetheless, after a summer stint at the University of California Irvine (UCI) Writing Project, I realized the assignment had other possibilities: The creation of an extraterrestrial led very naturally to writing in domains other than the sensory/descriptive, and its value as a subject for writing could be extended and enriched.

The Original Assignment

Here is a brief overview of the original sensory/descriptive assignment. Then I will suggest how it might lead to writing in the other domains.

Designing Your Own Extraterrestrial

Prewriting

1. Students define *extraterrestrial.* Can they think of other words that have the same root? Of other names for extraterrestrials?

2. Cluster on the chalkboard the names of all the outer space creatures students can think of from films, books, and television.

3. Ask students to invent categories for some of the creatures clustered on the chalkboard. For example, they might say that some of them are robots, some look like humans, or that some are good while others are evil.

4. Give them these categories suggested by a professor who has taken hundreds of phone calls from people who think they have seen outer space creatures:

   Human (indistinguishable from humans)
   Humanoid (having body parts analogous to humans)
   Animalistic
   Robotic
   Exotic (having bizarre anatomical features)
   Apparitional (ghostlike)

   See how many of the creatures in the group cluster they can fit into one of these categories.

5. Cluster on the chalkboard the features of one well-known extraterrestrial, such as E.T. Press them for precise details on size, shapes, colors, textures, and proportions. (For suggestions on clustering, see the "Prewriting" section of this book.)

6. Have the class members create a creature on the chalkboard. As they call out the creature's features, you draw them on the chalkboard. Make students be specific in their oral language as to the size, shape, number, and proportion of features they suggest.

7. Having discussed and described a variety of extraterrestrials, tell students that they are now going to visualize an alien that no one has ever seen before.

8. Take them through the following guided imagery:

   GUIDED IMAGERY.
   Close your eyes. Imagine that it is a cool, clear night. The stars burn brightly in the sky, and you are in a quiet, beautiful setting. It might be at the beach, in the mountains, or in the desert. Picture that setting. You are

there with friends or family, but at this moment you have decided to be alone; and you have gone for a walk away from the group. As you walk, you realize that it has been some time since you have been able to hear the distant voices of your friends and family. You pause for a moment to enjoy the still beauty of the night. Suddenly, you hear a sound. What is it? What does it sound like? You walk around a huge rock, and there you see it—an extraterrestrial. You are surprisingly calm and unafraid. The creature seems interested in you, and it is likewise calm and friendly. You have at least a full minute to study the creature.

- What does it look like?
- What kind of an extraterrestrial is it?
- What is its size? Shape? Weight? Coloration?
- What type of body covering does it have?
- Does its body have a variety of textures?
- What kind of limbs or appendages does it have? How many?
- How does it move? By what means does it move?
- Can it take in food? How?
- Does it make a noise? What kind of noise? How does it make this noise?
- Does it have any particular smell?
- Does it have a head?
- Does it have eyes?
- A smelling apparatus (a nose)?
- Auditory adaptions (ears)?
- Does it have any extrasensory capabilities?

After you have had a good look at it, it turns away and vanishes into the night! You realize that since you are the only one who has seen this creature, you are the only one who can describe it.

9. Cluster the features of your creature.

Prompt. Describe the extraterrestrial you encountered in as much specific, vivid detail as possible. Your description should be so clear and detailed that a classmate can draw a reasonably accurate picture of your creature just from reading your description.

Writing and Drawing. Students use their clusters to write descriptions of their creatures. When they have finished, each should draw a picture of the imagined creature. If they add features to the drawing that are not in the written sketch, they must also add them to the writing.

Sharing

1. After putting their drawings away, students exchange their written descriptions with peer partners.
2. Peer partners read the descriptions they have received.
3. Each peer partner then writes on a blank piece of paper a positive comment about some feature of the piece she or he has just read.
4. On the other side of the blank piece of paper, each peer partner will make a drawing of the creature she or he has read about, basing it as closely as possible on the written description.
5. Peer partners return to the writers the original pieces of writing accompanied by their comments and their drawings.
6. Writers take out their sketches and compare them and their writings with the sketches from their peer partners.
7. The writers determine where their partner's sketch differs from theirs or does not portray the creature as they saw it. They go back to their text and determine where and how to make their text clearer and more specific.

> **To use language, as language, is to be human; to use it with kindness, grace, and dignity is to be humane.**
> ALBERT UPTON

Revising. Revision takes place based on the pictorial and written feedback the writer has received and analyzed. Writers make the additions, deletions, substitutions, and rearrangements necessary to ensure that their pieces are more specific, vivid, and precise.

Editing. Students will edit their papers for the conventions of English which the teacher values and has taught for this assignment.

Evaluating. In part your evaluation of the piece should be based on the number of clear, vivid details the writer has provided. You may also wish to consider other elements that you may have taught, such as the creation of details that appeal to other senses, logical organization, and the use of the conventions of standard English.

Postwriting. Student writings and drawings make great classroom displays.

Springboard for Other Writing

Once students have completed the sensory description of the extraterrestrial, this assignment may profitably serve as a springboard for other types of writing. Here are some suggestions for prompts that enrich the extraterrestrial experience and extend it into other domains:

Sensory/Descriptive. Describe the experience with the extraterrestrial from the point of view of the creature itself. Write a sensory description of yourself (the terrestrial) as the extraterrestrial sees you. Remember, an extraterrestrial may perceive things about you that you do not see (or smell, hear, taste, or touch).

Imaginative/Narrative. The opportunities for storytelling about this creature are endless. Here are just a few suggestions:

- Have the creature tell the story of what life is like on its own planet.
- Write a monologue from the point of view of the extraterrestrial in which you tell why the creature came to earth. You might also tell of the journey itself and relate at least two specific incidents that happened along the way. Likewise, you might have the creature explain when and why it intends to leave the earth, where it is going next, and what it expects to encounter.
- Write a diary of the creature's stay here on earth.
- Tell the story of how you helped the extraterrestrial get out of a difficult situation here on earth, or of how the extraterrestrial helped you.

Practical/Informative. Analyze three of your creature's basic needs (food, rest, an occasional back rub to keep its heart beating, and so forth). Design a step-by-step informative guide in list form for the care and feeding of your extraterrestrial. Present the steps in logical, sequential order; and describe all the special equipment and material needed for the proper care of your creature.

Write a letter to your mother or father in which you try to persuade your parent to let you keep the extraterrestrial.

Analytical/Expository. From the point of view of the extraterrestrial, write a report to the creatures on your planet in which you analyze and draw conclusions about some feature you have observed here on earth (cars, telephones, human clothing, and so forth). Your report can follow simple expository form: introduction, body, and conclusion.

In expository form write a "scientific" paper which analyzes and draws conclusions about the functions of three anatomical or behavioral features of your extraterrestrial.

Again, in a scientific paper, speculate about how some of your creature's physical features were geared or adapted to the environment on the creature's home planet. What characteristics of the environment helped shape the features you see in your creature?

Exploring the domains with an extraterrestrial can be a profitable, entertaining, and broadening experience for students. Generating extended writing assignments focused on a central topic, the extraterrestrial, will allow students to concentrate on how various domains of writing differ in form, construction, and organization. Once these skills are practiced and internalized, students should be able to develop and elaborate on ideas related to any central subject.

Writing the Saturation Report

Using Fictional Techniques for Nonfiction Writing

By Ruby Bernstein
English Teacher, Northgate High School,
Mt. Diablo Unified School District;
and Teacher/Consultant, Bay Area Writing Project

By using saturation reporting, you can encourage students to write about real events, people, places, and new experiences that they can observe firsthand. When you employ this technique, you ask your students to make all the sophisticated choices professional writers make: which points of view to use; which details and dialogue to include; which research, if any, to pursue; and, finally, how to structure the nonfiction experience.

Tom Wolfe, contemporary essayist, coined the term "new journalism" (saturation reporting) when he discovered in the 1960s that newspaper and magazine nonfiction journalists had borrowed fiction writers' techniques for preparing their feature stories. Today, examples of new journalism can be collected from the daily press, *The New Yorker,* Sunday magazine sections of major newspapers, and monthly magazines.

Giving students opportunities to practice observing, interviewing, separating fact from opinion, and using the library will result in better saturation reporting when the major assignment is made. These prewriting activities are particularly helpful in sharpening the students' focus in their writing. It is also helpful to have them brainstorm and ask lots of questions before they leave the classroom to carry out their prewriting activities, and it is equally helpful to have them share their experiences and pieces of their reports after they have made their observations or conducted their interviews.

My own experience with saturation reporting occurred several years ago at a summer writing class for teachers at the University of California, Berkeley, taught by Jim Gray, Director of the Bay Area Writing Project. I had been making daily trips to a weight-loss clinic, one of those advertised in the daily newspaper. The 30-day experience lent itself to saturation reporting, especially since I had reservations about the weight-reduction method, and my intent was to be a modern-day muckraker.

My purposes for writing, my underlying theses, were: (1) to show that taking shots for weight loss was harmful to one's health; (2) to affirm that this particular clinic was directed by professionals with questionable credentials; and (3) to point out to my readers that the public generally wants quick solutions to

problems, such as obesity, which may have taken years to develop.

After I had brainstormed my ideas for the paper with my six-member writing group, my paper's scenario took the shape shown in Figure 23.

The scenes surrounding my experiences with the weight-loss clinic, which were described separately, were put in final order, as indicated by the letters A—G in Figure 23. Hopefully, the total effect of this collage of scenes achieved my purposes.

After this experience with saturation reporting, I enthusiastically brought the assignment to my class. In my junior/senior composition elective course, which is one semester long, the saturation report became the major assignment, culminating the first quarter's work. Among the topics my students chose to saturate themselves with were: revisiting junior high school, fast-food jobs, the senior prom ritual, department store dressing room gossip, cruising the Main, the school orchestra's bus trip to Modesto, riding on Bay Area Rapid Transit, bartending at a publisher's cocktail party, the local hangout after a football game, the final week of rehearsals for a community play. The possibilities for writing were limited only by time and sometimes transportation.

Provided below is a list of the features of a saturation report that I share with my students before they select a topic:

SATURATION REPORTING

Features—A "saturation" report involves:

1. Writing about some place, some group, or some individual that you know well or can get to know well firsthand. You "saturate" yourself with your subject.

2. Writing a nonfiction article using fictional techniques. There will be scenes, characters and characterizations, dialogue, and a subtle, rather than overt, statement.

3. The appeal of information and facts. You are writing nonfiction, and the reader will want to "know" about your subject; in short, be sensitive to this thirst for facts on the part of your reader.

4. Author identification. Your point of view can be quite flexible. You can be an active participant in the action; you can remove yourself; or you can come in and then move out.

5. Microcosm. You are focusing on some particular subject, but in so doing you are saying something more. As you capture an isolated segment of today's world, you say something about the total world.

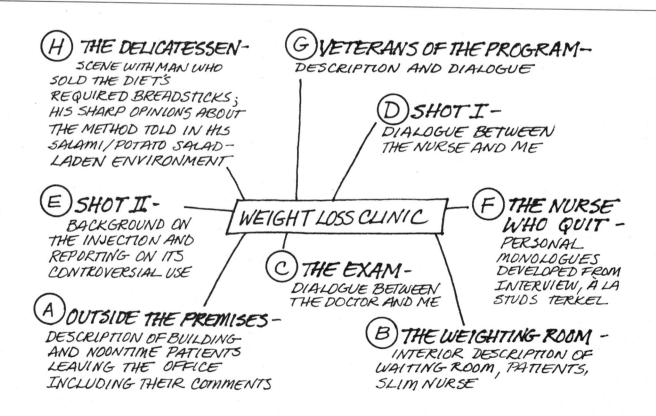

Fig. 23 Brainstorming of Observations for Saturation Reporting

6. Implication. Much of what you attempt to "say" in your article (because of your use of fictional techniques) will be said through implication—through dialogue and through your manipulation of details.

7. Reporting. You will observe your subject with a keen eye. You will note interesting "overheard" conversations. You might want to interview someone.

8. Form. You might write your article in pieces—conversations, descriptions, interviews, facts—and then piece it together, finding the best form for your subject (time sequence and so forth). A "patchwork"—working sections together with no transition—can be quite acceptable.

9. Choice of subject. You can pick some subject from the present or recreate some subject from your past.

Saturation Report—Triple Credit Paper

This paper will bring together some of the techniques you have practiced this quarter: use of descriptive detail, dialogue, narrative, close observation. For the saturation report you may do one of the following:

1. Teach or be taught a task.
2. Visit a place.
3. Capture an event.
4. Vividly describe a person.
5. Show your job in action.

No matter what you do, you will need to bring in an abundance of notes in which you have recorded your feelings, your detailed observations, conversations that you have heard, people you have spoken to, and descriptions. After all your visiting, looking, and listening, bring your notes in (more than you need, please), focus on your subject, and then write. Remember that your paper should make some kind of statement about lesson, place, event, person, or job. That statement may be stated or unstated as your material demands.

I also hand out a three-week schedule so that every student knows at what point in the writing process he or she should be on any given day:

Time Schedule for This Project

NOTE: Prior to the first week, students will have had experiences with *showing* writing, James Moffett's sensory reporting, ordering details, writing descriptions, and interviewing.

Week 1

Mon.—Introduce saturation reporting. Read Tom Wolfe's *The New Journalism*—scene-by-scene construction, use of detail, point of view, use of dialogue.[1]

Tues.—Read student examples. Read more of Tom Wolfe's explanations.

Wed.—What are you going to write about? Check topic with teacher. Get your assignment for the on-campus group saturation report. Bring lunch to class

today because you will be working during the lunch period.

Thur.—During the class period write your description of the campus scene.

Fri.—Read and discuss the group's report. Use student models.

Week 2

Mon.—Work with clauses.

Tues.—Work with tightening.

Wed.—Notes are due.

Thur.-Fri.—Confer with teacher. Bring complete notes. We will discuss your focus, including underlying ideas and point of view. While conferences are in progress, complete exercises in parallel structure, sentence combining, and clauses. Key will be available.

Week 3

Mon.—Every student brings page one of report to share.

Tues.—Write in class.

Wed.—Completed rough drafts are due at the beginning of the period for peer evaluation and assistance.

Thur.—Bridge to the essay.

Fri.—**Your finished paper is due.**

Saturation reporting can be adapted to grade and ability levels and to locale. Whether the students are asked to write a description of a scene, an interview, or multiple scenes, or whether they are responsible only for collecting facts with their tape recorders that their classmates will transcribe and edit with them, the finished product will be writing that the students will be proud they have done and that you will enjoy reading.

---

[1]Tom Wolfe and E. W. Johnson, *The New Journalism.* New York: Harper & Row Pubs., Inc., 1973.

Preparing Students to Write the Saturation Report

By Carol Booth Olson
Codirector, UCI Writing Project

The saturation report is one of the most popular writing assignments I give to students in my freshman composition class. Because the topic is of their own choosing, students almost always get *into* their subject. Moreover, they are challenged to come up with unique approaches to communicating factual information in an almost cinematic style. The task of capturing an actual person, place, or event and bringing the subject to life through fictional techniques will naturally lead students to blend the sensory/descriptive, imaginative/narrative, practical/informative, and analytical/expository domains of writing.

In order to ensure that students put the most in and get the most out of their saturation reports, I take them through a sequence of steps that will prepare them to select a topic, organize their ideas, and write their papers. The sequence is as follows:

- *Step 1.* Explain to students several weeks in advance (so they have some "think time") that they will have opportunities to immerse themselves in a person, place, or event and bring their subject to life by presenting factual information, scene by scene, using description, characterization, dialogue, and so forth. Pass out the list of key features of a saturation report, as outlined by Ruby Bernstein at the beginning of this section.

- *Step 2.* Provide students with a model of a saturation report and a list of criteria on which their papers will be evaluated. (Note: The rubric

should be created by each teacher to fit his or her objectives and classroom situation.) I usually begin by reading a paper to the class that I wrote about Houlihan's bar on Friday nights. Then I pass out one of my favorite student samples, a report on "Female Mud Wrestling," written by Dave Meltzer in a class I taught at Saddleback College, North Campus. I include it here in its entirety because it is such a well-written saturation report that conveys the "you are there" feeling very effectively.

FEMALE MUD WRESTLING

"Good evening, ladies and gentlemen. Welcome to KRAZ's YOU ASKED FOR IT.

"Dave Meltzer reporting live from McChonahay's in Costa Mesa. Tonight, my crew and I are going to broadcast a most unusual spectacle—FEMALE MUD WRESTLING.

"Excuse me, sir, would you mind telling the viewers what your occupation is and why you are attending this event tonight?"

"Not at all," he said. "My name is Jim Jacobsen and I'm a Professor of Psychology at the University of California at Irvine."

"That's very interesting, Jim. Are you conducting some research?"

"Are you kidding?" He smiled as he spoke. "I'm here for the same reason that most people are here—to have a good time."

(Shrugging my shoulders . . .) "Well, so much for our system of higher education.

"Excuse me. Why are you here?"

A young man with blonde hair, wearing a cowboy hat replies, "To watch the chicks wrestle in the mud."

"You look like an attractive lady. Why are you here?"

"To find a man, honey."

"In that case, try the blonde with the cowboy hat."

A dazed-looking man at the bar suddenly spills his drink onto his lap.

"Sir, I noticed you sitting here in the corner. You don't seem that interested in the entertainment. Why are you here?"

"OOPS . . . I . . . Um . . . drinking . . . mud."

Well, so much for the clientele.

Bob Barison, the master of ceremonies for female mud wrestling, enters the room.

"Bob, over here.

"Ladies and gentlemen, this is Bob Barison, this evening's master of ceremonies. Bob, how did you ever get involved with this crazy event?"

"Well (slight pause), it began about four months ago when I was traveling across the Midwest. I happened upon a little bar in Kansas that was displaying a banner advertising Thursday night female mud wrestling. My curiosity got the better of me and so I decided to stick around and watch. I was truly amazed at the way the girls really put their all into mud wrestling and at the crowd's reactions. I thought to myself that it would go over big in southern California. When I returned to California, I approached a number of bar owners about my ideas, but McChonahay's was the only one willing to listen. We decided to give it a try. There you have it. Business has tripled so far and there's no end in sight."

"That's very interesting, Bob. Do you enjoy this line of work?"

"Hell, yes," he answered. "Where else can you drink for free, say and do anything you want while the customers scream for more, see beautiful ladies wrestle, and be able to collect a paycheck for it?"

"I have to admit, it sounds great. Thanks for spending a few minutes with us, Bob."

> *The writer should not follow rules, but follow language towards meaning, always seeking to understand what is appearing on the page, to see it clearly, to evaluate it clearly, for clear thinking will produce clear writing.*
> DONALD MURRAY

The "grounds crew," as they are called, start preparing the ring. The ring consists of four foam blocks approximately six feet long and one foot wide that are hooked together by nylon straps to form a square. Inside the square, the "ground crew" lays some more foam and covers it with plastic. Then the whole area inside the square is filled with cool, slimy mud. A bathtub arrangement is located off to the right where the girls will be washed off after the match.

"It is time for tonight's main event." (The cameras turn to Bob who is making the announcement.)

"Awright! Awright!" he yells. "Good evening, ladies and gentlemen. Welcome to McChonahay's for a very, very crowded Tuesday night. Let me introduce myself. I am Bob Barison, your emcee for the evening. I will give you folks the play-by-play action until the very end. Are you ready for female mud wrestling?" (The crowd starts chanting "mud, mud, mud.")

"Awright! How many of you here tonight have seen female mud wrestling before?" (Lots of whistles and yells from the audience.) "How many of you are here tonight for your first time?" (About half the crowd raises their hands while the rest continue chanting "mud, mud, mud.")

"For those of you who do not know what this is, this is female mud wrestling.

"We have three different weight categories: the lightweights, the middleweights, and the heavy-weights. The lightweights we call the Cream-puff Cuties, the middleweights are called the Middleweight Ms., and the heavyweights are called the Hefty Hunnies."

"Awright! Awright!" the audience yells.

"This is an audience participation sport. Your cheers, boos, and financial support are all greatly appreciated. Let me give you the rules and regulations of female mud wrestling. This sport is sponsored by the Female Mud Wrestlers Association of Southern California:

"Rule Number 1—The ladies must be in the mud at all times." (The crowd begins whistling and chanting to start.)

"Rule Number 2—The ladies cannot remove each other's clothing." (The crowd begins booing and chanting, "Skin to win, skin to win!")

"Rule Number 3—No scratching, no pulling of each other's hair, and no biting." (Crowd continues booing.)

"Rule Number 4—No poking in the eyes, ears, nose, or any other hole." (More booing from the audience—also some laughter.)

"Rule Number 5—There will not be any men allowed in the mud (still more boos) unless, of course, they are invited." (Crowd begins whistling and cheering.)

Bob yells, "Are you ready for mud wrestling?"
The crowd screams, "We are ready. Skin to win."

"Is that the best you can do? Are you ready for female mud wrestling?

"Ladies and gentlemen, to start things off this evening, we will begin with the Hefty Hunnies." (The crowd begins chanting, "Here comes the beef, here comes the beef.")

Bob introduces the challenger for the event. "Our first lady is reminiscent of those wonder women, bionic women, and other strange looking chicks—Wild Wilma." (As she enters, the disc jockey starts playing the song by the group Queen, "Sheer Heart Attack.") She makes her way to the ring dancing, taking off bits and pieces of her Wonder Woman outfit until all that is left is her wrestling suit which consists of a one-piece bathing suit and some dark-shaded nylons. While she limbers up, the crowd goes crazy—throwing dollars, slipping them into runs in her nylons, shoulder straps, and some other areas.

Bob says, "Awright, let's have a big hand for the challenger. Now it is a great honor to introduce to you the champion for the past five weeks, Smooth Movin' Sam." (The crowd begins chanting, "Sam, Sam, Sam.") As she makes her entrance, the D.J. starts playing the song by Foreigner, "Cold as Ice." Sam goes through a similar routine, collecting the money and stripping down.

"Okay, ladies, in the mud," Bob says to them.

Are you ready? Let's count it down—everyone together. You've got 5 . . . 4 . . . 3 . . . 2 . . . 1 . . . mud wrestle!"

Right away Wilma's in trouble. The champ has her shoulders in the mud. She is trying desperately to free herself from the champ's powerful grip. All of a sudden, Wilma throws her legs up and catches Sam around her neck. The whistle sounds.

Bob yells, "Did you see that? Wild Wilma got out of that mess smooth as silk. Can she upset the champ tonight? We will have to wait and see. Are you ladies ready? Wrestle!"

Sam charges at Wilma, pulling her power play, trapping the challenger in a full body press between her powerful shoulders and thighs. Wilma doesn't stand a chance.

"She is down; it's a pin." The referee sounds the whistle.

In the second round, Wilma tries desperately to gain some points after that last pin but to no avail. But in round three, Sam is beginning to show signs of fatigue. Wild Wilma is all over Sam, toying with the champ as if she were a rag doll.

Bob announces, "The champ is in trouble now. Wilma has Sam on her back. She is positioning for the pin. 3 . . . 2 . . . 1 . . . It's a pin!" (The whistle sounds, signaling the end of the match.)

The crowd is going crazy—screaming, hollering, and throwing dollars into the air. Someone from the audience yells, "One more round."

And soon, the entire crowd picks up the chant, "One more round. One more round. One more round."

Bob asks, "How many of you work overtime for nothing? You want another round? Then give these girls some encouragement. Let's see those greenbacks." (The crowd begins to cough up the dough.)

"Thank you, folks."

"No, we don't accept VISA," Bob chuckles.

"Well, that's it for tonight, ladies and gentlemen. We'd like to stay for that extra round, but we've got to get back to the studio. Thank you for tuning in tonight. This is Dave Meltzer, live at McChonahay's for FEMALE MUD WRESTLING, signing off."

- *Step 3.* Once students have a clear idea of what the saturation report entails, ask them to brainstorm about the people, places, and events they could write about and to place the names on a chart like this one:

People	Places	Events

Then, have them put a *GI* next to the topics they are *genuinely interested* in and *MC* by the topics they are *mildly curious* about. After eliminating all the MCs from their lists, students can set priorities for their GIs and select the most promising topic.

- *Step 4.* Enable/require students to begin planning early by asking them to write a one-page abstract that explains what their topic is, why they selected it, and how they intend to go about getting the information they need. Review these abstracts while students share their ideas and get feedback from their peer groups. Meet with any students who still need to narrow their focus.

- *Step 5.* The students are now ready to go out and observe their person, place, or event. Encourage them to record everything they hear, see, touch, smell, taste, and so on and to note their own impressions and reactions. Allow a week for the information generating stage of the process. (You may find the accompanying chart helpful for showing your students how the data they collect can relate to the domain of writing.)

- *Step 6.* When students come back to class with their notes, help them to organize their ideas by asking them to think of themselves as photographers or cinematographers. If they were filming this, what kind of camera angles would they use? What focus? What kind of lighting? How often

Sensory/Descriptive	*Imaginative/Narrative*	*Practical/Informative*	*Analytical/Expository*
RECORD: Sights, smells, tastes, textures, sounds, action words, atmosphere words, character description	*RECORD:* Dialogue, time frame, ideas for scenes, transition words, dramatic effects, mood	*RECORD:* Historical background, interesting facts and statistics, "how to" information, interview questions, and responses	*RECORD:* First impressions, reactions, afterthoughts, opinions, judgments, criticisms

would they change the scene? Then show them Ruby Bernstein's cluster of her exposé of fat doctors (Figure 23), and ask them to create a scene-by-scene cluster of their report. Walk around the room to review these and offer suggestions.

- *Step 7.* Finally, to make sure that the students are off to a good start, have them write their opening scene and bring copies to class for sharing. Jenee Gossard's read-around technique (in the "Sharing/Responding" section of this book) works particularly well for bringing to the students' attention papers that look particularly promising. These papers can be read aloud to the whole group (in addition to being read silently by all) and discussed in terms of their special merits. Students can then go back to their own papers with a fresh perspective on their own writing, some new ideas gained from seeing other students' work, and the motivation of writing for their peers.

Even with all this preparation, some students will still write flawed saturation reports, but those students will be in the minority. My experience has been that the saturation report brings out the best in student writers. I always look forward to reading them because they are as diverse as one's students are—interesting, educational, and wellcrafted.

The Add-on Saturation Report

By Linda Bowe
Teacher, Evergreen Elementary School, Walnut Valley Unified School Distrct; and Teacher/Consultant, UCI Writing Project

Saturation reporting is a natural outgrowth of a writing exercise I use in my second grade classroom: writing add-on-books. This five-day writing experience helps students develop complete, detailed stories, each with a beginning, a middle, and an end. Once familiar with the add-on technique (described below), students can write saturation reports in any unit of study. Science and social studies are particularly appropriate. Reports can easily be done with science lessons on the following subjects: fruit flies, tadpoles, snails, tide pools, earthworms, or any similar subject that generates student interest and investigation.

My science unit on silkworms has provided an excellent opportunity for students to use the knowledge they have acquired through the enjoyable process of storywriting. Following intense weeks of observation and discussion as the silkworms hatch, grow, molt, spin, emerge as moths, lay eggs, and die, the students become thoroughly immersed in the life cycle of the silkworm. At this point, they are very capable of writing about the experience.

Students may take one of two approaches in writing their add-on saturation reports. They can describe a different life cycle of the silkworm each day, or they can concentrate on one cycle and write daily about a different aspect. Limiting the daily topic helps students to focus on the subject and to produce more descriptive pieces of writing than they might otherwise produce.

In a more creative vein, the students can fantasize and write imaginative stories about pet silkworms. The following format works well for this assignment:

Day 1: The students describe the silkworm's character.
Day 2: They describe the silkworm's habitat.
Day 3: They put the silkworm in an exciting situation that involves some kind of problem or conflict.
Day 4: They propose a solution to the problem or a resolution to the conflict.
Day 5: They tell about the feelings of the silkworm after its exciting experience.

Using this day-by-day add-on technique, the students develop an ongoing story in which they integrate fac-

When you employ saturation reporting, you ask your students to make all the sophisticated choices professional writers make: which point of view to use; which details and dialogue to include; which research, if any, to pursue; and, finally, how to structure the nonfiction experience.

RUBY BERNSTEIN

tual information and imaginative ideas. Often, students become so involved in the study of their silkworms that they choose to write their stories from the first person point of view.

Once the students have prepared a draft of their add-on saturation reports, they can revise them and put their final versions in booklets made of brightly colored construction paper. They should also be encouraged to illustrate what they wrote. Students love to share their new found knowledge with their classmates, parents, or community members at an open house. (For other suggested postwriting activities, see page 24 of the *Handbook for Planning an Effective Writing Program.*)

I have found that once students write an add-on saturation report by blending science with creative writing, their enthusiasm for classroom study in all curricular areas grows, as does their desire to communicate what they have learned to an audience.

The Saturation Research Paper

By Cathy D'Aoust
Codirector, UCI Writing Project

I was teaching intermediate composition at the high school level when Ruby Bernstein introduced saturation reporting to our writing project. I was immediately interested in adapting this approach to some type of research paper. I thought that utilizing fictional techniques in a research paper would be both challenging and interesting to students.

Basically, the assignment was to choose a famous person and to research a specific time in that person's life. Famous meant that there was sufficient research material available on this person to write a paper. In the paper itself the student writers were to capture in detail a moment in that character's life and to include a physical description of the person, details of the setting, narration (action), and interior monologue of the character.

To facilitate the collection of reference materials, I held several class sessions in the library. Students were required to record on 3″ x 5″ cards the footnote and bibliographical information they would need for their saturation research paper. I met with students individually while their research was in progress to make certain they were consulting a range of secondary sources and to discuss how to go about selecting one moment in their subject's life from the biographical information they had compiled.

Once the students had completed their research and narrowed their focus to one significant event in a famous person's life, I gave them the following directions:

Your paper will focus on one particular moment in your subject's life. Describe what your person looks like, identify and describe where he or she is, and explain what is going on at the time. Include, through interior monologue, what your character is thinking during this moment. Footnote all material obtained from research. Several successful papers have followed this order:

- Description of the setting
- Description of the action in the setting
- Introduction of the famous person
- Interior monologue of their thoughts

You are attempting to capture one minute or so in the life of your subject. There is no maximum or minimum paper length.

As an example of the above format, one student described a moment in Louis XVI's life. She focused on his execution in Paris, the tension on the scaffold, and his final moments of consciousness. Here is that student's description:

A Moment in Louis XVI's Life

A man standing on a scaffold, in the Place de la Révolution in Paris, is watched by thousands of people. He has been driven to this highly reputed location by carriage, in the company of an Irish priest, the Abbé Edgeworth. The troops are out in full force, and there are national guards as well as a strong military escort positioned by the condemned monarch's carriage.

The man who seems to be caught in the spotlight is Louis XVI. He was the King of France during its renowned Revolution. Although his clothes were somewhat disheveled, it was obvious, as one might judge from his habit, that he was definitely one of the hierarchy. At the age of forty, he was a thickset man with a puffy face. He possessed a long protruding nose, full, curved lips, and a broad forehead, over which his dark hair peeped out from under a curly, white wig. His large, dark eyes sent forth an expression that was not totally unsympathetic to the reasonable demands of his people for elementary justice; however, the peasantry's cry of, "Something has to be done by some great folk for the likes of us," had been ignored, and now they stood watching as their rage took vengeance upon their King. (2;21)*

As they readied Louis XVI's body for the guillotine, he lost consciousness and was as one already dead. From this state he was awakened—ages later, it seemed to him—by the piercing cries of the angry people. Keen, poignant agonies seemed to shoot from his neck downward through every fibre of his body and limbs. They seemed like streams of pulsating fire heating him to an intolerable temperature.

As to his head, he was conscious of nothing but fullness—of congestion. These sensations were unaccompanied by thought. The intellectual part of him had departed; he had power only to feel, and feeling was torment. Suddenly, his unconscious mind was awakened. He thought of escaping. To die at the guillotine—the idea seemed ludicrous.

He opened his eyes and was now in full possession of his physical senses. They were supernaturally keen and alert. He saw the scaffold, the captain, the sentinels—and he saw the executioners. They shouted and gesticulated, pointing at him. He felt ashamed and wondered, "Could it be through some fault of mine that France has been famine stricken, its finances turned chaotic, and its institutions ruined?" He sought for the answer and reassured himself that he wasn't to blame. He thought of the two previous Louises and remembered, "It was Louis XIV, who undermined the stability of France. Louis XV, whose sloth took France to the edge of abyss." (4;522)

As his mind searched for more proof of innocence on his part, he thought, "After all, it was I who sought to repair this damage to France. I am being punished for the deeds of others before me!"

It was unfortunate that he had to begin his reign as King of France at its worst moment, and to make matters worse, very little preparation was made to fit him for his destiny. He had received a sketchy education, and all knowledge of state affairs had been withheld from him by his insensate grandfather, Louis XV. Consequently, he had misjudged the magnitude of the problem and the temper of his people. Overwhelmed by the current situation, he thought to himself, "I had no idea that things would come to this!" Sadly he realized, "It's too late. Nothing more can be done at this place in time."

For Louis XVI, the end was near, and he could feel it for certain. In the final moments, a sudden urge swelled within him to speak to his people. Louis XVI's last

© 1986 DENNIS HEARNE

words were, "Frenchmen, I die innocent, and I pray to God that my blood will not fall upon my people." (1;237)

The executioners proceeded with their duties, although somewhat disconcerted by his proud bearing and fearlessness. As the knife fell, cries of thousands of people filled the air, willing the King's death. People dipped their fingers in the royal blood, and one tasted it saying, "It is vilely salty." (1;237)

There was no mourning in Paris that day. The theaters were full and much wine was drunk. The body was taken to the cemetery of the Madeleine and covered with quicklime.

Later I used this same assignment in an advanced composition course. These students were, of course, much more concerned with style. They were able to blend the elements of fictional writing into nonfiction more successfully. Many of them began with action or interior monologue; they all tried different ways of mixing narration, description, characterization, and dialogue.

Regardless of their skill level, my intermediate and advanced composition students enjoyed my research-oriented version of the saturation report. They immersed themselves in the life of a famous person of their choice and were able to recreate one moment in that person's life. To do this successfully, they had to do more than just state the facts; they had to bring research to life by dramatizing it. Reading these papers was a special pleasure because the students tapped all of their descriptive, narrative, and expository writing skills to make their saturation research papers interesting and informative.

*Note: The parenthetical notations refer to the following footnotes and the page references in these works:

1. Duc de Castries, *Lives of the Kings and Queens of France*. New York: Alfred A. Knopf, Inc., 1979.
2. Gwynne Lewis, *Life in Revolutionary France*. New York: G. P. Putnam's Sons, 1972.
3. Douglas Liversidge, *The Day the Bastille Fell*. New York: Franklin Watts, Inc., 1972.
4. Frank Usher, "Louis XVI," in *100 Great Kings, Queens, and Rulers of the World*, edited with an introduction by John Canning. New York: Taplinger Publishing Company, 1968.

Point of View in Writing

A Lesson on Point of View . . . That Works

By Carol Booth Olson
Codirector, UCI Writing Project

To make the concept of point of view comprehensible to students, I include a writing assignment in my composition class that enables each student to become a literary character and to speak through that character's voice. The emphasis of the lesson is two-fold. First, it provides an experiential, "learn-by-doing" approach to improving writing skills. As the British researcher on writing James Britton points out in *The Development of Writing Abilities (11-18)*, when writing becomes a genuine mode of learning instead of just a vehicle for showing what one has already learned, there is more opportunity for the student to discover his or her own personal voice as a writer.[1] Second, this kind of assignment fosters critical reading skills because the student must think deeply about a piece of literature in order to assume the point of view of one of the characters.

To begin, I introduce the following aspects of point of view: *who* (first person, third person, omniscient narrator, and stream of consciousness narration); *when* (past, present, future, and flashback); and *where* (from a distant perspective, in the midst of the action, from beyond the grave, and so forth). I then ask the students to read John Steinbeck's novella *Of Mice and Men*. This book works well for a variety of reasons. Since the majority of my students do not read for pleasure and need to be encouraged to discover the value of a good book, the brevity and pacing of *Of Mice and Men* is attractive for an initial reading and

writing assignment.[2] The universal themes of the novella are also readily accessible and lend themselves to a class discussion that everyone can contribute to. Finally, the authorial voice that John Steinbeck uses to set the stage for his drama is quite distinct from the dialogue in which his main characters, two itinerant farmhands, speak for themselves—revealing their hopes and dreams, frustrations and limitations.

Because of my exposure to the California and National Writing projects, I am a believer in teaching writing as a process and, whenever possible, structure my assignments in such a way as to include instruction and "think time" for each stage of composition: prewriting, writing, sharing/responding, rewriting, editing, and evaluating. As a prewriting exercise for my lesson on point of view, I use Gabriele Rico's clustering technique to generate ideas for discussion. (See Dr. Rico's description of clustering that appears earlier in this publication.)

During the clustering session the instructor writes a stimulus word on the chalkboard and asks students to make free associations to conjure up words, images, and phrases in bubbles around that stimulus word. These clusters are then used as a basis from which to create short paragraphs about the designated topic. For this particular prewriting exercise, I ask the students to take ten minutes to jot down anything that comes to mind in relation to Lennie and George, the protagonists in *Of Mice and Men*. We share these

---

[1]James Britton and others, *The Development of Writing Abilities (11—18)* (Schools Council Research Studies). Houndmills Basingstoke Hampshire: Macmillan Eduation Ltd., 1975.

[2]John Steinbeck, *Of Mice and Men*. New York: The Viking Press, Inc., 1972; © 1965 by John Steinbeck.

associations as a group and develop clusters, such as the one shown in Figure 24. Then, rather than asking students to write freely, using their clusters as a point of departure, I try to elicit one sentence from our discussion, such as, "Lennie's mind is not right," which students must illustrate in a paragraph using Rebekah Caplan's strategy of "showing, not telling" (see Rebekah Caplan's section earlier in this book); that is, of showing Lennie's mental infirmity rather than directly telling about it, as in the sample that follows:

Lennie's mind is not right.

Towering over all like a giant, ignorant of his strength, Lennie crushes the life out of the objects of his affection like so many paper dolls. And then he looks at George, helplessly, questioningly, burning with shame because he has done another bad thing and terrified that there will be no more soft, fuzzy creatures to fondle. He's kind of like those puppies he smothers with love—filled with need, anxious to please, obedient to his master. George just shakes his head and wonders what's to become of them. "Tell me again about the rabbits!" The broken record is stuck on the same groove. Lennie smiles dreamily as the nightmare unfolds—oblivious to all but the pretty picture in his head.

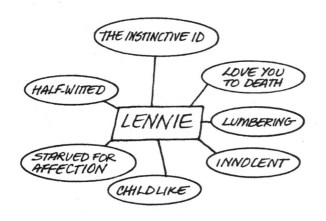

Fig. 24. Clustering of Lennie from *Of Mice and Men*

We follow the same procedure of sharing cluster words about George, although more emphasis is now placed on comparing and contrasting the two characters. But when it comes time to show that "George is his brother's keeper," I ask the students to write their paragraphs as monologues from George's point of view, as was done in this example:

He ain't smart but he's a worker, old Lennie is. He can do anything once you tell him how. Sometimes he makes me so mad, I just tell him to jump in the lake. But he

does it. Pathetic! How can you deal with a guy like that? I know I'd probably be better off without him. Trouble is, I think I'd probably miss him, crazy as it sounds. And I'd always be wonderin what kinda trouble he was gettin into with no one to get him out of it. I guess we gotta stick together.

Having established this foundation for writing, I give the students the following assignment:

At the conclusion of *Of Mice and Men*, Slim leads George away from the river and up towards the highway, reassuring him that he had to kill Lennie; there was no way out. Imagine that Slim and George head into town for some stiff drinks and deep conversation. Please begin your paper at this point.

Writing assignment: In George's words explain to Slim why *you* killed Lennie. Remember that you must *become* George to write this paper. You are limited to his vocabulary, his perspective on life, and his level of sensitivity. In your dialogue suggest either directly or indirectly: what Lennie meant to you, what significance the dream of the land and the farmhouse has or had for you, and your perception of what life will be like without Lennie.

To clarify what is expected of the student on this assignment, I hand out a two-page scoring guide based on a 1 to 9 holistic scale that outlines the characteristics of a successful and unsuccessful paper:

9—8 This paper is clearly superior—well written, coherent, clearly organized, and insightful. A 9—8 paper does most or all of the following well:

- Maintains a clear point of view; i.e., speak through George's voice and see through George's eyes.
- Portrays George in a manner that is consistent with John Steinbeck's depiction of him.
- Shows insight into George's character and into the main themes Steinbeck presents in the novella.
- Responds to the questions of: why you killed Lennie, what he meant to you, what significance the dream of the land and the farmhouse has or had for you, and what you think life will be like without Lennie.
- Displays the writer's own voice through the description that is external to George's and Slim's dialogue (such as establishing setting).
- Uses descriptive, precise, and appropriate diction.
- Handles dialogue effectively.
- Varies sentence structure and length for effect.
- Uses the conventions of written English (spelling, punctuation, grammar, complete sentence structure, proper format for using dialogue, and so forth) correctly. (*NOTE:* Grammar may be violated and slang words used in this case in the dialogue portions of your paper.)

My task . . . is, by the power of the written word, to make you hear, to make you feel—it is, before all, to make you see.
JOSEPH CONRAD

7   This paper is a thinner version of the 9—8 paper. It is still impressive and interesting but less well-handled in terms of point of view, organization, or diction. The 7 paper is also apt to offer less insight into George's character and into Steinbeck's main themes.

6—5   These scores apply to papers that are less well-handled than the 7, 8, or 9 paper. A 6—5 paper may be less insightful, more loosely organized, or less comprehensible to the reader. A 6—5 paper will exhibit some or all of the following:

- Speaks through George's voice but is not entirely clear in terms of the message conveyed.
- Portrays George in a manner that is generally consistent with Steinbeck's depiction of him but in such a way that the character does not sound real.
- Responds directly to why *you* killed Lennie but only touches on the other three subquestions.
- Tends to say the obvious and does not display any special insight into the characters.
- Displays little or none of the writer's voice through description of setting.
- Uses less descriptive, precise, or appropriate diction than in the 7, 8, or 9 paper.
- Handles dialogue less effectively than the 7, 8, or 9 paper. (The dialogue may either drag or be too sketchy.)
- Uses little or no variation in sentence structure and length.
- Contains some problems with the conventions of written English but none that seriously impairs the message.

4—3   These scores apply to papers that follow the general idea of the writing assignment but that are weak in thought, language facility, or the conventions of written English. A 4—3 paper exhibits some or all of the following:

- Speaks through George's voice only intermittently or not at all. Who is speaking may be unclear.
- Portrays George in a manner that is inconsistent with Steinbeck's depiction.
- Fails to respond to the four questions posed in the writing assignment.
- Displays very little insight into Steinbeck's characters or main themes.
- Uses overly general diction not suited to George's character.
- Uses dialogue ineffectively or not at all.
- Presents the purpose of paper unclearly.
- Contains little or no differentiation between style and sentence patterns in the "George portion" of the paper and in the writer's description of setting. Contains serious problems in the conventions of written English that impair the author's message.

2—1   These papers:

- Fail to speak through George's voice.
- Neglect the four questions posed in the writing assignment.
- Have superficial and/or fragmented and cloudy content.
- Indicate that the writer has misunderstood or perhaps has not read the book.
- Contain serious problems in the conventions of written English.

NOTE: An extremely well-written paper in terms of the conventions of written English may receive a point higher from the scorer than it would on the basis of content alone. A paper that is strong or satisfactory in content but that has serious problems in the conventions of written English should be docked up to two points, depending on the nature and frequency of the errors committed.

I give students one week to write rough drafts of their point of view papers and ask them to bring four photocopies of their work to class for discussion. I then allow one class session for students to meet in their groups to make critiques, read their papers aloud, get feedback from their group members, and make notes for revision. Early in the semester I train my students to use the following techniques adapted from Peter Elbow's *Writing Without Teachers* (see Peter Elbow's section that appears later in this book):

- Pointing to the words—Trying to remember key words or phrases that seem strong or weak
- Summarizing the writing—summarizing the piece of writing in a single sentence or choosing one word that captures it to help the writer determine whether the message he or she intended comes across clearly
- Telling the writer what happened—describing the thoughts and feelings that come to mind as the writer shares his or her work

I also stress that students should be descriptive rather that evaluative in their remarks, and I remind the class that there is no right and wrong in writing—

only what communicates and what does not. While students are sharing their papers, I call them up one by one and offer my comments and suggestions.

The revised paper is to be scored in class the following week. Using the scoring guide I provided, members of writing groups must score the papers, come to a group consensus, and fill out an evaluation sheet for papers written by four students from another writing group. The papers are then handed in to me for my score (which I average with theirs) and my written feedback.

> *The choice of a point of view is the initial act of a culture.*
> *JOSE ORTEGA Y GASSET*

I was particularly impressed with the quality of the papers that were turned in for this assignment. The students demonstrated a clear grasp of point of view, a depth of feeling for the character whose voice they were assuming, and an overall understanding of John Steinbeck's underlying themes. Ultimately, I feel that this lesson positively affected future papers, because it not only made students more aware of point of view in literature, but it also increased their recognition of their own voices as writers. A sample of a student paper written by Charles Wrightson, who was in my English 1A class at Saddleback Community College/ North Campus, follows:

GEORGE SPEAKS

The sun had fallen through the soft, dusty haze when they finally reached Soledad. Slim let the other farmhands come along but told them to leave George and him alone. They went to Suzy's Place, their boots kicking up little dust clouds and scraping on the gravel at the side of the rutted old road.

Suzy met them at the door and looked them up and down. But before she could say anything, Slim said softly, "The boys can do what they want. Me an' George want a quiet table alone."

After reading Slim's face and tone, she looked at George, lowered her eyes, and slowly nodded her head with its lovely blond curls. She led the way to the side table, brought a whiskey bottle and two shot glasses, and left after a slow look at Slim.

It seemed that George had sat there for hours, slumped, looking deep into the dark grain of the wood table for an answer. All he saw was the gun shaking in his nerveless hand, Lennie's head exploding from the impact, his body twitching as it fell over, and the blood pool beginning to grow like water from a slow spring.

"I been lookin' after Lennie my whole life," he finally whispered, still staring into the table.

Slim poured two shots of whiskey and handed George one. George downed it and felt like throwing up but kept it down because he needed not to think for awhile.

"You done all you could, George," Slim softly said. "All you could."

As he looked into Slim's eyes of steel, George felt the shock starting to leave him, but anger was welling up: "I had to shoot 'im! I had no choice. I couldn't let 'im alone for a minute. That bastard Curley was just waitin' to string 'im up."

George grabbed another shot of whiskey and downed it, trying to calm his nerves: "He was jus' like a big kid, but so strong an' he didn't know what he was doin! I couldn't let 'im go on like that."

George felt his eyes begin to burn, but he wasn't going to cry in front of Slim. So, he kept talking: "That poor kid couldn't a' been mean if it meant his life! Poor kid."

Again, George downed the refilled glass. Slim didn't say anything—just poured another and another. George kept talking. He felt like telling Slim everything. Without Lennie, there was no secret to be kept.

"I kept tellin' 'im about a place—a beautiful, green place all our own. At first it was jus' to keep 'im in line, ya know; but he'd get me talkin' and dreamin' and soon I'd start to ask myself, 'Why not? We could do it.' Oh, I knowed it probably wouldn't never of happened, but it was all that kep' us goin'."

George stopped, feeling the burning in his eyes again, thinking about living without Lennie. Lonely. Just drifting from place to place—with no friends. Terribly lonely.

"Yeah, all we had . . .," he said, "except each other. Now I ain't even got him no more."

"What you gonna do now, George?" Slim asked.

"Don' know, Slim, I jus' don' know. He was all I had. But I had to shoot 'im. You see that, don' you Slim?"

Without responding, Slim stood up, deciding it was time to leave. "Come on, George, we'd better be gettin' back," he urged.

Slowly wavering, George got to his feet. He was pretty drunk, but his head was clear: "I guess I'll work the month out an' then move on, Slim."

Slim looked at George for a minute, put his arm out to brace his friend, and helped him outside. "I guess that's best, George," he agreed. They moved out into the deep night with the rich smell of barley on the dry, whispering breeze and headed down the dusty road.

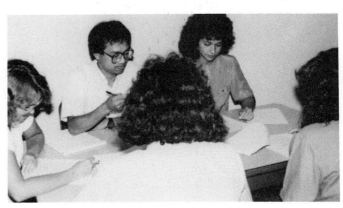

Teaching Point of View Through Characters from a Novel

By Elizabeth Williams Reeves
Teacher, Pine Middle School,
Los Alamitos Unified School District;
and Teacher/Consultant, UCI Writing Project

As readers, we often tend to discount story characters of minor significance and focus on either the protagonist or antagonist. By enabling students to consider the points of view of all characters, we may help them establish a clearer understanding of varying personality traits, emotions, and actions.

A lesson I have designed to increase students' awareness of point of view comes from *The Hobbit*.[1] In one segment of the novel, Bilbo, his dwarf friends, and Gandalf, the wizard, are captured by the goblins and taken prisoners in the goblin cave. I ask students to place themselves in the positions first of Bilbo, then Gandalf, and finally, a goblin, and to consider the following questions:

1. After Gandalf, Bilbo, and the dwarfs entered the cavern to find shelter from the thunder battle, how did you feel?
2. How did you feel when the cave opened up?
3. How did you feel as you stood in the great cavern before the Great Goblin? What did you do?
4. How did you react when the Great Goblin was smote before your eyes?

Student models of the beginning paragraphs written from each character's point of view follow:

1. *From Bilbo's point of view:*

   I was dumbfounded to find that my nightmare had come true. The wicked monsters led the dwarfs and myself down into their lair. There, the Great Goblin sat. My knees knocked, one against the other.

2. *From Gandalf's point of view:*

   Bilbo's scream provided me with just enough warning to escape the clutches of the goblins. I grabbed my wand, and with a flash of lightning, killed a few of the wicked monsters. Then, I quickly slipped into the long, dark corridor which led to the cavern below.

3. *From a goblin's point of view:*

   I heard the voices of intruders in the cave overhead and grabbed my goblin friends to see what we had

---

[1] J. R. R. Tolkien, *The Hobbit*. Boston: Houghton Mifflin Co., 1977.

caught. Luscious dwarfs and ponies lay within our grasp. With hoots and hollers, we began to gather them up, when out of a corner came a mighty burst of lightning, killing several goblins. We hastily took our new-found treasures (captives) down into the cavern and began to celebrate.

After the students have explored three different points of view, their assignment is to assume the role of one of these characters and to write a more lengthy narrative/monologue recounting the adventure in the goblin cave. I find that they have a much easier time becoming a character after exploring the same scene from several different perspectives.

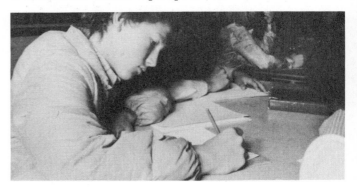

A Seventh Grade Approach to Point of View

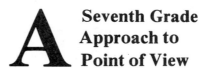

By Marie Filardo
English Teacher, Serrano Intermediate School,
Saddleback Valley Unified School District;
and Teacher/Consultant, UCI Writing Project

Point of view is one of the most difficult techniques of fine writing to teach seventh graders. To simplify teaching the technique, I take a two-step approach. First, I assign my students a novel entitled *A Special Gift* by Marcia L. Simon, which I ask them to summarize.[1] The ability to summarize is not just a reading skill but a critical thinking skill. According to Edward Fry, Director of the Reading Center and Professor at Rutgers University, summarizing is more than merely finding the main idea; it also involves the production of a message, a concise statement that is spoken or written. For most seventh graders, summarizing is the mere reproduction of a story. I attempt to teach them

---

[1] Marcia L. Simon, *A Special Gift*. New York: Harcourt Brace Jovanovich, Inc., 1978; © 1978 by Marcia L. Simon.

to internalize thoughts and emotions evoked by the author and to generate new ideas.

A Special Gift is the story of a teenage boy named Peter who is torn between two talents. He is an excellent basketball player as well as an excellent ballet dancer. At first, ballet is something Peter does as a young boy simply because he accompanies his sister to lessons. As Peter matures and becomes more sensitive to the feelings of others, he realizes his sister's enjoyment of the art is readily approved of, whereas his is not only disapproved of, but frowned on. Nevertheless, he pursues his love for dancing, insisting that the strenuous exercises enhance his basketball performance. His dad is thrilled with the prospect of his son's becoming the school's star basketball player but has difficulty accepting the fact that he enjoys ballet. Peter finds himself torn between winning his dad's admiration and bearing his rejection. Peter is also aware that he has kept his dancing a secret from his friends and classmates. When his father's friend, Pearson, discovers Peter's talent for ballet, he calls his enjoyment of dancing "weird." Peter realizes the horror facing him if and when his double life should be revealed.

As the story unfolds, Peter is chosen to dance in the *Nutcracker* ballet. He admits that he is thrilled with the opportunity, finally sensing how much dancing really means to him. All of Peter's difficulties become compounded when basketball season overlaps with ballet season. Rehearsals for the games and performances are scheduled for the same times, and Peter is caught in a dilemma. He must come to terms with himself, his values, and his friendships.

After we have summarized the story orally, I ask my students to embark on step two, the critical thinking stage, which has as its ultimate goal the production of a written statement. When students are fully immersed in the plot and characters of the story, I ask them to employ Gabriele Rico's technique of cluster-

> **The student must think deeply about a piece of literature in order to assume the point of view of one of the characters.**
> CAROL BOOTH OLSON

ing. (See Dr. Rico's description of clustering as a prewriting process, which appears earlier in this book.) As Dr. Rico points out, clustering is a visual, nonlinear development of ideas. It helps the students find and generate ideas. It is the discovery or brainstorming stage of writing sometimes labeled prewriting. Given a nucleus word, the writer is asked to associate satellite words. Later, the writer discovers struc-

ture in these thoughts. In this lesson we use clustering to focus on Peter's problems. The intent is to have the students project themselves into Peter's mind and to brainstrom about his dilemma, using Peter's voice.

To do this activity successfully, the students must adhere to the issue at hand; i.e., how Peter feels. I emphasize that their success depends on how well they get into Peter's mind. The writers must be objective and unbiased in their reactions. They must be willing to suspend their own thoughts and feelings and to refrain from judging Peter. Instead they must think as Peter thinks. They must strive to sense the emotional turmoil that Peter is experiencing. The physical movements Peter engages in must be as realistic to the students as are Peter's mental and emotional states. Given the word *dancing* as a nucleus word, we arrive at a cluster, as shown in Figure 25.

Fig. 25. Clustering *Dancing* from *A Special Gift*

Then I present a scene from the book to use as a springboard for the students' writing. It is one in which Peter has given in to his father's pressure to play basketball when he should have been attending an important rehearsal for the ballet. Because he plays poorly, his coach yells at him, and then he hurts his ankle. He uses the accident as an excuse to leave the game and rush to the rehearsal. While hectically changing clothes in his dad's car, he feels frustration and resentment. Marcia Simon writes:

> He was angry with his father for making him go to the game, and angry with the coach for scolding him. Most of all he was angry with himself—for agreeing to play in the game in the first place when he should have been at the ballet rehearsal, for playing like a clumsy idiot, and for leaving the game to go to ballet when any kid in his

right mind would have wanted to stay at the game and help his team win.[2]

Using this scene as a point of departure, I give my students the following prompt:

> Imagine you are Peter riding in your dad's car. You have just returned from a humiliating game, which you did not want to play in the first place. You were manipulated by your dad, your coach, your team members, classmates, and friends. You are furious because no one has shown any regard for your feelings or rights as an individual. You are tired of being ignored. You love your father and want him to understand that you are a young adult capable of making intelligent decisions. Prove that you are your own person. Convince your father that you have reviewed all the pros and cons before making this decision to quit the team and dance. You know beyond a shadow of a doubt that playing basketball will make you a hero, whereas dancing will make you a laughing stock.

A Special Gift is especially geared to junior high school students who are beginning both the school year and an examination of themselves and their place in the world. Writing about Peter's decision allows these students to examine the importance of being themselves—even if it is at the expense of fitting in. This book also provides them with the opportunity to explore the challenges, decisions, and difficulties of growing up, as viewed from the standpoint of a young person. Remaining anonymous allows young students to express their innermost feelings without the burden of repercussions from their peers.

[2]Marcia L. Simon, *A Special Gift*. New York: Harcourt Brace Jovanovich, Inc., 1978, p. 65. © 1978 by Marcia L. Simon; reprinted by permission of the publisher.

A Parent's Point of View

By Dale Sprowl
English Teacher, Irvine High School,
Irvine Unified School District;
and Teacher/Consultant, UCI Writing Project

To teach point of view, I use "Charles," a very short story by Shirley Jackson, which tells of a young boy's conflicts in his first days of kindergarten.[1] Narrated from his mother's point of view, the story unfolds as her son, Laurie, comes home each day to tell his family about another boy, Charles, who causes persistent trouble at school. In the course of the story, Charles becomes less naughty and more congenial and productive at school. Curious to find out who Charles's parents are, the mother attends a P.T.A. meeting only to find that there is no Charles in the class and, thus, that her son has been talking about himself.

After I have read the story aloud to my low-ability-level ninth grade students, we discuss Laurie's motivation in creating Charles, his transition into becoming a cooperative member of the class, clues the author gives of what the mother will discover, and the mother's point of view. Then the discussion moves away from the short story to the students' own experiences. I ask questions about the students' feelings on the first day of school, about conflicts with teachers, and about saying, "I have a friend who _____," to test a parent's reaction to a predicament. Why do we try to protect our parents from who we truly are? We discuss the need for acceptance.

After the discussion I give the writing assignment. I have the students write a letter to themselves from either their mother's or father's point of view. The students write the letters to themselves ("Dear Sean") and sign it from one of their parents ("Love, Mom"). I explain the proper format for a friendly letter and write criteria for the letter on the chalkboard.

The students responded well after they had completed the prewriting exercises of reading and discussing. Their responses, however, indicated that they perceived their parents as critical and rule conscious: "P.S. Clean your room." "Please don't forget to clean your room, make your bed, take the trash out, and stay in the house until everyone comes home." Fewer responses contained affection and acceptance. This outcome helped me to understand my students and their perception of authority. They were motivated to

[1]Shirley Jackson, "Charles," in *The Lottery: Or the Adventures of James Harris*. New York: Farrar, Straus & Giroux, Inc., 1949.

write by the switch in point of view (and perhaps, they felt power in becoming a parent). A lesson plan on my "point of view" assignment follows:

SUGGESTED LESSON PLAN ON POINT OF VIEW
(Ninth grade English, one to two days in class)

First—Read Shirley Jackson's short story "Charles."

Second—Discuss the story.
1. Why did the boy create Charles?
2. How did the boy grow as the story progressed?
3. What clues did the author give of how the story would end?
4. What is point of view? (Teach this concept if the students cannot derive a good definition.)
5. From whose point of view was the story written?
6. What is the mother's point of view toward Charles's behavior?
7. How did the author use the mother's point of view?

Third—Discuss the students' personal experiences.
1. How do you feel about starting school, a new job, or summer camp?
2. What conflicts do you have with teachers?
3. Have you ever covered up by creating a "friend" to blame for something you did that was wrong? Do you test your friends' or your parents' reactions before you tell the truth?
4. What is acceptance? Why does it motivate us?

Fourth—Teach the friendly letter form.

Fifth—Present the written assignment.
1. Pretend you are either your mother or your father.
2. Write a letter to yourself from one of your parent's points of view.
3. Use the proper friendly letter format.

Sixth—Read five or six papers aloud to the class, and make comments about what was effective in the writing.

Suggested follow-up activities:
1. Discuss how the students perceive their parents.
2. Discuss insights the students may have about their parents after experiencing their point of view.
   a. What do you do that annoys your parents?
   b. What do you do that worries your parents?
   c. How can you please your parents?
   d. Do you feel accepted by your parents?
   e. How can you help your parents to understand your point of view?
3. Have the students give the letter they wrote to their parents, and ask them to respond, taking the student's point of view.

On the whole, this has been a successful assignment for me because my students have been motivated to write fluently, to learn the letter form, and to experience the point of view of another person and to describe it in their writing.

> **Achilles exists only through Homer. Take away the art of writing from this world, and you will probably take away its glory.**
> *FRANÇOIS RENÉ de CHATEAUBRIAND*

An Inside Look at Fear: Point of View in *The Crucible*

By Julie Simpson
English Teacher, Sunny Hills High School, Fullerton Union High School District; and Teacher/Consultant, UCI Writing Project

You never really understand a person until you consider things from his point of view . . . until you climb into his skin and walk around in it.

from Harper Lee's *To Kill a Mockingbird*

I want my students to be able to transfer Atticus Finch's advice to his daughter in *To Kill a Mockingbird*[1] to their reading of Arthur Miller's play *The Crucible*.[2] I want them to identify with John and Elizabeth Proctor, Abigail Williams, Reverend Parris, and the others to the point that they can feel what it was like to be a Puritan. Moreover, I want them to know that the same fears that caused these people to become fanatics, making them believe that they had some control over the uncontrollable, are still motivating people today.

> *The students must look into the character's fears and motivations to determine why this person's actions were justifiable in terms of his or her values.*
> *JULIE SIMPSON*

I believe that underlying Arthur Miller's criticisms of the actions of the witch hunters, he has a sense that these people of Salem were living the best way they could in the world as they saw it. Virtually every character reaches a point when, because of some personal sense of inadequacy, he or she panics. Some exploit this panic to give themselves power. These people become self-righteous toward others and attempt to destroy them through a false representation of goodness. To appear in control, others try to become a part of the fanatical crowd and condone the manipulations of power. Still others, the stronger, overcome their personal fears and sacrifice themselves for what they consider a higher value.

---

[1] Harper Lee, *To Kill a Mockingbird*. New York: Harper & Row Pubs., Inc., 1960.
[2] Arthur Miller, *Collected Plays*, Vol. I. New York: Viking Press, Inc., 1957.

> *Good writing is disciplined talking.*
> JAMES BOSWELL

This examination of fear and the ways we handle it make Arthur Miller's play more than merely an historical account of the witchcraft trials of Salem, Massachusetts, or a sociological attack on paranoia.

To enable the students to understand the characters, we first read the play aloud in class. I go over Arthur Miller's explicit introductions of the various characters and (with considerable guidance) ask the students to choose who they want to be.

Then I give all of my students a list of questions to consider after they select their respective parts and prepare to give a dramatic presentation in class. The questions, which follow, are designed to help the students examine their chosen character's fears, find each situation that causes panic, and understand how the character copes with fears and panic:

- What does your character think of himself or herself?
- What is he or she most afraid of?
- What does he or she think of the people of Salem?
- What behavior or belief shows that he or she is a good Puritan?
- What decision does he or she face?
- What several choices does he or she have?
- Why does your character make a particular choice? (Deciding not to choose is also a choice.)
- Why does your character believe that his or her choice is right?
- Does your character consider the consequences when he or she make a choice?
- Does your character's choice change his or her personality or values at all?

Of course, we discuss the play as we read it. I preface each discussion with short writing and discussion problems that make the students consider real-life decision-making situations. For example, in Act I when the girls are caught conjuring in the forest, they become hysterical and finally accuse Tituba of bewitching them. To help the students with the assignment, I give the following prompts:

- Think of a time when you were caught doing something you were strictly forbidden to do. What did you do to get yourself out of trouble?
- Think of someone you resent. Write a paragraph explaining what this person says and does that make you feel he or she is out to get you.
- Describe a situation when you got carried away in a crowd and did something you would not have done had you been alone.

For Act II, to further the students' understanding of the relationship between Elizabeth and John Proctor,

I ask the class members to consider their own interpersonal relationships:

- Think of a time when you have hurt someone you love. What did you do to regain his or her affection? How carefully did you plan your actions and comments? How long did it take for things to become normal again?
- Have you ever lost trust in someone you love? How did your behavior with that person change? How were you able to regain that trust?

For Act III, which deals with the power of heresay and rumor, I pose the following questions:

- Think of a rumor you heard recently. At the moment of your hearing it, what did you believe? Who had control—the one who spread the rumor or the one about whom the rumor was spread?
- How can you stop a rumor that has damaged your reputation?
- Would you lie or go against some firm belief you hold to save the one you love?

Finally, for Act IV, when John Proctor has to decide to die for truth rather than to live a lie, I urge the students to look within themselves and examine their own beliefs and convictions:

- Can you think of any situation or idea that is important enough to you that you would die for it?

After we finish reading and discussing the play, I ask the students to think as their character would and write an explanation, in the character's own words, about the reason for his or her choice. (They may select any form of writing and write to any audience they think most appropriate for their character.) The students must write from the assumption that the

character behaved in the best way he or she possibly could. Thus, the students must look into the character's fears and motivations to determine why this person's actions were justifiable in terms of his or her values.

The students are enthusiastic about this activity. Consequently, the papers they write are often the most perceptive, the most creative, and the most detailed ones they write all year. They feel that they have stood in their character's skin and walked around for a while.

The New Kid

By Mark Reardon
Teacher, Gardenhill Elementary School,
Norwalk-La Mirada Unified School District;
and Teacher/Consultant, UCI Writing Project

One way to approach point of view is through an eyewitness account. I use the short story, "The New Kid," by Murray Heyert, focusing on the event where the main character, Marty, and the new kid are forced into a fight by their peers.[1]

Prior to reading the selection, students, who are formed into groups, cluster the word *bully,* focusing on motives, attitudes, and personality traits. These clusters are shared by each group's spokesperson as I write the ideas on butcher paper, which can be referred to later.

Knowing the power of creative dramatics, I involve the students in improvisations as the next step in prewriting. Volunteers are solicited to participate in the following sketches:

- Students gathered around a locker as a person walks by and slams the locker door shut
- A school lunch line when someone cuts in
- A private game in which a person steals the ball
- A person or persons who will not let someone be part of a game or group

As these improvisations unfold, I freeze the actions and ask the characters to tell what they are thinking and feeling. These words are added to a "Thinking-Feeling" list.

At this point, I share this portion of the prompt with my students: "We will be reading a story about a bully in a situation you may find to be familiar. As we read the short story, you will be looking closely

at the characters' actions, feelings, and thoughts, much as we have done with these improvisations."

To help the students identify immediately with the characters of the story, especially with the characters' actions, feelings, and thoughts, I lead my class through two guided imagery journal writings as part of the precomposing stage. The first guided imagery has the students recall a time when they were bullied:

- Recall a time when you were bullied or picked on by someone who was perhaps older, stronger, or smarter. This experience should stand out clearly in your mind. It may have happened at school, in class, in a line, in a store, or on a street.
- Now that you have this experience in your mind, recall specific details, such as the place, time, sounds, and so forth.
- Remember the person's words, tone of voice, facial expressions, the look in his or her eyes, attitude, and so forth.
- Repeat the entire episode in your mind.
- Now, focus on your feelings. Remember how your nerves, heart, and skin felt. Recall your thoughts. Perhaps you spoke aloud. Hear what you said.
- Now, recall the entire episode once again in your mind.

As if the incident were a journal entry, have students write about the time they were bullied. When the students are finished, have them make a list of their feelings during and after the experience and of their reactions, both emotional and physical. Here is an example:

FEELINGS		REACTIONS	
During	*After*	*Emotional*	*Physical*
scared	embarrassed	cried	knot in stomach
nervous	threatened	yelled	tense
		swore	

Have students share their journal entry with the class.

In the second guided imagery, I have my students recall a time when they were the bullies:

- Recall a time when you were a bully, when you picked on or intimidated someone because you were tougher, smarter, or older. This should be an experience that stands out clearly in your mind.

[1]Murray Heyert, "The New Kid" in *Stories.* Edited by Frank G. Jennings and Charles Calitri. New York: Harcourt Brace Jovanovich, Inc., 1957.

- Now that you have remembered that experience, recall the setting—place, time, and sounds. Hear what people were saying; see what they were doing.
- Listen to what you said, your tone of voice. Think about your attitude.
- See what you did.
- Replay the entire episode in your mind.
- Now, focus on your feelings. Remember what you did.
- Remember what your body felt like, your heart, your nerves. Focus on how the experience made you feel. Recall your thoughts.
- Now, replay the entire episode once again in your mind.

As if this experience were a journal entry, have students write about it. When they are finished, have them make lists as before. Have students also share this experience with the class.

Up to this point, the students have been writing from the first-person point of view. To help them move from that standpoint to third-person observation, I assign the following showing, not telling, sentence: "The person was a bully." They are to include the person's actions, attitudes, and feelings, creating a half to three-quarter page vivid description that leads the reader to conclude that the person was indeed a bully.

Before reading the selection, I share the remainder of the prompt with the students:

> After reading the short story "The New Kid," you will re-create the bully incident that occurred between the main character, Marty, and the new kid. You will want to create an accurate account of what happened by being precise, vivid, and detailed so that someone who has never read the story will have a clear picture of the incident. By not being directly involved, you are in a good position to understand why this person did what he or she did. After re-creating this incident, tell the reader why you think Marty did what he did. Include what Marty was possibly thinking and feeling. Finally, tell your reader what you learned from observing the incident.

We read the story in three parts, with close reading for actions, attitudes, feelings, and traits of each of the characters: Marty, Eddie and the boys, and the new kid. We use an observation sheet (see the accompanying illustration), with each of the characters listed as a major category. Subcategories of actions,

attitudes, feelings, and traits are listed for each. We read the first three pages, focusing on Marty and Eddie and the boys. Through the next three pages, we look for additional material on Marty and Eddie and the boys and begin, with the introduction of the new kid, to fill in words for this category. The remaining pages reveal the incident between Marty and the new kid. We add to the observation chart, especially noting feelings and actions to help students better understand why the characters did what they did.

After reviewing the prompt, the students write an eyewitness account of the incident between Marty and the new kid. They write from a third-person point of view in the first part of their paper as they describe the incident. Then they move into first-person reaction during the second part of their paper when telling why they think Marty did what he did, and they reflect on what they learned from observing the incident.

One to two class days are given to write the first draft. One day is given for students to share those drafts with their response groups. Members of each group complete a response sheet that includes *what, why,* and *how* sections. (See the "Sharing/Responding" section of this book for suggestions on writing-response groups.) Students write specific descriptive responses to the writer's description of the event (*what*), the writer's reason for Marty's action (*why*), and their perceptions of how the incident affected the writer (*how*).

Observation Sheet for "The New Kid"

Reader/Writer _____

Observations											
of Marty				*of Eddie and the boys*				*of the new kid*			
Actions	*Attitudes*	*Feelings*	*Traits*	*Actions*	*Attitudes*	*Feelings*	*Traits*	*Actions*	*Attitudes*	*Feelings*	*Traits*

I provide time in class for revision and encourage students to make use of the comments on their response sheets and to pay careful attention to the specifics of the prompt. I also use this day to work with individual students.

Before the papers are turned in for my evaluation, students form into read-around groups and evaluate papers using a holistic scoring guide like the one that follows:

Primary Trait Scoring

3 A 3 paper clearly and logically describes the event, explains why the writer thinks the persons did what they did, and considers the significance of this event for the writer. It:

- Re-creates an accurate account of the bully incident between Marty and the new kid, using vivid, precise description
- Gives reasons for Marty's actions based on his possible thoughts and feelings
- Responds with an evaluation of what the writer learned from observing the event

2 A 2 paper contains all the features of a 3 paper, but it is not as strong in details. It gives reasons for Marty's actions, but it is weak in supporting them with examples of Marty's possible thoughts and feelings.

1 A 1 paper is missing the basic features needed for an eyewitness account. It lacks description, reasons for actions, or a personal response to the event.

Secondary Trait Scoring

2 A 2 paper follows conventions of proper grammar and syntax, margins, paragraph structure, spelling, capitalization, and end punctuation.

1 A 1 paper has minor errors in the conventions named previously.

0 A 0 paper has gross errors in the previously listed conventions.

Basing an eyewitness account on a familiar situation, such as a peer-induced fight, proves very motivating. Students identify easily with the characters, adding to their depth and insight as they move from third-person observation to first-person reaction.

Writing the I-Search Paper

The Reawakening of Curiosity: Research Papers as Hunting Stories

By Ken Macrorie
Professor Emeritus of English
Western Michigan University

We need to smile at what we and our students have been doing in the name of research all these years. Repeated several times in almost every student's educational career, the assignment to prepare a research paper may produce a full-fledged *dunderhead,* which according to my *Webster's New World Dictionary,* comes from the Dutch *donder,* meaning thunder—associated by rhyme with *blunder.* That is a fascinating chain: The new word has lost all relation with *thunderhead* and fits the writer of a conventional research paper, who makes no great sound or light in the sky. I cannot think of a righter word than *blunderer* to describe the conventional student reseachers staggering through the card catalog and the stacks with their 3″ x 5″ cards, copying passages from books and journals they do not understand, as if they were boring test holes and removing core samples from the heads of authors.

When I first broached these notions to teachers around the country a few years ago, I was met by laughter and squeals of agreement. I found that many high school and college teachers, out of anger and frustration, had asked students to do something like what I call an I-Search paper. I use the term *I Search* rather than *research* not to convey that this paper is written to search an I or me, to come to "know oneself," but rather to remind the reader and writer that there is an *I* doing the searching and writing who affects the bend and quality of truth in the work. And

so the *I* affects all conventional research papers inside and outside school, although that straight-standing, cocky little word seldom appears in the writers' texts.

Since I published a whole book on the I-Search called *Searching Writing* in June, 1980, I rarely speak of the idea publicly now, but teachers want to tell me of their own and their students' sense of newfound freedom in writing papers which record a search that has had meaning for them. For example, Bernadette M. Glaze, a Teacher-Consultant at the Northern Virginia Writing Project, wrote an 18-page, single-spaced story of teaching I-Search papers in American civilization at Lake Braddock Secondary School in Burke, Virginia. I call her report a "story" because it was written in the narrative form of an I-Search paper,

> *Happy the man who can search out the causes of things.*
> *VIRGIL*

proceeding naturally from: (1) what she knew and did not know about her topic when she started out; to (2) what she wanted to find out; to (3) the story of her search; to (4) what she learned. The point of using this archetypal story pattern in reports and research papers is that it shows the reader where the writer is coming from, whether it be a storehouse of experience or the height of naivete, and thus enables the reader better to judge the course and conclusions of the writer. In Bernadette Glaze's report she quotes some students' answers to her question (delivered before she returned the graded I-Search papers): "What would you tell a rising eleventh grader about I-Search?" Here are two students' responses:

- This paper is essentially a story of how and what you're finding out about a topic.

- It sounds like a lot to do an I-Search paper. Just forget about how long the final form will be; in fact, don't even think about it. First think of a subject—not just any subject but something that really interests you. Pick your subject with care, one that you don't know everything about. Then start the fun! See how creative you can get trying to figure new and different ways of searching out your topic. After you find something out, write it so you don't forget details. It's awful hard to sit down and write your whole search after you're done. Write a few sentences here and there—before you know it, you'll be done. Remember to keep a record of your sources.

Another teacher, Susan Bussard, a Fellow of the Northeast Texas Writing Project, described in the journal *English in Texas* (spring, 1981) her experience teaching the I-Search paper, and she quoted students' responses. One student noted, "The people I interviewed liked the idea because they knew I was really interested." Another recommended that "the I-Search should be mandatory for everyone to write at least once in life."

Again and again, the words *fun* and *easy* come up in students' comments. These words are not dignified enough for the conventional aims of education, although Alfred North Whitehead wrote a great deal about pleasure in his book *The Aims of Education,*[1] and the powerful searchers I have talked with outside school frequently speak of the fun they are having.

Most of the I-Search papers I have read from my classes and those of other teachers from around the country are easy and organic in form and have one authentic voice. The assignment carries with it a natural form that comes easily to a searcher. And since the assignment is the story of the writer in action, he or

[1]Alfred North Whitehead, *The Aims of Education.* New York: Free Press, a Division of Macmillan Publishing Co., Inc., 1967.

she does not need to cultivate a voice. It is there. Teachers who have assigned I-Search papers, including me, have been pleasantly shocked by the excellence of the writing. Almost never do we detect plagiarism, because the project is weighted so heavily toward reporting the writer's searchings and talks with authorities. And almost never do we find *Engfish* (the pretentious word-wasting dialect of school) in the paper. For example, a mother returning to school wrote:

> I wonder if becoming an R.N. is worth disrupting our family life for two years. Jason is only two years old, and I would really love to be able to stay home with him. Preteenage Vanessa frequently needs a mother around, and my husband has often said he didn't marry to exchange notes on the refrigerator.

There are three poles in the I-Search: the student searcher, the authorities to be consulted, and the persons likely to read the paper. What determines the validity and appropriateness of the material discovered and reported is the particular needs of the searchers. Once their reasons for searching, their requirements, and their degree of knowledge are put down on paper, then what they give the reader from the authorities they have consulted or interviewed is charged—carries a current that lights a particular lamp. No readers will be likely to think that the findings are supposed to illuminate all of their world, or all of the world of others. Properly directed, the I-Search is an exercise in intellectual modesty, a characteristic of most of the great inquirers.

The form of the I-Search enterprise is ancient, in some ways prehuman, like an animal hunting. "Tell the story of the hunt" is the instruction. Pompous ill-founded generalizing must be brought into such a paper by a great act of will. These kinds of statements are not inherent in the narrative of a quest dominated by face-to-face encounters with human beings talking about things dear to them.

One of Bernadette Glaze's students said, "This paper was a new experience in writing. It wasn't hard

at all. Once I started writing, everything flowed right out. It sounded natural because I just wrote what I thought without having to translate into a higher vocabulary bracket."

An uneasy teacher might say, "But isn't that what school is for—to extend the use of students' language beyond the conversational?"

I am reminded of a paper I saw one summer by a visitor to the Teaching Writing Program at the Bread Loaf School of English, where I was teaching. In it, Roger Shuy of Georgetown University pointed out that children learn to speak in stages, from intimate cooing with mother to casual and consultative talk and, eventually, to formal language. But in writing instruction in schools, children are expected immediately to jump to the formal level without first using the vernacular in narrative or in dialogue or in a special form Jana Staton of the Center for Applied Linguistics in Washington calls "complaining." To write in their own voices about things that count in their lives is surely the basic step for students learning to write.

Some I-Searchers have learned a great deal but have been content with one good source. They needed to search for several opposing views so that they would face the challenge of deciding among differing experts' opinions. But even this group has learned more from their searches than do most writers of conventional research papers.

Almost all the other weaknesses in papers, of whatever topic, have been traceable to an initial failure of students to choose a topic that represented a need rather than simply an interest. I believe this to be the crucial and most difficult point in aiding students to carry out an I-Search. The teacher must not allow an idle interest to become the motive for a search. "Something you *need* to find out in your life, however small or large," should be the ruling passion. But a teacher must persuade rather than dictate, for at the same time freedom to go after what counts for the writer rather than for the teacher is one of the pivots on which the whole project swings.

In reading papers written by my own students and those of many other teachers, I have usually been able to tell in the first paragraph whether or not the paper will be strong. "I've always been interested in handguns and so thought I would investigate the current controversy on banning and registering guns" does not sound like the beginning of a powerful I-Search paper. Such a beginning is usually composed by a student making the conventional school response to an assignment—guessing what the teacher wants him or her to be interested in. Or the student may be following the long traditions of phony scholarly detachment and not revealing his or her true needs. A mean-

ingful search grows from seeds in the writer's life, which need to be revealed immediately to the reader. Perhaps the writer's father and mother have just battled rawly over the presence of a gun in their house. Or a boy has a collection of firearms, and his priest has told him he should get rid of it. Where there is no genuine need or itch to know, the search will be half-hearted or desultory and the paper vague and *Engfishy*.

The search must answer a question that fits the *I* who began it. In that particularity, then, the searching becomes thoughtful and the findings refined. The enterprise begins to parallel, if not to match, the hardheaded search of a professional. One of the most fascinating experiments in I-Search writing was carried out by Glenn Irvin, a Director of the Northeast Texas Writing Project. After his students had completed I-Search papers, he asked them to remove the *I* and all personal details and experiences and to write a second version as a conventional research paper. As the papers grew more abstract in statement, they became markedly shorter, and to my mind, lost their authority as well as liveliness. My first reaction was fright: Did this prove that the original I-Search papers, shorn of their personal qualities, were embarassingly superficial? After sleeping on that question and looking again at the papers Glenn Irvin had sent me, I decided that the exercise proved something different: that conventional student research papers and I-Search papers without all the hopes, fears, attitudes, and experience of the *I* in them are half reports or less.

In the time available to high school and college freshman classes, students cannot thoroughly search a question or subject so as to speak authoritatively on it. In research paper assignments we are teaching students to pretend to unqualified authority and to pretend to have discovered something valuable (when almost all of them know they have not). I have always thought that if one is to look at a whole book or a long magazine article and excerpt material from it alone to present to someone else, the act is a charade. Lest anyone who has not read *Searching Writing* think that I am saying that the effort toward objectivity is not valuable, I want to stress that I speak rather against the extreme detachment from one's subject and the pretense of absolute objectivity characteristic of many student and professional research reports. In my chapters about the *Oxford English Dictionary,* the *Encyclopaedia Britannica,* the *Reader's Guide to Periodical Literature,* Noah Webster and Samuel Johnson, and the history of spelling, I tried to break down students' hatred of the school library by showing that the people whose reference works they encounter there were frail and inconsistent at times, brilliant and accurate at others. I have not yet had much teacher or student response to that considerable part of the book, and I would like to receive more comments.

My most recent book, *Twenty Teachers* (Oxford University Press, 1985), is my I-Search into the question, "What is excellence in teaching?"

For all the responses to the I-Search project, I thank hundreds of teachers in the country. We have found that students do not have to approach a research project with aversion or numbness. We do not have to teach them to labor at a work that counts for no one, while investing it with clumsily crafted trappings of serious and consequential human inquiry. Rather than killing their curiosity, we can reawaken it by enabling them to produce searching writing that both we and they can respect.

EDITOR'S NOTE: For further information on the I-Search paper, see Ken Macrorie's book *Searching Writing,* published in 1980 by Hayden Book Company, Inc.; and distributed by Boynton-Cook Publishers, P.O. Box 860, Upper Montclair, NJ 07043.

Practical Ideas for Using the I-Search Paper

Adapting the I-Search Paper for the Elementary Classroom

By Anita Freedman
Teacher, Fairhaven Elementary School,
Orange Unified School District;
and Teacher/Consultant, UCI Writing Project

Nothing is more scandalous in school and colleges than what we call "writing a research paper."
KEN MACRORIE

Remember the old saying, "Copy from one author and it's plagiarism; copy from several and it's a research paper." Well, it is still true. We think we are teaching students how to do research when all we are actually showing them is how to assemble scattered pieces of information. It is time to redefine our goals and change our methods. We need to start at the beginning, in the elementary school, where we first tackle making a report.

What are our objectives when we assign reports? We are trying to help our students develop:

- The ability to recognize responsible sources of information and ideas
- The ability to distinguish between fact and opinion
- A knowledge of the accepted forms of writing research
- The habit of testing facts and drawing conclusions

A new approach suggested by Ken Macrorie, Allan Edwards, Iris Tiedt, and others is the I-Search paper. Here are some ideas for using the approach in the third grade and above.

Before you begin, be sure your students are ready. Can they write expository paragraphs? Expository paragraphs, in contrast to what we commonly call creative writing, must be tightly constructed. A topic sentence and two or more sentences to back up the topic sentence are required.

Dr. Tiedt suggests that teachers ask their students to write five "I think" statements. For example:

I think purple is a beautiful color.
I think my brother should get a haircut.
I think *Mork and Mindy* was a good television program.
I think we should have a school cafeteria.
I think dogs make better pets than cats.

After writing these statements, each student chooses one to develop into a paragraph. The first sentence becomes the topic sentence that is then followed by sentences supporting the statement made by the author.

Then, work with these formal paragraphs in different ways so that your students become familiar with them and write them easily. Have your students rewrite their paragraphs, placing the topic sentence at the end. Using the chalkboard, help the class develop paragraphs together. Duplicate and distribute to your class paragraphs taken from articles, and discuss the way the authors developed them. Find selections in your textbooks, and go over them with the class.

Now you are ready to start the I-Search paper. There are three steps to developing this paper:

1. Identifying a problem to be studied
2. Searching for information
3. Writing the report

As a prewriting exercise, each student can write several statements beginning with, "I would like to know . . . ." These can be written about anything at all or specifically related to a topic the class is studying. After writing four or more statements, the students choose one topic that interests them. This warm-up activity stimulates thinking and assures students of having the key ingredient of the I-Search paper: finding a problem which they can get involved in.

Next, show students how to find information. Take them to the library so that they can investigate different reference books. Help them with the use of encyclopedias, atlases, almanacs, biographies, and the card catalog. Perhaps the library has a picture file or filmstrips available for them. Teach older boys and girls how to use the *Reader's Guide to Periodical Literature.* However, do not stop with the use of the library. Give the students practice in interviewing, in using the telephone book and then in telephoning resource people, and in writing letters to obtain information. Suggest sources for finding people who may be helpful to the students.

Here is a format for the actual report that elementary school students can follow:

1. Statement of the problem: What did I want to know?
2. Procedures followed: How did I find the information?
3. Summary of findings: What did I learn?
4. Conclusion: What will I do with this information?

Do not forget to have the students practice notetaking and to guide them in writing their final report.

All of this preparation will enable the students to tackle a report with confidence; the structure will guide them, and most important of all, they will learn how to do actual research. Pages copied from the encyclopedia will not appear in the students' papers when this plan is followed.

An I-Search topic has to be of high interest to the child; yet in our crowded curriculum, we often feel we must cover certain topics. We can combine the two demands. For example, instead of assigning the topic Indians, let the children tell about the tribe to which they would like to belong. Perhaps someone will report on why he or she would not like to be an Indian.

The children can write about whatever region you are studying in social studies and share with the class, "I would like to live in . . . ," and give their personal reasons for wishing to do so. In my class we talk about what qualities we want where we live, make a class list together, and duplicate it for each child. One class studying the Southeast had astounding results with this approach: Jill wrote to her grandmother for more information about Miami, and Glen wrote to all of his relatives in Atlanta for firsthand facts. The children did thorough research on amusement parks and beaches, the number of school days in the year, and what kinds of jobs their parents could get. Blair chose Washington, D.C., because, "My mom could take my brother to the hospital for his special treatments. They have excellent hospitals there [he listed some]. And my dad could be President."

When American history is taught, each child can research his or her own family. Parents and grandparents may appreciate the results. "Why My Family

Came to the United States" or "Why All My Neighbors Moved to California" would interest many reluctant writers, as would "Why Orange County Is a Great Place to Live." Career education can be the source for much research when the children write about what they want to be. Science fits in with "My Trip to Outer Space" (or "Under the Sea . . ."). A health unit could get the class involved in checking school lunch habits or exercise programs among the adults they question. Students might also enjoy researching a favorite holiday or solving a local problem. Other suggestions are "My Favorite Sport," "How the Students in Our School Feel About Mathematics," "What We Watch on Television," or "The History of Our Street." The topics are endless, limited only by the interests of the children.

The information the students gather in the I-Search should be shared with the class and perhaps with other classes as well. I often publish the I-Search papers in a class or a school newspaper, or I send them to the local paper or magazine. I may display them on a bulletin board, bind several for the school library, or feature the reports during open house for parents. In one way or another, I make sure that the research serves a purpose other than being read and graded by the teacher. I want the students to become so involved that their search becomes an end in itself, and my evaluation is confirmation of work well done. The password in this form of a research paper is *I*.

My Search

By Laurie Opfell
Former English Teacher, Irvine High School; Teaching Assistant, Department of English, University of Kentucky; and Teacher/Consultant, UCI Writing Project

Scott was a teacher's nightmare. He did not walk into a room; he pushed, shoved, and kicked his way in, leaving behind a wake of at least five outraged students, who reacted by howling and throwing their books at him or running to tell me. He was constantly stealing—pens, backpacks, teachers' editions of textbooks, or the coffee creamer. He was not selective. Since in all the time I knew him he never once did an assignment, he naturally had a great deal of spare time to throw spitwads, make nasty suggestions to the girls,

The best teachers of teachers are other teachers who are believable as consultants, because their ideas and the specific teaching strategies they demonstrate have been developed with real students in real classrooms.
JAMES R. GRAY

and make loud, obnoxious comments about anything and everything that went on in my classroom.

However, because Scott directed his hostility primarily toward the other students, he was actually easier to deal with than the ones who considered school a boring war with the teacher—private enemy number one. The ones who were openly defiant, who called me names under their breath, who accused me of losing their work, who threw tantrums if confronted by their unacceptable behavior—these were the ones I lost sleep over. As this was my first year of teaching, I found that all my ideals and enthusiasm about "the learning experience" seemed to be getting lost under this issue of control. I found myself feeling confused, angry, somewhat powerless, and totally outraged over this onslaught of emotional behavior. I could not imagine how or why I was allowing this group of thirteen-year-olds to terrorize my life, but one thing I did know was that teaching could be an intense and often painful experience.

When I decided to do an I-Search paper along with my eighth grade English class, a topic readily occurred to me: frustration in teaching. After deciding to go on a quest of my own, I identified three questions that I knew I needed some answers to:

1. What made the students show so many negative behaviors?
2. What made me respond in stress-producing ways?
3. What could I do to handle their behavior more constructively?

As I went through the various stages of the search, I found myself enjoying the opportunity to find some solutions to problems that were bothering me. I interviewed the school counselor and the assistant principal on the topics of coping with student behavior, understanding games the students play, and maintaining discipline in class. I was quite pleased to get some humorous and practical advice that really worked. I studied various psychologists' views on adolescent behavior and gained some relevant information. After typing my research, I read it and tried to decide what to say in my conclusion.

I found that I had answered each of my questions but that, in the process, I had learned some fairly disturbing things about myself. One was the concept that we dislike most in others what is also hidden somewhere in ourselves. This meant that the emotional, irrational, attention-getting behavior of the students was also there, in some form, in myself. This was an uncomfortable idea that I had to admit was true. I also learned that adolescents who show especially outrageous behavior are often stuck at a painful stage in the growth process. In some ways being stuck was something I could look back and see in my own life.

Finally, I learned that all adolescents are expected to answer the questions who am I? and where am I going? to reach successful maturity. These are difficult questions that I realized I had not answered myself. I came away from the finished report feeling that there were some important unfinished issues still left to be dealt with. But I was now better able to deal with them. I had gained a new self-awareness and a sense of compassion for the struggles of my students.

When I compare my first year of teaching in an intermediate school to this year, I realize that I still have a few Scotts and a few who direct their rebellion at me, but somehow they do not seem intimidating. I know that it is my search that has made the difference.

A Sample Prompt, Scoring Guide, and Model Paper for the I-Search

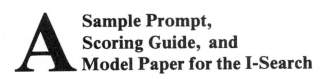

By Carol Booth Olson
Codirector, UCI Writing Project

I first learned about the I-Search paper at a California Writing Project Conference in Monterey. Allan Edwards, a Consultant from the Redwood Writing Project, had been experimenting with the concept that Ken Macrorie would introduce later that year in a book called *Searching Writing*. He was so excited about the results he was getting that I decided to try the idea.

What I like best about the I-Search assignment is that it encourages research that the student conducts out of a genuine need to know. So often, the traditional research paper is a passive enterprise in which the student merely analyzes and restates the results of someone else's intellectual inquiry, an inquiry that he or she may have no personal involvement in. When I think of research, I think of more than a visit to the card catalog and weekends spent in the library stacks. I think of firsthand activities like writing letters, making telephone calls, initiating face-to-face interviews, and going on field trips—supplemented by the valuable information that can be obtained from pertinent journals and books.

I agree with Ken Macrorie that the dictionary defi-

nition of research as a "patient study and investigation in some field of knowledge, undertaken to establish facts and principles" leaves out "the basic motivation for the whole effort" *(Searching Writing,* p. 162). My students are rarely patient about anything. I would rather have them get so involved in a topic that they launch their search for information in several different directions simultaneously than have them become bored before they begin, dragging their bodies down to the library, simply going through the motions of searching. Because the students have a stake in this paper, I find that after the initial excitement of getting started, they will sit down and take an objective look at what needs to be done and avail themselves of all the accessible secondary sources.

Based on Allan Edward's handouts and on Ken Macrorie's book, I developed a prompt describing the I-Search paper, which I distribute to students along with a scoring guide delineating criteria for evaluation, and a model student paper. Samples of all three items follow.

A Sample Prompt

THE I-SEARCH PAPER

DESCRIPTION

The I-Search paper is designed to teach the writer and the reader something valuable about a chosen topic and about the nature of searching and discovery. As opposed to the standard research paper in which the writer usually assumes a detached and objective stance, the I-Search paper allows you to take an active role in your search, to hunt for facts and truths firsthand, and to provide a step-by-step record of the discovery process.

TOPIC

The cardinal rule of the I-Search paper is to choose a topic that genuinely interests you and that you need to

EDITOR'S NOTE: For a more detailed account of how to implement the I-Search concept in the classroom, see this author's article, "Personalizing Research in the I-Search Paper," in the November, 1983, issue of the *Arizona English Bulletin.* Portions of this commentary have been reprinted from that article.

know more about. You may want to research teenage alcoholism, whether to pursue a second career in interior design, the effects of divorce on the American family, the pros and cons of several popular diets, and so forth. The important point is that you choose the topic you will investigate rather than having the instructor select a topic or even provide a number of options.

> *A meaningful search grows from seeds in the writer's life, which need to be revealed immediately to the reader.*
> KEN MACRORIE

FORMAT

The I-Search paper should be written in three sections: (1) What I know, assume, or imagine; (2) The search; and (3) What I discovered.

What I know, assume, or imagine. Before conducting any formal research, write a section in which you explain to the reader what you think you know, what you assume, or what you imagine about your topic. For example, if you decided to investigate teenage alcoholism, you might want to offer some ideas about the causes of teenage alcoholism, provide an estimate of the severity of the problem, and create a portrait of a typical teenage drinker, and so on.

The search. Test your knowledge, assumptions, or conjectures by researching your topic thoroughly. Consult useful books, magazines, newspapers, films, tapes, and other sources for information. When possible, interview people who are authorities on or who are familiar with your topic. If you were pursuing a search on teenage alcoholism, you might want to check out a book on the subject, read several pertinent articles in a variety of current magazines, make an appointment to visit a rehabilitation center for alcoholics, attend a meeting of Al-Anon or Alcoholics Anonymous, and consult an alcoholism counselor. You might also ask a number of teenagers from different social and economic backgrounds what their firsthand exposure to alcohol has been and whether they perceive any alcohol problems among their peers.

Write your search in narrative form, recording the steps of the discovery process. Do not feel obligated to tell everything, but highlight the happenings and facts you uncovered that were crucial to your hunt and contributed to your understanding of the topic. Document all your sources of information, using formal footnote form when it is appropriate.

What I discovered. After concluding your search, compare what you thought you knew, assumed, or imagined with what you actually discovered; and offer some personal commentary and draw some conclusions. For instance, after completing your search on teenage alcoholism, you might learn that the problem is far more severe and often begins at an earlier age than you formerly believed. You may have assumed that parental neglect was a key factor in the incidence of teenage alcoholism, but you now find that

peer pressure is the prime contributing factor. Consequently, you might want to propose that an alcoholism awareness and prevention program, including peer counseling sessions, be instituted in the public school system as early as the sixth grade.

BIBLIOGRAPHY

At the close of the report, attach a formal bibliography listing the sources you consulted to write your I-Search paper.

A Scoring Guide[1]

9—8 This paper is clearly superior. It is well-written, clearly organized, insightful, and technically correct. A 9—8 paper exhibits most or all of the following characteristics:

- Writing the paper was a genuine learning experience for the writer, and a person would benefit greatly from reading the paper.
- The paper displays evidence of critical thinking and offers special insight into the topic discussed.
- The topic lends itself to investigation and discovery.
- The paper is written in three sections. (The format may be explicit or implicit):
  - What I know, assume, or imagine (prior to the search)
  - The search (testing knowledge, assumptions, or conjecture through documented research)
  - What I discovered (comparing what you thought you knew with what you learned and offering commentary and conclusions)
- The author takes an active role rather than a passive role in the search.
- The writer uses research effectively as a supplement to, but not as a substitute for, his or her own ideas.
- The paper's tone and point of view convey a clear sense of the author's voice, or style.
- The writer uses precise, apt, or descriptive language.
- The main points of the essay are well-supported with examples.
- The writer uses ample transitions between ideas, paragraphs, and sections.
- The writer varies sentence structure and length.
- The search portion of the essay is properly documented with footnotes in correct form.
- The paper includes references to a minimum of two primary and two secondary research sources.
- The paper includes a formal bibliography.
- The writer generally uses effectively the conventions of written English.

7 This paper is a thinner version of the 9—8 paper. A paper rated 7 is still impressive and interesting, but it is less thoroughly researched, more loosely organized, less insightful, and not as informative as the 9—8 paper.

---

[1] *Note:* This scoring guide can be modified according to the grade level that you teach. For more information on evaluation, see the last section of this book and Chapter 5 of *Improving Writing in California Schools: Problems and Solutions,* which the State Department of Education published in 1983.

6—5 Scores of 5 or 6 apply to papers that are less well-handled than the 7, 8, or 9 paper. A 6—5 paper may be less interesting and informative, more superficially researched, and less insightful. It may contain problems in the conventions of written English. A 6—5 paper will exhibit some or all of the following characteristics:

- Writing the paper was a learning experience for the writer, but the paper is less informative than the 7, 8, or 9 paper, and thus, the lesson is less valuable for the reader.
- The paper does not display as much critical thinking or insight as the 7, 8, or 9 paper.
- The paper is written in three sections, but they are not equally complete or well-handled.
- The author does not seem genuinely involved in his or her topic.
- The writer may rely too heavily on the research rather than use it to augment his or her own thoughts.
- The paper does not convey a clear sense of the author's voice or style.
- The language is not as descriptive, precise, or apt as that of a 7, 8, or 9 paper.
- The main points of the report are not as well-supported with examples as they might have been.
- The three sections of the report are not tied together effectively with transitions.
- The sentence structure and length need more variation.
- The writer uses very few footnotes indicating that little research has been conducted, and the bibliography is sketchy.
- The paper does not refer directly to at least two primary and two secondary research sources.
- Some problems in the conventions of written English occur, but none that seriously impairs the message.

4—3 These scores apply to papers that maintain the general idea of the writing assignment, but they are weak in content, thought, language facility, or the conventions of written English. A 4—3 paper will exhibit some or all of these characteristics:

- Writing the paper was not a genuine learning experience for the writer. A person would not benefit from reading the paper.
- The paper demonstrates little or no evidence of critical thinking.
- The paper is not written in three sections, or the sections do not follow the guidelines set up in the assignment's description.
- The writer either relies too heavily on research or conducts very little, if any, research.
- The writer's "voice" does not come across.
- The language is vague and imprecise.
- The discussion is overly general or superficial.
- The main points are not supported with examples.
- The research sources are not documented in the bibliography or footnotes.
- The reader may have a problem understanding the paper.
- The paper has serious problems in the conventions of written English that impair the writer's message.

2 This score applies to papers that do not follow the writing assignment and contain weakness of the paper rated 4—3.

1 This score applies to a paper that is completely off track and has no redeeming qualities.

An extremely well-written and well-prepared paper may receive a rating of 10. If a paper has serious problems in the conventions of written English that impair the writer's message, it can receive up to a two-point deduction.

A Model Student Paper

Caren Rice, English 1A (Olson)
Saddleback Community College, North Campus

CANINE PARVOVIRUS

Just recently, I experienced the pain and trauma of almost losing a loved pet. Mandy was only a four and one-half month old puppy when, on a Friday night in October, she was suddenly struck with a severe illness.

The sickness first began with the loss of her appetite, followed by severe, convulsive vomiting. This went on for 24 hours, when I decided to call the emergency pet clinic.

"What are the dog's symptoms?" asked the nurse.

"Constant vomiting, loss of appetite, and lethargy," I replied.

"Does she have diarrhea?"

"No, not at all."

"Oh, thank goodness! She isn't showing the symptoms of parvo. Just give her some Pepto Bismol, and she'll be fine in a few hours."

Well, Mandy was given the antacid, and she still wasn't "fine." I thought perhaps that my eyes were betraying me, but in the short time that she had been sick, Mandy looked as if she had lost half of her weight. Her eyes were

bright red and to walk took all of her effort and strength. She refused to eat and drink.

This was only the beginning of what was to be a sleepless, heartsick week, and an eye-opener to the deadly dog-killing disease known as canine parvovirus.

What Is Parvo?

With a heavy heart and a guilty feeling, I took Mandy to the vet on Monday. I had heard of this disease and of the vaccine being given to ward it off. But I didn't take it seriously enough. I assumed that Mandy wouldn't get parvo since all of our neighbors' dogs had been vaccinated against the illness. Where else could she get it? Little did I know that Mandy could contract the disease just from walking on the grass outside our door. This was the beginning of my education on parvovirus.

Canine parvovirus was first identified at a Louisville, Kentucky, dog show in the spring of 1978 and spread to other dog shows throughout the country.[1] As a result of these dog shows, the disease soon spread overseas to Europe and Australia. Parvo was thought to have been a mutation of cat distemper, though it did not seem to affect cats in the same way. According to Dr. Martin Levin, scientists of veterinary medicine are still not sure what causes this almost always fatal disease.[2]

The question remains: How did canine parvovirus suddenly appear? The *Australian Veterinary Journal* has suggested openly that a contaminated batch of vaccine was responsible for the mutant virus.[3] Many doctors disagree with this theory because serial production lots of the vaccine are routinely monitored by the U.S. Department of Agriculture, which has yet to find a bad batch.

Now we are back to the same question: How did Parvo suddenly appear? From what I could gather at the clinic where Mandy was being treated, they still know very little about this disease.

Parvo and Its Cure

By Tuesday, it was confirmed that Mandy definitely had parvo, and her chance of survival was 15 percent. This really depressed me. I wanted to know why, what, and how. I pressed the doctor for more information.

"My knowledge is limited on this disease," he told me.

I asked him if he thought that Mandy would survive. Dr. Levin said that it was hard to determine. They knew that she had intestinal parvo, which if it could be called a plus, was one.

There are two known types of canine parvovirus. One is intestinal parvo. This virus grows in the intestinal tract of the dog, causing severe vomiting, loss of appetite, and diarrhea.[4] This can last for several weeks before the dog dies of malnutrition and exhaustion. If the disease is caught in its early stages, there is a chance of stopping it from spreading further, and a good chance of saving the animal. Mandy had suffered with the illness for 48 hours before I took her to the vet.

The other type of this disease is cardiovascular parvovirus. This virus starts in the arteries of the dog's heart and can kill the animal in as short a time as eight hours. The cardiac parvo is what usually strikes the very young puppies. The chance of survival of this form of parvo is almost zero.

Before veterinarians and pet owners became familiar with parvovirus, the mortality rate reached 40 percent among dogs with serious cases of the disease.[5] Puppies under ten weeks and older dogs are the most vulnerable.

Since parvo was first identified in the warmer months of spring and summer, it was hoped that perhaps cold weather would bring an end to the disease. But parvo proved to be a hardy virus, unaffected by temperatures.

When this disease began to break out in near epidemic proportions, many pet owners kept their dogs close to home, afraid that a trip to the vet might put a healthy animal in dangerous proximity to one carrying the virus.[6] Most pet owners, such as I, were naive to the fact that the shoes we wore could carry the virus into the house via contact with the feces of an infected animal.

Therapy is basically palliative—drugs to control vomiting and diarrhea, and fluids to prevent dehydration.[7] Without treatment, dogs often die of parvovirus within three days. It is one of the quickest killers of dogs known.

This was the therapy given to Mandy, as by Wednesday she still had not taken in any food or water, and her weight was dropping rapidly. I kept in close contact with Dr. Levin, and he, in turn, informed me of the effects of the disease on her. Her condition was stable, and despite loss of weight, there was a remote possibility that she would survive. After five days of being caught in a dark tunnel, I could see a spot of light in the distance.

The best protection against parvo is a new vaccine called parvocine. The lab that is producing it is working around the clock, turning out 1.5 million doses a month.[8] But there are 3 million doses on back order as clinics across the nation are operating at full capacity.

[1]Jean Seligman, "A Viral Epidemic Without a Cure," *Newsweek,* (August 19, 1980), 57.

[2]Martin Levin, Doctor of Veterinary Medicine, El Toro Animal Hospital, El Toro, Calif., December 11, 1980.

[3]Mike Macbeth, "Dogs, That Virus Is Still Loose," *MacLeans,* (March 3, 1980) 14.

[4]Seligman, p. 57.

[5]*Ibid.*

[6]*Ibid.*

[7]Martin Levin, December 11, 1980.

[8]Seligman, p. 57.

The vaccine does not cause immunity to parvo. Booster shots must be given every four to six months. It is not known just how effective the vaccine is, but there have been fewer cases of illness in immunized dogs than in ones that went untreated.

A Summary of Parvo

By Thursday, Mandy began to show signs of recovery. She became more responsive to the treatment and ate a small amount of food. I was told that if all went well, I could bring her home on Friday. I breathed a sigh of relief and thanked my lucky stars.

Mandy was one of the few dogs that survived this ravaging disease. The symptoms were still in their early stages when I brought her in and, therefore, the disease could be stopped from spreading further. When I picked her up on Friday, she was extremely thin, having lost half of her weight. But Mandy was alive and very glad to see me.

I can now reflect on the situation and realize how little we, as pet owners, know about our pets and their illnesses. We tend to take for granted that dogs are always healthy and need no help from us when they are sick. I realize now just how severely harsh diseases can affect our pets, especially when they cannot communicate their pain to us.

I am now well informed on canine parvovirus and through my own experience have learned a valuable lesson. The vaccine only costs about $7 to $14, but I chose not to buy it out of my own ignorance. Instead, I suffered a week of fear at the thought of losing my dog and a bill from the vet totaling over $140.

© 1984 ROY CHRISTIAN

I cannot recommend highly enough that teachers of writing who are unfamiliar with the I-Search paper learn more about it and assign it on a trial basis in at least one of their classes. When you personalize research and encourage students to bring everything they know about writing to their project, they produce some of their best work. In addition, they often discover something that is far more valuable to them than a letter grade or a numerical score.

The I-Search Paper: A Perfect Compromise

By Norma Tracy

English Instructor, California State University, Fullerton; and Teacher/Consultant, UCI Writing Project

Feeling somewhat guilty about never having assigned a research paper to my students in English composition at California State University, Fullerton, because of a lack of time and my own dread in having to read the boring topics, I seized on Ken Macrorie's I-Search paper as the perfect compromise.

Luckily for me and my students, Carol Olson's handout (which is included in her commentary in this section) was extremely clear-cut and complete. While skimming the syllabus with my students on the first day of classes, I explained briefly that this paper (not due until the last week of the course) would be a modified research paper that would be explained in fuller detail with handouts and examples as the semester progressed. I could see the raised eyebrows and hear the barely audible groans. Something about a research paper seemed to induce these predictable displays. Was I wrong in tackling this paper along with all the other required compositions?

By the third or fourth week of the course, I spent time in class discussing the paper, read some examples of I-Search papers, and asked the students to begin seriously considering a topic, one which they knew comparatively little about, but one which they wanted to pursue. One by one, topics were given to me as possibilities, and in spite of themselves, the students began to get caught up with their searches. These questions and discussions continued throughout the semester: "You mean I can use *I*?" "I don't have to give you a formal outline?" Relief permeated the class, and the most overheard question now became, "What are you doing your paper on?"

The "Saturation Report" (one of the required essays assigned the second month), interview sessions in and out of class, exercises in dialogue, and the various kinds of essays—narration, description, persuasion, classification, and so on—helped give students the confidence necessary for embarking on a new venture. By the time my students had completed the "Saturation Report" and discovered how they could apply different types of writing skills to the I-Search paper, they became very enthusiastic about the assignment.

Of course, my students, being human, were a mixture of those who worked hard and thoroughly as well as those who procrastinated. Yet all the students turned in an I-Search paper, and interestingly enough, no one wrote on the same subject. Many students personally told me how much they benefited from the assignment, even though they resented the extra work in the beginning. For many, this assignment was the first time they had really enjoyed looking for information because they did not have to worry about an overly structured format. Others felt the choice of subject matter finally allowed them to spend their valuable time earnestly searching out an interest, such as diabetes (in the case of the student who had just found out she had the disease) or mining (in the case of the student whose mother had just remarried to a miner).

For me the best part of this assignment was that I actually looked forward to reading the students' papers that were filled with their enthusiastic searches. And the students, who had enjoyed their superior position in almost always knowing more about their individual subjects after the search than I, had gained confidence in a mode of writing that will be useful to them in other classes. The compromise research paper worked.

Research Made Fun: Students' Responses to the I-Search Paper

By Joan Bower
English Instructor, Saddleback Community
College, South Campus;
and Teacher/Consultant, UCI Writing Project

"You know something? I had to narrow my focus down again! But I found this guy who gave me all this information, and he talked to me for an hour."

"I'm really learning about this Beverly Hills diet! I interviewed three girls yesterday who'd gotten sick on it even. This is so much more fun than just reading books from the library!"

"I almost feel like committing suicide! Well—not really. But after trying to phone the suicide crisis line for three days just to see how they'd react, I'm frustrated. The super 'run-around' and busy signals would drive anyone crazy! No wonder so many kids give up!"

Just what kind of assignment provoked such remarks? It was my first experiment with the I-Search paper. Although I had always spent time on controversial subjects to stimulate interesting topics for persuasive research in freshman composition courses, one semester I decided to change the emphasis and stress a first-person approach to research.

The result proved to be a smashing success. Students became aware of numerous resources beyond the marvels of the library. One student said, "I really enjoyed looking up sources in the library, then contacting that one author by phone. I'd never have found my major field of emphasis for the next four years without his long-distance advice." In addition, the difference between primary and secondary sources sharpened.

"Doing the actual experiments with the Ouija board sure made the book's information easier to verify. The firsthand research seemed so much better," an experienced encyclopedia researcher observed. Best of all, persuasive research papers proved to be enjoyable and educational for almost everyone involved.

The comments from some of the first-time researchers included these:

> Writing about the bad effects of smoking so my family would know really made this paper worthwhile. I'm sure my brothers will learn something, too.

> Interviewing other older women about their college enrollments really strengthened my determination to forge ahead. I realize I'm not alone either!

> After I talked to those guys in jail and some of my neighbors, I really hope now that I don't end up beating my wife someday. All of the men I interviewed had been abused children just like I was.

Because of all the enthusiasm on the part of students, plus the fascinating diversity of subject matter generated by the I Search, I decided to continue to use the assignment in future classes. My students made the following suggestions for implementing it the second time:

- Encourage the use of the first person whenever possible, but do not exclude an objectively written final draft if the paper is to be presented in another course as well.

- Require that a topic lend itself to persuasion so that the paper is not just a "learning about" experience.

- Require at least two authentic interviews to preclude the use of most previously written or purchased papers.

- Provide ample time in class for careful and thoughtful recommendations about classmates' papers during the "What I Think I Know" and rough draft read-arounds. (For a description of the read-around technique and suggstions on its use, see Jenee Gossard's article that appears in the "Sharing/Responding" section of this book.)

- Emphasize the value of careful proofreading.

Yes, the I-Search paper is a true learning experience. I say this because my students recommended it as the most beneficial assignment of the course.

Sharing/Responding

Some Guidelines for Writing-Response Groups

By Peter Elbow
Director of Composition,
State University of New York,
Stony Brook

To improve your writing, you do not need advice on what changes to make, and you do not need theories of what is good and bad writing. You need *movies* of people's minds while they read your words. But you need the movies for a sustained period of time—at least two or three months. And you need to get the reactions of not just a couple of people but of at least six or seven. And you need to keep getting them from the *same* people so that they get better at transmitting descriptions of their experiences and you get better at hearing them. And you must write something every week. Even if you are very busy, even if you have nothing to write about, and even if you experience writer's block, you must write something and try to experience it through those other people's eyes. Of course the writing may not be good; you may not be satisfied with it. But if you learn only how people perceive and experience words you are satisfied with, you are missing a crucial area of learning. You often learn the most from reactions to words that you hate.

In the paragraphs that follow, I will try to help you set up and use a writing-response group. If you get confused, remember that everything is designed to serve only one utterly simple goal: The writers should

EDITOR'S NOTE: We are grateful to Oxford University Press for permission to reprint excerpts from *Writing Without Teachers* by Peter Elbow. Copyright © 1973 by Oxford University Press, Inc. For further information on the use of writing-response groups, see *Writing Without Teachers* (1975) and *Writing with Power: Techniques for Mastering the Writing Process* (1981), both published by Oxford University Press, Inc., 200 Madison Avenue, New York, NY 10016.

learn how their words were *actually* experienced by their particular readers.

Setting Up the Class

Learning to make use of a class that depends heavily on students' responses to each other's writing is a struggle. To develop this kind of class, you need a committed group of students. You need the same people writing and taking part every week so that they have the time to get better at giving reactions and hearing them. You need to maintain the initial commitment of the class so that everyone continues to participate.

The main thing to remember in setting up the class is that *what* you and your students write does not matter as long as you write something. Treat the rigid requirement as a blessing. Since the class must produce something every week, expect some of the writing to be terrible. You and your students cannot improve your writing unless you put out words differently from the way you put them out now and find out how your readers experience these new kinds of writing. You cannot try out new ways of generating words unless many of them feel embarrassing, terrible, or frightening. But you and your students will be surprised in two ways. Some passages that you currently hate you will discover to be good later. And some of the reactions that most improve your writing are brought on by terrible writing—writing you would not have shown to someone if you had had more time to rewrite the material.

Use whatever procedure you think is best for deciding what to write. Write the same kind of thing over and over again—even the same piece over and over again if you wish. Or try out wildly different things. There is no best or right way. If you have the desire to write, you probably dream of doing some particular kind of writing. Do it. Or if there is something differ-

> *I always try to write on the principle of the iceberg. There is seven-eighths of it under water for every part that shows. Anything you know, you can eliminate, and it only strengthens your iceberg.*
> ERNEST HEMINGWAY

ent that you believe you should work on first, follow your own advice.

Should you hand out copies of what the class has written or read the writing out loud? Both ways have their advantages. Giving out copies to the class saves class time because silent reading is quicker; you can stop and think, go back, read more carefully, and if the piece of writing is long, you can let students take it home and read it there. This procedure may be more possible than you think. Many photocopying processes are cheap; or making three to five copies from carbon paper is easy, and writing or typing onto duplicating masters is easy. Class members may leave a single copy of their writing where everyone else can read it carefully before class.

But reading out loud is good, too. When you and your class read your writing out loud, you often hear things in it that you do not experience any other way. Hearing your own words spoken gives you the vicarious experience of being someone else. Reading your words out loud stresses what is most important. Writing is really a voice spread out over time, not marks spread out in space. The audience cannot experience words all at once as they can a picture. They can only hear one instant at a time, as with music.

When you read something out loud in class, always read it twice and allow at least a minute of silence after each reading for impressions to become clearer for your listeners.

Giving Movies of Your Mind

As a reader giving reactions, keep in mind that you are not answering a timeless, theoretical question about the objective qualities of those words on that page. You are answering a time-bound, subjective but *factual* question: What happened in *you* when you read the words *this time?*

Pointing to the words. Start giving your reactions by simply pointing to the words and phrases which most successfully penetrated your skull: Perhaps they seemed loud or full of voice, or they seemed to have a lot of energy, or they somehow rang true, or they carried special conviction. Any kind of *getting through* is possible. If I have the piece of writing in my hand, I tend to put a line under such words and phrases (or longer passages) as I read. Later when telling my reactions, I can try to say which kind of *getting through* it was if I happen to remember. If I am listening to the piece read out loud, I simply wait until the end and see which words or phrases stick in my mind. I may jot them down as they come to me in the moments of silence after the readings.

Point also to any words or phrases which strike you as particularly weak or empty. Somehow they ring false, hollow, or plastic. They bounce ineffectually off your skull. (I use a wavy line for these when I read with a pencil.)

Summarizing the writing. Another way to give your reactions to a piece of writing is to summarize it. This can be done by following these procedures:

1. First, tell very quickly what you found to be the main points, main feelings, or centers of gravity. Just sort of say what comes to mind for 15 seconds; for example, "Let's see, very sad; the death seemed to be the main event; um . . . but the joke she told was very prominent; lots of clothes."
2. Next, summarize the writing in a single sentence.
3. Then choose *one word* from the writing which best summarizes it.
4. And finally, choose a word that is not in the writing to summarize it.

Do this procedure informally. Do not plan or think too much about it. The point is to show the writer what things he or she made stand out the most, what shape the thing takes in your consciousness. This is not a test to see whether you got the words right. It is a test to see whether the words got *you* right. Be sure to use different language from the language of the writing. This ensures that the writing is filtered through your perception and experience, not just parroted. Also, try this test a week later: Tell someone what you remember of his or her last week's piece.

Pointing and summarizing are not only the simplest ways to communicate your perception but also the most foolproof and the most useful. Always start with pointing and summarizing. If you want to play it safe and make sure your class is successful, if you are terribly short of class time, or if your class is coming apart, try skipping all the following ways of giving feedback.

Telling the writer what happened. Simply tell the writer everything that happened to you as you tried to read his or her words carefully. It is usually easiest to tell what happened in the form of a story. First this happened, then this happened, then this happened, and so on. Here is an example of *telling* from the tape recording of an actual class:

> I felt confused about the man in the gray suit and the men gathered around you. I suppose they're the cops and the escorts. I had first thought [that] the [person in the] gray suit was a cop, but then I thought he was a dignified person who got arrested. I was uncertain about it. And then you talked about the men gathered around at one point—fairly early. I felt like they were cops, and I wanted you to contrast them to the fantasies.
>
> There was one point where you talked about—I think you were going down the stairs—and I felt like that whole part with the father of the bride and the gown was like the flash a person has supposedly, when he's going to drown and his whole life flows before him. I thought it

was like an initiation of a girl—or a woman, particularly—out of her whole parental, social, ball-gown past into this new thing. And I was, I just, I was *surprised.* I didn't expect you to describe things that way. I was really happy. Then for some reason I felt like when you talked about the men who were gathered around—I felt like they were cops—and if I heard it again I might feel like I didn't need to have you say it, but at the time, as you said it, I wanted them to be blue-suited or something contrasting. Perhaps that wouldn't be necessary for some other reader.

> I had a very sort of happy feeling when you went to drinking songs. But it felt like the whole history of someone's life from being a young bride to becoming an old fishwife. I felt like it was a social comment in a way. One gets brought up and goes from the ideal fantasies to being fat and a drinking companion in pubs. And I was just very happy at that change in age. It seemed like the whole thing was—if it were a movie it would be going around like this—but the history of a whole person in a way retold in capsule form.

The important thing in telling is not to get too far away from talking about the actual writing. People sometimes waste time talking only about themselves. But on the other hand, do not drift too far away from talking about yourself either, or else you are acting as though you are a perfectly objective, selfless critic.

To help you in *telling*, pretend that there is a whole set of instruments you have hooked up to yourself that record everything that occurs in you, not just pulse, blood pressure, and so on, but also ones that tell every image, feeling, thought, and word that happens in you. Pretend that you have hooked them all up and that now you are just reading the printout from the machines.

> *To the man with an ear for verbal delicacies—the man who searches painfully for the perfect word, and puts the way of saying a thing above the thing said—there is in writing the constant joy of sudden discovery, of happy accident.*
> H. L. MENCKEN

Showing the writer your reaction. When you read something, you have some perceptions and reactions which you are not fully aware of and thus cannot "tell." Perhaps they are very faint, perhaps you do not have satisfactory language for them, or perhaps for some other reason you remain unconscious of them. But though you cannot *tell* these perceptions and reactions, you can *show* them if you are willing to use some of the metaphorical exercises listed below. These may seem strange and difficult at first; but if you use them consistently, you will learn to tap knowledge which you have but which is usually unavailable to you:

- Talk about the writing as though you were describing voices; for example, shouting, whining, whispering, lecturing sternly, droning, speaking abstractedly, and so forth. Try to apply such words not only to the whole thing but also to different parts.

- Talk about the writing as though you were talking about weather; for example, foggy, sunny, gusty, drizzling, cold, clear, crisp, muggy, and so forth. Use this approach not just with the whole thing but with different parts.

- Talk about the writing as though you were talking about motion or locomotion; for example, as marching, climbing, crawling, rolling along, tiptoeing, strolling, sprinting, and so forth.

- Other ways to use this approach to talk about writing are as follows:

  Clothing: for example, jacket and tie, dungarees, dusty and sweaty shirt, miniskirt, hair all slicked down, and so forth.
  Terrain: for example, hilly, desert, soft and grassy, forested, jungle, clearing in a forest, and so forth.
  Color: for example, what color is the whole? the parts?
  Shape: for example, square, round, oblong, triangular, cylindrical, and so forth.
  Animals: for example, cat, lion, mouse, frog, moose, bear, elephant, gazelle, and so forth.
  Vegetables: for example, carrot, broccoli, cauliflower, lettuce, and so forth.
  Musical instruments: for example, trumpet, flute, drum, clarinet, tuba, trombone, violin, oboe, and so forth.
  A body: for example, what kind of body? which parts are feet, hands, heart, head, hair, and so forth?

- Think of the piece of writing as having magically evolved out of a different piece of writing, and it will eventually evolve into some other piece of writing that again is different. Tell where it came from, where it is going.

- Describe what you think the writer's intention was with this piece of writing. Then think of some crazy intention you think he or she might have had.

- Assume that the writer wrote the piece that is being discussed *instead* of something very different from what was really on his or her mind. Guess or fantasize what you think was really on the writer's mind.

- Assume that soon before the author wrote this piece, he or she did something very important or something very important happened to him or her—something that is not obvious from the writing. Say what you think it was.

- Pretend that this piece was written by someone you have never seen. Guess or fantasize what he or she is like.

- The writing is a lump of workable clay. Tell what you would do with that clay.

- Pretend to be someone else—someone who would have a very different response to the writing from what you had. Give this other person's perception and experience of the writing.

- Draw quickly the picture or doodle that the writing inspires in you. Pretend that the writing was received only by your arm with its pencil; now let them move.

- Make the sound the writing inspires or imitate the sound of the writing. Make different sounds for different parts.

- Jabber the writing; that is, make the sound you would hear if someone were giving a somewhat exaggerated reading of it in the next room—in a language you had never heard (also compress the writing into 30 seconds or so).

- Let your whole body make the movements inspired by the writing or different parts of it. Perhaps combine sounds and movements.

- Do a ten-minute writing exercise on the writing, and give it to the writer.

- Meditate on the writing and try to tell the author about what happened. Do not think about his or her writing. Try, even, to make your mind empty, but at the same time fully open to the writing. It is as though you do not chew and do not taste—just swallow it whole and noiselessly.

These *showing* procedures are not very useful until you get over being afraid of them and unless you give two or three at a time. Therefore, I make it a rule that for your first four classes, you make at least a couple of these oblique, metaphorical statements on each piece of writing. This procedure may seem strange and uncomfortable at first. Indeed, the reason I make this an explicit demand is that I have discovered that people in some trial writing-response groups were too timid to use them. In other classes where people did use them, almost everyone came to enjoy them and find them useful.

Do not struggle with these procedures. Try to let the words just come. Say the thing that comes to mind, even if it does not make any sense. And for the first few weeks, do not expect satisfactory results.

There is an easy way to think of the relation between telling and showing. Telling is like looking inside yourself to see what you can report. Showing is like installing a window in the top of your head and then taking a bow so the writers can see for themselves. There is no need to try to remember what was happening as you read. Just bow. Showing conveys more information but in a more mixed and ambiguous form than telling.

Further Advice to Readers

The following additional advice is given to help readers become more effective in the writing-response group:

- Make sure you have had a good chance to read the writing.
- Never quarrel with someone else's reaction.
- Give specific reactions to specific parts.
- No kind of reaction is wrong.
- Though no reactions are wrong, you still have to try to read well.

- Sometimes you may not want to give your reactions; respect this feeling.
- You are always right and always wrong. (You are always right in that no one is ever in a position to tell you what you perceive and experience. But you are always wrong in that you never see accurately enough, experience fully enough.)

Advice to Writers on Listening

The following advice is given to help writers benefit from their readers' comments in a writing-response group:

- Be quiet and listen.
- Do not try to understand what people tell you; just listen and take it all in.
- But do try to understand *how* they make their comments.
- Do not reject what readers tell you.
- Do not stop them from giving you reactions.
- But do not be tyrannized by what they say.
- Ask for the specific feedback you want, but do not play teacher with them.
- You are always right and always wrong. (You are always right in that your decision about the writing is always final. But you are always wrong in that you can never quarrel with their experience—never quarrel even with their report of their experience.)

Practical Ideas for Sharing/Responding

Implementing Sharing Groups in the First-Grade Classroom

By Michael Carr
Teacher, Los Alamitos Elementary School,
Los Alamitos Unified School District;
and Teacher/Consultant, UCI Writing Project

Writers of all ages need feedback in order to develop a concept of audience. Students of all ages can be trained to be an audience and to give specific, meaningful responses to each other's writing. This is true as early as the first grade.

I have been implementing peer sharing groups in my classroom since my exposure to Peter Elbow's response group techniques during the 1981 UCI Writing Project. One major modification to the model for children in the first grade is to have one large rather than several small groups. After the children have

completed their writing, they assemble on the rug and sit in a large circle. Our rules are simple. The author reads his or her piece of writing, and the group listens. There can be no talking during the reading, as that takes away from the piece of writing. The reader needs to have the center stage. Because of this rule, the children have developed a sense of mutual respect and trust—both of which are essential elements in a sharing group.

After completing the reading, the author can choose three people to respond to the writing. All comments, to begin with, have to be positive in nature. Later I hope to show the children how to tell whether or not the piece of writing was on the topic and whether the writing worked for them as listeners. The group must respond to certain parts of the writing or corresponding illustration and cannot make general, evaluative statements, such as, "I like your writing." The children must be very specific about what words or sentences they liked by using Peter Elbow's pointing techniques. This approach gives the writer specific feedback and increases the ability of the group to recognize vivid

language, effective use of details, and so forth. After three people have shared their reactions, the writer has the option of responding to the sharing group or letting the next writer share his or her work.

This process of sharing has given the first graders in my room a sense of purpose for their writing, an audience for sharing, and a forum for positive feedback. The enthusiastic attitude toward writing in my classroom can be traced back to the successful sharing group.

An Argument for Sharing in Triads

By Charles L. Reichardt
English Teacher, Pine Middle School,
Los Alamitos Unified School District;
and Teacher/Consultant, UCI Writing Project

Of the stages of the writing process inherent in the model advocated by the California Writing Project, I believe that the concept of sharing is the most important. As I sit down to write this commentary, I am thinking of my audience, mentally anticipating the needs of those individuals with whom I will share my thoughts, and remembering that my experience with peer groups was the most positive aspect of my participation in the UCI Writing Project.

I first heard of Peter Elbow's writing-response groups at a weekend conference over two years ago. When I first attempted writing groups with my sixth grade class, I followed Mr. Elbow's model closely and found that the logistics of the process did not suit my

classroom situation. The meeting time was too lengthy, my students had trouble remaining on task, and it was hard to form groups of five or six members without moving a great deal of furniture. Having the students prepare five or six copies of their work was difficult. Photocopies were costly for the students to make and carbon copies were messy. Eliminating these problems took over a year, yet finding the correct formula for my classroom's needs has been both creative and rewarding.

My groups now meet in threes, forming a triangle with the reader at the apex and the response partners at the base, as shown in Figure 26.

When sharing, the writer reads his or her piece aloud to the two peer responders and then passes it to them to read silently. This reading process eliminates the need for either photocopies or carbon copies and means that my class has only to move chairs to form the groups. Time is very easy to control because the process of reading, rereading, and sharing rarely takes more than seven minutes. The three members of the group can share in about 20 minutes. Rewriting often begins during the remaining minutes of a 45-minute period. My students love that!

There are other benefits of meeting in groups of three. With about ten groups in a class, you can disperse your best writers, making them leaders in the group. At the same time, your weakest writers are not congregated together, and they have the leadership and talent of a peer to rely on when there are problems. I was also able to control problems of concentration arising from close friends discussing topics other than writing by separating friends and making sure that each group had at least one girl and one boy. Careful grouping can help students, especially junior high school students, stay on task and promote meaningful interaction among the writer and his or her peer partners. While these triads meet, I can hold confer-

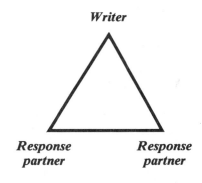

Writer

Response partner   *Response partner*

Fig. 26. Sharing in Triads

ences with individual students, circulate from group to group, or simply make myself available as a response partner when a group requires a third opinion.

Sharing in triads remains a key component of my writing class. I have found that limiting the size of peer groups to three students makes sharing more efficient for my classroom situation and student population without lessening the quality of the feedback. I recommend that other teachers who have found larger peer groups too unwieldy or the paperwork too cumbersome try sharing in triads rather than abandoning this valuable group interaction.

At First . . . And At Last

By Julie Simpson
English Teacher, Sunny Hills High School, Fullerton Union High School District; and Teacher/Consultant, UCI Writing Project

When it came to writing, I had considered myself to be the epitome of the expression, "Those who can, do; those who can't, teach." I was the one in college who invariably turned in her term papers late and who knew full well they were not good. I was the one who shopped around for years to find a master's program in her field that did not require a thesis. So it was with great trepidation that I applied to become a UCI Writing Project Fellow. I wanted to learn about teaching writing; I just did not want to have to do any of it in the process.

In the first paper I wrote for my writing group, I explored my frustrations:

> So much fear surrounds the idea of writing—fears of mediocrity, fears of criticism, fears of rejection. What if I "dare disturb the universe?" What if I open my gut and expose my sincerest thoughts and efforts to the world—and it yawns?
>
> Here I am, supposed to write something. Anything. And it's Sunday night, and I've been thinking for days and have nothing to say. No creative Ah-ha's have come at the end of any of the various clusters I've begun. I have a few ideas. But no faith. And thus no words. I sit—imageless, plotless, metaphorless. Empty.
>
> It's so much safer to be an audience, to read and react to others' writings—to find people who speak for me and who do it better than I ever could. Obviously, my ideas can't be as significant as those of the greats who have gone before me. I have nothing new to say. When I think of things to write, other people's lines and characters and

plots surge through my mind, drowning any spark of originality I might hope for.

I suppose I should have confidence enough to realize that since no one has seen the significant truths of the universe through my eyes, I could at least add my per-

> *Showing is like installing a window in the top of your head and then taking a bow so the writers can see for themselves.*
> *PETER ELBOW*

sonal vision to the ocean of visions already written. I have subjects. I want to write about having to endure aloneness and continual loss—the process of living. But I am no Alan Watts. I want to write about "passion" and how it is essential, even though it creates all the pains of life. But I am no Peter Shaffer. I want to write a story or poem about the exquisite pain of being separated from the one you dearly love. I want to create the eternity of a day without him. And to describe the surprise of recognizing that moments passed when you actually thought of something other than him, when you actually entered the world for a little while. But I am no Emily Dickinson or Edna St. Vincent Millay.

I want to write a story juxtaposing the interior, real, reality with the exterior game of reality we all play. I want to be able to create a slice of life that would portray the struggle of getting through another outward day, pretending to focus on it and to thrive in it, while all the while living only in a secret, emotional other world that is the true reality. But this is so personal that it would take the perfect words to communicate precisely what I mean. And I have no plot in mind. And I don't know how to create characters or dialog. And, and, and . . . .

And I'm afraid that someone might stop midsentence and complain, "How boring!" I'd feel "pinned and wriggling on the wall," and it wouldn't have been worth it, after all.

That is how I began. I understood, firsthand now, my students' hesitations and anxieties about writing. I felt as inferior as they did. But within the five weeks of the Writing Project, I learned to deal with my fears. Having a supportive, interested writing group that responded to my work from a personal as well as a professional perspective made all the difference.

Here is an excerpt from my final position paper:

> Besides reinforcing a couple of truisms I have always known, the Writing Project has exposed me to essential new ideas that will permanently affect my teaching. Learning about developing fluency through the domains of writing has taught me a most valuable awareness: Students must be viewed as writers. The fact that I was considered a writer from the start of the Writing Project was undoubtedly the biggest learning experience of the summer. I tried to fight it and insist that I had nothing to say, but I got hooked, nonetheless. I have learned that,

either inside me or outside in the world through my eyes, there *is* something that I can write about. And every time I come up with an idea, I feel proud: Hey! I can do that. I have learned that a subject doesn't have to be unique to be writable. And I've learned that I can conquer the battle of how to show an idea once I have it: I can always make it more concrete—to communicate. I feel proud about my own words; I no longer demand that they be great. I look forward to sharing them with others.

I want my students to discover the same sort of satisfaction in writing and sharing and to experience the same sort of pride in their work as I do in mine.

When I treat students as writers, I accept that they have a warehouse of experiences, sensations, ideas, and reactions to write about. My job, then becomes one of a facilitator more than an evaluator. I can help them tap their resources. I can help them view themselves as writers and, in a way, as more significant people.

Response Groups in the Business Writing Class

By Sheila Koff
Instructor of English, Orange Coast College:
and Teacher/Consultant, UCI Writing Project

Dashing up the steep two flights of stairs to my business writing class at California State University, Fullerton, clutching my latest transparencies and duplicated copies, I wondered whether this day's lesson might possibly create that rare, authentic learning environment that was so satisfying for my previous composition students. Although I had taught business writing as a component of other classes on other college campuses, I had never had a class of junior and senior business majors, focusing entirely on business writing. As I struggled to get my fingertips around the slippery door knob, I was not sure whether my gasping resulted from my sprint up the stairs or from the fear that the lesson might not work. These strong-willed, opinionated, future business leaders just might balk at sharing their hard work with a group of peers, even if the spirit of cooperation is encouraged in this competitive world.

Since it was the first Friday of the spring semester, I did not yet know their 28 names, nor did they know each other, which only increased my apprehension on entering the room.

"Good morning. Hello," I nodded to blurred strangers, trying to manufacture a smile. "Today, as I explained to you this past Wednesday, I would like you all to arrange your desks in circles of five." Chairs rumbled and screeched as metal scraped more scuffs into those already marking the ancient gray linoleum. Uncomfortable and embarrassed faces now nervously perused pens, rough drafts, and peeling nail polish.

"Before you begin this assignment, would you please take about five to ten minutes to introduce yourselves to your group. Go counter-clockwise until all have been introduced."

In spite of several years of using Peter Elbow's response groups from his *Writing Without Teachers,* I have yet to willingly let go of my need for teacher control. As always, at first, the students were ill at ease in their unfamiliar circles—and so was I. My confidence disintegrated a little more with each of their dubious or painful side glances to one another.

Just to reassure myself, I reviewed my notes from Wednesday about why the response group is used. The majority of these students were unfamiliar with group sharing. But they had agreed on Wednesday that since writing is a process of continually refocusing for clarity, it would be beneficial to read their first and second drafts aloud in groups. They also agreed that writing for a real purpose, to convey a message, and for their peers, whom they would soon know, was more realistic than writing for a letter grade and for an instructor they would probably know only formally.

While I was passing out duplicated copies of Peter Elbow's pointing steps, I listened to some laughter and inquiring comments rising from the group members' introductions. Breathing a little easier, I began to

review gently and carefully with them Peter Elbow's pointing steps, along with the writing rubric on the overhead transparency. Because they were anxious to begin sharing their first drafts of business memos, I then instructed one writer in each group to pass out his or her four copies to the other group members.

Sometimes while weaving unobtrusively around the sharing and pointing circles, I would catch and correct potential problems. Some reticent American and shy foreign-speaking students tried to avoid reading aloud by suggesting that the group members silently read their papers. Some groups forgot the positive commenting phase and immediately began making negative comments. As expected, others focused on grammatical problems that are better reserved for a later editing stage of the process. It was easy to help individual responders point to specifics in each person's writing and to suggest that they keep an eye on the rubric adapted for that particular writing assignment. Although initially I felt shaky in my new observer-facilitator role, I soon reaped the benefits from gently insisting on strict adherence to Peter Elbow's guidelines. The students were better able to help each other, and I quickly adjusted to their not regularly needing me. I was impressed by the intense cooperation shared by these highly competitive students as they helped each other toward individual excellence.

During the last five minutes of class, after at least three papers had been shared in each group, I asked the students to write anonymous accounts of how they felt about their first interaction with group members. My fears were all for naught. Here are some reactions:

I feel that the group meeting is a very effective idea. It gives people in the class a good way of having a peer review of their work. Also, it gives students a chance to participate in the class on a group and on an individual basis.

I like the idea of meeting in groups to discuss our papers. It helps to see how other members in the group have approached the assignment and exposes the different styles of writing they have acquired. The group meetings should continue, as everyone in the group benefits from the experience.

I feel quite comfortable with my group. They make constructive comments and offer good ideas for improvement.

I have found the group interaction most helpful. We have been able to generate a lot of ideas about our assignment. These ideas will help me in preparing my final draft. In addition, my group is friendly and therefore not shy about offering criticisms, as well as compliments. We all get along well, so I think we will be able to help one another more as the semester continues. (I think I should also mention that prior to this semester, I had a negative attitude about group work, but that has changed as a result of this class.)

I believe working with a group is a good way to improve your writing. Everyone can help each other in organizing structure, word choice, and grammar. In addition, people in a group always give you good ideas or suggestions to make your essay better. However, we should have a group leader so he or she can pull us back to reality when we go too far outside the topic that we're discussing.

Other than the last comment about the need for a group leader, the only other suggestion was that groups should be carefully monitored by the instructor to ensure that all members participate.

Many weeks later, after several kinds of group interaction had occurred, I knew that the students needed less of my intervention to facilitate their group process. And the problem with inactive members resolved itself simply from group pressure and the high expectations of individual members.

My business writing students adapted easily to Peter Elbow's peer-response groups, energetically teaching each other—a few even pleading for the chance to do third drafts. Meanwhile, I warily eye my multiplying stack of papers to be graded, but I am comforted by the fact that I will be reading writing that has evolved and improved because of peer group responses.

> *You and your students cannot improve your writing unless you put out words differently from the way you put them out now and find out how your readers experience these new kinds of writing.*
> PETER ELBOW

RAGs for Sharing/Responding

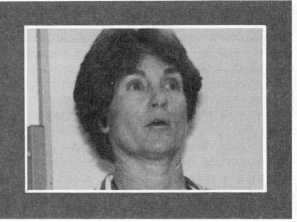

Using Read-Around Groups to Establish Criteria for Good Writing

By Jenee Gossard
Chairperson, Department of English, Culver City High School;
and Teacher/Consultant, UCLA Writing Project

A few years ago, I realized that the only way my students were ever going to learn to write better was for them to write more often, revise more willingly, and edit more effectively than they had been doing in the past. In addition, they needed a wider and more "real" audience to write for and a clearer sense of the purpose for each piece of writing. In short, their entire writing experience needed to be much more extensive and much more realistic than it had been.

On the other hand, I definitely did not want to read and mark any more papers of the kind my students typically handed in—dashed off the night before, bloated with generalizations and cliches, and riddled with irritating errors of expression and conventions. As I began to experiment with solutions for this dilemma, I found myself relying more and more on a modified small-group technique that seemed ideally suited to the special needs of a writing class.

The Read-Around Group Approach

Basically, the read-around group (RAG) approach gives students the opportunity to read and respond to each other's writing at several stages in the process of any assignment. For example, they read each other's first drafts to discover how others solved the problem of finding a subject and getting started. They read second and third drafts to note progress in shaping the paper according to criteria established in discussions of earlier drafts. Later, they help each other edit nearly finished papers for specific requirements of form, language use, and conventions of writing. At the end of the process, they evaluate final drafts, complementing improvements and editing for surface errors.

With each reading, the students develop a more precise idea of what they want to say, to whom, and how. They experience writing as a process, and they discover that good writing rarely springs full-blown from the author's brow, but must be carefully shaped over a period of time. They begin to recognize the importance of their audience as they become accustomed to writing for real readers—their classmates—instead of just for the teacher—a most unreal creature, in their eyes. From the student's point of view, perhaps the most helpful aspect of using the RAG method is that, for the first time, each student has a clear notion of what other students do to solve writing problems. Papers written by their peers provide much more useful models than do the professionally written examples in textbooks.

For the teacher, one of the most important advantages of using RAGs is that the students read, discuss, and revise their papers three or four times before ever handing them in, which means not only that the submitted papers are at a fairly advanced stage of development but also that they are relatively free from gross errors in language and mechanics. As a result, the teacher can comment more directly on issues of composition—organization, development, tone, point of view, and effective use of language—rather than devoting so much red ink to matters of spelling, grammar, punctuation, and other conventions.

The Steps in the RAG Process

As I began to use RAGs regularly, I devised several procedures to streamline the process and make it more effective. I learned that small groups work best when they have a very specific task to perform and not quite as much time to complete it as they would like. Several of the procedures are so useful to me that I will describe them for you in some detail.

The first day. On the first day, after a brief prewriting activity (clustering or brainstorming—anything open-ended), students write for ten minutes on the given topic, using code numbers instead of their names to identify their papers. Then they form groups of four to read all the papers. At my signal, each group leader passes his or her group's papers to the next group, where they are distributed and read quickly—30 seconds for each paper. At the end of each 30-second interval, I give the signal to pass the papers to the next reader in the group. As soon as the set of four papers has been read, each group chooses the paper it liked the best in that set. Each group's recorder notes the code number of the chosen paper, while the leader holds up the set of papers to indicate that the group has finished making a choice. When all groups have made a choice (generally, in less than a minute), I give the signal for the leaders to pass the papers on. We repeat this process until all groups have read every set except their own.

> *We write to explore the constellations and galaxies which lie unseen within us waiting to be mapped with our own words.*
> DONALD MURRAY

When all the sets of papers have been read, I print the code numbers chosen by each group on the chalkboard. Students enjoy seeing how often their papers were chosen as best in the sets of four papers they traveled with. Inevitably, some code numbers appear several times. I call for these and read them aloud as I ask the students to identify the qualities of the best papers they read. As they enumerate the specific "best" qualities they noticed in reading around, I write them on the chalkboard. Their list usually includes such items as good details and description, interesting beginning, consistent tone, good beginning, and so forth. The list on the chalkboard becomes a simple rubric which the students are to follow in revising

their ten-minute paper for the next day. In their new versions, I require them to include from the rubric two or three specific items related to organization and development. New versions, stapled on top of the originals, must be at least one full page, but no longer than one and one-half pages.

The second day. On the second day I use the same RAG procedure, but this time I ask my students to use the criteria from the rubric in choosing the best paper in each set. Among the second day's "best" papers will be several that had not been chosen in the first day's RAG. Thus, students who worked hard to improve their original versions are rewarded for their efforts, while some of the first day's "stars," who rested on their laurels by simply recopying their popular originals, find themselves back in the middle of the pack.

After this second RAG, I generally spend a few class sessions discussing sample copies of some of the papers the class chose most often in order to refine the rubric on which their third versions will be based.

The third day. On the day the third version is due, I use a modified RAG procedure in which I ask the students to focus on very specific elements of the rubric. In this first editing phase, students pass their papers within their own group only, checking and marking each other's papers at each reading. For example, in the first turn, readers may be asked to make a note in the margin next to the opening and closing lines if these lines contain the required content or form. In the second and third turns, I may ask readers to underline concrete details, specific examples, or lines of dialogue—whatever the rubric specifically requires in terms of organization and development.

The second phase of this editing RAG requires the students to pass the papers around their groups again to identify problems in language use. This time, on the first turn, readers are to circle all forms of *to be*. On the second turn they circle all *dead words* (e.g., *thing, very, so, really, a lot,* and other overused words), while on the third turn readers bracket all repeated words at the beginnings of sentences. Later in the semester, I may ask them to star all repeated words and bracket short, choppy sentences for sentence combining work. After this session, their final version is due. It must incorporate any changes suggested by the marks of the student editors.

The fourth day. When the students submit the fourth version of their papers, I repeat the RAG procedure from the first day, allowing a little more time for the reading of each paper (up to 45 seconds), as the new versions tend to be more concentrated than earlier ones. After posting the chosen numbers, I have the students proofread each other's papers for spelling and sentence errors before handing them in. Then I read aloud the best of the best, compliment the writers on a job well done, and take the whole set home to read for the first time. And a pleasant reading it is, too, compared to what it might have been if I had taken home their first or second drafts. Because all earlier versions are handed in along with the newest ones, I can easily see the changes that have been made from the original writing. Thus, I can praise a student's efforts to revise, even if the overall quality of the latest version is only average in comparison with others in the class.

For longer papers (over two pages), or more complex assignments, I use variations of the RAG method. Often, students will read their longer papers aloud to their group, followed by a discussion of each paper's strengths and weaknesses. For essays of argument, I use RAGs to teach thesis paragraphs, counterarguments, supporting arguments, and concluding paragraphs, spending one RAG session on each element separately. In remedial classes I use the editing-style

RAG procedure, requiring readers to find and note margins, paragraph indentions, capitals and end punctuation, dead words, contractions, fragments, run-ons, and other specific items related to the skills we have been working on. The read-around group technique can be easily modified to suit almost any situation arising in a composition class.

> *Students must learn that writing is a process that requires time for ideas to incubate, often through draft after draft.*
> BILL HONIG

Suggestions for RAG Sessions

Here are some general considerations for setting up a successful RAG session:

1. Students should use code numbers instead of names on their papers to reduce anxiety by preserving anonymity.

2. Groups should be as nearly equal in size as possible. If your class number is not divisible by four or five, be certain that the odd-sized group(s) is smaller than the rest rather than larger. Groups of four or five students are best for most tasks; fewer than four provide too little interaction; more than five may have difficulty sticking to the task.

3. Appoint a leader and a recorder in each group; define their duties clearly.

4. Give the groups a specific task to perform in a strictly limited amount of time; (e.g., read quickly and select the best in the set, circle all forms of *to be*).

5. Keep close track of time. I use a stopwatch so that students learn to pace themselves against a fixed time period. Do not let students pass papers on until you give the signal; otherwise the reading process will quickly become chaotic.

6. Set up a simple system for accomplishing the task. When reading a class set, my students follow this system:

   a. Group leaders collect papers from their own group members and, at my signal, pass the set to the next group in a counter-clockwise direction.

   b. Students read each paper in the prescribed time, passing it to the person on their *right* when I give the signal to pass—not before and not after.

c. When the set has been read (I keep a tally as I time the reading so that I know when each set is finished), I tell the groups to choose the best paper, reminding them of the specific criteria for that day.

d. Recorders write the number of the chosen paper on the small slip of paper that I provide for each group. Leaders then collect the papers and hold them up to signal that their group is finished.

e. When all the leaders indicate readiness to continue, I say, "Change groups," and the leaders pass the set on to the next group.

7. Do not ask students to choose the best paper from among the papers in their own group; it is too threatening, at least at first.

8. Keep the papers short for whole-group read-around sessions; papers longer than two pages can be handled better by being read aloud in a small group, followed by discussion.

Advantages of Using Read-Around Groups

There are many advantages to using read-around groups. For the student, the following advantages are most important:

1. Writing for, and getting response from, a "real" audience
2. Gaining useful ideas, approaches, and perspectives from reading and hearing other students' writing
3. Sharpening editing skills
4. Revising their papers several times before having them graded
5. Knowing where they stand in relation to other students
6. Gaining a clearer understanding of writing as a process

For the teacher, these advantages stand out:

1. Students write more often, but the teacher does not read more papers.
2. Gross errors decline significantly with each revision following a RAG session and discussion.
3. Papers are better written and more interesting to read.
4. Students learn to evaluate their own and others' work.
5. Students have fewer complaints about grades.
6. Student handwriting improves. This last phenomenon occurs when students with good ideas but poor handwriting realize that their papers are being passed over in the choosing process because they are too hard to read.

Of all the techniques I have used over the years, the RAG has been the most useful and the most versatile. Though it requires careful advance planning and strict monitoring, the extra effort pays off in better writing and improved attitudes. Students enjoy it, too, for it gives them a chance to share. Most important, it focuses attention on the act of composing itself, demystifying the process and thereby giving students more confidence in their abilities to write better at every new step.

Practical Ideas for Read-Around Groups

Using RAGs to Teach Revising and Editing at the Elementary Level

By Diane Dawson
Coordinator of Programs and Curriculum,
Beverly Hills Unified School District;
and Teacher/Consultant, UCLA Writing Project

It has been my impression that the revising and editing stages of the writing process are rarely emphasized at the elementary school level. As a fifth-grade teacher in a self-contained classroom, I have found the read-around group (RAG) to be a powerful tool for teaching these skills. In fact, of all the techniques I have used to encourage my students to revise and edit, none has been as successful as this procedure. It provides students with a "real audience" of their peers, and it creates for them the personal motivation to rethink and rework a piece of writing. For the first time, I feel that my elementary students see writing as a valuable process.

I use the first few exposures to RAGs as a way to get students thinking about what constitutes effective writing. After selecting the "best" papers, we talk about what specific elements make certain papers stand out from the rest. The list we generate from this discussion and print on the chalkboard becomes a rubric we use for revising our papers. Students can then be trained to look for and mark particular items in papers as they read around in groups. For example, I teach them to mark a plus (+) in the margin to indicate an excellent topic sentence, to draw two lines under a strong, vivid verb, and to put parentheses around effective sensory descriptions. Other notations can be used to call attention to a particular aspect of the writing assignment while the papers are being read, such as the use of transition words in a narrative or the clarity of instructions in a "how to" paper.

During later stages of the writing process, as revising moves into editing, I have found RAGs particularly effective when I have been focusing on specific skills, such as using quotation marks and correct end punctuation, eliminating forms of *to be* in favor of strong, vivid verbs, identifying basic sentence patterns (declarative, interrogative, and so forth), and checking spelling after sentence dictation.

RAGs serve as outstanding support for teaching writing. Students working in groups not only learn the stages of the process but also analyze what they have written and come up with ways to make it better. The total success of this approach can be measured by the fact that my students do not believe that the writing task is complete unless they have had at least one read-around experience to help them revise their papers.

Students' Reactions to the Read-Around

By Sheila Koff
Former English Teacher, Irvine High School;
Instructor of English, Orange Coast College;
and Teacher/Consultant, UCI Writing Project

"Please take out some paper and a pen to begin writing," I shouted above the restless din of my high school composition class.

"Oh, no, do we have to write already?" moaned Eddie from the back of the room.

Although I did not want to admit it, my fourth period class was my least favorite writing class, and the 100° F. Santa Ana weather condition, along with the broken air conditioner, did not help. The students were tired and restless from roasting and sitting for three straight periods, and I was drained from roasting and standing for the same amount of time.

Their uncomfortable tedium subsided somewhat as we began to cluster on the chalkboard descriptions of numerous vivid memories.

"What about a first kiss? Is that a vivid memory?" roared athletic Greg to successive embarrassed giggles.

"Of course, Greg," I responded, "if that kiss has already been obtained." A few more chuckles arose. "Now, I want you all to write for ten minutes about just one of these memorable events. Don't worry

about grammar, spelling, or punctuation. But do realize that almost everyone in this room will be reading your anonymously labeled paper. Keep your pens moving as quickly as possible, trying to describe your story with much detail. Have you any questions? Then begin."

A rare hush visited the room as 35 minds settled down to ponder what to write. The heat did not feel quite so suffocating.

"Now that your ten minutes are up, pass your papers to your table's group leader. That person is to pass the set clockwise to the next table."

Further specific read-around instructions were given. A few more questions were answered as many impatient students eagerly began reading their peers' writing. Debbie, usually bored with existence, twittered behind her first paper. Other eyes, often glazed from daydreaming, now glinted while hurriedly dancing back and forth across the pages.

"Stop. Your minute is up. Pass your paper to the right and begin the next story," I said, glancing at my stopwatch.

"What? A minute can't be up! I just started!" howled Rosemary.

"Ah, come on, Ms. Koff. I'm just getting to the best part," complained Eddie again.

"Can't we have more time?" asked another.

"I'm sorry, but the class period is almost over, and you still need to finish reading at least one full set of papers and to pick your favorite. I promise to let you finish them tomorrow." I could barely believe what I had said.

Waves of heated protests from my once yawning crew greeted each of my orders to "stop" and to begin reading a new paper. Jennee Gossard's minute read-around captivated not only the hearts but also the imaginations of my composition students. And this enthusiasm remained for the second and third days of subsequent sharing, revising, and peer group responding.

To my relief and joy, this scene repeats itself every time, no matter what level of class I am teaching. Need any more be said about the significance of peer review, peer modeling, and peer recognition—all evolving from the read around in the English composition classroom?

Using Read-Around Groups in a Biology Class

By Judith Sanderson
Biology and English Teacher,
Culver City High School;
and Teacher/Consultant, UCLA Writing Project

Read-around groups are highly effective for improving my students' understanding the content of the biology course as well as helping them to express themselves accurately and clearly when writing about science. In my biology class, students write for a variety of purposes, including reporting laboratory experiments, reviewing films, and summarizing articles. I may ask them to describe a process or to explain the use and care of laboratory equipment. A typical writing assignment may involve summarizing what they have learned about a major topic, such as "enzymes" or "photosynthesis," and I give my students a list of vocabulary words they must use in their papers. They must also illustrate their major points with specific examples drawn from their laboratory work or reading. The best papers contain the correct information, illustrated with pertinent examples, and written in the most readable format.

In a read-around session, students code their papers with identification numbers to preserve anonymity. They work in groups of three or four, reading and passing the coded papers at my signal. When they finish each set of papers, each group picks the best paper in that set and then passes the papers to the next group. As the papers are passed around the room, students quickly notice that the good papers are similar in content, organization, and style. This experience gives them an inductive model for good writing on this assignment.

While students are sharing papers in read-around groups, I may ask them to do several different tasks, depending on the purpose of the assignment and the time available. The simplest procedure is to ask students to pick the best of each set as they read around. At the end of the session, I tabulate the results and read aloud two or three of the papers that were chosen most often. A more involved approach is to ask students to focus on and mark a single element at each turn: bracket the main idea, underline correctly used terminology, and star effectively written sentences. These two activities can also be combined: a basic read-around followed by the marking session. Whenever appropriate, students are encouragd to revise their papers based on the good models they have read. After a read-around session on final drafts, I distribute copies of the best student-selected papers to the class and post a set of them in a display case.

I find read-around groups useful for teaching biological concepts as well as for evaluating finished pieces of writing. For example, I may ask each student to generate a large cluster around a key term, such as *organelle* (For suggestions on clustering, see Gabriele Lusser Rico's section earlier in this book.) Then my students circulate copies of their clusters until each student has read several samples. When they get their own clusters back, I tell them to add appropriate items "stolen" from the clusters they have seen. Such an activity might precede a discussion of the topic, lead to a written definition of the term, or serve as a review for a test. As a matter of fact, whenever a read-around occurs before a major examination, I encourage students to "steal" useful information by making notes as they read.

Used in a high school biology class, read-around groups work effectively to clarify course content and to reinforce a scientific approach to problem solving. The read-around group procedure connects students to course content in ways that teacher-student interactions do not. The process is a kind of peer teaching; when students read what other students write, they see how others organize information, use vocabulary, and follow directions. When they know that their audience is composed of their peers, they want to do a better job; they increase the level of their performance if they know peer judgment will follow. Most important, without risking exposure, they see their written work in relation to the work of others in the class. For some, this is a rewarding experience; for others, it is an enlightening shock.

Through using the read-around process, my students learn to distinguish between writing that expresses a concept clearly and accurately and writing that does not. In addition, they increase their understanding of the course content through sharing ideas in groups. Thus, the process improves not only their writing skills but also their mastery of basic biological concepts.

Using Read-Around Groups for Holistic Scoring

By Trudy Beck
El Toro High School,
Saddleback Valley Unified School District;
and Teacher/Consultant, UCI Writing Project

Having first learned about read-around groups (RAGs) second or third generation, I did not know the finer details of RAGs; so I took the essence of the approach, as I knew it, and improvised. What I ended up with was a RAG that incorporated holistic scoring, too. Thus, in one final-stage RAG, I get the top papers in the class and scores for all papers.

I have been training my students to score compositions holistically for several years, and I recognize the critical need for a clear, strong rubric. At the same time that it must reflect the individual assignment, I prefer a rubric that is standard in form and mechanics. As a result, I use a basic six-point rubric as the foundation for the individualized versions. (For more information on holistic scoring, see the evaluation section later in this book.) The students become quite skilled at focusing on the specifics of an assignment, so we can agree on a final rubric quite rapidly. Once it is in final form, the rubric gets three to four minutes of silent attention from everyone. If the students request additional time to internalize the rubric, they are given it without question.

Ideally, students are placed in groups of four or five. I often sit in to round out the number, and my participation in the process lends a measure of formality that seems to encourage an even more conscientious attitude from my students. A group leader and clerk distribute papers and materials and record scores.

> *From the student's point of view, perhaps the most helpful aspect of using the RAG method is that, for the first time, each student has a clear notion of what other students do to solve writing problems.*
> *JENEE GOSSARD*

The leaders gather the papers from the members of their groups. (Students do not score their own papers.) Attached to the back of each set of papers are seven or eight score sheets, one for each group in the room. Each student writer has entered an identification number at the top of each score sheet and has written the letters *A* through *E* on the sheet (if there are five in the group) for the readers' scores. Each leader passes the group's papers clockwise to the next group, and they are redistributed there. Each member of each group has an assigned letter (again, usually *A* through *E*, depending on the number in the group), and the clerk records the letters on an index card for future reference. The group leader is always *A;* the person on the leader's left is always *B.* Then the holistic read-around begins.

I allow one minute for the reading of each paper. This provides ample time for the students to read the papers and to determine holistic scores. Each student turns the paper over, records in pen a holistic score on the top score sheet beside his or her letter and holds the paper until given the signal to pass the paper to the person on the left. After all papers have been read by the group, the leader records the best paper of the stack and collects the papers. Then the clerk collects the completed score sheets and clips them together. (Because the scores given by any one group are not seen by the next group, it is easy for me to tell if one group is grading consistently high or low and to remedy the situation rapidly. Using the clerk's record of readers' letters assigned before the RAG began, I can also tell if any one student is grading inconsistently.) The scored stack of papers is passed to the next group, and the process is repeated until the stack is returned to the originating group.

The final step is for the clerks to hand the clipped score sheets to the leader of the appropriate group, who then distributes them to the writers. Each student can immediately figure his or her average score. The students staple their score sheets to the back of their papers before they turn them in.. I also call for the best paper from each stack, and we discuss those papers, focusing on their outstanding aspects.

With a well-trained class and an efficient handling of the papers, a class of 35 can complete the entire RAG process in a 50-minute period. While my students are scoring, they are internalizing criteria for evaluating the papers of others; they can apply the criteria to their own first and final drafts of subsequent papers. At the same time, I am lightening my own paper load without reducing the number of writing assignments. I can then respond to selected papers or particular assignments in more depth and can provide the kind of content-based feedback that will genuinely help students improve their writing.

Rewriting/Editing

Competence for Performance in Revision

By Sheridan Blau
**Vice-Chair, Department of English, and
Director, South Coast Writing Project,
University of California, Santa Barbara**

Once we begin to think seriously about revision, we are likely to feel some confusion about what acts of mind or writing behavior ought to be called by that name. All composition theorists warn us against making the easy mistake of thinking of revision as merely the last stage in a linear three-stage composing process. That is because, in composing, revision can and does take place at any time. Studies of the thinking processes of writers show that nearly every writer is constantly reviewing, evaluating, and changing words and ideas at every moment in the composing process—as much perhaps while the writer is planning what he or she might want to say as when the person has already begun to write sentences on paper.

> *I scarcely ever read my published writings, but if by chance I come across a page, it always strikes me: All this must be rewritten; this is how I should have written it.*
> LEO TOLSTOI

Our conception of revision will be only momentarily clarified if we forget about when it takes place in the linear organization of the composing process and define it more operationally as the thinking and behavior that writers engage in whenever they rework any piece of a text that they have already drafted or partially drafted. As every writing teacher knows, however, not all redrafting entails revision. For many students, rewriting means copying a draft over neatly in ink. And if nothing counts as revision except what gets written and rewritten on paper, what will we call the mental activities of writers who in their minds perform the same operations of selecting, altering, and deleting that less experienced writers might have to carry out in more obvious stages on paper?[1]

Toward a Unified Theory of Revision

In spite of all these complications in our understanding of revision—or perhaps because of them—there has begun to emerge a fairly clear picture of what revision—in any and all of its manifestations—entails as a thinking process or set of intellectual skills. These are skills that can be taught and learned or at least encouraged and nourished in the context of an instructional program in composition.

We can take an important step toward a unified theory of revision by recognizing that all of the various activities we might want to call revision can probably be said to belong to one of the two classes of revision that Donald Murray has designated "internal" and "external."[2] Internal revision refers to the

---

[1]Donald H. Graves and his colleagues at the University of New Hampshire noticed precisely such a progression as a mark of development in the young writers they studied. That is to say, they observed children at one stage making language choices and alterations on paper which, at a later stage in their development, they would make mentally.

[2]Donald M. Murray, "Internal Revision: A Process of Discovery," in *Learning by Teaching: Selected Articles on Writing and Teaching.* Upper Montclair, N.J.: Boynton Cook Pubs., Inc. 1982.

process through which writers, in the production, evaluation, and amendment of their own emerging texts, gradually discover for themselves what it is that they mean to say. External revision, in contrast, entails the amending of an already written text *for the sake of a reader,* so that the reader will be able to understand it as unambiguously and efficiently as possible.

Virtually every theory of the composing process implicitly or explicitly postulates internal and external revision. Sondra Perl speaks of them under the headings of "retrospective" and "projective" structuring.[3] She defines the first as the process through which writers, in composing, use their language not to communicate something they already know but to come to

> **Editing is easy. All you have to do is cross out the wrong words.**
> *MARK TWAIN*

know for themselves something they do not yet know except as a vague feeling or "felt sense." She points out, furthermore, that when we discover and give articulate shape to our inchoate felt sense of a meaning, we necessarily restructure our sense of what the meaning is that we are trying to articulate. Retrospective structuring, then, refers to the way in which during composition we oscillate between expression and revision—attempting to express what we do not yet know and, through that attempt, revising our sense of what it is we are trying to come to know.

Projective structuring, on the other hand, is directed not to the discovery and construction of our emerging meaning for ourselves, but to the communication of a meaning we already know to our readers. It refers to the effort writers make to accommodate the expression of their ideas to the needs of their auditors or to the requirements of a situation. It would include revising in order to use more acceptable diction, to achieve mechanical correctness, or to meet the requirements of a specialized form (a laboratory report, research paper, and so forth).

All competent writers engage in some projective structuring. All want to meet the needs of their readers. However, studies of the differences between the composing processes of competent and incompetent writers consistently reveal that competent writers, in most of their composing, are principally engaged in retrospective structuring, turning more to projective structuring only after they have discovered the sub-

stance of their ideas in a fairly complete form. Incompetent writers, on the other hand, seem to give most of their attention to form rather than content from the moment they begin writing. Typically, poor writers pause so frequently to amend their language or correct real or imagined mechanical errors that they are unable to develop or follow any continuous line of thought long enough to see what it is. Their thinking, therefore, appears to be discontinuous and impoverished.

The Dimensions of Competence in Revision

If we reflect on the kind of thinking that is entailed in revising, in any of its modes or stages—that is, in the early stage of revising to discover one's ideas, in the later stage of amending a text to suit the needs of one's readers, or even in the stage of copy editing and proofreading—we will see that two apparently opposite acts of mind are required. These are *commitment* and *detachment*.

In identifying the writer's commitment as a dimension of his or her competence to engage in revision, I am acknowledging the fact that writing—insofar as it calls for revision—is characteristically a difficult, frustrating, and time-consuming process. Inexperienced writers frequently experience the difficulties of the task as evidence of their own incompetence as writers. Experienced writers know that frustration and feelings of incompetence are among the most difficult challenges any writing task is likely to pose for any writer.

Only if we attribute enough value to what we have to say are we likely to make the effort required to get our ideas straight, even for ourselves. The less commonplace our ideas and the more they derive from our own independent thinking, the more difficult it is likely to be for us to discover them for ourselves or to articulate them precisely for our readers. When the task of articulation feels impossible or too arduous to endure (as it often will in composing any piece worth writing), then we must depend in spite of such feelings on our faith that the job we have taken on for ourselves can be completed and that we are capable of completing it. Thus, of the two qualities of mind that account for a writer's competence in revision, the first of them, commitment, requires two underlying acts of the will—one finding value in the completion of the writing task and the other, consisting of faith (despite feelings to the contrary) in one's capacity to meet the challenge of the task.

The second enabling or prerequisite skill for competence in revision is the intellectual skill of *detachment*. This entails distancing ourselves from our own writing in order to take the perspective of a reader. Such a perspective is especially necessary as writers move

---

[3]Sondra Perl, "Understanding Composing," *College Composition and Communication,* Vol. 31 (December, 1980), 363-369.

from retrospective structuring to projective—from getting their ideas straight for themselves to getting them straight for a reader, or in moving from writer-based to reader-based revising. To the degree that writers appear able to make such a shift in perspective, we may say that they are exhibiting *empathy*. As a competence underlying detachment, *empathy* refers to a writer's or speaker's ability to see things from someone else's point of view. The more writers want to have an impact on their readers, the more they need to understand how readers are likely to respond to their discourse.

Empathy does not quite describe the underlying skill that enables writers to achieve the kind of distance or detachment that is necessary for internal revision—the revision through which writers gradually discover and take possession of their own emerging ideas. Here it is not necessary to imaginatively project oneself into the mind of some other reader, but to assume the detached perspective of oneself as reader rather than writer of the text being produced. Competent writing and revising requires writers, at intervals, to step back from the production of their texts with sufficient distance to judge whether or not the words appearing on the page match their sense of the intended meaning. When writers as readers find a mismatch, they also find opportunities to work further to discover their intended meaning or, just as likely, to revise their intention.

Competence in revision, as I have defined it, may therefore be said to have two principal dimensions: an affective dimension, which I have called *commitment*; and a cognitive dimension, which I have called *detachment*. The first is a function of writers' attitudes toward themselves and their tasks; the second, of their cognitive abilities to perform the tasks. For any task of composing, writers will be committed to the degree that they value the assignment they are engaged in and

retain faith or confidence in their capacity to complete it. Their capacity for the competent completion of the task will, in turn, be a function of their having learned to detach themselves sufficiently from their text to engage in the evaluative and empathic procedures that revising entails as they attempt to discover their ideas for themselves and adjust their discourse to the needs of their readers. Graphically, we may represent the dimensions of competence in revision as shown in Figure 27.

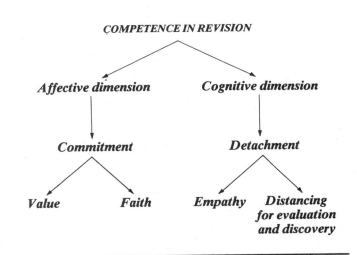

Fig. 27. Dimensions of Competence in Revision

Strategies to Develop Competence in Revision

A variety of instructional strategies are available for the teacher who is intent on helping students acquire the disciplines of commitment and detachment that underlie competence in revision. Many of them are described elsewhere in this book. They include the use of writing-response groups of the sort proposed by Peter Elbow; the use of "read-around groups," as described by Jenee Gossard; and considerable effort at following Mary K. Healy's advice about finding genuine situations that call for real communicative writing for students instead of "dummy runs." Taken together, activities like these help students discover the value of writing as a genuine communicative act directed toward a real audience whose differing perspectives must be taken into account.

Building Communities of Writers. Students in writing-response groups, in particular, learn to become more empathic readers, not simply from getting the responses of others to their own work, but from reading the work of peers and thereby seeing through their own experience what readers need and can expect from writers like themselves. Writing-response groups can also be important for what they contribute to turning the writing class into a community of writers. In such a community, much of the conversation and instruction are focused on the difficulties and challenges that the student writers encounter while they are engaged in the composing process. Through such discussions, students usually find themselves better able to work out the self-management strategies they need to sustain the effort that revision often requires.

Ideally, teachers will become active members of their classroom communities of writers by writing along with their students and sharing their experiences of anxiety, frustration, and satisfaction in the composing process. Students need to see their teachers write in order to see that the most accomplished writers are not those who write most easily. They need to see how much it is the case that the competence of most writers consists less of facility than of staying power—a power that derives from their recognition of the value of the enterprise they are engaged in and from their faith in their capacity to continue making progress in it, even after they begin to feel defeated by it.

Inviting Drafting and Redrafting. If we want our students truly to revise, we need to give them opportunities to get a number of writing projects started so that they may choose to revise only those that hold the most interest or promise for them. Most of us produce many starts—a few notes, some pages of an early draft—on projects that are simply not worth revising or else need to be put aside for the months or years it might take before we ripen to the challenge they pose. Teachers who want to make their classes into authentic environments for writing and revising will, therefore, deliberately cultivate the production of a great many starts on pieces in progress, quick rough drafts that may or may not be taken any further. Only when students have had the opportunity to produce three or four such pieces in rough first-draft form (and

perhaps received some responses on them from peer readers) should they be required to commit themselves to the further revision of their most promising pieces in progress. Real *reseeing* (revision), rather than obedient tinkering with the surface features of the text, will occur when writers have a sense of the value of their thoughts and have a need to enhance, clarify, recast, or elaborate on their original messages.

> *To most composition teachers and researchers, revision is regarded as an isolated noncreative activity, as interesting, perhaps, as an autopsy.*
> NANCY SOMMERS

A related way to nurture revision as an integral part of the composing process for our students is to provide them with lots of experiences in experimental and exploratory writing in journals or notebooks. These can serve as repositories for ideas, lists, clusters, and starts on drafts that writers may return to selectively to find material worth developing into completed pieces of writing. Students will benefit particularly from being encouraged to do a good deal of free-writing (nonstop recording of a writer's continuous thoughts on a subject) in such notebooks. The virtue of free-writing in teaching revision is that it helps writers discover the value of their "naked" thoughts—thoughts that can sometimes be discovered most fully when the writers attend only to them, putting aside momentarily the distractions of a concern for correctness or form or the needs of a reader. Even for very young writers, one of the first steps toward learning to revise seems to come with the recognition that in the initial stages of one's writing, it is an acceptable and proper procedure to produce messy, incorrect, and hastily composed work that is intended as material for revision.

Authorship as a Motive for Revision

Among the most effective strategies teachers can use to help students discover the value of their own ideas (and hence the value of clarifying and communicating them) is that of taking those ideas seriously—examining them not with the eye of a corrector but with the respect of one who would learn from them. A teacher who can give the time and concentrated effort required to respond to student writing as a partner in an intellectual dialogue will find that several benefits flow from it. First, the teacher's actions testify to the value of a student's ideas. Second, the teacher will be modeling a mode of response that students would do well to imitate in responding to each other's work as well as to literature and other assigned readings.

Finally, the dialogue between student-writer and teacher-respondent (which can be continued with an answering response from the student and another from the teacher) offers both participants an opportunity for additional learning through their continuing exchange and clarification of ideas—an exchange that continues to take place in writing.

School writing assignments often subvert the normal relationship that emerges between the writer and reader by asking students to write on subjects about which they are less well-informed than their teachers are. In such a transaction the writer is relieved of most of the responsibility that a real author bears for accommodating what he or she has to say to the understanding of his or her readers. Teachers who would have their students develop a capacity for detachment will therefore encourage them to write on topics about which they (the students) have more authoritative knowledge than their readers.

Metaprocessing as a Strategy for Revision

Aside from having their students write about what they know with some authority (i.e., as "authors"), teachers can help students develop their ability for detachment or perspective-taking by employing a number of instructional methods that may be loosely characterized as *metaprocessing* activities. These are activities that call on students to treat their own texts and writing processes as objects of inquiry. Metaprocessing describes most of the talk that takes place in writing-response groups and in teacher-student conferences. Such talk can sometimes become more focused and productive if students are asked to keep writing-process logs in which they record and reflect on their composing processes, including their responses to each of their own completed drafts for each writing task they undertake.

Most of the revising and editing tricks that experienced teachers are fond of showing to their students also entail metaprocessing. One such trick is to have students outline drafts of their essays after they finish them. From such an outline students can gain new perspectives on the structure of their essays—on the relative emphasis they have given to main and subordinate points and on the progression of their arguments.

> *Pruning writing is the same as pruning apple trees: The point is not so much to get rid of the dead branches (which are easy enough to spot) as it is to shape the tree to produce the best possible fruit.*
> BRUCE O. BOSTON

In another metaprocessing activity students write brief summary statements of each of their completed drafts (or of each paragraph) in the form of what Linda Flower calls a *WIRMI* statement: "What I Really Mean Is . . ."[4] Having written WIRMIs, students may be able to stand far enough back from their essays to ask productively if they actually said in the essays what they meant to say. An exceptionally promising activity of this sort is to ask students to write revised drafts of their essays without looking back at their first drafts and then to have students write a comparison of the two versions. Since the two versions will tend to be very different (especially for the poorest writers), the task of comparing them forces the writers to pay close attention to the written content of their two essays, separate from whatever intentions may have informed either or both of them.[5] This distancing exercise provides practice in assuming the detached perspective that one needs to revise effectively.

A much simpler distancing assignment, yet one that almost always yields surprising benefits for unskilled writers, is to have students read drafts of their essays aloud before they revise or submit them. This can be done in the presence of another person, in the context of a writing group, or even in private. When writers read their texts out loud—to themselves or to other persons—they become more apt to hear the text themselves. Unskilled student writers rarely reread their texts out loud as they compose. Skilled writers almost always do.

Publishing as a Strategy to Encourage Revision

Publishing is the last instructional strategy I want to mention here for its role in encouraging revision. However much we may want through our writing to gain possession of our thoughts or to communicate with our readers, no inducement to revision is likely to carry us as far through the difficulties of the process as the prospect of having our work published. Many forms of publishing are possible within the context of a classroom, particularly if we think of publication in its root sense of "making public." These forms can range from having students read their work out loud to the entire class, to posting work on bulletin boards or in school display cases, to producing dittoed, mimeographed, or photocopied anthologies of student work from a single class. Many teachers have found that in working on long-term projects, students will be encouraged to revise carefully when they know that they will individually make a hard-cover binding

---

[4]Linda Flower, *Problem-Solving Strategies for Writing*. New York: Harcourt Brace Jovanovich, Inc., 1981.

[5]Will Garrett-Petts of the University of British Columbia has experimented with the technique of withholding first drafts while students create a second version.

for their completed work so that it might be kept in the classroom or library for reference by future students. The promise of publication is a promise of fame, however limited. If that makes it appealing to a student's vanity, it is surely a tolerable vanity and one that can do a writer much good.

The strategies I have identified here are all aimed at fostering in students the commitment necessary to communicate something of value and the detachment required to discover, articulate, and reformulate an intended meaning for an intended audience. Taken together they imply a respect on the part of the teacher for the process of composing and an appreciation of the importance of a humanly rich communicative context, both for the acquisition of competence in composition and for its realization in performance.

Practical Ideas for Revising

Stages in the Revising Process

By Michael O'Brien
English Teacher, Foothill High School,
Tustin Unified School District;
and Teacher/Consultant, UCI Writing Project

Good writers are "schizophrenic," some claim. Certainly, they tend to be fluent, imaginative creators; on the other hand, most writers also seem to be meticulous, disciplined craftsmasters. William Blake, the English artist, poet, and visionary, actually created his own complex mythology. Yet what book of poems has such exquisite, careful symmetry as his *Songs of Innocence and of Experience*?[1] Wild William must have been a careful reviser. Likewise, we teachers want student fluency and creativity; yet we also preach, "Revise! Revise! Revise! The way to Heaven is through revision!" But how can we teach revision? And are the acts of creation and revision really that opposite?

I am not sure that we can teach revision any more than we can teach creativity. However, we can give guidelines, we can model behavior, and we can provide opportunities where effective revision, like creativity, can take place. Revision is a recursive process within the larger writing process. I would like to describe the opportunities for effective revision that have been working for my students.

Students should not revise too early in the writing process. I ask them to refrain from revising or editing while they are prewriting and doing the rough draft. Revising at this stage can seriously hamper fluency. Instead, they should be carving out big blocks of thought and trying to fit them together into a coherent structure. They should be using the mallet and chisel, not the jeweler's file.

When they have completed their rough drafts, we review the rubric (the criteria on which the paper will be evaluated), which was initially introduced before the first draft. The students then examine their own papers, asking themselves, "Okay, how does my rough draft measure up?" After reviewing the rubric, we discuss typical problems with that assignment. For a descriptive paper, I might warn students against telling rather than showing, for example. At this stage, I am trying to help them to envision their ideal paper that might evolve from the rough draft, much as a sculptor might imagine a supple human figure emerging from a marble block. (Whether done consciously or subconsciously, this is, I believe, a creative act.) With the rubric and my comments as guides, I ask them to revise for content and form, cautioning them not to worry much about editing at this stage. They will probably still be doing some shaping and rough work. The delicate stuff comes later.

> *When you and your class read your writing out loud, you often hear things in it that you do not experience any other way.*
> PETER ELBOW

After this stage or revision is completed, we spend a period grading and discussing sample papers according to the rubric. In the following period my students score and write comments on each other's revised copy in peer-response groups. By this time, they have read quite a few papers. This, along with comments on their revisions, helps them move closer to that ideal paper still forming in their minds.

Now they are ready to write a semifinal copy and to edit. I am also prepared to help them individually by giving oral evaluations at my desk. Research indicates that the teacher's comments have the most impact *now*, while the students work on their papers, not after they have written final drafts. I see myself here as

[1]William Blake, *Songs of Innocence and of Experience*. New York: Oxford University Press, Inc., 1977.

a sensitive audience and partner; I can give them insight into what works and what does not.

The final in-class step occurs when the semifinal copies are done. I ask them to edit each other's papers in their response groups, equipped with dictionaries and grammar books. I do not answer questions that they can find by "looking them up." (This was a tough lesson for me, the big dad, to learn—to discover that in the long run I was not helping them by being a walking reference book.) In this last step, they polish and tinker and adjust. Then they write final copy, which probably means even more fine tuning.

These techniques work for my students. Since they must turn in material from all of the stages of revision for the assignment, I can see that the difference between the rough and final drafts is usually vast. I have also noticed that as the semester progresses, they not only get better at revising, but they also become firmly convinced of the need for it. They have also had the satisfaction of seeing the refined paper unfold from the rough copy. And I do not know of one student who has become schizophrenic from using this process.

Yes, There Is a Better Way: Revising on the Word Processor

By Russell Frank
English and Journalism Teacher,
Chaparral Middle School,
Walnut Valley Unified School District;
and Teacher/Consultant, UCI Writing Project

I remember the drudgery of learning how to write as a child—of painfully scratching out letter after letter with sore, tender red fingers. Meanwhile, my mind raced ahead of my hand, and, as a result, only I could interpret the scrawl left on the page. There had to be a better way.

My typing ability quickened my composing process, but revising and editing remained just as tedious. I remember the times just before a paper was due—when it was no longer worth the pain of erasing and retyping a page to clarify a vague point or argument buried in the text. There had to be a better way.

In the summer of 1982, I experienced how word processing could improve my composing and revising skills. My writing kept closer pace with my thoughts, and I no longer needed to type draft after draft, shaping my ideas on a typewriter. Now I believe this technology could improve many students' writing by making composing and revising physically less demanding.

A word processor is any type of system for typing text material into a computer and editing, changing, or correcting the text easily and efficiently. Essentially, a word processor is a computer loaded with a word processing program, written on a storage device—usually a floppy disk. With a word processor, the author discovers or creates content and shapes and edits this content while the computer holds the text in memory. The author can revise and edit his or her piece by pushing the appropriate keys. When the piece is finished, the author presses other keys to obtain a paper copy that is clean from cross-outs, inserts, carets, smudges, and deletion marks. The process is simple, legible, and immediate and leads to easier and faster writing and revision.

Word processing is a potentially powerful tool in the quest to improve student writing. In order to explain how word processing can be used to help students, I would like first to review the characteristics of competent and incompetent student writers. Research shows that competent writers generally write longer essays, spend more time on writing tasks, and pause more often to reflect on their writing. Competent writers also revise their texts while rereading them and are far more concerned with planning, more aware of audience, and more considerate of purpose and stylistic concerns of an assignment than incompetent writers are. Competent writers also view revision as restructuring of content and ideas. These characteristics reflect the high degree of commitment competent writers feel for their writing.

Incompetent writers generally are concerned too soon during their writing with form and mechanics and, therefore, spend less time developing the content of their piece. They try to "follow the rules" of writing in an attempt to make their first draft their final draft. Incompetent writers view revision as a patchwork—of getting what was written worded correctly and of correcting mechanics and spelling. These writers, according to Sheridan Blau, are deficient in two dimensions of writing and revising: an affective dimension that includes commitment and a cognitive dimension that includes detachment. Incompetent writers generally

Word processing is a potentially powerful tool in the quest to improve student writing.
RUSSELL FRANK

have a low sense of commitment to their writing because (1) they do not value the piece's importance; or (2) they do not believe in their ability to complete the writing task. They also usually lack detachment from their writing—an ability to step back from their piece and view the content from a reader's point of view.

The word processor can help students to improve their writing in both the affective and cognitive dimensions of writing and revision by making the writing act easier, faster, and more efficient. Word processing enhances the affective dimension by increasing the student's faith in his or her ability to complete the writing task. Additions, deletions, substitutions, and

> *If we want our students truly to revise, we need to give them opportunities to get a number of writing projects started so that they choose to revise only those that hold the most interest or promise for them.*
> *SHERIDAN BLAU*

the reordering of words, phrases, sentences, and paragraphs can be executed immediately without cluttering the page or necessitating the recopying of an entire text. This power for immediate revision is the word processor's greatest power, because students are freed from early concerns regarding correctness and form. Students know they can make editing corrections as well as reshape entire paragraphs late in the process with the same ease that they made earlier modifications. Writing now becomes a mode of discovery of thought and meaning—of creating and developing content—what Sondra Perl labels retrospective structuring.[1,2] I have seen a child move from total rejection of writing to intense interest and involvement within a few weeks of being introduced to the word processor. Clearly, that child's ability, desire, and commitment to complete a writing task increased with the mechanical advantages of the computer.

The word processor can also be used in conjunction with peer response groups to develop the cognitive dimension of writing and revising, because it encourages detachment from a piece of writing in order to see an audience's point of view. During small group interaction, students read their work to each other to

---

[1] In my own personal experience, I am aware of how much more I utilize retrospective structuring when I write with my computer. In this article, for example, each paragraph and many sentences have been restructured during my initial composing during my search for the "right" meaning. In contrast, I am less willing to experiment with ideas and text when I am composing with pen and paper.

[2] Sondra Perl, "Understanding Composing," *College Composition and Communication,* Vol. 31 (December, 1980), 369.

obtain feedback on its effectiveness. My own observation of writing response groups without accessibility to a word processor indicated that, even after successful group interaction, many students failed to incorporate their classmates' suggestions in their second drafts, probably because it was too much to bother to write the extra text needed to clarify a point. With electronic editing, such revisions become simple and quick. Instead of taking home an essay to revise overnight, students can obtain some feedback from their groups, incorporate the suggestions in the essay, and often obtain a paper copy within the same class period. By allowing students to incorporate peer feedback immediately, the word processor enables the writer to see his or her work from the perspective of a reader. As this concept of audience broadens, the student may gain enough critical distance (or detachment) to begin to anticipate how the reader will respond or, better yet, to plan his or her writing to manipulate the reader's response.

The teacher can also play a role in helping students achieve enough detachment to revise what they have written. By writing comments in the electronic text that require clarification or explanation, teachers can encourage students to see their writing as a reader might interpret it. And because revision is easy on a word processor, one can expect a student to rethink a paper and make appropriate changes as a result of a peer group's or teacher's feedback.

For word processing to have a significant impact on the quality of student writing, teachers as well as students must internalize what is meant by revision—that it is not just copying over or correcting mechanical errors but reseeing and reshaping an intended message for an audience. A teacher's own sense of what revision is will probably have the greatest influence on students' attitudes. After all, the human being is still more of a motivator than a machine is. But the word processor can contribute greatly to the writing process if it is used wisely.

Yes, there is a better way!

EDITOR'S NOTE: For additional information on the use of computers in writing, see pages 8, 9, and 59—62 in *Handbook for Planning an Effective Writing Program*, which was published by the California State Department of Education in 1983.

Revising with Sentence Combining

By Jerry Judd
English and Journalism Teacher,
Venado Middle School,
Irvine Unified School District;
and Teacher/Consultant, UCI Writing Project.

Writing is one of the few communication processes that allows the communicator the luxury of revision. This can involve revision of thought, of structure, of style, of writing to an audience, and generally of writing to produce a certain effect on the reader. When one is transforming initial thoughts to print, ideas do not generally flow in an orderly, linear, well-planned manner. In fact, many writers need to generate ideas on paper in the form of fragments, jottings, and disconnected sentences before they can make composing decisions that are compatible with their purpose and their audience.

Sentence combining can be an invaluable tool in the evolution of a piece of writing from prewriting to rough draft to finished product. Teaching sentence combining is not, in itself, teaching writing; rather, it is a means of increasing a writer's options in terms of fluency, form, and correctness, enabling the writer to create his or her own style.

> *Rewriting is when playwriting really gets to be fun. . . . In baseball you only get three swings and you're out. In rewriting, you get almost as many swings as you want and you know, sooner or later, you'll hit the ball.*
>
> NEIL SIMON

I have found the practice of sentence combining in my classroom to be beneficial for a variety of reasons. If sentence combining is introduced early in a writing class and practiced regularly, it can have a positive influence on the attitudes of writers, especially beginning writers. Generally, there is a built-in tension and pressure in the act of composing a piece of written text. This anxiety is often self-imposed by the writer who is struggling to "get it right" the first time around. Mina Shaughnessy points out in *Errors and Expectations:*

> The practice of consciously transforming sentences from simple to complex structures . . . helps the student cope with complexity in much the same way as finger exercises in piano or bar exercises in ballet enable performers to work out specific kinds of coordination that must be virtually habitual before the performer is free to interpret or even execute a total composition.[1]

This practice, or prewriting, not only raises the ability of student writers to manipulate language, but it also raises the level of confidence that student writers have in their ability to manipulate language. This releases them to generate more fluent first drafts that can be reworked and polished in the later stages of composing.

Sentence combining can enhance form and correctness as well as fluency. Sentence patterns, pronoun usage, and punctuation can all be introduced and mastered through practice and problem solving. I

---

[1]Mina P. Shaughnessy. *Errors and Expectations: A Guide for the Teacher of Basic Writing.* New York: Oxford University Press, Inc., 1977, p. 77. Used by permission of the publisher.

> *Style is not a fashionable garment you put on; style is what you are; what you have to say as well as how you say it.*
>
> DONALD MURRAY

usually begin with the first part of Charles Cooper's "An Outline for Writing Sentence-Combining Problems."[2] I write sample sentences, such as the ones below, and challenge students to combine them in as many ways as they can.

> The people on the boat asked us to come aboard.
> The boat was *alongside*.
> We sailed in the boat.
> The boat was the one *with the blue sail*.

To encourage students to experiment with language use and sentence structure, I give full credit for each variation of the initial sentences.

Once students are adept at sentence combining, I use it as a means to teach not just sentence variation and length but also style. Using the literature we study as a resource, I either select or let students choose passages that they must break down from complex into kernel or base sentences. Then they must recombine them by adding their own modifiers and clauses. As they "reconstitute" the styles of professional writers, they begin to internalize elements of successful writing through imitation.

After students are practiced in the sentence-combining technique, I turn their attention to its use in the revision of their own prose. To begin the process, I take a section from one of my own stories, which I originally wrote with short, choppy sentences and then later revised using sentence-combining techniques:

> His hair was dark, matted, and graying. It was pushed back and was shiny with hair oil. It was wavy and neatly trimmed around his ears and neck.
>
> His dark, matted, wavy hair was shiny from hair oil and neatly trimmed around his ears and neck.
>
> A newspaper was on the stool next to Spence. He picked it up after the first shot of whiskey. He read the names of writers given by-lines on the first page.
>
> After Spence downed his first shot of whiskey, he picked up a newspaper on the stool next to him and read the names of writers given by-lines on the front page.

We discuss the differences between the two versions, and we point out the changes in style created by longer, more complex sentences.

---

[2]Charles Cooper, "An Outline for Writing Sentence-Combining Problems," in *The Writing Teacher's Sourcebook*. Edited by Gary Tate and Edward P. Corbett. New York: Oxford University Press, Inc., 1981, p. 372.

To integrate sentence combining into the revision of their own writing, I have students select an earlier journal entry or free-writing exercise that they are interested in revising. They find paragraphs, sentences, or sections from their writing which are short and choppy and need work. They pull these excerpts from their papers and experiment with revising them in a variety of ways through sentence combining. Peer groups can provide valuable feedback for the author when he or she must decide which of the new variations represents the greatest improvement over the original. These selections are then inserted in the revised version of the student's writing.

Having students make up their own sentence-combining exercises from spelling lists, vocabulary lists, or other units of study can also be done. Here is an example of part of a student-produced sentence-combining activity from an eighth grade spelling list:

Spelling List	Student-Produced Sentence Combining Activity
1. sophomore	He was a wrestler.
2. wrestler	He fought on Wednesday.
3. colonel	He was full of haughtiness.
4. Wednesday	She was a sophomore.
5. laboratory	She works in a laboratory.
6. haughtiness	He was an old colonel.
7. yacht	He liked sailing his yacht.
8. autumn	He sails in autumn.

After having the students do the activities described previously for several weeks, I have found that an instructional unit on the different sentence patterns can be invaluable. When I am about halfway through my sentence-combining unit, I teach students the simple, compound, complex, and compound-complex sentences over a several-week period. Once students are writing longer sentences, they want to know whether their longer sentences are correct and not run-ons.

In the end, perhaps the single most important criterion in teaching writing is the amount of time students spend thinking about writing. The more students write, the more they begin to think like writers. Sentence combining is an excellent teaching tool to help students gain control and confidence over their own writing. When students write often and have confidence in themselves as writers, they begin to do more offstage thinking about writing, composing, and revising in their heads before committing pen to paper. They also have more options in how to go about communicating an intended message and can consciously plan not only what they want to say but also how they can best express it. Revising, then, becomes an integral component of each stage of the writing process.

Two Activities That Encourage Real Revision

By Trudy Beck
English Teacher, El Toro High School,
Saddleback Valley Unified School District;
and Teacher/Consultant, UCI Writing Project

I spend considerable time and energy each year fighting the same battles, and one that I never seem to win is the battle over rewrites. I say, "Rewrite," and somehow it is translated as "recopy." However, I have come up with a solution. It is not infallible, but it has been successful. Simply stated, I collect and keep the draft, and then I ask for a rewrite.

The reactions are what one might expect them to be. Looks of horror and disgust abound, and someone almost always cries, "Foul." It is then that we discuss one more time, for the record, the variety of approaches one can make to a topic. We review voice, point of view, and methods of organization and development. I follow this discussion with an extensive precomposing phase during which I introduce a variety of topics that the students orally practice writing.

I may suggest a potentially suspenseful event to begin the discussion. One student will invariably arrange the parts of that event in chronological order while another might offer a news story account with the most important information first. Given a controversial issue, one will attempt to persuade, and one might choose to remain objective. One approach may be to begin with the least significant items; another will lead with the most important. One may support with facts; another could offer examples. The students spot avenues open to them that they would not have considered before.

> *No inducement to revision is likely to carry us as far through the difficulties of the process as the prospect of having our work published.*
> SHERIDAN BLAU

Often the goal is for the writers to revise their work in essentially the same form. In this instance, the earlier draft has been a rehearsal for the purpose of blocking and pacing. When the student writers are forced to act without their original scripts, they become more familiar with their purposes and their unique messages; their rhythm becomes more even and their style more apparent. The writers move more ably within their topics, and their writing develops tones of confidence and authority.

An adjunct activity is to have one student rewrite another's paper. This exercise is especially useful for response partners. Each has a clearer understanding of the weaknesses in the other's draft and of the difficulties in handling the topic. The writer then has the benefit of a peer model when he or she begins his or her own revision. The partner's version may offer fresh ideas; it may also expose unworkable alternatives. Either way, it is helpful.

These revision activities seem to bring about the most consistent change when repeated several times early in my course and then resurrected at random intervals thereafter. Probably the greatest long-range effect is an increased opportunity for the students to gain some distance from their work. With this distance, students take command of the subject. Without it, they do not control their writing; their writing controls them.

I tell my students that to bury an idea, a sentence, or even a topic may be to give it an honorable death, and that to keep a poor draft in its flawed form is to condemn it to a life of pain and distortion. I like to draw an analogy between the revision process and an incident in which a ceramics instructor admonished me to destroy the first hundred pots I threw on the potter's wheel. He said, in effect, "To keep each pot is to treat it as your child. It is not, and you are not obligated to love it or to give it a home. Work until you create something that deserves your admiration."

Revising for Correctness

Some Basics That Really Do Lead to Correctness

By Irene Thomas
Educational Consultant, IOTA, Inc.

When many English teachers hear the word *basics*, they think of drills on grammar; that is, drills that lead to the identification of nouns, adverbs, subjects, and so forth. When parents and the society at large call for *the basics,* however, what they usually mean is that students should be able to correct such usages as "we was" and "he done," write in complete sentences with proper punctuation and spelling, and so on. We have been led to believe by the writers of textbooks and traditional English curricula that a connection exists between these two definitions of the basics; indeed, it is assumed that a teacher's drills on grammar will satisfy society's demands for correct performance. I question that assumption. In fact, I would attribute much of the so-called writing crisis in our schools to that very assumption. When drills on grammar are used as *the* means toward better writing, precious time is wasted—time that could be better spent on actual writing tasks. First, let me suggest some reasons why drills on grammar are a waste of time.

> *. . . the teaching of formal grammar, if divorced from the process of writing, has little or no effect on the writing ability of students.*
> HANDBOOK FOR PLANNING AN
> EFFECTIVE WRITING PROGRAM

Grammar—the analysis, or parsing, of sentences—is an abstract skill. It bears little or no relationship to the production of a correct sentence. Anyone who has taught knows that children or adolescents who can locate an adverb in a sentence do not necessarily use

effective or correctly formed adverbs in their writing. And the reverse is also true: Many students who write well do not necessarily perform well on standardized grammar tests. The fact is that the two skills are indeed just that—two different skills. Here are several examples of modern research that support that assertion:

1. Controlled studies attempting to link the teaching of grammar with improvement in writing ability have so far been unsuccessful.[1]

2. The work of Piaget, the prominent cognitive psychologist, strongly suggests that preadolescents are not developmentally ready for the levels of abstraction demanded in the process of parsing. (That may be why so many ninth graders come to you still not knowing what a verb is, much less a predicate.)

3. The most recent studies of right and left brain domains suggest that the tasks involved with composing are right brain tasks and those of analyzing are left brain tasks. We can at least hypothesize, at this early stage of the research, that the two kinds of skills, when taught simultaneously, may create a neurological conflict during the acquisition of writing skills.

4. Finally, from what researchers know about the acquisition of oral language, we can safely say that oral language is acquired biologically and

---

[1]*EDITOR'S NOTE:* For specific citations on the research regarding grammar and the teaching of writing, see pages 3 and 4 of *Handbook for Planning an Effective Writing Program,* which the Department of Education published in 1983.

with data provided by the normal linguistic environment. In other words, children are biologically equipped to learn a language quickly. The language spoken around them serves as the data and the input to their language *computer*. They know, for example, that *er* comparative endings are added to only one class of words. And they will add the *er* to those words predictably, even though they may not understand the term *adjective* until they are fifteen years of age.

Now you might say that oral language and written language differ considerably, even though the latter is roughly based on the former. Moreover, the special requirements of the written forms and conventions (spelling, punctuation, sentence structure) require practice—even drill. Yes, I fully agree; but it is the kind of practice needed that we should consider carefully.

All too often in the language arts, we spend our time allotted for *revising* skills on practice material that is essentially impractical. We use textbook drills on verbs or "grammar games" and then, we are led to believe, our students will write correct sentences. What tends to be missing in the process are those intermediate steps of copying, imitating, and manipulating good models. Such models, in fact, can provide the linguistic input to writing skills that is analogous to the "natural language data" necessary to oral language development. Many teachers have found that working with models tends to encourage carry-over of the information conveyed in models—information about punctuation, spelling, sentence structure, verb forms—into the students' independent composing. And do not miss an opportunity to use the students' own writing as a learning tool. The idea of being "correct" takes on a new importance when a student is genuinely concerned about communicating his or her message to an audience.

Listed below are some examples of practical sentence-exercises that you can use almost daily in either your prewriting activities or your warm-up to the revising stage of the writing process. They can be adjusted for any grade level. The overall objective of these exercises is to develop students' *eyes and ears* for identifying the correct written form of sentences. If you have students keep these exercises in a permanent notebook, you can refer to a specific exercise or specific sentence when they need to "correct" something in their independent work. In almost every case, your demonstrating an example first is enough instruction to allow students to work on their own or with a partner. Whenever possible, create examples that relate to actual people, places, and activities to capture the interest of your class. Use the sentence-exercises to reinforce the curriculum you are teaching.

Most teachers have found that when they integrate the basics with other content areas and present them as they occur naturally in written expression, the need for grammatical terminology is substantially reduced—even eliminated. Here are 12 practical sentence-exercises that I hope you find helpful:

1. Copying a sentence or two from the chalkboard or from a specific passage in a text. What could be more basic? (These can later serve as models to imitate, as in exercise 2.)

2. Replacing a word or phrase in a sentence with some other word or phrase—also a very practical way to recycle a spelling list.

   Third grade example: Jill sat on my **hat.**

   Ninth grade example: We won the competition because of our **tremendous** speed.

3. Unscrambling a scrambled sentence to produce a real sentence.

   Third grade example: like We boats. to sail (Punctuation and capitalization clues can be dropped later.)

   Ninth grade example: are faster than he and I Harry (three possibilities)

   A series of these scrambled sentences with pronouns helps to establish the relationship between form and position.

4. Replacing nonsense words with real words.

   The **tizz** is **mimming** in the **fass.**
   The **tizzes** are **mimming** in the **fass.**
   The **tizz mims timly.**
   The **tizzes mimmed** yesterday.

   This kind of exercise focuses attention on structural clues and subject-verb agreement.

5. Changing declarative sentences into negations, questions, or imperatives. (Again, you can recycle spelling words.)

6. Using the sentence machine. Make a sentence by choosing one word from each column, as in the examples below. Then repeat the process and make as many other sentences as you can.

EXAMPLE FOR GRADE THREE

They	made	the	same	game
We	ate	a	eight	cages
Ray		an	late	lunches

EXAMPLE FOR GRADE NINE

Because	I	were	late	we	were	punished.
Since	we	was	sick,	I	took	medicine.
Although	they		obedient,	they	was	

7. Mixing and matching (subjects and predicates) to produce as many sentences as possible.

EXAMPLE FOR GRADE THREE

Those girls		was naughty.
Henry	+	is silly.
My cat		are my friends.
		were away today.

8. Punctuating sentences in discourse.

   Third grade example: I want some bubble gum may I go to the store

   Ninth grade example: Reproducing any series of sentences, or a paragraph, from a text everyone has (eliminate capitalization and punctuation). Read the sentences aloud so that students can associate punctuation with intonation clues. Then ask them to proof and correct the copy. Finally, let the students compare their corrected versions with the original text.

9. Writing sentences, later whole paragraphs, from dictation. At any grade level, read a passage from a common text and then compare with the original to allow for self-correction.

10. Playing the why game (invented by Frank O'Hare). This game both teaches and reviews mechanics. Have students look at a paragraph in the text they have. Begin by asking a question about a specific use of punctuation or capitalization; e.g., "Why is there a period after the word 'time'?" The student who answers correctly may then ask a similar question of the class and so on. You can provide the answer when students cannot.

11. Expanding the world's shortest sentence. This technique works well in grades four and above to help students develop a sense for the two-part structure of the English sentence. The terms subject and predicate can be added, if you wish, once the students can easily perform the tasks involved.

Example for grade four: Children/play. Have students add one word at a time to each part of the sentence, always keeping it a real sentence. You can write their suggestions on the chalkboard, always retaining the line between subject and predicate. You can invite prepositional phrases (treating them as single word adverbials) by asking the questions beginning with where, when, and how.

If you are concerned about the recognition of predicates on standardized examinations, you can point out that the second part of a sentence almost always begins with a verb (a word that can take past tense). To draw attention to helping verbs, you can follow up the original exercise by demonstrating the variations of *play*—played, have played, are playing, will play, and so forth—all of which have a time dimension. The reverse of this whole process, perhaps most appropriate to upper grades, is the paring down of an expanded simple sentence to its barest essentials. This is a most practical way to aid the conceptualization of subject/predicate.

> *The starting point in the teaching of writing must be the teacher's belief that children possess the requisite linguistic knowledge.*
> OWEN THOMAS

12. Sentence combining. This is probably the best method yet developed for teaching all the important skills of sentence building. See the illustration on the next page for a suggested sequence of sentence-combining exercises that are appropriate for students in grades three through six. Additional material on sentence combining may be found in *Sentence Combining: Improving Student Writing Without Formal Grammar Instruction* by Frank O'Hare,[1] in *Sentence Combining: A Composing Book* by William Strong,[2] and in the commentaries by William Lomax and Jerry Judd that appear in other sections of this book. Sentence-combining exercises have also been adapted for computer instruction.[3]

---

[1]Frank O'Hare, *Sentence Combining: Improving Student Writing Without Formal Grammar Instruction.* Urbana, Ill.: National Council of Teachers of English, 1973.

[2]William Strong, *Sentence Combining: A Composing Book.* New York: Random House, Inc., 1983.

[3]Irene and Owen Thomas, *Sentence Combining I and II.* (Consists of six diskettes, teacher's guide, reproducible masters, and a binder.) St. Louis, Mo.: Milliken Publishing Co. (P.O. Box 21579, St. Louis, MO 63132), 1984.

Note: The grammatical terminology used here is directed to the teacher, not the pupil.

GRADE THREE

1. Inserting adjectives and adverbs

   Examples:

   I ate the hamburger.
   The hamburger was *soggy.* } *I ate the soggy hamburger.*

   Harry is a roller skater. }
   He is *good* at it.

   Harry roller skates. [good ⟶ well] }
   He is good at it.

   Children are playing. }
   They are playing *in the school yard.*

2. Producing compound subjects and objects

   Examples:

   Maria wanted some bubble gum. [and] } *Maria and Jose wanted some bubble gum.*
   Jose wanted some bubble gum.

   Maria wanted bubble gum. [and] }
   Maria wanted *popcorn.*

3. Producing compound subjects and objects with pronouns.

   Examples:

   He likes bubble gum. [and] } *He and I like bubble gum.*
   I like bubble gum.

   Peter gave her a puppet. [and] }
   Peter gave *me* a puppet.

GRADE FOUR

   Review of the above, plus:

1. Producing compound sentences with *and* and *but.*

   Example:

   John went to the movies. [, but] } *John went to the movies, but I didn't want to go.*
   I didn't want to go.

2. Producing parallel sequences

   Example:

   Maria wanted a bike.
   Maria wanted *a doll.* [___,___and___] *Maria wanted a bike, a doll, and a baseball bat.*
   Maria wanted *a baseball bat.*

3. Producing possessive nouns

   Example:

   I like the sailboat. } *I like Henry's sailboat.*
   It is *Henry's.*

4. Producing sentences with adverbial clauses, using connecting words, such as *because, after, until,* and *when.*

   Examples:

   We went to the store. [because] } *We went to the store because we wanted some bubble gum.*
   We wanted some bubble gum.

   I finished the book. [when___,___] }
   I went back to the library.

Review of the above, plus:

1. Producing sentences with relative clauses

   Example:

   The girl will win a prize.
   The girl *is the best player.* [who] }   *The girl who is the best player will win a prize.*

2. Inserting participial phrases

   Examples:

   My favorite book *is **Charlotte's Web.*** }
   It was *written by E. B. White.*   *My favorite book is **Charlotte's Web**, written by E. B. White.*

   My father is busy. }
   He is *playing football.* }

3. Inserting appositives

   Example:

   Grandma is coming to visit.
   Grandma is *a famous cook.* [,——,] }   *Grandma, a famous cook, is coming to visit.*

4. Multiple combinations (with more than one possible answer)

   Examples:

   I ate the hamburgers.
   Henry also ate the hamburgers.
   They were *soggy.* }   *Henry and I ate the soggy, stale hamburgers quickly.*
   They were *stale.*
   We ate them *quickly.*

   A Wrinkle in Time is a book.
   It is written by Madeleine d'Engels. }
   I would recommend it.
   People my age would like it.

By way of a conclusion, I offer two suggestions to those teachers who agree that the approaches I have described are both basic and sound alternatives to traditional grammar:

1. If your school district uses standardized examinations, ask for a periodic review and evaluation of these examinations. If their measure of writing ability is limited to the skill of identifying subject and verb, press for the elimination of such examinations. A district-made test that uses the kinds of tasks described above, combined with a writing sample, will provide much sounder indices of a student's writing ability.

2. If your district and community insist that grammar be taught somewhere in the curriculum, press for the creation of an elective course in grammar (perhaps two semesters) at the high school level. Such a course, highly recommended to students studying foreign languages or preparing for college, can be designed for pure grammar instruction as an intellectual exercise. We all know that a course like this taught by someone who is enthusiastic about parsing and diagramming can be great fun as well as a rewarding challenge.

In these ways, we will be "putting grammar in its place," doing no one a disservice, and realizing our mutual priorities at a time when our profession is being called on to do so.

Making Correctness Creative: The "Snurdles" Project

Sandra Barnes
Riverbank High School,
Oakdale Joint Union High School District;
and Teacher/Consultant, UCI Writing Project

As English teachers, we are usually required to teach grammar because, supposedly, it will help students write better. However, research indicates that a knowledge of grammar has very little effect on how well students write. Despite these data, most public schools still give instruction in grammar. With that in mind, I tried in my "Snurdles" project to bring the teaching of grammar and writing together. I postulated that if students were challenged to apply what they knew about grammar in their own compositions, then correctness could be a creative enterprise that would foster long-term editing abilities.

I was inspired to make correctness creative by a set of posters called "Snurdles," published by the Perfection Form Company.[1] The set tells a short funny story, with each poster emphasizing one part of speech. I thought it would be educational and entertaining to have students create their own posters illustrating the parts of speech.

I use the original "Snurdles" posters as models for the students. They read the posters and use them as points of departure to create their own characters and stories. After providing a working definition of the parts of speech, I ask the students to work in groups of six to collaborate on a "Snurdles" project.

Each group decides on a character and a series of events or adventures for their story. Each student in the group writes one paragraph that emphasizes one part of speech. The whole group then reviews what has been written and polishes the writing to provide transitions and continuity between the parts. When the story is finished, each paragraph and its part of speech are written and illustrated on posters. The entire group is responsible for the correctness of the finished product.

When working on this unit, I have the students do most of the writing in class with their groups. I move among the groups giving help and advice and monitoring their progress. Usually, the project takes about five class periods. I give each student two letter grades—one for his or her contributions to the group and one for the individual poster.

I have found that students enjoy this project and have much greater success in identifying parts of speech in their own work than in isolated examples written by someone else. Because the students are applying grammatical knowledge to their own writing, they become more aware of when and where parts of speech are used in sentences. The need for transition to build in continuity is also important in the project and helps students in future writing assignments. Overall, the project can positively affect the students' attitudes toward grammar as well as their aptitudes for using parts of speech appropriately in their own writing.

The following is a sample of an eighth grade group's "Snurdles" project, as written by the students and with the parts of speech underlined by the students:

CLOSE ENCOUNTERS OF THE ITCHY KIND

NOUNS

This is a <u>story</u> about a poor <u>canine</u> named <u>Butch</u>, who had a terrible personal <u>problem</u>. Well, you see, he had a <u>flea</u> <u>family</u> of who knows how many living in his <u>fur</u>. They began "living in" <u>Butch</u>, well, his <u>fur</u> that is, last <u>summer</u> while he was at an annual <u>flea</u> <u>market</u>. Now there are millions of them infested in <u>Butch</u>. <u>Butch</u> had gone so crazy because of these <u>fleas</u> that he had even tried to get an <u>exterminator</u> to exterminate him. He figures that if he

[1] *NOTE:* The address for the Perfection Form Company is 100 North Second Ave., Logan, IA 51546: telephone 800-831-4190.

jumps in a <u>pool</u>, he will drown all of these <u>fleas</u> and that will be the <u>end</u> of this "itchy" ordeal!

ADJECTIVES

All of a sudden the <u>little</u> fleas saw a <u>mean</u> looking dog named Butch, running toward a <u>deep</u> pool. The <u>tiny</u> fleas decided to try to build a <u>giant</u> ark very quickly. They spent all of the <u>long</u> day chopping down <u>big</u> <u>thick</u> trees (his <u>thick</u> hair) and trying to put their <u>huge</u> ark together. The <u>big</u> ark had <u>five</u> <u>little</u> rooms—one for Mr. and Mrs. Fleaster, one for <u>little</u> Fleapé, one for baby Please, and one for their pet tick, Toc. They all got in the <u>large</u> ark, when suddenly a <u>huge</u> <u>tidal</u> wave came. They all started screaming loudly and they started floating faster and faster to who knows where.

INTERJECTIONS

As the fleas jumped on the ark, there was noise and excitement. Everyone was yelling things back and forth. As baby Please walked aboard the ark, she yelled, "<u>Yippee!</u> This is fun." Then a huge wave came upon the ark, and Fleapé exclaimed, "<u>Hey!</u> I am getting seasick." Later, Mrs. Fleaster sat down and yelled, "<u>Yea!</u> This is great." But as soon as Mr. Fleaster looked on the deck of the ark, he screamed, "<u>Ugh!</u> There is a leak." Five minutes later Grandma Fleaster slowly started walking toward the ark and said, "<u>Nuts!</u> I'm still hungry," in a very screechy, high voice. Following her, baby Please yelled, "<u>Hey!</u> Wait for me." A few minutes later everyone was on board, and all were happy till Mr. Fleaster saw a big waterfall close by. (The waterfall was really some water going down into the jacuzzi from the pool.)

VERBS

As the fleas <u>sailed</u> down the waterfall, sudden panic <u>fell</u> over all the Fleaster family. Please, one of the fleas in the Fleaster family, <u>lost</u> her hat. The hat <u>glided</u> into the big ocean lying before her. One of the fleas <u>was</u> <u>chatting</u> to another about new hairstyles. They probably <u>did</u> not <u>realize</u> what danger they soon <u>would be facing</u>. I <u>think</u> they <u>started</u> to <u>get</u> the hint when they <u>were submerged</u> in water from their little tiny toes to their teeny little arms. I <u>imagine</u> the fleas at least <u>felt</u> safe when they <u>reached</u> the bottom of the waterfall.

PREPOSITIONS (PHRASES)

Then, all <u>of the sudden</u>, there was another big tidal wave. The flea ark was floating <u>in the violent sea</u> for what seemed <u>like hours</u>. The four little fleas and their pet "tick," Toc, were becoming very seasick. Mr. Fleaster saw a drop <u>in the water</u>. They were coming <u>to another waterfall</u>. <u>Down the falls</u> went the flea ark <u>into a giant whirlpool</u>. They started <u>in a big spin</u>.

CONJUNCTIONS

The fleas were jumping <u>and</u> falling all over the place. They were stunned by the whirlpool, for it was spinning <u>and</u> turning around <u>and</u> around. The fleas were going down <u>and</u> down. Finally, the spinning stopped (because the jacuzzi, which they were in, was turned off), <u>but</u> the fleas didn't stop spinning.

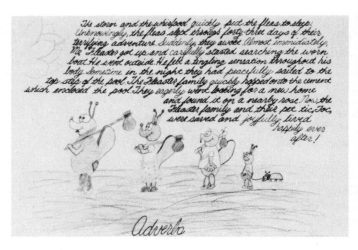

PRONOUNS

The flea family's ark was drenched from going through the whirlpool. Please got dizzy. <u>She</u> was sick to <u>her</u> little flea stomach. <u>They</u> saw only misty and slightly foggy weather. Suddenly a light shone. <u>They</u> realized <u>it</u> was the sun shining. Then <u>they</u> emerged from the wet wonderland. Slowly rising out of the water <u>they</u> all rejoiced. After rejoicing, father flea was very tired and ordered <u>them</u> all to bed.

ADVERBS

The storm and the whirlpool <u>quickly</u> put the fleas to sleep. <u>Unknowingly</u>, the fleas slept through 43 days of their terrifying adventure. <u>Suddenly</u>, they awoke. <u>Almost immediately</u>, Mr. Fleaster got up and <u>carefully</u> started searching the worn boat. He went outside. He felt a tingling sensation throughout his body. <u>Sometime</u> in the night they had <u>peacefully</u> sailed to the top step of the pool. The Fleaster family <u>quickly</u> hopped onto the cement which enclosed the pool. They <u>eagerly</u> went looking for a new home and found it on a nearby rose. Now, the Fleaster family and their pet tick, Toc, were saved and <u>joyfully</u> lived <u>happily</u> <u>ever</u> <u>after</u>!

Teaching Correctness with Competition Day

By Russell Frank
English and Journalism Teacher,
Chaparral Middle School,
Walnut Valley Unified School District;
and Teacher/Consultant, UCI Writing Project

I know my students need to master the conventions of written English, but I have always dreaded the task. In every lesson it seemed as if I were dragging a group of tug-of-war opponents through the mire.

"Well, class, today we are going to study the use of the comma in setting off an introductory dependent clause." When you make a statement like that to a group of courteous students, you are probably greeted with a combination of yawns and blank stares. In my eighth grade classes, the moans of pain remind me of milking time at the dairies in nearby Chino. However, because of Competition Day, the thought of teaching correctness now excites me. I get a big kick out of seeing "terminally cool" eighth graders leap from their seats in their enthusiasm to answer questions.

Competition Day is designed around a game format that puts motivation theory to practice while encouraging class participation in learning. It is based on the following principles:

1. High interest through the use of competition (This is especially effective at the intermediate level.)
2. Immediate knowledge of results (This reinforces learning.)
3. Success according to level of difficulty (The teacher can individualize the game to make success easier for each student.)

In addition, Competition Day will encourage discussion in small groups. In essence you will be using the students in your classroom as teachers.

> *The idea of being "correct" takes on a new importance when a student is genuinely concerned about communicating his or her message to an audience.*
> IRENE THOMAS

At some time, we have all made the mistake of asking our class a question and immediately picked one person to answer it without allowing "think" time. Meanwhile, the others in class have stopped thinking about the question. "Johnny has to answer it," they are thinking. "I don't have to worry about this one." At that point, effective learning is diluted. In Competition Day everyone is responsible for answering a question and earning points for his or her respective team.

To start the competition, you must have first introduced a correctness skill: the use of commas, appositives, difficult spelling words, capitalization rule, and so forth. The necessary materials include an overhead projector, chalkboard space, chalk, scorekeeper, and a set of small numbered cards. You divide the class into groups of between four and eight members, depending on the size of your class and the number of teams you wish to have. Assign a number to each person on each team. If you have four teams competing, you will have four people from opposing teams with the same number. Each player must have a sheet of paper and pencil and must answer each question.

This paper is turned in at the end of the game, and you can review the paper to check a student's mastery of a particular skill.

Basically, students compete against students who have the same number on the other teams. This allows you to group students according to ability levels if you wish to do so. Highly skilled or highly competitive students can all be given the same number and, thus, will compete against each other. In like manner less skilled or shy students can be given the same number.

After assigning numbers, I may ask the teams to punctuate or capitalize a sentence properly. I dictate the sentence or write it so that it is projected on the overhead projector. As the students are writing their answers, I draw a numbered card (1—4 or 1—6, depending on the number of players on each team), and anticipation mounts. Nobody knows what number I will call. Finally, I read the number.

At this point, I can ask all those people who have the number to give their answers orally or write them on the chalkboard. Another option is to have them hold up their papers, which I can check at their desks. Correct answers earn a point for that person's group; incorrect answers receive no score.

In a variation of the game, I ask a question and have each group come to consensus regarding its answer. This option is especially useful when I ask the students to do higher level thinking, such as composing sentences that contain certain grammatical structures. Group discussion also provides students with opportunities for evaluation. In sentence combining, for instance, I ask my students to select the most effective sentence combination written by group members. These can be put on the chalkboard for display and compared with sentences chosen by other teams.

When the competition comes to a close, I tally up the scores of each group and pronounce a winner. In

the event of a tie, I give a trivia quiz as a tie breaker. This may consist of a variety of questions from other disciplines—names of state capitals, dates of historical events, names of famous people, mathematical problems, and so forth.

Although Competition Day can be used in any content area, I have had success in using the approach to reinforce skills in punctuation, capitalization, spelling, grammar, vocabulary, and sentence combining. Using this game to help my students gain mastery over correctness skills has kept student motivation high when it usually ebbs. I no longer feel as if I am having to drag my students through a mire of tedium. By putting the learning of the conventions of written English into a game and making students responsible for each other's success, I have found that the competition can be with me rather than a tug-of-war against me.

Creative Practice with Sentence Patterns

By Laurie Opfell
Former English Teacher, Irvine High School;
Graduate Student, University of Kentucky;
and Teacher/Consultant, UCI Writing Project

Can working with sentence structure patterns positively influence students' writing? I think it can if it is presented in a way that is motivating, interesting, and meaningful.

In my mind, nothing is less relevant or duller for students to do than completing work sheets on commas or parts of speech. Having students correct errors in punctuation and grammar or work sheets rarely

results in fluent, error-free writing, because students cannot make the connection between such isolated exercises and their own prose. However, certain activities do help students transfer what they learn in manipulating sentence structures to writing in more practical ways. First, however, you have to put away the books and work sheets on grammar.

After taking the important step of putting away the books and work sheets, inform your students in understandable terms exactly what it is they are learning. Too often, the grammatical language alone will hopelessly confuse them. The accompanying chart contains a list of patterns I give my students to learn, and they have found the patterns workable and clear. Next, it is important to stimulate the students mentally so that as they practice and apply the patterns, their interest and motivation is high. Finally, ensure that they transfer what they learn in practice to "real" writing. Two activities that I use to help my students get interested and learn to make that transfer are described in the paragraphs that follow.

After presenting to my students a pattern such as *N-V, and N-V,* I write it on the chalkboard and give examples of sentences in which the pattern is used. For example:

Fred chased the dog, and Alice followed.

Then I show the students slides so that they will have subjects for their writing.[1] I usually get prepackaged sets of slides from the library; art slides are good for creating interest and discussion, but vacation slides can also be used. After I show a slide, I give my students approximately a minute to write a sentence that fits the pattern and is based on the slide. I also encourage creativity by involving the students in imagining and predicting. For example, if I show a slide of a door in a wall, I might ask my students to imagine what is going to come suddenly through the door.

As I show each new slide, I usually walk around the room and monitor the activity. This is a very friendly activity; the students suggest ideas to each other, react to the pictures, laugh, and come up with wild ideas; yet at the same time they must concentrate because I change the slides every minute or two.

As I show the slides, I also change sentence patterns. After showing ten or more slides for the *N-V, and N-V* pattern, I may ask the students to add three adjectives and one adverb to the pattern, or I may introduce a completely new pattern. To avoid having this exercise become routine, one should have diversity both in slides and in sentence patterns.

---

[1]If slides are difficult for you to secure or use, this activity also works well with a set of magazines. Having a picture to view seems to make the activity easier for students.

CHART OF SOME SENTENCE PATTERNS*

Pattern (N=noun; V=verb)	Grammatical term	Use
(Compound) N-V, and N-V. N-V and V.	Coordinating conjunctions	and, but, or, for, nor, yet
(Complex) While N-V, N-V. N-V while N-V.	Subordinating conjunctions	while, if, as, because, since, so, when, until, etc.
N-V; however, N-V. N-V; N, however, N.	Transitions Connectors	however, moreover, whereas, thus, on the other hand, etc.

*This was adapted from material prepared by Cathy D'Aoust, a Teacher/Consultant in the UCI Writing Project and the author of material appearing elsewhere in this book.

A good way to end the class session is to have students exchange papers and check each other's sentences for correct structure and other matters. This provides each writer with an audience and also helps reinforce the lessons on structure and the punctuation associated with each pattern. Later, it will be important to ask the students to use the patterns in some kind of writing. It does not necessarily matter whether you have them write a paragraph for the purpose of using several patterns or you have them make the patterns part of a rubric for an assignment. The important thing is to emphasize that the *purpose* of working with patterns is to give variation and correctness to the writing, which leads to the development of comprehensible, interesting papers.

Another activity that helps students make the transfer from practice to "real writing" is to have them use specified structures in letters to each other. As with the previous activity, show the students a sentence pattern, give examples, and then have the students select a partner. Each partner writes, Dear *(his or her partner's name),* at the top of the paper. Then each one writes a sentence that follows the pattern and that could logically be found in a letter. (Sometimes, a connector sentence will be necessary.) For example, if the pattern is *N-V: N,* then the beginning of the letter might be:

Dear Lisa,

Hi, how are you? Please come to the party tonight and bring the following: Cokes, candy, and chips.

After each partner has started the letter using a pattern, have the students exchange letters and write a reply using the same or another pattern. They should keep following the pattern and switching back and forth until they have finished their dialogue. This activity is especially good to use as a test or a review because your students should be able to write a very coherent letter and still effectively use eight to ten patterns.

As with the activity involving slides, this letter writing activity is also fun and motivating. As you walk around the classroom, you get an unusual glimpse into how students spend their time and what they consider important. After all, note writing is a popular and naturally relevant activity for them anyway. When the students are finished with the activity, I usually ask for several volunteers to read their letters to the class. This is received with interest and a great deal of humor.

By teaching sentence manipulation in the manner I have described, students can be creative while practicing a variety of grammatical patterns. Instead of filling in the blanks or responding to meaningless drills, students are generating authentic writing for an audience. The transfer from practice to written communication has already been made! Finally, these activities are fun and inexpensive to implement; they can be used in grades seven through twelve; and they motivate students to learn.

Building Vocabularies

Word-Sprouting: A Vocabulary Building Strategy for Remedial Writers

By Barbara Morton

English Teacher, Villa Park High School,
Orange Unified School District;
and Teacher/Consultant, UCI Writing Project

Gabriele Rico coined the term *clustering* to describe a writing warm-up exercise that she developed as a result of her research in right brain functioning at Stanford University. Briefly, clustering is a formalized kind of brainstorming. The writer encircles a nucleus word, such as *blue* in Figure 28, and arranges the words he or she associates with the nucleus word in a free-form diagram around the nucleus. (For more information on the clustering technique, see Dr. Rico's essay in the "Prewriting" section that appears near the beginning of this book.)

Dr. Rico's research indicates that through the process of clustering, writers, particularly those at the remedial level, can generate a network of related thoughts from the nucleus word; i.e., clustering assists them in writing coherent paragraphs. Visualizing the relationships between the nucleus word and its satellites helps these students organize their thinking, eliminate nonessential elements, and write in an orderly, systematic manner. It is particularly useful as an alternative to outlining for students who have difficulty developing their thoughts sequentially. Similarly, a distant cousin of the clustering technique enables remedial writers to bypass the often counterproductive grammar lesson and deal directly with usage and word manipulation, as you will see as we examine the procedure of word-sprouting.

In Figure 29, which closely resembles Dr. Rico's clustering diagram, you will find an assortment of words related to the nucleus word *fool*. However, instead of random associations, the cluster is limited to inflections of the nucleus word.

Because the method of identifying inflections departs substantially from the clustering technique, I have substituted the term *sprouting* for Dr. Rico's *clustering*. Language teachers, already familiar with the linguistic terms *root* and *stem,* will readily comprehend the metaphor of *sprouts*, or grammatical variations, growing from *wordseeds*.

As each sprout is labeled and classified according to its grammatical identity, the fickleness of grammar becomes apparent, as shown in the following chart:

Verbs/ Verb variations	Nouns/ Noun variations	Modifiers (adjectives and adverbs)
fool	fool	foolish
fools	fools	foolishly
fooling	(to) fool	fooling
fooled	fooling	fooled
	foolishness	
	fools	

The confusion that results from attempts at arbitrary classification might discourage the most able of students. *Fool* appears as both a noun and a verb, as does *fools*. And *fooling* is included in all three categories, because the participial form qualifies as a modifier as well.

Until the word is considered in the context of the sentence, its grammatical classification is, of course, impossible. Even then, frustrated remedial learners flounder in a morass of linguistic terminology with no improvement in their usage skills.

The word-sprouting approach abandons the traditional grammarian's approach to language and capitalizes on the student's inherent ability to distinguish the appropriate inflection of a familiar word according to its position in a spoken phrase. It is a vocabulary expansion and usage drill that deals with nouns, verbs, and modifiers without labeling them. Spared the burden of learning new definitions and assigning grammatical categories, as is often the procedure in standard vocabulary lessons, the student concentrates on the usage that "sounds right" for a given problem structure.

To introduce this exercise, the teacher generates a diagram of sprouts from a familiar word on the chalkboard or transparency as the class spontaneously provides them, adding new forms of the seedword. Before assigning the written segments of the exercise, the teacher must determine that the diagram includes an exhaustive list of sprouts. With speakers of substandard English, it may also be necessary to repeat the words with appropriate examples: "We don't say, 'I fooling you,' we say, 'I _____?'"

Even though the word may be familiar, it is also important for the class to decide on a working definition. Remedial students often have a great deal of difficulty arriving at simple definitions, particularly if they are not allowed to use a form of the word to phrase the definition.

Next, using the completed diagram of sprouts, students work with a partner to select the most appropriate sprout for use in carefully structured sample sentences. Allowing them to complete the exercise aloud with a partner reinforces aural perception and provides an opportunity for peer involvement.

In the final phase of the exercise, students are expected to write original sentences, developed from a list of words and phrases that incorporate the sprouts in a variety of syntactic problems. They are allowed to use the sample sentences as models, and they may refer to a set of sentence-grading criteria that will later be used to determine their letter grades. While they are expected to work independently, a peer-evaluation session in which students read their sentences aloud to one another allows them to correct errors before submitting their papers for final grading.

The teacher's use of the grading criteria allows for a rapid, "no surprises" return of papers. Students who score less than 89 should choose two sentences to rewrite as a follow-up.

> *Only if we attribute enough value to what we have to say are we likely to make the effort required to get our ideas straight, even for ourselves.*
> SHERIDAN BLAU

Phase One: Word-Sprouting

The group session in which the class provides sprouts of the seedwords combines auditory, visual, and kinesthetic modes of learning. Because remedial learners need constant reinforcement in all modes, the

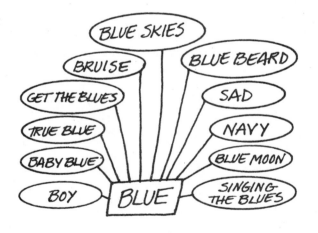

Fig. 28. The Clustering of *Blue*

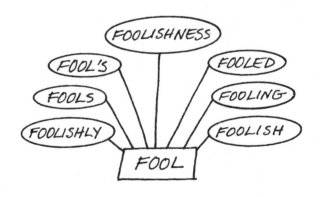

Fig. 29. Clustering with Inflections of the Nucleus Word

teacher's presentation should be painstakingly thorough. In the first phase of the exercise, the teacher must help the students create the most complete word-sprout.

For example, the sprouts the group might create for the seedword *decide* are shown in Figure 30. Even though the definition of a familiar word like *decide* may seem obvious, a brief session to arrive at a consensus is necessary before continuing with the written segments of the exercise.

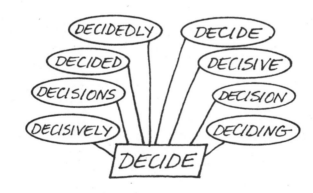

Fig. 30. Word-Sprouts of a Seedword

Phase Two: Completing Sample Sentences

In phase two of the word-sprouting exercise, the students are asked to use the words they sprouted from the seedword *decide*, and they are given the following instructions:

- Write the most appropriate form of *decide* in the blanks provided in the accompanying sample sen-

tences. Use each word from our word-sprout at least once.
- Say each sentence aloud to help you decide on the correct form.
- You may work with a partner. Refer to the word-sprouting diagram if necessary.

SAMPLE SENTENCES

1. Louise always has difficulty making her own _____.
2. Yesterday, Louise _____ to give up the tennis team to take a job at a fast-food restaurant.
3. She had to _____ whether the money she would make was important enough to take the place of her first love, tennis.
4. "I just can't _____," she told me unhappily.
5. Louise always talks things over with me when she has trouble _____ .
6. I usually _____ carefully to avoid making a mistake.
7. That is why _____ is usually easy for me.
8. Leaving the tennis team was a tough _____ for Louise.
9. Louise has never been a very _____ person; now she wants to change her mind and go back on the tennis team.
10. Coach Burns will not let favoritism be a _____ factor.
11. Having already _____ to remove her name, he's not likely to change his mind.
12. He is _____ today whether to let Louise come back on the team.
13. I hope he _____ in favor of Louise.
14. Louise just called to tell me it has all been _____.
15. Coach Burns said he _____ that he would give Louise one more chance.
16. It is _____ in the team's best interest to have Louise as a starter.

Phase Three: Writing a Sentence

In phase three of the word-sprouting exercise, the students are given a list of words and asked to create their own sentences. They are given these instructions:

- Using the words or word groups suggested below, write a sentence at least eight words long:

1. decide	9. decisions
2. to decide	10. deciding is
3. they decide	11. is deciding
4. decides	12. Mary, deciding
4. Mary decided	13. was decided
6. had decided	14. decisive
7. having decided	15. decisively
8. decision	16. decidedly

- Do not change the form of the word, and do not separate or rearrange the word groups.
- You may refer to the "Sample Sentences" and the "Grading Standards for Sentences" as guidelines.

GRADING STANDARDS FOR SENTENCES

Possible score

90—100 (Superior)

To earn maximum points, you must show the following in each sentence:

- An understanding of the meaning of the vocabulary word.
- Correct use of the form of the vocabulary word.
- No spelling mistakes.
- No punctuation mistakes.
- Construction according to the rules of standard English.
- Originality and inventive use of language.

80—89 (Good)

This paper does not receive maximum points because of one or more of the following:

- Minor confusion about the meaning of the vocabulary word.
- Mistaken use of the form of the vocabulary word.
- Minor errors in grammar, punctuation, or spelling.
- Little apparent effort and originality in sentence construction.

70—79 (Fair)

This score is reserved for sentences that:

- Show uncertainty about exact meaning or use of the word in three or more instances.
- Have occasional awkward grammatical constructions.
- Show difficulty with internal punctuation.
- Have frequent spelling errors.

60—69 (Weak)

This score is reserved for sentences that:

- Show that the writer has little understanding of the vocabulary word.
- Have abundant errors in spelling, including the word being studied.
- Show elementary punctuation errors, indicating failure to proofread.
- Are elementary in structure; run-on sentences or fragments.

> *Too often we tell students to listen to what we have to say when students should listen to their own drafts.*
> DONALD MURRAY

SAMPLE SEEDWORDS— HIGH SCHOOL REMEDIAL LEVEL

Verbs/ Verb variations	Nouns/ Noun variations	Modifiers (adjectives and adverbs)
separate	separation	separate
separates	separations	separately
separating	(to) separate	separating
separated	separating	separated
	separator	separable
obey	obedience	obedient
obeys	(to) obey	obediently
obeying	obeying	obeying
obeyed		obeyed
anger	anger	angry
angers	(to) anger	angrily
angering	angering	angering
angered		angered
create	creation	creative
creates	creations	creatively
creating	(to) create	creating
created	creating	created
deceive	deceit	deceitful
deceives	deception	deceitfully
deceiving	(to) deceive	deceptive
deceived	deceiving	deceptively
		deceiving
		deceived
pursue	pursuit	pursuant
pursues	pursuits	pursuing
pursuing	(to) pursue	pursued
pursued	pursuing	
change	change	changeable
changes	changes	changeably
changing	(to) change	changing
changed	changing	changed
picture	picture	picturesque
pictures	pictures	picturesquely
picturing	(to) picture	picturing
pictured	picturing	pictured
analyze	analysis	analytical
analyzes	analyses	analytically
analyzing	(to) analyze	analyzing
analyzed	analyzing	analyzed
experiment	experiment	experimental
experiments	experiments	experimentally
experimenting	(to) experiment	experimenting
experimented	experimenting	experimented

Deceptive Definitions: Making the Dictionary a Treasure Chest

By Mindy Moffatt

**English Teacher, Walker Junior High School,
Anaheim Union High School District;
and Teacher/Consultant, UCI Writing Project**

The dictionary is a treasure chest, but too often students see it only as Pandora's box. The mere mention of a dictionary often suggests punishment, or it is associated with boring, endless, mindless ditto sheets which ineffectively "teach" vocabulary skills. Unfortunately, the dictionary may also be viewed the same way by some teachers. (Contrast the availability of dictionaries in teachers' workrooms and in a school's detention halls.)

When I was confronted with the dilemma of turning Pandora's box into a treasure chest, one of my eighth grade students gave me the key—a game called Deceptive Definitions. I have been told that a version of this game, called "Fictionary," which has slightly more elaborate scoring rules, is popular with many teachers.

Although the explanation for Deceptive Definitions was complicated, one of my students and I had played the game a few times, and we became aware that the treasure was *ours*. The more often the game is played, the more self-motivated students become in order to improve their own skills of dictionary use (especially

with pronunciation key and guide), vocabulary building, imitative writing, listening and reading comprehension, memorization, and spelling. The directions for playing the game are presented in the accompanying chart.

After playing two rounds of the game with the teacher, the students can play the game without additional guidance. Each student can have a turn at selecting a word from the dictionary, for which deceptive definitions can be written and then presenting the definitions to a peer group of four to five students. (Note: To promote listening comprehension skills, the definitions can be read aloud and then written on the

> *The word-sprouting approach capitalizes
> on the student's inherent ability
> to distinguish the appropriate inflection
> of a familiar word according to its position
> in a spoken phrase.*
> BARBARA MORTON

chalkboard or notepaper.) Or, working in small groups, students can select an intriguing vocabulary word; each student can then contribute a definition for the word and let other groups in the class come to consensus on which is the true definition. The rules remain the same: 1 point for each group that chooses the correct definition and 1 point for the small group each time one of its deceptive definitions is chosen by another group.

The point of Deceptive Definitions in the first few rounds of the game is simply to get students interested in the dictionary and excited about learning new words. While they may not use the specific words gained in the Deceptive Definitions game in their own writing, they may reach for a new words to convey what they do want to say. In subsequent games, the teacher can supply a list of words that relate more directly to the content of the course. At the same time that they are building vocabulary skills, students are also practicing imitative writing. The deceptive definitions they write must sound as if they came from the dictionary in order for their definitions to stump their classmates. This aspect of the game can be a rehearsal for the stylistic writing they will do later in the semester.

Deceptive Definitions is, indeed, a treasure chest. It can be adapted to any grade level and tailored to any student population. It promotes active rather than passive learning and it is fun.

Directions	Example

Introduction to the Game
The teacher arranges to play two rounds.
 	
Round 1
1. The teacher chooses a word from the dictionary and writes it on chalkboard with pronunciation guide (if needed for review of skill).
2. The teacher writes four deceptive definitions and the true definition on chalkboard.
3. Students write down the letter identifying the definition that they believe is the correct one.
4. The teacher identifies the correct answer.
5. Each student who chose *blackbird* earns 1 point.
 	
Round 2
1. The teacher writes a new word on the chalkboard and selects four students to write deceptive definitions for the word.
2. The teacher collects the definitions.
3. The teacher writes all the definitions on the chalkboard.
4. The students again choose the definition that they believe is the true definition and write the identifying letter on their papers.
5. The teacher announces the correct definition and the names of students whose deceptive definitions were chosen.
6. Scoring: Each student who chose the true definition earns 1 point. Any student whose deceptive definition was chosen by others earns 1 point for every student who was fooled.
	1. merl (mərl)
	
	2. a. to rotate in a counterclockwise direction d. fiber used in elastic
	   b. blackbird e. Neanderthal weapons
	   c. corner spring in a mattress
	4. merl
	   b. blackbird
	
	1. anlace (an ləs)
	
	3. a. tropical flower
	   b. type of sour cherry having blue-green fruit
	   c. therapeutic psychologist
	   d. leather strip used for tying
	   e. a tapering medieval dagger
	5. anlace
	   e. a tapering medieval dagger

Teaching Vocabulary Through Competition

By Michael O'Brien
English Teacher, Foothill High School,
Tustin Unified School District;
and Teacher/Consultant, UCI Writing Project

"All right, the period is almost over. Both teams are even. Buker is up for the South . . . ."

"Yea, Buke!" his teammates shout.

". . . and Kelly is up for the North . . . ."

"You can do it, Kelly!" one of her teammates yells encouragingly.

". . . and at stake is an all-expense paid trip to Enid, Oklahoma, for the Miss Oil by-Products Beauty Pageant!"

"Hooray!" some students shout. Others simply roll their eyes at me.

If you visit my class on vocabulary day, you will find that my students yell a lot—probably because I use team competition.

Most of my vocabulary program is boringly standard. In fact, I have some reservations about "teaching" vocabulary through the use of lists. I have, however, always bowed to community pressure. For years, I got the words from class-related reading, dictated the words and the meanings (which, I found, promotes listening skills) on Monday, and then held a test on Friday. Lately, however, I have changed my approach to try to help students on the *Scholastic Aptitude Test (SAT)*. Therefore, I have been focusing on prefixes, suffixes, and roots and choosing words in which they appear—the more advanced the class, the more difficult the words. Remedial classes not only get easier but also fewer words. Two books that I have found helpful in this work, although I have done a lot

of adapting, are *Vocabulary for the High School Student*[1] and *Vocabulary for the College-Bound Student*.[2] These also have analogy exercises, which are helpful for the *SAT*.

Before the day of the test, I set aside half of a period for the competition. To give variety, I often divide up teams in different ways. One day it might be a battle of the sexes; the next time it might be a competition between the rows or even between people wearing blue versus those wearing brown. I let the students choose their team names, which often give insight into the peculiarities of the adolescent mind. Then I announce the prize, which is hopelessly fabulous or silly or sometimes as prosaic as being able to leave first when the lunch bell rings.

To begin the competition, I call team representatives to the chalkboards; I arrange them so that they are facing away from each other to make "borrowing" difficult. I give them a word at random and ask them to write the word and its definition on the chalkboard. For a correct spelling of the vocabulary word, the team gets a point; for an accurate, correctly spelled definition, the team gets another point. I have also

> *The knowledge of words is the gate to scholarship.*
> WOODROW WILSON

tried Las Vegas Vocabulary in which I set betting limits based on word difficulty. Depending on the confidence of the player, he or she can bet cautiously or bet

[1]Harold Levine, *Vocabulary for the High School Student.* New York: AMSCO School Publications, Inc., 1983.
[2]Harold Levine, *Vocabulary for the College-Bound Student.* New York: AMSCO School Publications, Inc., 1983.

the limit. The team with the most "money" at the end of the class period is the winner. I hope I have not led any students to a life of moral degeneration through Las Vegas Vocabulary. But if I have, at least they will be articulate degenerates.

Other competitive approaches can be used successfully. I have a colleague who uses Vocabulary Charades. The student teams try to guess the vocabulary word through animated silent clues given by a teammate. The team with the lowest combined times for guessing the words is the winner. He reports that the students are wildly imaginative and easily get caught up in the enthusiasm of the game. And why not make something that is as tedious as memorizing vocabulary as stimulating as possible?

I have used the competition method successfully with the whole spectrum of high school age and ability groups. Even the students who are passive and uninterested in school seem to respond to this activity. After having these contests for awhile, peer pressure becomes high for the students to study. Those who know their words are cheered; those who do not know them let down their teammates. By making the prize something silly or fantastical, I minimize the disappointment of losing and maximize the entertainment and challenge of competing. Usually, my students are so caught up in the contest that they do not even realize how much they are learning in the process.

Verbal Density: Expanding Students' Use of Verbs

By Evelyn Ching
English and Fine Arts Teacher,
Villa Park High School,
Orange Unified School District;
and Teacher/Consultant, UCI Writing Project

Although I stress several aspects of vocabulary to show high school students how diction contributes to a mature writing style, one of the most useful concepts I have found is that of verbal density, or the ratio of verbs and verbals to the total number of words in a piece of writing. It is an easy concept to demonstrate in the writing of various authors and becomes simple for the students to use in evaluating their own or others' writing styles.

For the lesson I first explain the rationale: that *moving pictures* created by interesting active verbs are far more fascinating to read than almost any still *portrait* that depends largely on the verb *to be* and its various forms. Even John Steinbeck's descriptions in which very little *happens* are full of evocative verbs that move the reader's mental eyes around the picture much as an artist, such as Cezanne, skillfully manipulates the eye of the viewer in one of his still lifes.

After the rationale is explained, students need to be reminded of what a verb and a verbal are; e.g., any verb, its conjugational parts and constructs, gerunds, participial and infinitive phrases, and participles used as modifiers. Also counted are those words in which the noun form and verb form are the same: *strike, slide, ride, smile,* and so forth. Do not be surprised by how many of these words come from sports. Encourage students to make this connection, because sports broadcasting, particularly on radio, has a high verbal ratio.

Next, it is useful to show how the process works by providing several samples. I distribute a selection in which I have previously counted the total number of words (between 200—300 is best). Then I *walk* my students through the selection by reading it aloud, emphasizing the verbs and verbals, which they underline on their copies. I purposely *forget* several to encourage them to look actively, not just listen to me. Here is one of the selections I have used:

1904—The Forgotten Games

ST. LOUIS—It was late one spring afternoon. A watery sun tried fitfully to pierce the clouds that hung over the city. In Forest Park, the trees were bare, their branches tracing stark patterns against the dull gray sky.

In a far corner of the Washington University campus, great mudstreaked Caterpillar tractors and bulldozers eased their way between the ranks of parked cars, their exhausts sending puffs of dirty smoke into the afternoon air.

Workmen, warmly bundled against the cold, sloshed through the rain-filled potholes, already thinking about the end of another shift. Huge trucks, piled high with debris, carried away the results of the day's demolition.

Francis Field, its turf churned to mud by the treads of the giant earth movers, had a sad look about it. The black wrought-iron fence surrounding the field lay flat in places, as if having given up trying to keep the future from tearing away at the past. Already, the once-proud cement grandstand, the first of its kind in the United States, had been reduced to little more than a mound of broken concrete, twisted wire, and splintered wood.

Not so, however, for the giant stone pillars and ornate gates at the east end of the field. There they stood, as they had done for four-score years and more, and there they will remain.[1] (*220 words; verbal density = 1:7.3*)

Before counting the total number of words in the selection, I ask a volunteer to read aloud just the verbs and verbals. The students will be able to follow the

action with almost no help at all from nouns, adverbs, or their "great fabulous, fantastic" adjectives.

The verbal density is figured by dividing the total number of words by the number of verbs and verbals.[2] The resulting number will be the denominator of the verbal-density fraction. Studies have shown that professional writers consistently achieve a verbal density of about 1:6; college students, 1:10; and many high school students, 1:12—15.

> *Talking is a hydrant in the yard and writing is a faucet upstairs in the house. Opening the first takes all the pressure off the second.*
> ROBERT FROST

Usually, I follow the demonstration by distributing two selections, such as the following, for which I have already calculated the verbal density:

Excerpt from "The Most Dangerous Game"

An apprehensive night crawled slowly by like a wounded snake, and sleep did not visit Rainsford, although the silence of a dead world was on the jungle. Toward morning when a dingy gray was varnishing the sky, the cry of some startled bird focused Rainsford's attention in that direction. Something was coming through the bush, coming slowly, carefully, coming by the same winding way Rainsford had come. He flattened himself down on the limb, and through a screen of leaves almost as thick as tapestry, he watched . . . That which was approaching was a man.

It was General Zaroff. He made his way along with his eyes fixed in utmost concentration on the ground before him. He paused, almost beneath the tree, dropped to his knees and studied the ground. Rainsford's impulse was to hurl himself down like a panther, but he saw that the

---

[2]In counting the number of verbs and verbals, a verb and its helping verb are counted as one; infinitives, as one; hyphenated words, as one; gerunds, as one; participles, as one; and nouns that are identical with the verb form, as one.

---

[1]Grahame L. Jones, "1904—The Forgotten Games," *Los Angeles Times,* Part VIII, p. 4, July 24, 1984. Copyright, 1984, *Los Angeles Times;* used by permission of the publisher.

general's right hand held something metallic—a small automatic pistol.

The hunter shook his head several times, as if he were puzzled. Then he straightened up and took from his case one of his black cigarettes; its pungent incense-like smoke floated up to Rainsford's nostrils.

Rainsford held his breath. The general's eyes had left the ground and were traveling inch by inch up the tree.[3] *(212 words; verbal density = 1:5.05)*

Excerpt from *An Introduction to Shakespeare*

An actor also had to be a trained swordsman, for the London audiences knew a great deal about the art of fencing and the Theatre was often hired for exhibition matches by professionals. A good fencer needed years of training and a great deal of physical endurance, for the heavy Elizabethan rapier was a brutal weapon and the fencer was trained to make for his opponent's eyes or strike below the ribs. Actors had an even more difficult problem, since they had to face a critical audience on an open stage in the glare of the afternoon sun and stage a duel which was realistic enough so it would look as though a man had actually been killed.[4] *(118 words; verbal density = 1:5.9)*

After we have read the selection, we discuss it as a class. This follow-up makes students especially aware of the impact of verbals in a given selection.

---

[3]Richard E. Connell, "The Most Dangerous Game." Copyright, 1924, by Richard Connell; copyright renewed 1952, by Louise Fox Connell. Reprinted by permission of Brandt & Brandt Literary Agents, Inc.

[4]Marchette Chute, *An Introduction to Shakespeare.* New York: E. P. Dutton and Co., Inc., © 1951, p. 26. Used by permission of the publisher.

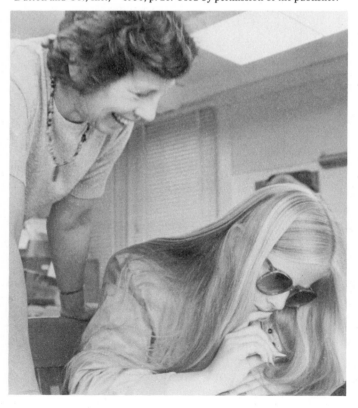

When students begin to have confidence in their own writing and, in particular, to feel secure about their ability to fix errors and to improve their effectiveness as writers, I have them run a verbal density test on a piece of their own writing or the work of an author they admire or enjoy.

At this point, I ask students to apply what they have learned by using an idea I picked up from Barbara Morton's word-sprouting technique—having students apply the missing words in a paragraph. But instead of having them use only forms of a root word, like *decide,* I encourage them to use as many original verbs and verbals as they can think of, as I did in the following exercises:

SUPPLY THE VERBS FOR THE BLANKS:

An ancient popcorn machine _____ the door, and a long glass counter _____ down the narrow aisle. Mounds and pounds of candies—most of them homemade—are in baskets gaily _____ with ribbons and red plastic roses.

A little boy _____ in his jeans for a dime—the price of an ice cream cone. Another youngster _____ down a dime for a bag of popcorn and _____ out. A man enters and _____ the walkways, _____ something, that special, certain something to _____ a sweet tooth.

Slowly he _____ toward the end of the counter.

At last the man's jaw _____ firm; he stands erect, no longer _____ over the stronghold of sweets, his decision _____ .

LIST THE VERBS AND VERBALS YOU SUPPLIED:	MORE ORIGINAL VERBS AND VERBALS:
_____	_____
_____	_____
_____	_____

We share the different student versions of the exercise as a class and, in the process, develop a word-bank of effective verbs and verbals that students can draw on in upcoming writing assignments. Having students perform this same task on the work of prominent authors (with the verbs and verbals removed) helps the students enlarge their vocabularies, increase their use of dictionaries and thesauruses, and gain a better understanding of the elements of style.

The final step in the lesson is to ask students to perform a verbal density analysis on something they have written. This concrete experience with their own work is the best motivator for using a more action-oriented vocabulary in the future. Invariably the ratio of verbs and verbals in my students' writing increases as a result of this lesson and, as a by-product, their vocabulary is enhanced and their style becomes more vital.

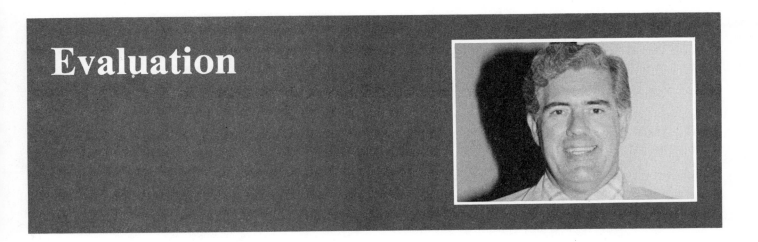

Evaluation

Holistic Scoring in the Classroom

By Glenn Patchell
Chairperson, Department of English,
Irvine High School, Irvine Unified School District;
and Teacher/Consultant, UCI Writing Project

Holistic scoring is a technique of evaluation that solves many of the problems of a writing teacher. The conscientious English teacher concerned with teaching writing effectively is often burdened with the obligation of reading several class sets of papers a week. Even the best intentioned and most dedicated teacher burns out after several weeks. I found that after 12 weeks I could hardly stand to look at a student paper. The results of the burnout were that students did not get immediate feedback; they did not write as often; and I felt guilty for offending the principles of good teaching. I welcomed the use of holistic scoring because it gave me needed relief from the paper load, involved my students in a more effective learning experience, and provided parents and administrators with concrete evidence of progress and program effectiveness.

Simply put, holistic scoring is evaluating the paper as a whole. It assumes that each writing skill is related and that no one skill is more important or should receive greater emphasis than another. The evaluation is achieved through the use of a rubric (scoring guide) which lists the criteria for each score. The rubrics that readers use may be based on various scales, usually ranging from nine points to four points. I personally find the four-point scale less desirable because it relates too closely to the common grading scale of A through F. Each rubric should be tailored to the specific writing task described in the prompt (assignment). Holistic scoring is used by school districts to evaluate proficiency tests, staff development projects,

class progress, and individual improvement. Holistic scoring also serves the English teacher or any teacher of writing in the classroom to facilitate evaluation of the students' work. I soon found that one of the most practical uses of holistic scoring was in the classroom with students as the readers.

As a tool for the teacher, holistic scoring provides more time to instruct because less time is spent evaluating the students' papers. For example, before I used holistic scoring, I spent most of my evaluation time marking errors and writing suggestions or basic comments on the papers. Unfortunately, the students rarely read or understood my comments. Through the use of the prompt and rubric, the teacher establishes a

> *Evaluation is only one aspect of the postwriting stage of the writing process; thus, it should be kept in perspective.*
> HANDBOOK FOR PLANNING
> AN EFFECTIVE WRITING PROGRAM

clear purpose for each assignment, the student is exposed to the criteria for evaluation of each writing assignment, and the writer is directed to the strengths and weaknesses of each writing sample. For instance, the UCI Writing Project used the following descriptive prompt in an evaluation of the writing skills of tenth, eleventh, and twelfth grade students in the classes of teachers trained in the Writing Project and in the classes of comparable teachers who had not been exposed to the Writing Project's techniques:

> Write a paper in which you describe a restaurant that you remember vividly. It could be the best, worst, or most unusual. Include in your description the senses (sight, smell, touch, hearing, and taste).

Note that the prompt was designed to stimulate writing and was broad-based enough so that every student could draw on his or her experience. Moreover, the student received specific directions as to what to include in the essay. Based on the prompt, a rubric was established that clearly delineates the criteria for scoring each writing sample:

RUBRIC: DESCRIPTION

9—8 This paper is clearly superior. The writer developed the topic with excellent organization, content, and insight, and he or she displayed facile use of language and mastery of mechanics. A person who has written a *9—8* paper has done most or all of the following well:

- Developed a good introduction.
- Maintained an appropriate point of view throughout the paper.
- Employed precise, apt, or evocative descriptive vocabulary.
- Did not shift in tense or person.
- Organized ideas effectively and provided an introduction, some closure, and an orderly progression from one idea to another.
- Varied sentence structure and length.
- Used effectively the conventions of written English—spelling, usage, sentence structure, capitalization, punctuation.
- Used at least three examples with specific supporting details.
- Used at least three of five senses.
- Wrote legibly.

7 This is a thinner version of the *9—8* paper—still impressive, cogent, convincing, but less well handled in terms of organization, insight, or language.

6—5 A score of 5 or 6 applies to papers in the upper-half category that are less well written than a *7* paper. This paper may exhibit less maturity of thought than was exhibited in the papers with higher scores, and the writer has not handled organization, syntax, or mechanics as well. The *5* paper is a thinner version of the *6*. A *6—5* paper will exhibit these characteristics:

- Has a clear introduction.
- Has an appropriate point of view.
- Communicates clearly.
- Shows some sense of organization but is not fully organized.
- Uses less variety of sentence structure and length.
- Contains some errors in mechanics, usage, and sentence structure.
- Usually has three examples with supporting details.
- Uses at least two of the five senses.
- Handwriting can be easily read.

4—3 These scores apply to a paper that maintains the general idea of the writing assignment, shows some sense of organization, but is weak in content, thought, language facility, and mechanics. A *3* paper is a thinner version of the *4* paper. A *4—3* paper has these characteristics:

- Introduction lacks clarity.
- Has shifts in tense and person.
- Displays a minimal overall organization.
- Has little variety of sentence structure and many sentence errors.
- Has some misunderstanding of the prompt.
- Contains serious errors in mechanics, usage, and sentence structure.
- Examples and supporting details are not clearly stated or defined.
- Uses at least one of the five senses.
- Handwriting can usually be easily read.

2 This score applies to a paper that makes no attempt to deal with the topic and compounds the weaknesses found in a *4—3* paper. A *2* paper exhibits several of the following:

- Has no sense of organization.
- Shifts constantly in tense and person.
- Shows little or no development of ideas; lacks any focus on specific and related details.
- Distorts, misreads, or ignores the topic.
- Contains disjointed sentences, lacks sense of sentence progression and variety, and contains many sentence errors.
- Shows serious faults in handling the conventions of written English to the extent of impeding a reader's understanding.
- Has no discussion of the five senses.
- Handwriting cannot be read easily.

1 This score is used for any response that is not on the topic and has almost no redeeming qualities.

Although the prompt and rubric described above were used for a large-scale evaluation, the same principles apply to holistic scoring in the classroom. Some students have a hard time understanding why they received a particular grade on a paper, but I have never had a student who had difficulty comprehending why he or she received a certain score when a rubric was available and clearly explained in advance. The careful use of a rubric will provide the student instruction in specific areas of usage, spelling, sentence structure, word choice, and so forth. For example, one area that always concerns me is the variety of sentence patterns. Most high school student writers have little understanding of the value of subordination. Requiring several complex sentences or the use of clauses beginning with *because, if, since, although,* and so forth and listing the use of subordination as a criterion on the rubric make the student aware of complex sentences. When writers find that their papers received scores that indicate a lack of sentence variety, they know that they must learn the concept of subordination.

One of the greatest boons of holistic scoring in the classroom is that it actually involves students in the evaluation process. As the students learn to use the rubric, I have discovered that they can be trained to score writing assignments effectively. The rubric is now viewed in a new light as they try to apply it to the papers of other students. Then, not only do they better understand the rubric, but they also become responsible for helping other writers improve by directing them to the appropriate criteria by the score they select for each paper. The experience of Carolyn is a case in point. Carolyn was one of those students who always excelled. She worked hard to complete each assignment and to produce quality work. Soon, her reputation earned her such respect that the presence of her name on an assignment often earned her an *A*. However, during a class holistic scoring session, Carolyn received a *3* from her peers. Because the scorers were all boys, she appealed to me for a second opinion. I inserted her paper in a group of papers to be scored by another class. A second scoring again produced a *3* evaluation. Carolyn was then convinced

to go back to the rubric and determine what the weaknesses in her essay were.

Training students to score holistically takes time and patience. Students will not become proficient overnight. But with the same training given to teachers, I have seen students score with the same consistency as adults. In the process of scoring, students also become aware of the criteria for good writing and learn to identify areas which need improvement not only in the papers of others but also in their own

We will write nothing but garbage if we do not practice critical thinking towards the end of the writing process, but it is dangerous to be too critical too early.
DONALD MURRAY

compositions. Significantly, in seeing their peers' writing and receiving group feedback on their own papers, student writers suddenly become conscious that they have an audience other than the teacher. This situation clearly lessens the burden on the teacher as the sole evaluator of student work.

Although holistic scoring is a valuable tool, I would never recommend it as the only method of evaluation. When I take the time to evaluate and completely edit a student's paper, I want to be able to have a conference with the writer about his or her paper. I now have the time for individual conferences because holistic scoring does help moderate the paper load, as well as provide specific criteria for evaluation, improve assignments, allow more writing, and motivate students to understand what constitutes good writing. The student writes with purpose, recognizes good writing, and learns to take responsibility for learning about the writing process through reading, scoring, and responding to the efforts of his or her peers through the use of holistic scoring.

I find that the longer I use holistic scoring the more I use it. My students respond to holistic scoring and learn from it. Much of the anxiety is removed from the act of writing, for the student writer is freed from the red pen of correction, and the teacher is freed from the stress of editing and grading excessive amounts of student work.

As an added plus, holistic scoring provides the teacher with a more objective means of evaluation, which can be demonstrated to interested parents and administrators. I have found the use of folders containing a sequential record of each student's prompts, rubrics, first drafts, and final scored papers as an effective means of documenting student progress as well as of making my short-term and long-term composition goals clear.

Practical Ideas for Using Holistic Scoring

Prompts and Rubrics for Second Grade Teachers

By Barbara Farrell Brand
Former Teacher, Sycamore Elementary School,
Orange Unified School District;
and Teacher/Consultant, UCI Writing Project

I have been using a modified version of holistic scoring in my classroom since 1978. By modified, I mean that I use the concept of holistic scoring but simplify the process to make it comprehensible to my students. I have found that I get much better writing from my students when I present them with a clear prompt that specifies exactly what I want them to include in the writing assignment. But rather than eval-

> *Holistic scoring provides more time to instruct because less time is spent evaluating the students' papers.*
> GLENN PATCHELL

uating them on any kind of involved point system, I have three basic categories: A Very Good Composition, A Good Composition, and a "Needs Improvement" Composition. Drawing from the directions in the prompt, I list the key elements a paper must contain in order to be very good and what elements the paper will lack if it falls short of the "very good" range. The important factor is to keep the prompt and rubric clear and simple.

Three sample prompts and rubrics that I have used with success in my class follow. My purpose in each lesson is two-fold: to give students practice in using the conventions of written English (capitalization, end punctuation, possessives, and so forth) and to use imaginative and problem-solving skills in composing.

"KEEP OUT" LESSON

PREWRITING

Review skills of sentence writing with capitalization and end punctuation.

Make available two pictures, such as girl and dog looking at an abandoned house, or boy and dog looking at a "KEEP OUT" sign.

PROMPT

Think of something that could happen if a child went into a place even when the sign said, "Keep Out." It could be dangerous or funny. Choose one picture to write about. Write a complete story. When you finish, mount your picture and your story on colored paper.

WRITING ASSIGNMENT

The teacher establishes heading, margin, and spelling standards.

Write a story of at least five sentences and:

- Tell what the child saw.
- Tell why the child went in or why the child stayed out.
- Tell what happened.

RUBRIC

- *A Very Good Composition*

  Has fewer than three errors in capitalization and end punctuation of sentences.

  Tells what child saw, why child went in or stayed out, and what happened.

- *A Good Composition*

  Has fewer than five errors in capitalization and end punctuation of sentences.

  Includes two of the three assigned items.

- *A "Needs Improvement" Composition*

  Has frequent sentence errors.

  Includes fewer than two of the items of information.

POSTWRITING

Share and display the stories.

ADD-ON STORY

PREWRITING

Enjoy the game of telling an Add-On Story (unrehearsed, with each person building on the previous sentences).

Example: The teacher or first person gives a starter:

I saw a strange animal yesterday.
Second person: The animal was eating my lunch.
Third speaker: He ate all the lunches in the school.
Fourth child: He got a terrible stomachache!
(Four or five sentences usually complete a story.)

Other starters: Once upon a time there were three spiders that lived in a big web . . .
My friend and I had two dollars to spend . . .
A shiny round spaceship landed on the lawn . . .

Identify *imagination*. Encourage its use. Review skills of capitalizing and centering a title. Share rubric before children write.

PROMPT

Use your imagination to write a story. Here are some starters:

My dad and I . . .
Once there was . . .
I heard a strange noise last . . .
In the spring . . .

WRITING ASSIGNMENTS

● Make a title for your story.
● Write an imaginary story using the starter you chose.
● Tell who is in the story.
● Tell what interesting things happened.

RUBRIC

● *A Very Good Composition*

Has a centered, capitalized title.

Has fewer than three errors in capitalization and end punctuation of sentences.

Utilizes one of the starter phrases, tells who is in story, and uses imagination in telling what happened.

● *A Good Composition*

Has a title.

Has fewer than five errors in capitalization and end punctuation of sentences.

Includes two of the three requirements.

● *A "Needs Improvement" Composition*

May have omitted a title.

Has frequent sentence errors.

Includes fewer than two of the items.

POSTWRITING

Partners read and hear each other's stories. Partner tells author a part he or she liked and what grade (Very Good, Good, or Needs Improvement, based on the rubric) he or she thinks it should receive. Share stories orally with class or "publish" copies.

STOREFRONT LESSON

PREWRITING:

Review skills of adding *s* for plurals and adding *'s* for possessive proper nouns.

Conduct class discussion and cluster the *businesses* and/or *services* that a town needs, as shown in Figure 31.

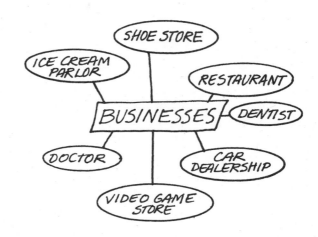

Fig. 31. Clustering of *Businesses* for Storefront Lesson

Students choose a kind of enterprise each might like to have, draw furnishings or counter and wares inside the store (on Sheet 1), and cover with a storefront (using Sheet 2) with door, plastic window, and space for signs, as shown in Figure 32.

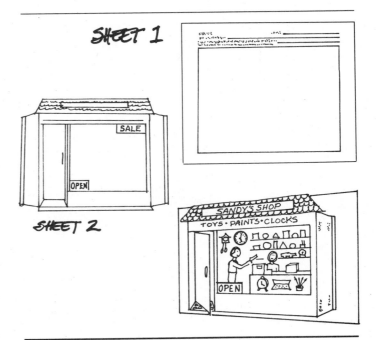

Fig. 32. The Storefront Lesson

NAME

STORE OR BUSINESS

WHAT DO YOU SELL, OR WHAT SERVICE DO YOU PROVIDE?

DRAW THE INSIDE.

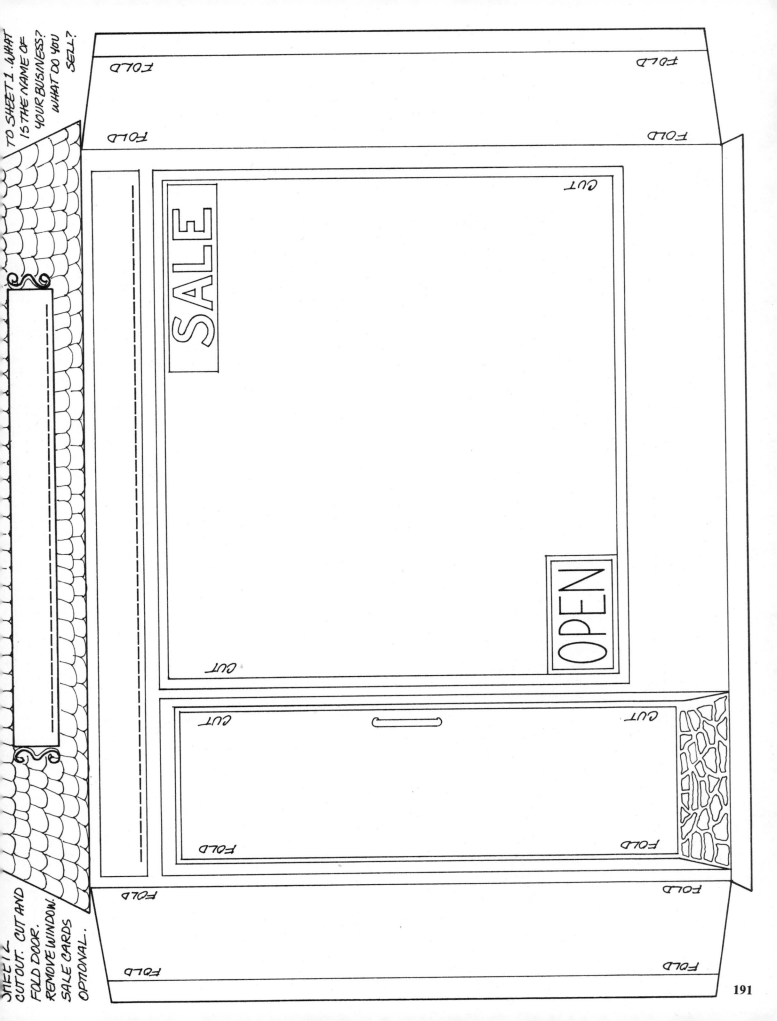

SHEET 1. WHAT
IS THE NAME OF
YOUR BUSINESS?
WHAT DO YOU
SELL?

SHEET 2.
CUT OUT. CUT AND
FOLD DOOR.
REMOVE WINDOW.
SALE CARDS
OPTIONAL.

SALE

OPEN

191

By Pam Burris
Teacher, Talbert Middle School,
Fountain Valley Elementary School District;
and Teacher/Consultant, UCI Writing Project

A picture is worth a thousand words. That is why I often use a visual motivator when I ask children to write.

Holistic scoring has been an integral part of my writing program for the last four years. It seems to me that we create a situation for children to fail when we require them to write and then neglect to provide them with a focus, a specific situation, and a list of criteria on which they will be evaluated. Holistic scoring lends itself to making these aspects of an assignment clear.

While working on a prompt, I usually share a picture as a springboard for writing to lower the anxiety of the children and spark their imagination. The picture is a rich resource for children who lack experiences, imaginative ideas, or confidence. It also provides the children with the follow-up activity of decorating or coloring the visual prompt or perhaps of creating a new picture of their own to illustrate what they have written.

The written and visual prompt appear as follows for an assignment I give called "Roller Boogie":

WRITTEN PROMPT

Imagine that you are able to skate anywhere you want to, even to a faraway country. Write a paper in which you:

- Describe your skates.
- Tell where you want to go.
- Describe your journey.

VISUAL PROMPT

Color your skates and turn in the picture with your papers. You may choose to draw a picture of the place you skate to in the background.

PROMPT

Think of a store or business you might like to have. Name your business, using your name and *'s*, and tell what you sell or do. It could be Jimmy's Supplies, and Jimmy sells pool supplies. It might be Garcia's Shop, and Miss Garcia sells records. In Jason's Development Company, Jason sells houses. Decide where you buy supplies and how many people work for you. Think of everything you will need to know in order to run a business.

WRITING ASSIGNMENT

- Make a title for your composition.
- Tell what your store or business is called.
- Write about your shop or office. Tell what you sell or do.
- Tell more about your business.

RUBRIC

- *A Very Good Composition*

  Has a well-written title and sentences.

  Has fewer than three *-s* or *-'s* errors.

  Includes name of business, what is sold or done, and thoughtfully written details.

- *A Good Composition*

  Has acceptable title and sentences.

  Has fewer than five *-s* or *-'s* errors.

  Includes name of business, what is sold or done, and a few other details.

- *A "Needs Improvement" Composition*

  May have no title. Has frequent sentence errors.

  Has frequent *-s* or *-'s* errors.

  Includes fewer than four of the required items of information.

POSTWRITING

Partners share "stores" and stories and suggest improvements. Display storefronts and interiors in class. Discuss how the businesses might be related and interdependent.

Many elementary teachers discount holistic scoring because it seems too complicated for the students they teach. But, if adapted, it can be just as effective at the second grade as it is at the high school or college level.

After the papers are written, the teacher has an instant "Roller Boogie" bulletin board. In fact, the pictures of the skates can be placed all over the room.

Many sources are available to get good pictures to use as a stimulus for writing. Magazines, student-oriented publications, and newspapers contain excellent materials. Political cartoons work well for those writing about current events. Diagrams and pictures from science and social studies textbooks can easily be adapted for interdisciplinary development of children's writing skills.

Holistic Scoring and Peer Rating Groups in the Elementary Classroom

By Lois Anderson

English Teacher, Fred L. Newhart Elementary School, Capistrano Unified School District; and Teacher/Consultant, UCI Writing Project

Although holistic scoring may seem complex and best suited for intermediate and high school students, it can also be successful at the upper elementary level. The use of holistic scoring and student rating groups has worked well for my fifth grade students. I find these activities to be worthwhile for a number of reasons. Students have an opportunity to analyze and evaluate writing similar to their own. In doing so, they gain a clearer picture of what works and what does not in their writing assignments. In addition, the process provides an audience of their peers to evaluate their writing. Often, they will take the comments received from their peers more seriously than any I make. Bonuses of the peer rating groups are the group interaction and the experiences students have of defending an opinion, reaching a compromise, and arriving at a group consensus.

The processes of introducing and using rubrics and rating groups may take several weeks. The first step is to teach the elements of the particular type of writing that the students are to learn. I usually begin with descriptive writing, so we study and practice using precise sensory descriptive words and figurative language. We then listen to several descriptive examples from literature, as well as to pieces I have written myself, and have a brainstorming session during which we list the ways the authors were able to create vivid descriptions.

At the next session, I present a rubric constructed from the most important elements of our brainstorming session. I explain the purpose of a rubric, and we clarify the meaning of the statements on the scale. We use a six-point rubric, but a four-point rubric would also work well.[1] I hand out a copy of a descriptive paper from a previous year, which we read orally and then rate as a group exercise. Reaching a consensus at this point is very informal. My goal is to introduce the rubric and show how it relates to a piece of writing.

After my students have written, revised, and edited their next descriptive papers, using the rubric as a guide, I score each piece. I also point to one or two elements of the paper that helped me determine the rating. Students then respond to my evaluation by writing, "I agree with my _____ rating because . . ." or "I disagree. I should have a _____ rating because. . . ." I sometimes give a letter grade to these rating responses, even though I have not graded the actual piece of writing. This approach takes some of my time, but it pays off in getting students to think carefully about evaluating their own writing.

In the next session, we take a look at another student paper. This time we break into groups of four, and I introduce the use of a rating sheet. I have taken spelling and penmanship out of the rating because if I include them, students tend to concentrate on those aspects of the paper rather than on the writing itself. Later in the year, we add a 1, 2, or 3 rating for the conventions of writing, in addition to the scoring of the piece of writing itself. Students use the rating sheet and rubric to rate the piece. Then each group of four spends several minutes comparing ratings and reaching consensus. Last, we compare the ratings from all the groups and reach a group consensus.

After I prepare my students to work in independent rating groups, I teach them the procedure to use in the groups. As soon as they complete their writing assignments, I divide the students into groups of four. Each group gets four papers to rate (none from their own group). Each student reads and fills out a rating slip for a paper; then he or she passes that paper to the next person in the group until all of the students in the group have rated the four papers. Nothing is written on the paper itself; comments and ratings are marked on the rating slip, which each scorer keeps until con-

---

[1]For sample rubrics, see the other articles in this section or Carol Booth Olson's article in the section on "Writing the I-Search Paper."

> *In the process of rating the papers as a group, the students sharpen their awareness of the elements of good writing and develop critical thinking skills.*
>
> LOIS ANDERSON

sensus time. During this session, I insist on silence in the classroom. Students or groups that finish early read silently or do other work silently.

When all groups have rated all four papers, I call for consensus time. At this point, the members of each group compare ratings and study each piece of writing to arrive at consensus. Students present arguments in defense of the score they marked. After a few minutes, a compromise is usually made and consensus is reached.

The group score is printed at the top of the piece, and the four rating slips are attached to the paper. I collect and redistribute them to the appropriate writers. The needs of the students determine whether papers are identified by secret number or by name. My students have always wanted their names on their papers.

When students receive their own papers back, they respond to the ratings; then they turn in their papers, rating sheets, and responses. At this point, the teacher has a number of options:

1. Read and rate each paper.
2. Read the students' responses and make comments.
3. Do 1 and 2 above.
4. Read the papers but do not rate or grade them.
5. Skim the papers and record that the work was done, but make no comments or ratings.

6. Record the students' ratings; read only those papers in which the responses disagree with the ratings.
7. Do any combination of the above or whatever suits the program.

My students respond seriously and enthusiastically to the holistic scoring/group rating sessions. They read and consider each paper carefully because they want others to do the same for their own writing. And in the process of rating the papers as a group, the students sharpen their awareness of the elements of good writing and develop critical thinking skills.

Holistic Scoring: The Good News and the Bad

By Michael O'Brien
English Teacher, Foothill High School,
Tustin Unified School District;
and Teacher/Consultant, UCI Writing Project

I have often used holistic scoring in my high school classroom over the last three years. While attesting to its partial effectiveness, I look with some disbelief at the claims that holistic scoring, like a patent medicine, cures everything from rambling run-on sentences to murky thesis statements.

One "miracle" of holistic scoring that I can attest to is the results of using a rubric. Students do appreciate being presented with a precise description of what is expected of their writing. The rubric is also a ready-made list of terms I repeat over and over to students so that "unified composition" and "specific, supporting details" become a part of their vocabulary, a necessary step toward writing more effectively.

Another claim of those who advocate holistic scoring is that it works "Fast! Fast! Fast!" Indeed, it is a quick way to evaluate a set of papers. Therefore, I can ask my students to write more, which is an important gain. There are, however, side effects. On the return of a paper, a typical reaction is, "Oh, I got a 5 on a scale of seven. Say, Mr. O'Brien, what were my problems here?"

"Look at the rubric," is my hopeful reply.

"Okay, but I still don't know if I've got excessive mechanical errors, a lack of specific details, ineffective organization . . . ."

So I have tried attaching checklists to the papers, indicating areas of strength and weakness, but I make the students find the errors. Yet, by the time I have completed the checklist and worked with students who cannot find their errors, this process has become as "Slow! Slow! Slow!" as the traditional marking of papers. However, since my experience with holistic scoring, I have heard of a strategy used by Cathy D'Aoust, a UCI Writing Project colleague, that I plan to try. Cathy returns papers to students with only a holistic score (no comments or checklists), and she requires them to write a one-page paper explaining to her why they received the score they did. Perceptive self-assessments earn an extra point for the overall paper. Students who are unable to specify the reasons for their score are called in for conferences so that Cathy can work one-on-one with those students.

Another claim for holistic scoring is that students can score each other's papers. I have found this partially true. It is valuable that they use the rubric as a criterion for judging, that they provide another audience for the writer, and that they learn by reading the work of others. One drawback, however, is that, again, even with the comments of other students written on their papers, the writers are still getting limited information. Another problem is that even after extensive training with samples, I have found that there are always a few students who are unreliable graders. Thus, a universal student concern is that the scores and comments on their papers may be inaccurate. Perhaps one way to alleviate this concern is to have both the teacher and student peer groups score the students' papers, and then average the two scores if they are one or more points apart.

Ultimately, I suppose the good news outweighs the bad. As I look over my list of pros and cons, I see that holistic scoring makes the criteria for writing clearer

> *Holistic scoring is evaluating the paper as a whole. It assumes that each writing skill is related and that no one skill is more important or should receive greater emphasis than another.*
> GLENN PATCHELL

to students, speeds up the evaluation process, allowing for more writing assignments, and enables students to participate in the process. Overall, it clearly benefits the students. As for teachers, it will not lighten the burden of the paper load as much as most of us would like. And it cannot (or should not) be used as a replacement for oral or written teacher feedback on student writing. But it provides the teacher with a variety of options in responding to students' writing: to score and comment, to score only and let the students comment, to comment only and let peer groups score, to score along with peer groups, and so forth.

No, holistic scoring is not a patent medicine for curing writing problems, but it can be a valuable supplement to good writing instruction.

Compromising with an Ideal: Rubrics Based on Grades

By Charles Schiller
English Teacher, Laguna Beach High School,
Laguna Beach Unified School District;
and Teacher/Consultant, UCI Writing Project

The classes that I teach at Laguna Beach High School are almost entirely college preparatory, and as anyone who has taught such classes already knows, letter grades are very important to college-bound students. They will not settle for a number from a rubric—or, at least, not for long. I had to deal with this in adapting the ideas and methods of the UCI Writing Project to my teaching. The result was a rubric based on letter grades.

I now use such rubrics all the time, both for the guidance of students before they write and as a handy reminder to myself as I grade. The "Rubric—Paper of Literary Analysis," which follows, is routinely given to students entering my Shakespeare classes and the "Rubric—Writing on the Title of Your Book," which also follows, is typical of those I use in my ninth grade English classes.

RUBRIC—PAPER OF LITERARY ANALYSIS

A Level Papers

Well structured

Introduction. Thesis statement with title, author, and your main idea about the subject of your paper

Development. Logically organized presentation of proof for thesis; references to incidents (using the plot selectively), quotes, discussion of ideas, and so forth

Conclusion. Sums up satisfactorily, repeats, and restates the ideas of the introduction

Fullfills the assignment

Shows good insight into the literature

Clear, easily understood; interesting to read

Few, if any, mechanical errors

Follows rules of stylebook and makes a good appearance in blue or black ink or typed, no ragged edges on paper, and so forth

B Level Papers

Thinner version of an *A* paper

C Level Papers

May not follow stylebook consistently

May have several mechanical errors, especially spelling

Will have thesis statement and recognizable structure, but development may be slight

Will deal with theme but may be heavy on plot

May show only surface understanding of the literature or even some confusion about it

D Level Papers

Little attention to the stylebook; may be in pencil and generally careless in appearance

Many mechanical errors

Structure weak, probably lacks thesis

Deals with plot almost entirely

Shows little understanding of the literature

RUBRIC—WRITING ON THE TITLE OF YOUR BOOK

A Level

Follows assignment, deals with title

Well structured:

Introduction, including *thesis*
Well developed
Recognizable conclusion

Excellent insight into literature

Discusses, does not tell

Few (two or three), if any, mechanical errors

Follows stylebook; has excellent appearance

B Level

Thinner version of the *A* paper

Structure good, but development is weaker than in an *A* paper (fewer examples, quotes, and so forth)

Insight into the literature less keen

Discusses, does not tell

Mechanical problems more serious (four or five of them)

Follows stylebook; has good appearance

C Level

Follows assignment, at least partially; deals with title but may retell story in doing so

Has fair structure

Thesis may not be clear.
Development may be poor (only one or two examples).
Conclusion may be hard to recognize.

More telling than discussing

Mechanics only acceptable (six or seven errors)

May not follow the stylebook consistently; appearance may be only fair

D Level

Attempts the assignment

Structure poor—may fail to paragraph

Tells the story

Poor mechanics (eight or nine errors)

Little attempt to follow the stylebook; appearance poor

F Level

Minimal effort; little or no attempt to follow the assignment

Hard to understand

Mechanics get between the reader and the understanding of the paper

Appears unaware of the stylebook; unacceptable appearance

The students' responses to such rubrics have been very good; they like knowing what is expected for those grades they value. I should add that I also preface their structured writing assignments with enough prewriting experiences (one can cluster even about Shakespeare, after all) that I am easy in my conscience about using what is admittedly a compromise with an ideal.

Primary Trait Scoring

By Virginia Baldwin
Teacher, Gifted and Talented Education
Del Cerro Elementary School,
Saddleback Valley Unified School District;
and Teacher/Consultant, UCI Writing Project

Primary trait scoring (PTS) is a versatile evaluation system in which the strengths and weaknesses of student writing are described. The system, developed by the National Assessment of Educational Progress, can be adapted for use in elementary, intermediate, and high school classrooms across the curriculum and can be used to:

● Measure the presence of particular characteristics or elements of style.
● Value content, yet consider correctness in assessment.
● Create a sense of purpose and audience during prewriting.
● Provide a focus for peer interaction during sharing and revising.

The PTS system is akin to holistic scoring because it is based on a rubric or set of criteria on which a paper will be evaluated, but the scoring system differs. With PTS the person evaluates a single characteristic, or primary trait, rather than a piece of writing as a whole. PTS scoring guides focus on the most important characteristic, or critical attribute, of a successful response to a given writing prompt. Other traits may also be identified as characteristics of a successful response and evaluated as secondary traits.

The following are two examples of teacher-generated prompts and primary trait scoring (PTS) guides at the elementary and high school levels:

NEWS ABOUT HANDS AT SCHOOL
(Kindergarten through grade three)

PROMPT

Today you are a newspaper reporter. Choose one person who works at our school that you would like to write a news story about. Choose one activity that the person does, and write a news story that describes and tells how the person's hands help him or her do the activity. Since your news story will be placed in the classroom's "News About Hands at School" book, it should be interesting and informative so your classmates and other people will want to read it.

EVALUATION

Primary Trait Scoring Guide

This news story is interesting to read. It accurately describes how a person who works at our school uses his or her hands to do his or her job.

This news story is not as interesting as it could be. It tells about some of the person's duties but does not accurately describe how he or she uses his or her hands to do a job.

This news story does not give enough information about how the person uses his or her hands to do the job. This lack of information made the story less interesting to read.

Secondary Trait Scoring Guide

This paper is neat and easy to read. Fewer than three total errors were made in capitalization, punctuation, and/or spelling.

This paper is not as neat or easy to read. Three to five total errors were made in capitalization, punctuation, and/or spelling.

This paper is not neat or easy to read. More than five total errors were made in capitalization, punctuation, and/or spelling.

PAC MAN OR KICK THE CAN?
(Grades seven and eight)

PROMPT

Interview your grandparents or other older adults who grew up during the Depression. Ask them to describe the toys and games they remember from their childhood. Then write a three-paragraph analytical/expository essay in which you:

● *Describe* one or more toys and/or games of the Depression era, and
● *Describe* one or more toys and/or games you enjoy.

After describing them, show the *similarities* and *differences* between the two types of toys and games. From your

study of toys and games, *compare* what it was like to grow up during the Depression to what it is like to grow up now.

EVALUATION

The teacher will evaluate according to the following rubric. The paper is worth a total of 10 points:

5 points—Drawing conclusions/Content
3 points—Structure
2 points—Mechanics/Format

PRIMARY TRAIT—DRAWING CONCLUSIONS/CONTENT

- A *5* paper draws conclusions—compares childhood during the Depression with childhood today by giving examples of one or more toys/games from each era and by analyzing the similarities and differences of each.
- A *4* paper draws only one conclusion but otherwise fulfills the same criteria as a *5* paper.
- A *3* paper discusses only the toys/games and distinguishes between the two eras without drawing conclusions.
- A *2* paper does not discuss the similarities and differences of the toys/games in each era.
- A *1* paper does not provide sufficient detail about the toys/games or does not give one example from each era.

SECONDARY TRAITS—STRUCTURE
AND MECHANICS/FORMAT

STRUCTURE

- A *3* paper follows a three-paragraph structure using topic sentences, details, and transitions.
- A *2* paper omits one of the elements of a *3* paper.
- A *1* paper omits two of the elements of a *3* paper.

MECHANICS/FORMAT

- A *2* paper has neat margins, handwriting, and indentions; it uses proper spelling and capitalization and has a title.
- A *1* paper is not neat or does not follow the format given in class.
- A *0* paper addresses neither neatness nor format.

In lessons of the type just cited, the teacher can design a scoring system that weighs more heavily on the primary trait he or she wishes to highlight. For

example, in the lesson on "News About Hands at School," the teacher made *an interesting story line and accuracy of description* the key elements; neatness and error-free writing were reinforced but considered as secondary to content. In the "Pac Man or Kick the Can?" scoring guide, the teacher stressed thinking skills, followed by organizational writing skills, appropriate paragraph form, and correct mechanics and grammar.

When creating the scoring guide, one must identify the purpose for writing, the audience to whom the writing will be addressed, and the domain or mode of the writing requested. Once these objectives are established, it is easy to determine the primary and secondary traits of the lesson. For instance, if the prompt asks the writer to explain how to make a peanut butter sandwich, it is of primary importance that the directions be clear and in the proper sequence in order for the reader to understand and follow them. If the writer fails to tell the reader to open the jelly jar, it will not matter how vividly he or she describes its contents.

The major goal of the PTS system is not to provide a grading or ranking device for writing. The goal is to describe the strengths and weaknesses of individual compositions so that students will understand clearly what the characteristics of a successful response are and be able to write and revise with those characteristics in mind. Having identified the primary and secondary traits, the teacher can plan prewriting activities which will help students achieve a successful response.

At the same time that the system clearly delineates for students the writing tasks they are being asked to perform, it enables the teacher to formulate his or her priorities in regard to writing instruction and to tailor assignments to foster the development of specific skills. Teachers who wish to stress fluency first and then form and correctness will find this system useful, as will teachers in curriculum areas other than English who wish to emphasize content. PTS can also be used to help transfer grammatical concepts, syntactical structures, and mechanical rules to students' writing, because mastery of a specific conventional skill (such as use of proper dialogue format in a narrative or the use of the colon in a descriptive essay) can be built into the scoring guide as a primary trait.

After some exposure to PTS, the students themselves will be able to contribute to the creation of primary and secondary trait scoring guides for future writing assignments. As their understanding of this process deepens, they will begin to develop an inherent set of criteria for what good writing is—not just on specific assignments, but good writing in general—and be better able to evaluate and revise their own papers before turning them in.

Evaluation Techniques

Some Techniques for Oral Evaluation

By Michael O'Brien
English Teacher, Foothill High School,
Tustin Unified School District;
and Teacher/Consultant, UCI Writing Project

Oral evaluation of student papers is like the bicycle in my garage: neglected but patiently waiting in the corner. Well, I decided to pull oral evaluation out of the cobwebbed corner, clean up the moving parts, and try it. With the help of a lecture I heard by Dorothy Bray of Sacramento City College, I found that oral evaluation was a very effective vehicle.

My motivations for trying oral evaluation were not entirely selfless: I got very tired of grading papers after school or at home. Also, I got frustrated about how my carefully written comments were either neglected or misunderstood. So I began to evaluate papers orally in class. I found through my own experience and listening to Dr. Bray at a meeting of the University of California at Irvine's Writing Project that the following techniques were effective:

1. I assign papers of about 400 words so I can evaluate six or seven of them in a 50-minute period and, thus, can plan on completing a class set in about five days.

2. While I work individually with a student at my desk, the others are working on writing assignments or on work sheets to help them in areas of weakness.

3. I structure the conference to the needs of each student by asking at the outset whether he or she had any problem or questions with the writing of the paper.

4. I try to give favorable comments early if I sense that the student has given a good effort. (The oral evaluation is a much more positive experience because written evaluations tend to be overwhelmingly negative, no matter how I try.)

5. In my criticisms I try to cover one or two major problems, realizing that this is about as much as most of the students can work on at one time.

6. I give the student a chance to respond and ask questions. Often, a short explanation can clear up major concerns.

> *The teacher is a facilitator of the writing/learning process by creating an environment that is conducive to learning; assigning writing is not the same thing as teaching writing.*
> JAMES R. GRAY

7. I have each student bring his or her journal to the conference to record my comments, both favorable and critical. Thus, the student has a log where he or she keeps all of my comments. This approach is very effective for isolating chronic problems and areas of improvement.

EDITOR'S NOTE: We are grateful to the National Council of Teachers of English for granting us permission to reprint this article, which appeared in the January, 1982, issue of the *English Journal.*

8. I do not grade the assignment. After doing two or more of the same type of paper, the student will choose the one that has the most promise and rewrite it. Then I evaluate the final copy and grade it in the traditional way.

After using this method in my three composition classes for one quarter of a school year not long ago, I asked the students to write their anonymous responses to the following questions:

1. Should we continue oral evaluations?
2. If so, why? If not, why not?
3. How would you suggest they be improved?

Out of 98 students, all but one felt we should continue. This was a typical comment about why we should continue:

> Yes, I would like to see oral evaluations continue. I get a much better understanding of whether or not my paper is well written. You can explain things in detail whereas you couldn't simply by writing down comments. I also like being able to tell you what I think is wrong with my paper and learning if it is or it isn't.

To the question regarding suggested improvements, most students had none to suggest. Some, however, were frustrated that it took me five days to get to the last students. Others felt that I should have taken more time with each paper. Both of these were valid concerns, but I could only solve these problems by

having smaller classes, a solution that was not in my power, unfortunately.

I do not purport that my informal survey is conclusive evidence that oral evaluation works. And, certainly, little in the professional literature either confirms or denies the effectiveness of oral evaluation. For example, the Educational Resources Information Center (ERIC) lists only one study from 1967—1980, and it was admittedly inconclusive. But in my experience oral evaluation has increased appreciably the effectiveness of my teaching while decreasing the time I spend after school grading papers. No, I do not spend my extra time bike riding. (My bike is still in the garage, the old tires rotting.) I spend it doing lesson plans.

Practical Ideas for Evaluation

Teaching Self-evaluation Skills to Student Writers

By Carol O. Sweedler-Brown
Assistant Professor, Study Skills Center
San Diego State University

Most students find it especially difficult to evaluate their own writing because (1) they have had no training or practice in applying evaluation skills; (2) they are too close to their own writing to be able to deal with it objectively; and (3) it is very threatening to admit deficiencies in their own work. A couple of years ago I devised an exercise that helps my students overcome these problems.

During the third or fourth week of the semester, after my students have done some writing, but while they are still fairly green, I assign an in-class essay. I read these essays at home, and from each of my classes I select three essays that present a range of

writing problems and strengths. I duplicate enough of these model essays for one class and set them aside.

Four or five weeks later (using essays from one class as models for another class), I distribute these model papers to each class. Students are asked to read and grade these three essays without any prior discussion. After they have graded them, I write on the chalkboard the range and frequency of grades assigned to each essay. Then we discuss both the problems and strengths of each paper, and I put on the chalkboard the reasons students give for grading each paper as they did. Once the students have committed themselves to a grade, class discussion of the relative merits of these essays is often very lively, even raucus. At the end of the discussion, I have many evaluation criteria randomly jotted on the chalkboard—all directly suggested by the students. Then we organize these in broad categories—clarity, structure, content, grammar, and so forth—and decide which categories of criteria are more important than others in determining the overall grade of the paper. (So this activity also becomes an exercise in organizing and categorizing.) At this point, I emphasize to the students that they are capable of establishing valid standards for good writing.

At the next class meeting, I bring in the essays that my students wrote four or five weeks earlier. By this time, I have duplicated copies of the criteria established by the class, and I leave plenty of room on the sheets for comments after each criterion and a place for an overall grade. I staple four of these to the back of each essay, put a code number on each essay and its criteria sheets, and remove the student's name from the paper. I distribute the essays to the class. (If a student receives his or her own essay, he or she passes it to someone else.) The students then evaluate the essays on the criteria sheet by commenting about each criterion, making any other comments that seem appropriate, and assigning the paper an overall grade. After a student finishes grading a paper, he or she tears off the evaluation sheet, puts that in a pile, hands the essay to someone else, and takes another essay to grade. In this way, no one's grading can be influenced by the grading or comments of someone else. This process is repeated by all students until each essay has only one of the four criteria sheets left. Then the essay, with no marks on it, is given to the writer who fills in the final and most important evaluation.

At this point the writers are in an excellent position to evaluate their own writing because they have just had at least two days of training and practice in performing the evaluation process. In addition, because the student writers have not seen the paper for at least a month, they will have lost a close identification with it (some students hardly recognize their own papers). Since the students wrote the papers several weeks

earlier, they are not as threatened by their shortcomings because they feel that they have improved.

After the students have evaluated their own papers (amidst groans and giggles, "Did I write this?"), I give them the three other evaluation sheets, and they compare their evaluations with those of their peers (unsigned). Usually, the assessments are surprisingly consistent. Then I ask the students to revise their essays in light of all the comments, especially their own. Some revisions will involve deep structural changes; and some, just mechanics.

I have found that this exercise shows students that they can determine what the qualities of good writing are, and they can apply evaluation techniques to their own essays as part of the revision stage of their writing.

The Writing Folder: A System for Responding to Students' Writing

By Jim Hahn
English Teacher, Armijo High School,
Fairfield-Suisun Unified School District;
and Teacher/Consultant, Bay Area Writing Project

If a teacher reads everything a student writes, the teacher is a bottleneck in the writing process. —JAMES MOFFETT

I have been marking papers and wrestling with the problem of responding to student writing for ten years. I have found that traditional systems of feedback trap us in the frustrating cycle of myriad comments and corrections aimed at students who continue to make the same errors. The frustration stems from these areas: there are too many papers to mark, the students do not read our comments, and the same students make the same errors again and again, regardless of how often we point them out. An analysis of the process of responding to students' writing will help illuminate some of the causes of these problems.

Part of the problem with providing feedback on papers is that we try to do too many things at once. If we take all the marks teachers put on students' papers, we could place them in three categories: (1) comments related to content and organization; (2) notations related to grammar, mechanics, and spelling; and (3) remarks related to evaluation. Each of these categories sends a different message to students. A comment on content implies that the students will rewrite the composition to correct the problem. A mark about grammar or mechanics implies that the students need to make minor corrections to solve the problems.

Marks of evaluation, such as grades or even statements like "Good work," imply that the composition is finished. When we consider all of these areas simultaneously, we are telling our students (1) rewrite and rethink the paper; (2) correct the paper, but do not necessarily rethink it; and (3) the paper is finished. Given the three choices, it is no wonder that our students seldom do more than look at the grade. I shudder every time I think of the number of hours I spent commenting on student papers only to find them in the wastebasket soon after I passed them back.

The frustration teachers often feel after responding to and returning papers is easily explained when one realizes that students and teachers are both trying to save time while dealing with the difficult task of writing. On the one hand, teachers, pressed for time, develop shorthand methods for communicating with the student: *awk. frag. rts. ⌒ ⁋*

On the other hand, students, who are also in a hurry, usually accept the grade, ignore the cryptic marks, relegate writing to the realm of things they will never master, and throw their papers in a nearby trash can.

If marking the papers for content and grammar, and evaluating them should not be done simultaneously, then the next step is to find out when to do what. (See Figure 33 for a diagram showing what you may want to emphasize during each stage of the writing process.)

Comments about content and organization are pertinent at several stages in the process. They can help clarify thinking anywhere from the prewriting to the revising stages. The conventions of writing belong to the editing stage. If you make notations to your student writers regarding conventions (spelling, grammar, and so forth) too early in the process, they will correct the word or sentence; but then they often will find it very difficult to revise the content of the paper later because they are committed to the correct form, regardless of the sense (or nonsense) of the passage. Since evaluations, especially letter grades, imply that the work is finished, they should be used only at the end of the process.

Acceptance of the preceding analysis leads us overworked teachers to the unwelcome conclusion that instead of marking papers once, they should be marked three separate times, with the student making changes after each step. If I had to teach only one person to write, I might do that; however, with 150 to teach each semester, I look for options. I have designed a system for responding to writing at different stages in the composing process, and the system, which I will describe in the paragraphs that follow, provides students with feedback they can use and alleviates some of the burden of the paper load.

Students are constantly collapsing the writing process by taking shortcuts. Our job as teachers is to expand the process—to get students to think and rethink their work as much as possible. By postponing evaluation as long as possible, the writing process (and, consequently, the learning process) is kept open. Instituting writing folders for all written work helps accomplish this. Students often wish to throw out old papers. (If the papers have been graded, why should they be kept?) However, if the papers are evaluated en masse at the end of the grading period, the writing folders can be evaluated by the teacher, by the teacher and student in conference, or they can be self-evaluated by the student. These folders have the added benefits of teaching students to be responsible for their work while demonstrating how much they have learned.

All of my students keep writing folders, which they must turn in to me at the end of a grading period (anywhere from two weeks to a semester in length) to

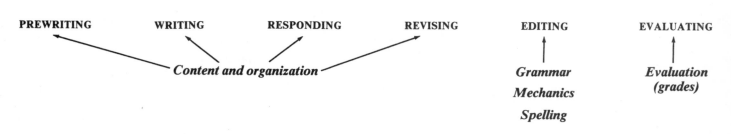

PREWRITING   WRITING   RESPONDING   REVISING   EDITING   EVALUATING

Content and organization

EDITING: *Grammar Mechanics Spelling*

EVALUATING: *Evaluation (grades)*

Fig. 33. Items to Emphasize in Each Stage of the Writing Process

get credit for their work. I collect these folders intermittently to provide feedback on the students' work; but I withhold grades until the end of the grading period. Prior to turning in work in progress for my review, I ask students to fill out a cover sheet that includes a self-evaluation of their paper, a classmate's comments on the piece, and a space for my response (see Figure 34).

COVER SHEET   *PROOFREADERS*

Name:_____ 1._____

Title:_____ 2._____

Date:_____ 3._____

AUTHOR'S COMMENTS

The thing I like most about this paper is:_____

The thing I like least about this paper is:_____
_____

The things I tried to improve in this paper are:_____
_____

STUDENT'S COMMENTS _____
_____
_____

TEACHER'S COMMENTS _____
_____
_____

*THINGS TO WORK ON IN YOUR NEXT PAPER ARE:*____
_____
_____

Fig. 34. Evaluation Sheet for Student's Writing

You will note that the cover sheet (Figure 34) also requires the signature of three proofreaders. When we teachers correct our students' errors, we train them to be lazy proofreaders. I transfer this responsibility to the students by making them the editors of each other's work. In the same way that students gain an intuitive sense of the criteria for good writing by participating as peer respondents to the work of others, they can improve their grasp of grammatical concepts and mechanical rules when they must be attentive to the conventions of written English in their classmates' papers. When a question arises, I can always serve as a resource.

In order for the students to track their progress, I also have them use a paper log sheet that is kept in each student's folder (see Figure 35). Students transfer

> *I also like being able to tell you what I think is wrong with my paper and learning if it is or it is not.*
> ONE OF MICHAEL O'BRIEN'S STUDENTS

the comments from the cover sheets of individual papers (theirs, a peer partner's, and mine) to this cumulative log. Now, they can begin to see that writing is a craft that one can improve with practice. In addition to gaining ideas for revising specific pieces of writing, they can recognize how the assignments fit together as a sequence and determine what skills they need to strengthen in future papers.

All of my students' writing goes into their folders, but I do not necessarily read or evaluate everything. Much writing is only for practice, and some rough drafts are not meant to be final copies. I can spot check the folders at intervals throughout the semester, establish a set grading period, and evaluate an entire body of work as a whole. I require that certain assignments be revised for evaluation, or I allow my students to select from their folders items for review that they believe represent their best work.

Once students become used to the writing folder and accept the idea that developing writing ability involves practice and that not every draft must be evaluated, teachers will no longer become "bottlenecks in the writing process," and students can write as much as they need to.

Name_____

Topic	Title	What I tried to improve	What I need to work on in my next paper

Fig. 35. Log of Student's Writing

Adding an Analytical Commentary to Holistic Scoring

By Carol Booth Olson
Codirector, UCI Writing Project

I have found holistic scoring to be a fair, fast, and efficient method of providing comprehensible evaluative feedback on student papers. But, in its pure form, it does not allow for the descriptive feedback that most students need in order to determine what specific skills they should work on to improve future papers. Not only do students need this input, but I feel *guilty* if I do not provide them with it. It just does not seem equitable for a teacher to require students to write and then not respond with some form of written commentary of his or her own. On the other hand, I do not want to fall back into my old habit of spending hours writing essays in response to students' essays.

I think I have come up with a workable solution to this dilemma. I read each student's paper, give it a holistic score, and then fill out a form which breaks down the paper into its key elements: quality of thought, structure, diction, syntax, and so forth. Each assignment requires a slightly different form.

The categories for my analytical response sheet come straight from the rubric on which the paper is evaluated. For example, here is the scoring guide I developed for a 9—8 paper (on a 1—9 scale) for "A Sample Prompt, Scoring Guide, and Model Paper for the I-Search," which appears earlier in this book:

9—8 This paper is clearly superior. It is well written, clearly organized, insightful, and technically correct. A 9—8 paper exhibits most or all of the following characteristics:

- Writing the paper was a genuine learning experience for the writer, and a person would benefit greatly from reading the paper.
- The paper displays evidence of critical thinking offers special insight into the topic discussed.
- The topic lends itself to investigation and discovery.
- The paper is written in three sections (the format may be explicit or implicit):
  - What I know, assume, or imagine (prior to the search)
  - The search (testing knowledge, assumptions, or conjecture through documented research)
  - What I discovered (comparing what you thought you knew with what you learned and offering commentary and conclusions)
- The author takes an active role rather than a passive role in the search.
- The writer uses research effectively as a supplement to, but not as a substitute for, his or her own ideas.
- The paper's tone and point of view convey a clear sense of the author's voice, or style.

- The writer uses precise, apt, or descriptive language.
- The main points of the essay are well supported with examples.
- The writer uses ample transitions between ideas, paragraphs, and sections.
- The writer varies sentence structure and length.
- The search portion of the essay is properly documented with footnotes in correct form.
- The paper makes reference to a minimum of two primary and two secondary research sources.
- The paper includes a formal bibliography.
- The writer generally uses effectively the conventions of written English.

I use an abbreviated list of the criteria from the scoring guide to establish the headings for my feedback:

Overall Comments and Suggestions for Improvement
Paper as Learning Experience
Analysis of the Three Sections
Research (Quality and Quantity)
Support with Examples
Transition
Author's Role
Footnotes and Bibliography
Diction
Syntax
Conventions of Written English
Paper's score _____

Although I feel compelled to provide students with a written reaction to their work, I am also one of those people who eagerly embraces almost any opportunity to procrastinate. I find that having a response sheet makes the task of evaluating students' papers seem less formidable. I get to the job earlier and keep on task because the headings and the limited space provided (I try to keep the form to one page) necessitate that I keep focused and to the point. When filling out the form, I write a brief paragraph of four to five sentences in length in which I share my general reactions to the piece—in terms of both its strengths and its weaknesses. Beyond that initial remark, I do not feel obligated to write in complete sentences. If an "OK," "Nice work," or "More specific examples needed" will do, I leave it at that. If more explanation is required, then I provide it.

Adding an analytical commentary to holistic scoring has eased my conscience in regard to my responsibility to give students feedback on their written work. The method is certainly not as fast as using holistic scoring alone. But it is still more efficient than coming to each student's essay with a blank piece of paper and an undefined set of expectations, on the one hand, or an elaborate system of points for each component of the writing assignment, on the other. In my opinion, this combination is the best of both worlds.

Selected References

This list of selected references was compiled from the publications cited in this document. The references are organized according to whether they are works of literature, other sources, or publications about writing.

Literature

Allinson, Beverly. *Mitzi's Magic Garden.* Westport, Conn.: Garrard Publishing Co., 1971.

Baylor, Byrd. *Everybody Needs a Rock.* New York: Charles Scribner's Sons, 1974.

Blake, William. *Songs of Innocence and of Experience.* New York: Oxford University Press, Inc., 1977.

Broun, Heywood. *The Fifty-First Dragon.* Edited by Ann Redpath. Mankato, Minn.: Creative Education, Inc., 1985.

Brown, Margaret W. *The Important Book.* New York: Harper & Row Pubs., Inc., 1949.

Chaucer, Geoffrey. *The Canterbury Tales.* Edited by A. Kent Hieatt and Constance Hieatt. New York: Bantam Books, Inc., 1981.

Connell, Richard E. "The Most Dangerous Game" in *Stories.* Edited by Frank G. Jennings and Charles J. Calitri. New York: Harcourt Brace Jovanovich, Inc., 1957.

Dickens, Charles. *Great Expectations.* New York: Bantam Books, Inc., 1981.

Doctorow, E. L. *The Book of Daniel.* New York: Random House, Inc., 1971.

Eliot, T. S. *The Waste Land and Other Poems.* New York: Harcourt Brace Jovanovich, Inc., 1955.

Golding, William. *Lord of the Flies.* New York: Putnam Publishing Group, 1962.

Hawthorne, Nathaniel. *The Scarlet Letter.* New York: Bantam Books, Inc., 1981.

Hemingway, Ernest. "Cat in the Rain," in *Short Stories of Ernest Hemingway.* New York: Charles Scribner's Sons, 1966.

Heyert, Murray. "The New Kid" in *Stories.* Edited by Frank G. Jennings and Charles Calitri. New York: Harcourt Brace Jovanovich, Inc., 1957.

Jackson, Shirley. "Charles," in *The Lottery: Or the Adventures of James Harris.* New York: Farrar, Straus & Giroux, Inc., 1949.

Jensen, Virginia A. *Sara and the Door.* Reading, Mass.: Addison-Wesley Publishing Co., Inc., 1977.

Katz, Bobbi. *Nothing but a Dog.* Old Westbury, N.Y.: Feminist Press, 1972.

Lee, Harper. *To Kill a Mockingbird.* Philadelphia: J. B. Lippincott Company, 1960.

London, Jack. *To Build a Fire.* Mankato, Minn.: Creative Education, Inc., 1980.

Lurie, Toby. *Conversations and Constructions.* San Francisco: 1429 Page St., Apt. E, San Francisco, CA 94117, 1978.

Martin, Bill, Jr. *David Was Mad,* one of the *Kin-der Owl Books.* New York: Holt, Rinehart & Winston, Inc., 1971.

Miller, Arthur. *Collected Plays.* Vol. I. New York: Viking Press, Inc., 1957.

Miller, Arthur. *The Crucible.* New York: Penguin Books, Inc., 1976.

Mizumura, Kazue. *If I Were a Cricket.* New York: Harper & Row Pubs, Inc., 1973.

Sandburg, Carl. "Summer Grass," in *Good Morning, America.* New York: Harcourt Brace Jovanovich, Inc., 1928, 1956.

Shakespeare, William. *Antony and Cleopatra.* Edited by E. Jones. New York: Penguin Books, Inc., 1981.

Shakespeare, William. *Romeo and Juliet.* Edited by T. J. Spencer. New York: Penguin Books, Inc., 1981.

Simon, Marcia L. *A Special Gift.* New York: Harcourt Brace Jovanovich, Inc., 1978.

Simon, Nora. *I Know What I Like.* Niles, Ill.: Albert Whitman & Company, 1971.

Steinbeck, John. *Of Mice and Men.* New York: Viking-Penguin, Inc., 1972.

Steinbeck, John. *The Red Pony.* New York: Viking-Penguin, Inc., 1966.

Swift, Jonathan. *Gulliver's Travels.* New York: Pocket Books, Inc., 1984.

Terkel, Studs. *American Dreams: Lost and Found.* New York: Pantheon Books, 1980.

Tolkein, J. R. R. *The Hobbit.* Boston: Houghton Mifflin Company, 1966.

Twain, Mark. *The Adventures of Tom Sawyer.* New York: Bantam Books, Inc., 1981.

Zolotow, Charlotte. *Janey.* New York: Harper & Row, Pubs., Inc., 1973.

Other Sources

Castries, Duc de. *Lives of the Kings and Queens of France.* New York: Alfred A. Knopf, Inc., 1979.

Chute, Marchette. *An Introduction to Shakespeare.* New York: E. P. Dutton and Co., Inc., 1951.

Lewis, Gwynne. *Life in Revolutionary France.* New York: G. P. Putnam's Sons, 1972.

Liversidge, Douglas. *The Day the Bastille Fell.* New York: Franklin Watts, Inc., 1972.

Usher, Frank. "Louis XVI," in *100 Great Kings, Queens and Rulers of the World.* Edited with an introduction by John Canning. New York: Taplinger Publishing Company, 1968.

Whitehead, Alfred North. *The Aims of Education.* New York: Free Press, a Division of Macmillan Publishing Co., Inc., 1967.

Publications About Writing

Britton, James, and others. *The Development of Writing Abilities (11—18).* (Schools Council Research Studies) Houndmills Basingstoke, Hampshire: Macmillan Education Ltd., 1975.

Caplan, Rebekah. *Writers in Training: A Guide to Developing a Composition Program.* Palo Alto: Dale Seymour Publications, 1984.

Caplan, Rebekah, and Catherine Keech. *Showing Writing: A Training Program to Help Students Be Specific.* Berkeley: Bay Area Writing Project, University of California, 1980.

Cooper, Charles. "An Outline for Writing Sentence-Combining Problems," in *The Writing Teacher's Sourcebook.* Edited by Gary Tate and Edward P. Corbett. New York: Oxford University Press, Inc., 1981.

Elbow, Peter. *Writing Without Teachers.* New York: Oxford University Press, Inc., 1975.

Elbow, Peter. *Writing with Power: Techniques for Mastering the Writing Process.* New York: Oxford University Press, Inc., 1981.

Flower, Linda. *Problem-Solving Strategies for Writing.* New York: Harcourt Brace Jovanovich, Inc., 1981.

Graves, Donald H. *Balance the Basics: Let Them Write.* New York: Ford Foundation, 1978.

Graves, Donald H. "We Won't Let Them Write: Research Update," *Language Arts,* Vol. 55 (May, 1978), 635—40.

Handbook for Planning an Effective Writing Program, Kindergarten Through Grade Twelve (Revised edition). Sacramento: California State Department of Education, 1986.

Healy, Mary K. *Using Student Writing Response Groups in the Classroom.* Berkeley: Bay Area Writing Project, University of California, 1980.

Improving Writing in California Schools: Problems and Solutions. Sacramento: California State Department of Education, 1983.

Levine, Harold. *Vocabulary for the College-Bound Student.* New York: AMSCO School Publications, Inc., 1983.

Levine, Harold. *Vocabulary for the High School Student.* New York: AMSCO School Publications, Inc., 1983.

Lomax, William. "Sentence Combining Across the Curriculum," *California English,* Vol. 16 (November-December, 1980), 18—21.

Macrorie, Ken. *Searching Writing.* Rochelle Park, N.J.: Hayden Book Company, Inc., 1980.

Macrorie, Ken. *Twenty Teachers.* New York: Oxford University Press, Inc., 1985.

Murray, Donald M. "Internal Revision: A Process of Discovery," in *Learning by Teaching: Selected Articles on Writing and Teaching.* Upper Montclair, N.J.: Boynton Cook Pubs., Inc., 1982.

O'Hare, Frank. *Sentence-Combining: Improving Student Writing Without Formal Grammar Instruction.* Urbana, Ill.: National Council of Teachers of English, 1973.

Olson, Carol Booth. "Personalizing Research in the I-Search Paper," *Arizona English Bulletin,* Vol. 25, No. 1 (November, 1983), 147—63.

Perl, Sondra. "Understanding Composing," in *College Composition and Communication,* Vol. 31 (December, 1980), 363—69.

Rico, Gabriele. *Writing the Natural Way: Using Right-Brain Techniques to Release Your Expressive Powers.* Los Angeles: J. P. Tarcher, Inc., 1983.

Rico, Gabriele, and Mary Frances Claggett. *Balancing the Hemispheres: Brain Research and the Teaching of Writing* (Monograph). Berkeley: Bay Area Writing Project, University of California, 1980.

Scardamalia, Marlene. "How Children Cope with the Cognitive Demands of Writing," in *Writing: Process, Development and Communication,* Vol. 2 of *Writing: The Nature, Development, and Teaching of Written Communication.* Edited by Carl H. Frederiksen and Joseph F. Dominic. Hillsdale, N.J.: Lawrence Erlbaum Associates, Publishers, 1981.

Shaughnessy, Mina P. *Errors and Expectations: A Guide for the Teacher of Basic Writing.* New York: Oxford University Press, Inc., 1977.

Stanford, Gene, and Marie Smith. *A Guidebook for Teaching Creative Writing.* Newton, Mass.: Allyn & Bacon, Inc., 1981.

Strong, William. *Sentence Combining: A Composing Book.* New York: Random House, Inc., 1983.

Thomas, Irene, and Owen Thomas. *Sentence Combining I and II.* St. Louis, Mo.: Milliken Publishing Co., 1984.

Wolfe, Tom, and E. W. Johnson. *The New Journalism.* New York: Harper & Row Pubs., Inc., 1973.

Index

Topics

Authors and Titles of Articles in *Practical Ideas*

Authors, Composers, and Works Cited in *Practical Ideas*

Publications Available from the Department of Education

This publication is one of over 650 that are available from the California State Department of Education. Some of the more recent publications or those most widely used are the following:

ISBN	Title (Date of publication)	Price
0-8011-0271-5	Academic Honesty (1986)	$2.50
0-8011-0722-9	Accounting Procedures for Student Organizations (1988)	3.75
0-8011-0272-3	Administration of Maintenance and Operations in California School Districts (1986)	6.75
0-8011-0216-2	Bilingual-Crosscultural Teacher Aides: A Resource Guide (1984)	3.50
0-8011-0238-3	Boating the Right Way (1985)	4.00
0-8011-0275-8	California Dropouts: A Status Report (1986)	2.50
0-8011-0783-0	California Private School Directory, 1988-89 (1988)	14.00
0-8011-0748-2	California School Accounting Manual (1988)	8.00
0-8011-0715-6	California Women: Activities Guide, K—12 (1988)	3.50
0-8011-0488-2	Caught in the Middle: Educational Reform for Young Adolescents in California Public Schools (1987)	5.00
0-8011-0760-1	Celebrating the National Reading Initiative (1989)	6.75
0-8011-0241-3	Computer Applications Planning (1985)	5.00
0-8011-0749-0	Educational Software Preview Guide, 1988-89 (1988)	2.00
0-8011-0489-0	Effective Practices in Achieving Compensatory Education-Funded Schools II (1987)	5.00
0-8011-0041-0	English-Language Arts Framework for California Public Schools (1987)	3.00
0-8011-0731-8	English-Language Arts Model Curriculum Guide, K—8 (1988)	3.00
0-8011-0710-5	Family Life/Sex Education Guidelines (1987)	4.00
0-8011-0289-8	Handbook for Physical Education (1986)	4.50
0-8011-0249-9	Handbook for Planning an Effective Foreign Language Program (1985)	3.50
0-8011-0320-7	Handbook for Planning an Effective Literature Program (1988)	3.00
0-8011-0179-4	Handbook for Planning an Effective Mathematics Program (1982)	2.00
0-8011-0290-1	Handbook for Planning an Effective Writing Program (1986)	2.50
0-8011-0224-3	Handbook for Teaching Cantonese-Speaking Students (1984)	4.50
0-8011-0680-X	Handbook for Teaching Japanese-Speaking Students (1987)	4.50
0-8011-0291-X	Handbook for Teaching Pilipino-Speaking Students (1986)	4.50
0-8011-0204-9	Handbook for Teaching Portuguese-Speaking Students (1983)	4.50
0-8011-0250-2	Handbook on California Education for Language Minority Parents—Chinese/English Edition (1985)	3.25*
0-8011-0737-7	Here They Come: Ready or Not—Report of the School Readiness Task Force (1988)	2.00
0-8011-0712-1	History–Social Science Framework for California Public Schools (1988)	6.00
0-8011-0782-2	Images: A Workbook for Enhancing Self-esteem and Promoting Career Preparation, Especially for Black Girls (1989)	6.00
0-8011-0227-8	Individual Learning Programs for Limited-English-Proficient Students (1984)	3.50
0-8011-0466-1	Instructional Patterns: Curriculum for Parenthood Education (1985)	12.00
0-8011-0208-1	Manual of First-Aid Practices for School Bus Drivers (1983)	1.75
0-8011-0209-X	Martin Luther King, Jr., 1929—1968 (1983)	3.25
0-8011-0358-4	Mathematics Framework for California Public Schools (1985)	3.00
0-8011-0664-8	Mathematics Model Curriculum Guide, K—8 (1987)	2.75
0-8011-0725-3	Model Curriculum for Human Rights and Genocide (1988)	3.25
0-8011-0252-9	Model Curriculum Standards: Grades 9—12 (1985)	5.50
0-8011-0762-8	Moral and Civic Education and Teaching About Religion (1988)	3.25
0-8011-0229-4	Nutrition Education—Choose Well, Be Well: A Curriculum Guide for Junior High School (1984)	8.00

*The following editions are also available, at the same price: Armenian/English, Cambodian/English, Hmong/English, Korean/English, Laotian/English, Spanish/English, and Vietnamese/English.

ISBN	Title	Price
0-8011-0228-6	Nutrition Education—Choose Well, Be Well: A Curriculum Guide for High School (1984)	8.00
0-8011-0182-4	Nutrition Education—Choose Well, Be Well: A Curriculum Guide for Preschool and Kindergarten (1982)	8.00
0-8011-0183-2	Nutrition Education—Choose Well, Be Well: A Curriculum Guide for the Primary Grades (1982)	8.00
0-8011-0184-0	Nutrition Education—Choose Well, Be Well: A Curriculum Guide for the Upper Elementary Grades (1982)	8.00
0-8011-0230-8	Nutrition Education—Choose Well, Be Well: A Resource Manual for Parent and Community Involvement in Nutrition Education Programs (1984)	4.50
0-8011-0185-9	Nutrition Education—Choose Well, Be Well: A Resource Manual for Preschool, Kindergarten, and Elementary Teachers (1982)	2.25
0-8011-0186-7	Nutrition Education—Choose Well, Be Well: A Resource Manual for Secondary Teachers (1982)	2.25
0-8011-0253-7	Nutrition Education—Choose Well, Be Well: Food Photo Cards (with nutrient composition charts) (1985)	10.00
0-8011-0254-5	Nutrition Education—Choose Well, Be Well: Teaching Materials for Preschool/Kindergarten Curriculum Guide (in color) (1985)	7.50
0-8011-0303-7	A Parent's Handbook on California Education (1986)	3.25
0-8011-0671-0	Practical Ideas for Teaching Writing as a Process (1987)	6.00
0-8011-0309-6	Program Guidelines for Hearing Impaired Individuals (1986)	6.00
0-8011-0258-8	Program Guidelines for Severely Orthopedically Impaired Individuals (1985)	6.00
0-8011-0684-2	Program Guidelines for Visually Impaired Individuals (1987)	6.00
0-8011-0213-8	Raising Expectations: Model Graduation Requirements (1983)	2.75
0-8011-0311-8	Recommended Readings in Literature, K—8 (1986)	2.25
0-8011-0745-8	Recommended Readings in Literature, K—8, Annotated Edition (1988)	4.50
0-8011-0214-6	School Attendance Improvement: A Blueprint for Action (1983)	2.75
0-8011-0189-1	Science Education for the 1980s (1982)	2.50
0-8011-0339-8	Science Framework for California Public Schools (1978)	3.00
0-8011-0354-1	Science Framework Addendum (1984)	3.00
0-8011-0665-6	Science Model Curriculum Guide, K—8 (1987)	3.25
0-8011-0668-0	Science Safety Handbook for California High Schools (1987)	8.75
0-8011-0738-5	Secondary Textbook Review: English (1988)	9.25
0-8011-0677-X	Secondary Textbook Review: General Mathematics (1987)	6.50
0-8011-0781-4	Selected Financial and Related Data for California Public Schools (1988)	3.00
0-8011-0265-0	Standards for Scoliosis Screening in California Public Schools (1985)	2.50
0-8011-0486-6	Statement on Preparation in Natural Science Expected of Entering Freshmen (1986)	2.50
0-8011-0318-5	Students' Rights and Responsibilities Handbook (1986)	2.75
0-8011-0234-0	Studies on Immersion Education: A Collection for U.S. Educators (1984)	5.00
0-8011-0682-6	Suicide Prevention Program for California Public Schools (1987)	8.00
0-8011-0739-3	Survey of Academic Skills, Grade 8: Rationale and Content for Science (1988)	2.50
0-8011-0192-1	Trash Monster Environmental Education Kit (for grade six)	23.00
0-8011-0236-7	University and College Opportunities Handbook (1984)	3.25
0-8011-0237-5	Wet 'n' Safe: Water and Boating Safety, Grades 4—6 (1984)	2.50
0-8011-0194-8	Wizard of Waste Environmental Education Kit (for grade three)	20.00
0-8011-0670-2	Work Experience Education Instructional Guide (1987)	12.50
0-8011-0464-5	Work Permit Handbook for California Public Schools (1985)	6.00
0-8011-0686-9	Year-round Education: Year-round Opportunities—A Study of Year-round Education in California (1987)	5.00
0-8011-0270-7	Young and Old Together: A Resource Directory of Intergenerational Resources (1986)	3.00

Orders should be directed to:

California State Department of Education
P.O. Box 271
Sacramento, CA 95802-0271

Please include the International Standard Book Number (ISBN) for each title ordered.

Remittance or purchase order must accompany order. Purchase orders without checks are accepted only from governmental agencies. Sales tax should be added to all orders from California purchasers.

A complete list of publications available from the Department, including apprenticeship instructional materials, may be obtained by writing to the address listed above or by calling (916) 445-1260.

89 79013

F88-256 (Third printing) 03-0148 300 12-88 10M